Autodesk
AutoCAD Architecture 2026
Fundamentals

Elise Moss

SDC Publications
P.O. Box 1334
Mission, KS 66222
913-262-2664
www.SDCpublications.com
Publisher: Stephen Schroff

Copyright 2025 by Elise Moss

All rights reserved. This document may not be copied, photocopied, reproduced, transmitted, or translated in any form or for any purpose without the express written consent of the publisher, SDC Publications.

It is a violation of United States copyright laws to make copies in any form or media of the contents of this book for commercial or educational purposes without written permission.

Examination Copies
Books received as examination copies are for review purposes only and may not be made available for student use. Resale of examination copies is prohibited.

Electronic Files
Any electronic files associated with this book are licensed to the original user only. These files may not be transferred to any other party.

Trademarks
The following are registered trademarks of Autodesk, Inc.: AutoCAD, AutoCAD Architecture, Revit, Autodesk, AutoCAD Design Center, Autodesk Device Interface, VizRender, and HEIDI.
Microsoft, Windows, Word, and Excel are either registered trademarks or trademarks of Microsoft Corporation.
All other trademarks are trademarks of their respective holders.

The authors and publisher of this book have used their best efforts in preparing this book. These efforts include the development, research, and testing of material presented. The author and publisher shall not be held liable in any event for incidental or consequential damages with, or arising out of, the furnishing, performance, or use of the material herein.

ISBN-13: 978-1-63057-739-1
ISBN-10: 1-63057-739-1

Printed and bound in the United States of America.

Preface

No textbook can cover all the features in any software application. This textbook is meant for beginning users who want to gain a familiarity with the tools and interface of AutoCAD Architecture before they start exploring on their own. By the end of the text, users should feel comfortable enough to create a standard model, and even know how to customize the interface for their own use. Knowledge of basic AutoCAD and its commands is helpful but not required. I do try to explain as I go, but for the sake of brevity I concentrate on the tools specific to and within AutoCAD Architecture.

The files used in this text are accessible from the Internet from the book's page on the publisher's website: www.SDCpublications.com. They are free and available to students and teachers alike.

We value customer input. Please contact us with any comments, questions, or concerns about this text.

Elise Moss
elise_moss@mossdesigns.com

Acknowledgments from Elise Moss

This book would not have been possible without the support of some key Autodesk employees.

Thanks to David Driver. His Autodesk University class on curtain walls was extremely helpful in providing guidance on that section of this textbook.

The effort and support of the editorial and production staff of SDC Publications is gratefully acknowledged. I especially thank Stephen Schroff for his helpful suggestions regarding the format of this text.

Finally, truly infinite thanks to Ari for his encouragement and his faith.

- Elise Moss

About the Author

Elise Moss has worked for the past thirty years as a mechanical designer in Silicon Valley, primarily creating sheet metal designs. She has written articles for Autodesk's Toplines magazine, engineering.com, AUGI's PaperSpace, DigitalCAD.com and Tenlinks.com. She is President of Moss Designs, creating custom applications and designs for corporate clients. She has taught CAD classes at Santa Clara University, Laney College, DeAnza College, SFSU, Silicon Valley College, and for Autodesk resellers. Autodesk has named her as a Faculty of Distinction for the curriculum she has developed for Autodesk products. She holds a baccalaureate degree in Mechanical Engineering from San Jose State. She is currently working as an adjunct professor, teaching in the Engineering Department at Santa Clara University.

She is married with two sons. Her husband, Ari, is retired from a distinguished career in software development.

Elise is a third-generation engineer. Her father, Robert Moss, was a metallurgical engineer in the aerospace industry. Her grandfather, Solomon Kupperman, was a civil engineer for the City of Chicago.

She can be contacted via email at elise_moss@mossdesigns.com.

More information about the author and her work can be found on her website at www.mossdesigns.com.

Other books by Elise Moss
Autodesk Revit Architecture 2026 Basics
AutoCAD 2026 Fundamentals

Table of Contents

Preface

Acknowledgments   i

About the Author   ii

Lesson 1: ACA Overview

Exercise 1-1: Setting the Template for QNEW	1-3
Exercise 1-2: Creating a New Geometric Profile	1-20
Exercise 1-3: Copying a Style to a Template	1-27
Exercise 1-4: Copying a Style using the Style Browser	1-31
Exercise 1-5: Creating a New Visual Style	1-34
Exercise 1-6: Creating an Autodesk Cloud Account	1-37
Exercise 1-7: Tool Palettes	1-39
Exercise 1-8: Exploring the Display Manager	1-54
Exercise 1-9: Creating a Text Style	1-58
Exercise 1-10: Using the Project Navigator and Project Browser	1-67
Exercise 1-11: Modifying a Project's Properties	1-73
Exercise 1-12: Using a Template to Create a Project	1-75
Exercise 1-13: Modifying the ACA Layer Keys	1-82
Quiz 1	

Lesson 2: Foundations & Site Plans

Exercise 2-1: Creating Custom Line Types	2-2
Exercise 2-2: Creating New Layers	2-5
Exercise 2-3: Creating a Site Plan	2-9
Exercise 2-4: Creating a Layer User Group	2-27
Exercise 2-5: Creating a 2D Layout Grid	2-30
Exercise 2-6: Creating a Custom Grid Bubble	2-35
Exercise 2-7: Insert Grid Lines	2-41
Exercise 2-8: Creating Constructs	2-47
Exercise 2-9: Convert Polylines to Column Grids	2-49
Exercise 2-10: Creating Slab Styles	2-52

Exercise 2-11: Creating a Gravel Fill	2-56
Exercise 2-12: Creating Member Styles	2-60
Exercise 2-13: Creating Member Shapes	2-62
Exercise 2-14: Copying Structural Member Styles	2-63
Exercise 2-15: Create Concrete Footings	2-66
Exercise 2-16: Create Element	2-68
Exercise 2-17: Create Main Model	2-72
Exercise 2-18: Defining a Low Detail Representation of a Framing Plan	2-78
Exercise 2-19: Adding Tags to the Tool Palette	2-82
Exercise 2-20: Adding Tags to Structural Members	2-87
Exercise 2-21: Adding Project Properties	2-98
Exercise 2-22: Creating a View in a Project	2-100
Exercise 2-23: Adding an Element to a Project	2-107
Exercise 2-24: Structural Detail	2-108
Exercise 2-25: Create a Foundation Deck Part 1	2-121
Exercise 2-26: Create a Foundation Deck Part 2	2-127
Exercise 2-27: Create Topography	2-130
Quiz 2	

Lesson 3: Floor Plans

Exercise 3-1: Creating a Floor Plan	3-2
Exercise 3-2: Adding Interior Walls	3-13
Exercise 3-3: Place a Grid	3-19
Exercise 3-4: Combining Constructs	3-23
Exercise 3-5: Create a Floor Plan - Reprised	3-26
Exercise 3-6: Place a Curtain Wall	3-37
Exercise 3-7: Create a Second Floor Plan	3-43
Exercise 3-8: Use the Style Browser to Add Doors	3-50
Exercise 3-9: Create a Door and Window Assembly	3-52
Exercise 3-10: Add an Overlay	3-59
Exercise 3-11: Create a Third Floor Plan	3-62
Exercise 3-12: Add Interior Walls and Doors	3-70
Exercise 3-13: Add Overlay- Reprised	3-72
Exercise 3-14: Add an Opening to a Wall	3-74

Quiz 3

Lesson 4: Space Planning

Exercise 4-1: Creating AEC Content	4-1
Exercise 4-2: Inserting AEC Content	4-10
Exercise 4-3: Inserting AEC Content - Reprised	4-13
Exercise 4-4: Inserting AEC Content – Second Floor	4-16
Exercise 4-5: Designing a Kitchen	4-19
Exercise 4-6: Modifying an Element	4-32
Exercise 4-7: Inserting an Element	4-37
Quiz 4	

Lesson 5: Roofs

Exercise 5-1: Creating a Roof Using Existing Walls	5-4
Exercise 5-2: Create Layer Filters and Layer States	5-8
Exercise 5-3: Roof Slabs	5-14
Exercise 5-4: Attach Walls to Roofs	5-24
Exercise 5-5: Creating Materials	5-28
Exercise 5-6: Roof Slab Styles	5-35
Quiz 5	

Lesson 6: Floors, Ceilings, and Spaces

Exercise 6-1: Creating Slab Styles	6-2
Exercise 6-2: Create Slab from Linework	6-11
Exercise 6-3: Create View Categories and Views	6-17
Exercise 6-4: Create Slab from Boundary	6-22
Exercise 6-5: Create a Reflected Ceiling Plan View	6-26
Exercise 6-6: Levels and Elevations	6-32
Exercise 6-7: Create an Elevation View	6-38
Exercise 6-8: Create Ceiling Grid	6-44
Exercise 6-9: Add Lights to Ceiling Grid	6-48
Exercise 6-10: Add a Space	6-51
Exercise 6-11: Add a Ceiling and Floor to a Space	6-54
Exercise 6-12: Add a Lighting Fixture to a Ceiling	6-58

Exercise 6-13: Placing a Stair	6-61
Exercise 6-14: Placing a Railing on a Stair	6-68
Exercise 6-15: Placing a Railing on a Slab	6-70
Exercise 6-16: Create Named Views	6-72
Exercise 6-17: Placing a Stair with a Landing	6-77
Exercise 6-18: Create a Stair and Railing Style	6-82
Exercise 6-19: Add Slabs to the Second Floor Plan	6-91
Exercise 6-20: Add Balconies	6-98
Exercise 6-21: Add a Hole to a Slab	6-101
Quiz 6	

Lesson 7: Curtain Walls

Exercise 7-1: Creating a Curtain Wall Style	7-6
Exercise 7-2: Create a Custom Profile	7-29
Exercise 7-3: Add a Door to a Curtain Wall	7-31
Quiz 7	

Lesson 8: Views, Schedules and Legends

Exercise 8-1: Creating a 3D Section View	8-4
Exercise 8-2: Creating a Detail View	8-11
Exercise 8-3: Creating a Wall Section	8-13
Exercise 8-4: Add Keynote Legend	8-20
Exercise 8-5: Create a Section View	8-24
Exercise 8-6: Add a Door Elevation	8-29
Exercise 8-7: Add a Callout	8-34
Exercise 8-8: Adding Door Tags	8-41
Exercise 8-9: Create a Door Schedule	8-48
Exercise 8-10: Create a Door Schedule Style	8-52
Exercise 8-11: Create Door Symbols for a Legend	8-59
Exercise 8-12: Convert Images to Blocks	8-63
Exercise 8-13: Create a Door Legend	8-67
Exercise 8-14: Creating a Custom Imperial Multi-Leader	8-73
Exercise 8-15: Create a Framing Plan View	8-84
Quiz 8	

Lesson 9: Rooms & Sheets

Exercise 9-1: Creating a View Drawing	9-1
Exercise 9-2: Adding Spaces	9-7
Exercise 9-3: Modifying Spaces	9-17
Exercise 9-4: Adding Room Tags	9-21
Exercise 9-5: Create a Custom Room Tag	9-24
Exercise 9-6: Create a Room Tag Tool	9-33
Exercise 9-7: Adding Room Tags - Reprised	9-35
Exercise 9-8: Create a Room Schedule Style	9-38
Exercise 9-9: Create a Room Schedule Tool	9-42
Exercise 9-10: Create a Room Schedule	9-44
Exercise 9-11: Create a Fire Rating Floor Plan	9-50
Exercise 9-12: Applying a Fire Rating Line	9-54
Exercise 9-13: Assigning Fire Rating Properties to Wall Styles	9-58
Exercise 9-14: Creating a Schedule Tag	9-63
Exercise 9-15: Adding a Schedule Tag Tool to the Document Palette	9-69
Exercise 9-16: Adding Property Sets to Walls	9-74
Exercise 9-17: Modify a Dimension Style	9-77
Exercise 9-18: Dimensioning a Floor Plan	9-81
Exercise 9-19: Creating a Custom Title Block	9-87
Exercise 9-20: Adding Views	9-96
Exercise 9-21: Creating a Sheet in a Project	9-103
Exercise 9-22: Creating a Framing Schedule Style	9-111
Exercise 9-23: Creating a Framing Schedule Tool	9-117
Exercise 9-24: Adding a Sheet	9-119
Exercise 9-25: Creating a PDF Document	9-125
Quiz 9	

Lesson 10: Rendering & Materials

Exercise 10-1: Modifying the Material Browser Interface	10-5
Exercise 10-2: Copy a Material from a Library to a Drawing	10-10
Exercise 10-3: Adding Color to Walls	10-14
Exercise 10-4: Adding Elements	10-20

Exercise 10-5: Adding Topography	10-22
Exercise 10-6: Camera View	10-24
Exercise 10-7: Create Rendering	10-30
Exercise 10-8: Render in Cloud	10-36
Exercise 10-9: Create an Animation	10-43
Exercise 10-10: Using the Sun & Sky	10-47
Exercise 10-11: Applying Materials	10-51
Exercise 10-12: Applying Materials to Furniture	10-60
Exercise 10-13: Replace a Block	10-64
Exercise 10-14: Using Artificial Light	10-66
Exercise 10-15: Mapping Materials	10-70
Quiz 10	

Lesson 11: Collaboration

Exercise 11-1: Set the Number of Backup Files in a Project	11-2
Exercise 11-2: Checking out and Checking In a Drawing	11-4
Exercise 11-3: Version History	11-8
Exercise 11-4: Shared Views	11-10
Exercise 11-5: Use Markup Import	11-15
Exercise 11-6: Use Trace	11-18
Exercise 11-7: Use Autodesk Docs	11-25
Exercise 11-8: Use eTransmit	11-28
Quiz 11	

Lesson 1:
ACA Overview

AutoCAD Architecture (ACA) enlists object-oriented process systems (OOPS). That means that ACA uses intelligent objects to create a building. This is similar to using blocks in AutoCAD. Objects in AutoCAD Architecture are blocks on steroids. They have intelligence already embedded into them. A wall is not just a collection of lines. It represents a real wall. It can be constrained, has thickness and material properties, and is automatically included in your building schedule.

AEC is an acronym for Architectural/Engineering/Construction.
BID is an acronym for Building Industrial Design.
BIM is an acronym for Building Information Modeling.
AIA is an acronym for the American Institute of Architects.
MEP is an acronym for Mechanical/Electrical/Plumbing.

The following table describes the key features of objects in AutoCAD Architecture:

Feature Type	Description
AEC Camera	Create perspective views from various camera angles. Create avi files.
AEC Profiles	Create AEC objects using polylines to build doors, windows, etc.
Anchors and Layouts	Define a spatial relationship between objects. Create a layout of anchors on a curve or a grid to set a pattern of anchored objects, such as doors or columns.
Annotation	Set up special arrows, leaders, bar scales.
Ceiling Grids	Create reflected ceiling plans with grid layouts.
Column Grids	Define rectangular and radial building grids with columns and bubbles.
Design Center	Customize your AEC block library.
Display System	Control views for each AEC object.
Doors and Windows	Create custom door and window styles or use standard objects provided with the software.
Elevations and Sections	An elevation is basically a section view of a floor plan.
Layer Manager	Create layer standards based on AIA CAD Standards. Create groups of layers. Manage layers intelligently using Layer Filters.
Masking Blocks	Store a mask using a polyline object and attach to AEC objects to hide graphics.
Model Explorer	View a model and manage the content easily. Attach names to mass elements to assist in design.
Multi-view blocks	Blocks have embedded defined views to allow you to easily change view.

Feature Type	Description
Railings	Create or apply different railing styles to a stair or along a defined path.
Roofs	Create and apply various roof styles.
Floorplate slices	Generate the perimeter geometry of a building.
Spaces and Boundaries	Spaces and boundaries can include floor thickness, room height, and wall thickness.
Stairs	Create and apply various stair types.
Tags and Schedules	Place tags on objects to generate schedules. Schedules will automatically update when tags are modified, added, or deleted.
Template Files	Use templates to save time. Create a template with standard layers, text styles, linetypes, dimension styles, etc.
Walls	Create wall styles to determine material composition. Define end caps to control opening and end conditions. Define wall interference conditions.

AutoCAD Architecture sits on top of AutoCAD. It is helpful for users to have a basic understanding of AutoCAD before moving to AutoCAD Architecture. Users should be familiar with the following:

- AutoCAD toolbars and ribbons
- Zoom and move around the screen
- Manage blocks
- *Draw* and *Modify* commands
- *Model* and *Paper space* (layout)
- Dimensioning and how to create/modify a dimension style

If you are not familiar with these topics, you can still move forward with learning AutoCAD Architecture, but you may find it helpful to have a good AutoCAD textbook as reference in case you get stuck.

The best way to use AutoCAD Architecture is to start your project with massing tools (outside-in design) or space planning tools (inside-out design) and continue through to construction documentation.

If you use the **QNEW** tool, it will automatically use the template set in the Options dialog.

Express Tools

Express Tools are installed with AutoCAD Architecture. If you do not see Express Tools on the menu bar, try typing EXPRESSTOOLS to see if that loads them.

Exercise 1-1:
Setting the Template for QNEW

Drawing Name: New
Estimated Time: 15 minutes

This exercise reinforces the following skills:

- Use of templates
- Getting the user familiar with tools and the ACA environment

1. Launch ACA.
2. Select the large A to access the Application Menu.

   Select **New→Drawing**.

You can also select **New** from the Start tab.

Click the down arrow next to New and select **Browse templates…**

3. Browse to the *Template* folder under *Program Data/Autodesk/*.

4. Right click on the left panel of the dialog.

   Select **Add Current Folder**.

   This adds the template folder to the palette.

ACA Overview

5. *Select the desired template to use.*

   Each template controls units, layers, and plot settings.

   Select *Aec Model (Imperial.Ctb).*

   This template uses Imperial units (feet and inches and a Color Table to control plot settings).

   Click **Open.**

6. Place your cursor on the command line.

7. Right click the mouse.

   Select **Options** from the short-cut menu.

8. Select the **Files** tab.
   Locate the *Template Settings* folder.

9. Click on the + symbol to expand.
   Locate the Default Template File Name for QNEW.

10. Highlight the path and file name listed or None (if no path or file name is listed) and select the **Browse** button.

11. Browse to the *Template* folder or select it on the palette if you added it.   This should be listed under *ProgramData/Autodesk/*

1-5

12. Locate the *Aec Model (Imperial Ctb).dwt* *[Aec Model (Metric Ctb).dwt]* file.

    Click **Open**.

    Note that you can also set where you can direct the user for templates. This is useful if you want to create standard templates and place them on a network server for all users to access.

    You can also use this setting to help you locate where your template files are located.

13. Click **OK**.

14. Select the **QNEW** tool button.

15. Note that you have tabs for all the open drawings.
    You can switch between any open drawing files by selecting the folder tab. You can also use the + tab to start a new drawing. The + tab acts the same way as the QNEW button and uses the same default template.

16. Select the **Model** tab of the open drawing.

17. Type **units** on the *Command* line.

    Notice how you get a selection of commands as you type.

    Click ENTER to select UNITS.

18. Note that the units are in Architectural format.

    The units are determined by the template you set to start your new drawing.

19. Close the drawing without saving.

Templates can be used to preset layers, property set definitions, dimension styles, units, and layouts.

AEC Drawing Options

Menu	Tools→Options
Command line	Options
Context Menu→Options	Place mouse in the graphics area and right click
Shortcut	Place mouse in the command line and right click

Access the Options dialog box.

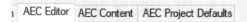

ACA's Options include three additional AEC specific tabs.
They are AEC Editor, AEC Content, and AEC Project Defaults.

There are two additional tabs: AEC Object Settings and AEC Dimension. These will become visible once you add some AEC Objects into your drawing.

AEC Editor

Diagnostic Messages	All diagnostic messages are turned off by default.
Similar-Purpose Dialogs	Options for the position of dialog boxes and viewers.
Use Common Position	Sets one common position on the screen for similar dialog boxes, such as door, wall, and window add or modify dialog boxes. Some dialog boxes, such as those for styles and properties, are always displayed in the center of the screen, regardless of this setting.
Use Common Viewer Position and Sizes	Sets one size and position on the screen for the similar-purpose viewers in AutoCAD Architecture. Viewer position is separately controlled for add, modify, style, and properties dialog boxes.
Optimize for Speed	Options for display representations and layer loading in the Layer Manager dialog.
Object Snap	Enable to limit certain display representations to respond only to the Node and Insert object snaps. This setting affects stair, railing, space boundary, multi-view block, masking block, slice, and clip volume result (building section) objects.

ACA Overview

Apply Common Property Sets to New Objects	Property sets are used for the creation of schedule tables. Each AEC object has embedded property sets, such as width and height, to be used in its schedule. AEC properties are similar to attributes. Size is a common property across most AEC objects. Occasionally, you may use a tool on an existing object and the result may be that you replace the existing object with an entirely different object. For example, if you apply the tool properties of a door to an existing window, a new door object will replace the existing window. When enabled, any property sets that were assigned to the existing window will automatically be preserved and applied to the new door provided that the property set definitions make sense.
Solution Tips 	Users can set whether they wish a solution tip to appear while they are drafting or plotting. A solution tip identifies a drafting error and suggests a solution.
Dynamic Dimensions Linetype	Set the linetype to be used when creating dynamic dimensions. This makes it easier to distinguish between dynamic and applied dimensions. You may select either continuous or dot linetypes.
Export to AutoCAD 	Enable Bind Xrefs. If you enable this option, the xref will be inserted as a block and not an xref. Enable Use Insert Method when binding Xrefs if you want all objects from an xref drawing referenced in the file you export to be automatically exploded into the host drawing. If you enable this option, the drawing names of the xref drawings are discarded when the exported drawing is created. In addition, their layers and styles are incorporated into the host drawing. For example, all exploded walls, regardless of their source (host or xref) are located on the same layer. Disable Use Insert Method when binding Xrefs if you want to retain the xref identities, such as layer names, when you export a file to AutoCAD or to a DXF file. For example, the blocks that define walls in the host drawing are located on A-Wall in the exploded drawing. Walls in an attached xref drawing are located on a layer whose name is created from the drawing name and the layer name, such as Drawing1|WallA.

	Many architects automatically bind and explode their xrefs when sending drawings to customers to protect their intellectual property.
	Enter a prefix or a suffix to be added to the drawing filename when the drawing is exported to an AutoCAD drawing or a DXF file.
	In order for any of these options to apply, you have to use the Export to AutoCAD command. This is available under the Files menu.
Unselected Grip Colors	Assign the colors for each type of grip.

Units for Legacy Drawings	Determines the units to be used when opening an AutoCAD drawing in AutoCAD Architecture.
	  Automatic – uses the current AutoCAD Architecture units setting
	  Imperial – uses Imperial units
	  Metric – uses Metric units

Option Settings are applied to your current drawing and saved as the default settings for new drawings. Because AutoCAD Architecture operates in a Multiple Document Interface, each drawing stores the Options Settings used when it was created and last saved. Some users get confused because they open an existing drawing and it will not behave according to the current Options Settings.

AEC Content

Architectural/Documentation/Multipurpose Object Style Path	Allows you to specify a path of source files to be used to import object styles; usually used for system styles like walls, floors, or roofs.
AEC DesignCenter Content Path	Type the path and location of your content files or click Browse to search for the content files.
Tool Catalog Content Root Path	Type the path and location of your Tool Catalog files or click Browse to search for the content files.
IFC Content Path	Type the path and location of your Tool Catalog files or click Browse to search for the content files.
Detail Component Databases	Select the **Add/Remove** button to set the search paths for your detail component files.
Keynote Databases	Select the **Add/Remove** button to set the search paths for your keynote database files.
Display Edit Schedule Data Dialog During Tag Insertion	To attach schedule data to objects when you insert a schedule tag in the drawing, this should be ENABLED.

IFC Content is an object-based building data model that is non-proprietary. It uses open-source code developed by the IAI (International Alliance for Interoperability) to promote data exchange between CAD software. IFC Content might be created in Autodesk Revit, Inventor, or some other software for use in your projects.

Using AEC Content

AutoCAD Architecture uses several pre-defined and user-customizable content including:

- Architectural Display Configurations
- Architectural Profiles of Geometric Shapes
- Wall Styles and Endcap geometry
- Door styles
- Window styles
- Stair styles
- Space styles
- Schedule tables

Standard style content is stored in the AEC templates subdirectory. You can create additional content, import and export styles between drawings.

AEC Project Defaults

Most BID/AEC firms work in a team environment where they divide a project's tasks among several different users. The AEC Project Defaults allow the CAD Manager or team leader to select a folder on the company's server to locate files, set up template files with the project's title blocks, and even set up a webpage to post project information.

ACA Overview

```
Select paths, file names and file locations:
☐ AEC Project Location Search Path
    ⇒ D:\Documents\Autodesk\My Projects\
    ⇒ D:\ACA 2026 Fundamentals\ACA 2026 Fundamentals exercises
☐ Default Project Template Files
☐ Default Project Bulletin Board
☐ Default Project Image
```

To add a path, simply expand the folder and use the Browse button to locate the desired folder.

You can add more than one path to the AEC Project Location Search Path. All the other folders only allow you to have a single location for template files, the project bulletin board, and the default project image.

I highly recommend that you store any custom content in a separate directory as far away from AutoCAD Architecture as possible. This will allow you to back up your custom work easily and prevent accidental erasure if you upgrade your software application.

You should be aware that AutoCAD Architecture currently allows the user to specify only ONE path for custom content, so drawings with custom commands will only work if they reside in the specified path.

☐ Close project drawings when switching projects	If enabled, when a user switches projects in the Project Navigator, any open drawings not related to the new project selected will be closed. This conserves memory resources.
☑ Show detailed drawing preview when dropping view on sheet	If enabled, then the user will see the entire view as it is being positioned on a sheet. If it is disabled, the user will just see the boundary of the view for the purposes of placing it on a sheet.
☐ Show Project Browser at startup	If enabled, you will automatically have access to the Project Browser whenever you start AutoCAD Architecture.

AEC Object Settings

Wall Settings	
Autosnap New Wall Justification Lines	Enable to have the endpoint of a new wall that is drawn within the Autosnap Radius of the baseline of an existing wall automatically snap to that baseline. If you select this option and set your Autosnap Radius to 0, then only walls that touch clean up with each other.
Autosnap Grip Edited Wall Justification Lines	Enable to snap the endpoint of a wall that you grip edit within the Autosnap Radius of the baseline of an existing wall. If you select this option and set your Autosnap Radius to 0, then only walls that touch clean up with each other.
Autosnap Radius	Enter a value to set the snap tolerance.
Do not display opening end cap styles	Enable Do Not Display Opening Endcap Styles to suppress the display of endcaps applied to openings in walls. Enabling this option boosts drawing performance when the drawing contains many complex endcaps.

ACA Overview

Stair Settings	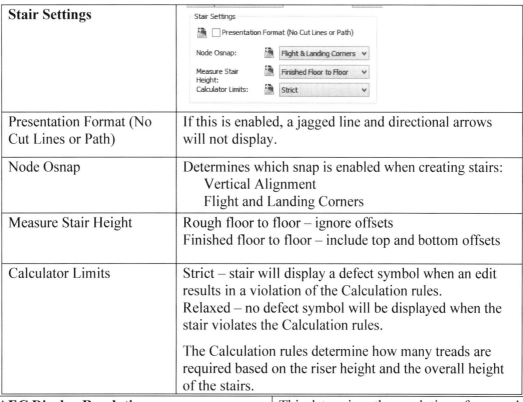
Presentation Format (No Cut Lines or Path)	If this is enabled, a jagged line and directional arrows will not display.

Node Osnap	Determines which snap is enabled when creating stairs:
	    Vertical Alignment
	    Flight and Landing Corners

Measure Stair Height	Rough floor to floor – ignore offsets Finished floor to floor – include top and bottom offsets
Calculator Limits	Strict – stair will display a defect symbol when an edit results in a violation of the Calculation rules. Relaxed – no defect symbol will be displayed when the stair violates the Calculation rules. The Calculation rules determine how many treads are required based on the riser height and the overall height of the stairs.

AEC Display Resolution	This determines the resolution of arcs and circular elements.
	Facet Deviation – The default is ½″. Facet Maximum – this can be set from 100 to 10,000. Higher settings use more memory and may affect screen refresh rates.
Space Settings	If *Automatically update associative spaces* is enabled, AutoCAD Architecture will automatically determine which spaces are adjacent to each other and update their association accordingly. The Maximum Gap Size is the allowable distance between spaces. The Maximum Automatic Adjacency sets the gap allowance between spaces for spaces to be considered adjacent. The Floor Boundary Thickness sets the value of the Floor Boundary Thickness. The Calculation Standard determines how

		the space values are calculated.
AEC Property Set Definitions 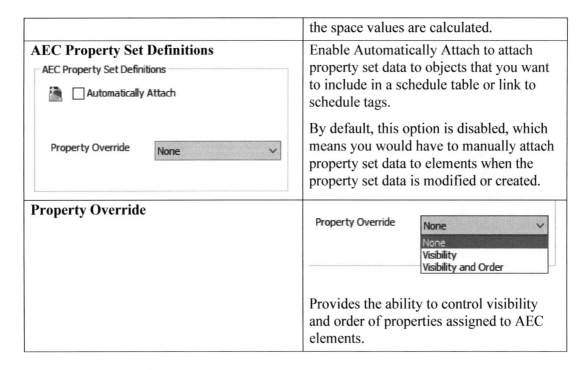		Enable Automatically Attach to attach property set data to objects that you want to include in a schedule table or link to schedule tags. By default, this option is disabled, which means you would have to manually attach property set data to elements when the property set data is modified or created.
Property Override		Property Override — None / Visibility / Visibility and Order Provides the ability to control visibility and order of properties assigned to AEC elements.

AEC Dimension

1-16

General	
Update Added/Removed points immediately	Enable to update the display every time you add or remove a point from a dimension chain.
Make Manual Dimension Points Associative	Enable if you want the dimension to update when the object is modified.
Override Display of Undefined Text	Enable to automatically underline each manually overridden dimension value.
Underline All	Enable to manually underline overridden dimension values.
Underline None	Enable to not underline any overridden dimension value.
Units	
Dimension in:	Select the desired units from the drop-down list.
Use Superscript mm	If your units are set to meters or centimeters, enable superscripted text to display the millimeters as superscript.
Trailing Zero Suppression for Superscript	To suppress zeros at the end of superscripted numbers, select Trailing Zeros Suppression for Superscript. You can select this option only if you have selected Use Superscript mm and your units are metric.
Automatic Scale of AutoCAD Dimstyles	Select the dimstyles you would like to automatically scale when units are reset.
Elevation Labels	Enable whether or not to display symbols next to the elevation value.

Dimension Label Prefixes	
	Dimension Label Prefixes are set based on the object selected from the drop-down. You can set label prefixes for Doors, Windows, Openings, and Stairs.
	Select the object, and then set the prefix for each designation. The designations will change based on the object selected.

Architectural Profiles of Geometric Shapes

You can create mass elements to define the shape and configuration of your preliminary study, or mass model. After you create the mass elements you need, you can change their size as necessary to reflect the building design.

- **Mass element**: A single object that has behaviors based on its shape. For example, you can set the width, depth, and height of a box mass element, and the radius and height of a cylinder mass element.

Mass elements are parametric, which allows each of the shapes to have very specific behavior when it comes to the manipulation of each mass element's shape. For example, if the corner grip point of a box is selected and dragged, then the width and depth are modified. It is easy to change the shape to another form by right-clicking on the element and selecting a new shape from the list.

Through Boolean operations (addition, subtraction, intersection), mass elements can be combined into a mass group. The mass group provides a representation of your building during the concept phase of your project.

- **Mass group**: Takes the shape of the mass elements and is placed on a separate layer from the mass elements.
- **Mass model**: A virtual mass object, shaped from mass elements, which defines the basic structure and proportion of your building. A marker appears as a small box in your drawing to which you attach mass elements.

As you continue developing your mass model, you can combine mass elements into mass groups and create complex building shapes through addition, subtraction, or intersection of mass elements. You can still edit individual mass elements attached to a mass group to further refine the building model.

To study alternative design schemes, you can create a number of mass element references. When you change the original of the referenced mass element, all the instances of the mass element references are updated.

The mass model that you create with mass elements and mass groups is a refinement of your original idea that you carry forward into the next phase of the project, in which you change the mass study into floor plates and then into walls. The walls are used to start the design phase.

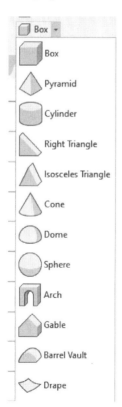

Mass Elements are accessed from the Home ribbon.

Mass Elements that can be defined from the Home tab include Arches, Gables, Cones, etc.

Exercise 1-2:
Creating a New Geometric Profile

Drawing Name: New
Estimated Time: 15 minutes

This exercise reinforces the following skills:

- Use of AEC Design Content
- Use of Mass Elements
- Use of Views
- Visual Styles
- Modify using Properties

Creating an arch mass element

1. Start a New Drawing.
2. 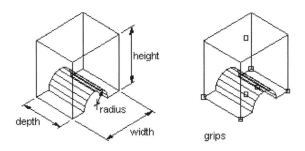 Select the **QNEW** tool from the Standard toolbar.
3. Because we assigned a template in Exercise 1-1, a drawing file opens without prompting us to select a template.

All the massing tools are available on the **Home** ribbon in the Build section.

4.

If you don't see the Properties palette:

Launch the **Properties** palette under Tools.

5.   Select the **Arch** tool from the Massing drop down list.

Expand the Dimensions category in the Properties palette.
Set Specify on screen to **No**.
Set the Width to **6'** [**183**].
Set the Depth to **6"** [**15**].
Set the Height to **6' 8"** [**203**].
Set the Radius to **2'** [**61**].

Units in brackets are centimeters.

You need to enter in the ' and " symbols.

6. 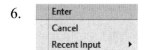   Pick a point anywhere in the drawing area.

   Click ENTER to accept a Rotation Angle of 0 or right click and select **ENTER**.

   Click **ENTER** to exit the command.

7.   Switch to an isometric view.
   To switch to an isometric view, simply go to **View** panel on the Home ribbon. Under the Views list, select **SW Isometric**.

   Or select the Home icon next to the Viewcube.

Our model so far.

8. Select **Visual Styles, Realistic** on the View panel on the Home ribbon to shade the model.

You can also type **SHA** on the command line, then **R** for Realistic.

9. To change the arch properties, select the arch so that it is highlighted. If the properties dialog doesn't pop up automatically, right click and select **Properties**.

10. Change the Radius to **9"** [15].

    Pick into the graphics window and the arch will update.

11. Click **ESC** to release the grips on the arc.

12. Save the drawing as *ex1-2.dwg*.

If you see this dialog, it means that the mass element just created (the arch) cannot be saved as a previous version file.

Click **Close**.

The Style Manager

Access the Style Manager from the Manage ribbon.

The Style Manager is a Microsoft® Windows Explorer-based utility that provides you with a central location in Autodesk AutoCAD Architecture where you can view and work with styles in drawings or from Internet and intranet sites.

Styles are sets of parameters that you can assign to objects in Autodesk AutoCAD Architecture to determine their appearance or function. For example, a door style in Autodesk AutoCAD Architecture determines what door type, such as single or double, bi-fold or hinged, a door in a drawing represents. You can assign one style to more than one object, and you can modify the style to change all the objects that are assigned that style.

Depending on your design projects, either you or your CAD Manager might want to customize existing styles or create new styles. The Style Manager allows you to easily create, customize, and share styles with other users. With the Style Manager, you can:

- Provide a central point for accessing styles from open drawings and Internet and intranet sites
- Quickly set up new drawings and templates by copying styles from other drawings or templates
- Sort and view the styles in your drawings and templates by drawing or by style type
- Preview an object with a selected style
- Create new styles and edit existing styles
- Delete unused styles from drawings and templates
- Send styles to other Autodesk AutoCAD Architecture users by email

Objects in Autodesk AutoCAD Architecture that use styles include 2D sections and elevations, AEC polygons, curtain walls, curtain wall units, doors, endcaps, railings, roof slab edges, roof slabs, schedule tables, slab edges, slabs, spaces, stairs, structural members, wall modifiers, walls, window assemblies, and windows.

Additionally, layer key styles, schedule data formats, and cleanup group, mask block, multi-view block, profile, and property set definitions are handled by the Style Manager.

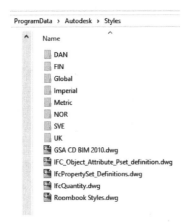

Most of the objects in Autodesk AutoCAD Architecture have a default Standard style. In addition, Autodesk AutoCAD Architecture includes a starter set of styles that you can use with your drawings. The Autodesk AutoCAD Architecture templates contain some of these styles. Any drawing that you start from one of the templates includes these styles.

You can also access the styles for doors, end caps, spaces, stairs, walls, and windows from drawings located in *ProgramData\Autodesk\Styles*.

Property set definitions and schedule tables are located in the *ProgramData\Autodesk\AEC Content* folder.

Exercise 1-3:
Copying a Style to a Template

Drawing Name: Styles.dwg, *AEC Model (Imperial Ctb).dwt*
Estimated Time: 20 minutes

This exercise reinforces the following skills:

- Style Manager
- Use of Templates
- Properties dialog

1. Close any open drawings.

   Go to the Application menu and select **Close → All Drawings**.

   *You can also type **CLOSEALL**.*

2. Start a New Drawing using plus tab.

3. Activate the **Manage** ribbon.

   Select the **Style Manager** tool.

4. Select the **File Open** tool in the Style Manager dialog.

5. Locate the *styles.dwg*.
   This file is downloaded from the publisher's website.
   Click **Open**.

Note: Make sure the Files of type is set to dwg or you will not see your files.

6. Styles.dwg is now listed in the Style Manager.

7. Select the **File Open** tool.

8. Set the Files of type to *Drawing Template (*.dwt)*.

You should automatically be directed to the Template folder.

If not, browse to the Template folder.

9. Locate the *AEC Model Imperial (Metric) Ctb.dwt* file. Click **Open**.

This is the default template we selected for QNEW.

10. You should see files open in the Style Manager.

11. Locate the **Brick_Block** Wall Style in the *Styles.dwg*.

12. Right click and select **Copy**.

13. Locate Wall Styles under the template drawing.

    Highlight, right click and select **Paste**.

14. You could also just drag and drop the Brick_block style from the Styles file to the template.

15. Click **Apply**.

16. Click **Yes**.

17. Close the Style Manager.

18. Look at the drawing folder tabs. The Styles.dwg and the template drawing are not shown. These are only open in the Style Manager.

19. Select the **plus** tab to start a new drawing.

20. Activate the Home ribbon.
    Select the **Wall** tool.

21. The Properties dialog should pop up when the WallAdd tool is selected.

    In the Style drop-down list, note that Brick_Block is available.

    If you don't see the wall style in the drop-down list, verify that you set the default template correctly in Options.

22. Click Escape to end the WallAdd command.

23. Close all drawing files without saving.

The Styles Browser

The Styles Browser can be launched from the Home ribbon under the Tools drop-down.

The Styles Browser displays the styles available for various elements.

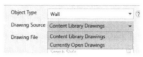 You can see the styles that are available in the Content Library as well as the active drawings.

You can use the Styles Browser to copy and paste styles between drawings.

Exercise 1-4:
Copying a Style using the Style Browser

Drawing Name: Stylebrowser.dwg
Estimated Time: 10 minutes

This exercise reinforces the following skills:

- Style Browser
- Use of Styles
- Importing a Style into a Drawing

1. Close any open drawings.

Go to the Application menu and select **Close → All Drawings**.

*You can also type **CLOSEALL**.*

1-31

2. 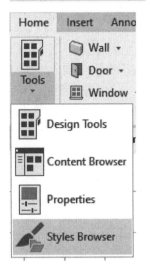 Start a New Drawing using plus tab.

3. Switch to the Home ribbon.

   Click **Styles Browser** under Tools to launch the Styles Browser.

4. On the Drawing Source field, click the down arrow and select **Currently Open Drawing**.

    Only one wall style is listed.

   If you modified the template used by QNEW, you will see two wall styles.

5. Open the *stylebrowser.dwg*.

   This file is downloaded from the publisher's website.

   The Styles Browser shows all the wall styles available in this file.

ACA Overview

6. Click on the **Drawing2** tab (the new drawing you created at the start of the exercise).

    Notice the Drawing Source has changed to Currently Open Drawings.

    The green check indicates any style being used in any of the open drawings.

7. Highlight the Stud-4 Rigid-1.5 Air wall style.

    Right click and select **Import styles**.

    Note you can hold down the CTL key to select more than one style to be imported.

    Close the *stylesbrowser.dwg* without saving.

8. Right click on the Stud-4 Rigid-1.5 Air wall style.

    Click **Add object**.

9. Click a point to start placing a wall.
    Drag the mouse to the right.
    Click to place an end point for the wall.
    Click ENTER to exit the command.

    Close the Style Browser.

10. Click the **Wall** tool on the Home ribbon.

11. Note that the imported wall style is available in the drawing now.

    Place a wall using the imported style.

12. Close without saving.

1-33

Visual Styles are stored with the drawing.

Visual Styles

Visual styles determine the display of edges, lighting, and shading in each viewport.

You can choose a predefined visual style in the upper-left corner of each viewport. In addition, the Visual Styles Manager displays all styles available in the drawing. You can choose a different visual style or change its settings at any time. ACA comes with several pre-defined visual styles or you can create your own.

Exercise 1-5:
Creating a New Visual Style

Drawing Name: visual_style.dwg
Estimated Time: 15 minutes

This exercise reinforces the following skills:

- Workspaces
- Use of Visual Styles
- Controlling the Display of Objects

1. Open *visual_style.dwg*.

2. Activate the **View** ribbon.

3. Launch the Visual Styles Manager.

   To launch, select the small arrow in the lower right corner of the Visual Styles panel.

4. 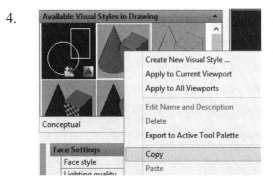 Highlight the **Conceptual** tool.

   Right click and select **Copy**.

5. 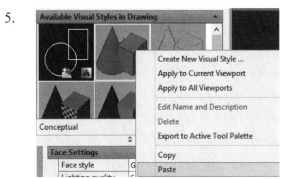 Right click and select **Paste**.

6. 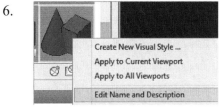 Highlight the copied tool.
   Right click and select **Edit Name and Description**.

7. Change the name and description to **Real Conceptual**.

   Click **OK**.

8. Under Face Settings:

   Set the Face Style to **Realistic**.

   Set Material display to **Materials and textures**.

   Under Environment Settings:

   Set the Backgrounds to **Off**.

   Under Edge Settings:

   Set the Show to **None**.

9. Verify that the Real Conceptual Style is highlighted/selected.

   Right click and select the **Apply to Current Viewport** tool.

   Note that the active visual style is listed in the upper right corner of the drawing.

10. Save the drawing as *ex1-5.dwg*.

Exercise 1-6:

Creating an Autodesk Cloud Account

Drawing Name: (none, start from scratch)
Estimated Time: 5 Minutes

This exercise reinforces the following skills:

❑ Create an account on Autodesk.

You must have an internet connection to access the Autodesk server. Many government agencies do not allow the use of cloud accounts due to security concerns. Autodesk's cloud account is useful for students, home users, and small shops.

1.

   When you first launch the software, you will be asked to sign in to your account.

   If you are in a school, the school may use a school ID account.

   If you have an existing Autodesk ID, you can use it.

   If not, select the link that says **Create Account.**

   You may have an existing Autodesk ID if you have registered Autodesk software in the past. Autodesk's cloud services are free to students and educators. For other users, you are provided a small amount of initial storage space for free.

   I like my students to have an on-line account because it will automatically back up their work.

2. Fill in the form to create an Autodesk ID account.

   Be sure to write down the ID you select and the password.

3. You should see a confirmation window stating that you now have an account.

4. You will see the name you selected as your Autodesk ID in the Cloud sign-in area.

Tips & Tricks

Use your Autodesk account to create renderings, back up files to the Cloud so you can access your drawings on any internet-connected device, and to share your drawings.

Exercise 1-7:
Tool Palettes

Drawing Name: tool_palettes.dwg
Estimated Time: 15 minutes

This exercise reinforces the following skills:

- Use of AEC Design Content
- Use of Wall Styles

1. Open the tool_palettes.dwg.

2. Activate the Home ribbon.

   Select **Tools→Design Tools** to launch the tool palette.

3. Right click on the Design Tools palette title bar.

   Click **New Palette**.

4. Rename the new palette **Favorite Walls**.

5. Click the **Design** tab on the tool palette.

   Use the scroll bar to scroll to the bottom of the tool palette.

   Locate the Content Browser icon.

   Click on the **Content Browser** icon to launch.

6. 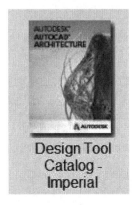 Locate the **Design Tool Catalog – Imperial.**

   Click on the **Design Tool Catalog – Imperial** to open.

7. Use the scroll bar to scroll down.

   Click on **Walls**.

ACA Overview

8. Click on the **Stud** link to look at the stud walls.

9. 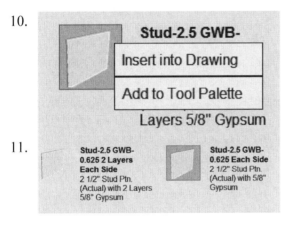 Locate the **Stud – 2.5 GWB – 0.625 2 Layers Each Side**.

10. 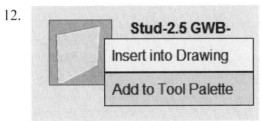 Click on the wall icon.
Select **Add to Tool Palette**.

11. Locate the **Stud – 2.5 GWB – 0.625 Each Side**.

12. Click on the wall icon.
Select **Add to Tool Palette**.

The two wall styles are now listed on the Walls palette.

13.

Right click below the second wall style.

Click **Add Separator**.

14.

A horizontal line is added to the tool palette.

ACA Overview

15. On the Favorite Walls tool palette:

Select the **Properties** button.

16. Select **View Options**.

17. Adjust the Image Size and select the desired View style.

You can apply the preference to the Current Palette (the walls palette only) or all palettes.

Click **OK**.

18. 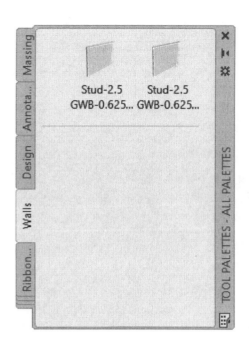 Verify that the tool palette is open with the Favorite Walls palette active.

19. Activate the **Manage** ribbon.

    Select the **Style Manager** tool.

20. Locate the **Brick-Block** wall style you created in the Style Manager.

21.   Drag and drop the wall style onto your Favorite Walls palette.

    Click **OK** to close the Style Manager.

ACA Overview

22. Highlight the **Brick_Block** tool.
Right click and select **Rename**.

23. Change the name to **8″ CMU- 3.5″ Brick [200 mm CMU – 90 mm]**.

24. Select the new tool and draw a wall.
You may draw a wall simply by picking two points.
If you enable the ORTHO button on the bottom of the screen, your wall will be straight.

25. Select the wall you drew.

Right click and select **Properties**.

Note that the wall is placed on the A-Wall Layer and uses the Brick-Block Style you defined.

26. Save your file as *Styles3.dwg*.

The wall style you created will not be available in any new drawings unless you copy it over to the default template. To make it easy to locate your exercise files, browse to where the files are located when you save the file. Right click on the left pane and select Add Current Folder.

A fast way to close all open files is to type CLOSEALL on the command line. You will be prompted to save any unsaved files.

Layer Manager

Back in the days of vellum and pencil, drafters would use separate sheets to organize their drawings, so one sheet might have the floor plan, one sheet the site plan, etc. The layers of paper would be placed on top of each other and the transparent quality of the vellum would allow the drafter to see the details on the lower sheets. Different colored pencils would be used to make it easier for the drafter to locate and identify elements of a drawing, such as dimensions, electrical outlets, water lines, etc.

When drafting moved to Computer Aided Design, the concept of sheets was transferred to the use of Layers. Drafters could assign a Layer Name, color, linetype, etc. and then place different elements on the appropriate layer.

AutoCAD Architecture has a Layer Management system to allow the user to implement AIA standards easily.

Layer Manager

The Layer Manager helps you organize, sort, and group layers, as well as save and coordinate layering schemes. You can also use layering standards with the Layer Manager to better organize the layers in your drawings.

When you open the Layer Manager, all the layers in the current drawing are displayed in the right panel. You can work with individual layers to:

- Change layer properties by selecting the property icons
- Make a layer the current layer
- Create, rename, and delete layers

The Layer Manager has a tool bar as shown.

ᴸ	*Layer Standards* You can import Layer Standards from an existing drawing or Export Layer Standards using the current drawing. 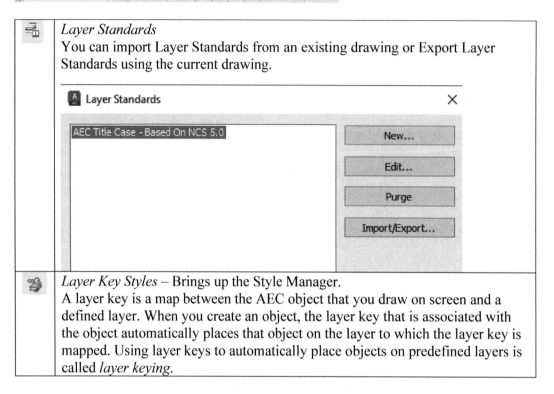
ᴸ	*Layer Key Styles* – Brings up the Style Manager. A layer key is a map between the AEC object that you draw on screen and a defined layer. When you create an object, the layer key that is associated with the object automatically places that object on the layer to which the layer key is mapped. Using layer keys to automatically place objects on predefined layers is called *layer keying*.

The layer key styles in Autodesk AutoCAD Architecture, Release 3 and above replace the use of LY files. If you have LY files from S8 or Release 1 of AutoCAD Architecture that you want to use, then you can create a new layer key style from an LY file. On the command line enter **-AecLYImport** to import legacy LY files.

	Layer Key Overrides 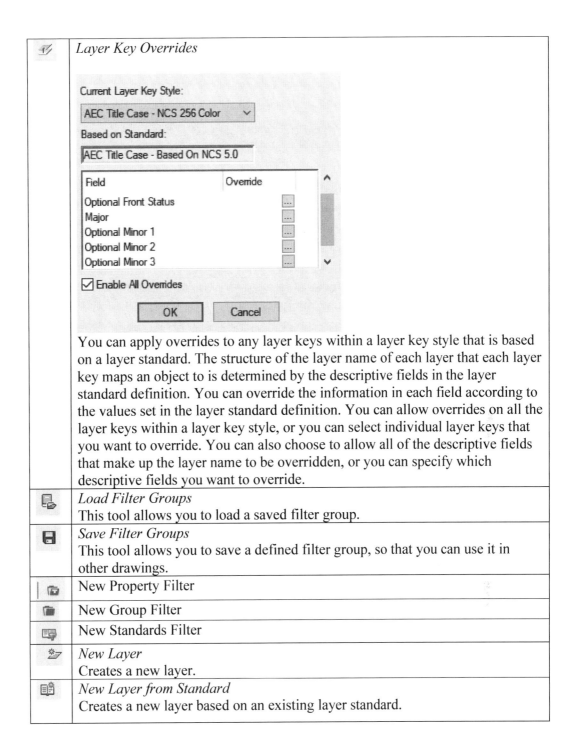 You can apply overrides to any layer keys within a layer key style that is based on a layer standard. The structure of the layer name of each layer that each layer key maps an object to is determined by the descriptive fields in the layer standard definition. You can override the information in each field according to the values set in the layer standard definition. You can allow overrides on all the layer keys within a layer key style, or you can select individual layer keys that you want to override. You can also choose to allow all of the descriptive fields that make up the layer name to be overridden, or you can specify which descriptive fields you want to override.
	Load Filter Groups This tool allows you to load a saved filter group.
	Save Filter Groups This tool allows you to save a defined filter group, so that you can use it in other drawings.
	New Property Filter
	New Group Filter
	New Standards Filter
	New Layer Creates a new layer.
	New Layer from Standard Creates a new layer based on an existing layer standard.

	New Layer VP Frozen in All Viewports Creates a new layer and automatically freezes it (makes it invisible).	
	Delete Layer Highlight the layer(s) you wish to delete and select this tool.	
	Make selected layer current Highlight a layer name in the list and Click this button to set current.	

The following are the default layer keys used by Autodesk AutoCAD Architecture when you create AEC objects.

Default layer keys for creating AEC objects

Layer Key	Description	Layer Key	Description
ANNDTOBJ	Detail marks	COMMUN	Communication
ANNELKEY	Elevation Marks	CONTROL	Control systems
ANNELOBJ	Elevation objects	CWLAYOUT	Curtain walls
ANNMASK	Masking objects	CWUNIT	Curtain wall units
ANNMATCH	Match Lines	DIMLINE	Dimensions
ANNOBJ	Notes, leaders, etc.	DIMMAN	Dimensions (AutoCAD points)
ANNREV	Revisions	DOOR	Doors
ANNSXKEY	Section marks	DOORNO	Door tags
ANNSXOBJ	Section marks	DRAINAGE	Drainage
ANNSYMOBJ	Annotation marks	ELEC	Electric
APPL	Appliances	ELECNO	Electrical tags
AREA	Areas	ELEV	Elevations
AREAGRP	Area groups	ELEVAT	Elevators
AREAGRPNO	Area group tags	ELEVHIDE	Elevations (2D)
AREANO	Area tags	EQUIP	Equipment
CAMERA	Cameras	EQUIPNO	Equipment tags
CASE	Casework	FINCEIL	Ceiling tags
CASENO	Casework tags	FINE	Details- Fine lines
CEILGRID	Ceiling grids	FINFLOOR	Finish tags
CEILOBJ	Ceiling objects	FIRE	Fire system equip.
CHASE	Chases	FURN	Furniture
COGO	Control Points	FURNNO	Furniture tags
COLUMN	Columns	GRIDBUB	Plan grid bubbles
GRIDLINE	Column grids	SITE	Site

Layer Key	Description	Layer Key	Description
HATCH	Detail-Hatch lines	SLAB	Slabs
HIDDEN	Hidden Lines	SPACEBDRY	Space boundaries
LAYGRID	Layout grids	SPACENO	Space tags
LIGHTCLG	Ceiling lighting	SPACEOBJ	Space objects
LIGHTW	Wall lighting	STAIR	Stairs
MASSELEM	Massing elements	STAIRH	Stair handrails
MASSGRPS	Massing groups	STRUCTBEAM	Structural beams
MASSSLCE	Massing slices	STRUCTBEAMIDEN	Structural beam tags
MED	Medium Lines	STRUCTBRACE	Structural braces
OPENING	Wall openings	STRUCTBRACEIDEN	Structural brace tags
PEOPLE	People	STRUCTCOLS	Structural columns
PFIXT	Plumbing fixtures	STRUCTCOLSIDEN	Structural column tags
PLANTS	Plants - outdoor	SWITCH	Electrical switches
PLANTSI	Plants - indoor	TITTEXT	Border and title block
POLYGON	AEC Polygons	TOILACC	Arch. specialties
POWER	Electrical power	TOILNO	Toilet tags
PRCL	Property Line	UTIL	Site utilities
PRK-SYM	Parking symbols	VEHICLES	Vehicles
ROOF	Rooflines	WALL	Walls
ROOFSLAB	Roof slabs	WALLFIRE	Fire wall patterning
ROOMNO	Room tags	WALLNO	Wall tags
SCHEDOBJ	Schedule tables	WIND	Windows
SEATNO	Seating tags	WINDASSEM	Window assemblies
SECT	Miscellaneous sections	WINDNO	Window tags
SECTHIDE	Sections (2D)		

Display Manager

The Display Manager is a utility for managing display configurations, display sets, and display representations: renaming them or deleting them, copying them between drawings, emailing them to other users, and purging unused elements from drawings.

The display system in AutoCAD Architecture is designed so that you only have to draw an architectural object once. The appearance of that object then changes automatically to meet the display requirements of different types of drawings, view directions, or levels of detail.

You can change the display settings for an element by using the Display tab on the Properties palette.

To change the display using the Display tab, click Select Components, select an object display component (like a hatch or a boundary), and then select or enter a new value for the display property you want to change (such as color, visibility, or lineweight).

Exercise 1-8:
Exploring the Display Manager

Drawing Name: display_manager.dwg
Estimated Time: 15 minutes

This exercise reinforces the following skills:

❑ Display Manager

1. Open *display_manager.dwg*.

2. Access the **Display Manager** from the Manage ribbon.

The display system in Autodesk® AutoCAD Architecture controls how AEC objects are displayed in a designated viewport. By specifying the AEC objects you want to display in a viewport and the direction from which you want to view them, you can produce different architectural display settings, such as floor plans, reflected plans, elevations, 3D models, or schematic displays.

3. Expand the *Representations by Object* folder.

   Locate Door.

   You see that there are different ways a door will appear depending on the display configuration selected.

   Highlight **Threshold Plan**.

ACA Overview

4. You see that the Threshold visibilities are turned off.

5. Highlight the **Plan** configuration.

6. You see that some door components are turned on and others are turned off.

7. Highlight the Model configuration.

8. You see that most door components are turned on and the swing is turned off. This means when you are viewing your building in 3D mode, you will not see the door swing symbol.

9. Go to the Sets folder. The Set highlighted in bold is the active Display Representation.

   Highlight **Plan**.

10. Select the Display Representation Control tab.
    Locate **Door** under Objects.
    Note that some display representations are checked and others are unchecked.
    A check indicates that the door is visible. Which door components are visible is controlled under Representations by Object.

    The three different folders – Configurations, Sets, and Representations by Object – are different ways of looking at the same elements. Each folder organizes the elements in a different way. If you change the display setting in one folder, it updates in the other two folders.

11. Expand the **Configurations** folder.

12. Expand **Medium Detail**.
    You see the different display sets. Note that Medium Detail does not hold all the different display sets. You can add or remove display sets.
    Close the Display Manager.

13. Close the drawing without saving.

Text Styles

A text style is a named collection of text settings that controls the appearance of text, such as font, line spacing, justification, and color. You create text styles to specify the format of text quickly, and to ensure that text conforms to industry or project standards.

- When you create text, it uses the settings of the current text style.
- If you change a setting in a text style, all text objects in the drawing that use the style update automatically.
- You can change the properties of individual objects to override the text style.
- All text styles in your drawing are listed in the Text Style drop-down.
- Text styles apply to notes, leaders, dimensions, tables, and block attributes.

All drawings contain a STANDARD text style which can't be deleted. Once you create a standard set of text styles, you can save the styles to your template file (.dwt).

Exercise 1-9:
Creating a Text Style

Drawing Name: new using QNEW
Estimated Time: 15 minutes

This exercise reinforces the following skills:

- CUI – Custom User Interface
- Ribbon
- Panel
- Tab

1. Start a new drawing using the QNEW tool.

2. Select the **Text Style** tool on the Home ribbon.

   It is located on the Annotation panel under the drop-down.

3. Click the **New** button in the Text Styles dialog box.

4. In the New Text Style dialog box, enter **TEXT1** for the name of the new text style and Click **OK**.

5. 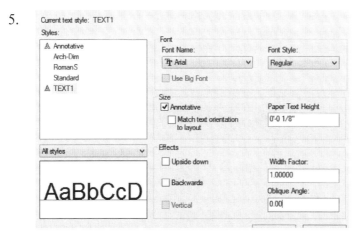 Fill in the remaining information in the Text Style dialog box as shown.

   Set the Font Name to **Arial**.
   Set the Font Style to **Regular**.
   Set the Paper Text Height to **1/8"**.
   Set the Width Factor to **1.00**.

6. Click the Apply button first and then the Close button to apply the changes to TEXT1 and then close the dialog box.

7. Save as *fonts.dwg*.

- You can use PURGE to eliminate any unused text styles from your drawing.
- You can import text styles from one drawing to another using the Design Center.
- You can store text styles in your template for easier access.
- You can use any Windows font to create AutoCAD Text.

Project Settings

The Project Navigator in AutoCAD Architecture gives us a way to Create, Access, Organize, and Coordinate all of our Project drawings in one palette.

The use of the Project Navigator begins with creating a Project in the **Project Browser**.

You can launch the Project Browser from the **Quick Access Toolbar**.

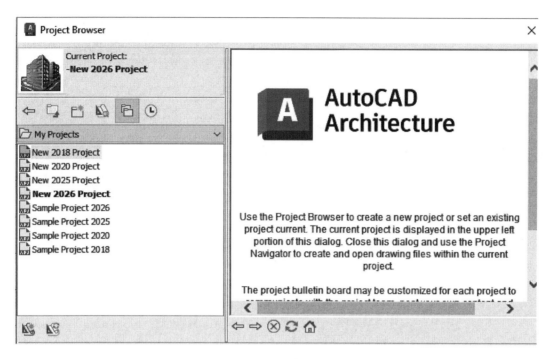

In the Project Browser, you create Projects and adjust their properties. Once a Project is created, you can right-click on it and in the pop-up menu, choose **Set Project Current**, and then click the **Close** button. This opens the **Project Navigator** palette. When you create a new project, you are also creating a folder sub-structure where all the files associated with the project will be stored. Projects rely on the use of external files all linked together to create the project. Companies that wish to use the Project Management system may opt to store all projects on a server so that team members can access the files easily. The Project Navigator also acts as a PDM server, where users can check in and out files, control file revisions, and roll-back drawings to previous versions.

When you organize your building using the Project Navigator, you have the following advantages:

- Organization of drawing and supporting files in one easily accessible location—Project Navigator
- Storage of project-based information such as the project name and number as well as site, utility, and financial data in a single location—Project Browser
- Updated sheet numbers to reflect changes made in the sheet set
- Notification of changes made to project drawings
- Control over project tools, project standard styles, and display settings
- Distribution of projects over a network with multi-user access

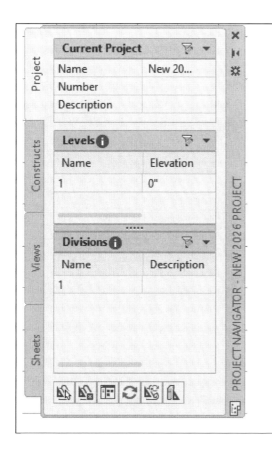

All the drawings in the project are displayed and organized in the Project Navigator.

These drawings are referenced into more complex drawings, for example referencing all individual level drawings into one drawing displaying a complete view of the building model. From these view drawings, you can create other drawings for sections, elevations and annotated plot sheets for the project.

You use the Project Navigator instead of the File Explorer.

The **Project Navigator** palette has four tabs: **Project**; **Constructs**; **Views**; and **Sheets**.

The **Project** tab is where you begin.

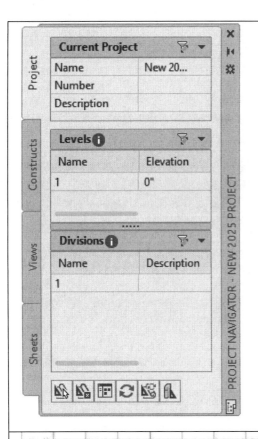

Here you can create the Project **Levels** and **Divisions**. Divisions are used to subdivide Levels into drawings. Levels represent the floors in a building. The construct drawings are assigned to a level of the building and the level height controls the elevation at which the drawings are inserted.

Divisions represent wings or plan areas within a building. The construct drawings are assigned to a division of the building as well as the level of that division. In a small project it is possible to have only one division.

The **Constructs** tab consists of two separate areas: **Constructs**, and **Elements**.

These are your Model files. These may be further subdivided into different Categories.

Constructs are for objects that are uniquely located at a specific Level. These might be columns, walls, windows.

Elements contain objects that are not associated with a specific Level. Elements are similar to blocks and contain objects that are repeated inside the building. The elements are referenced by the constructs within a project, for example, a typical toilet room that is located in the same spot on all floors.

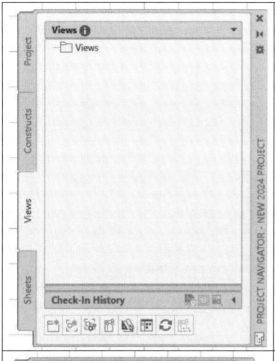	The views tab will be used to create Composite Trade Drawings which include notes, dimensions, tags and any other annotation necessary. To create one, right click on the views folder and select "New view dwg." Then select what type of view drawing you want to create. The options are general, section/ elevation or detail. Pick the type of view you need and follow the next set of prompts.
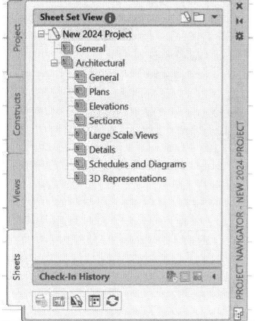	On the **Sheets** tab, you may establish **Subsets** for your drawings. For example, this project includes **General** and **Architectural** subsets. Under Architectural, there are additional Subsets. Each subset may consist of several sheets/drawings. The Sheets Tab is where all the dimensioning and plotting is done. Each file that is created will become the layout sheets used to print. This keeps the main construct files clutter free and smaller in size. The sheets drawing files are typically split up by trade. Under each trade you will create a new sheet for each new drawing. (Example: 01-DW-INSTALL)

> **Tips & Tricks**
>
> To quickly access the Project Navigator, use CTL+5.
> You can also type PROJECTNAVIGATORTOGGLE to toggle visibility on/off.

Project Management

The Project Browser is where you perform high-level project-related tasks, such as creating a new project, selecting the currently active project, and setting project properties. The Browser allows you to create a folder where you will store your project files, so they are easily located and managed.

Project Tab:

This is where you will set & get all the information about the project.

- Name
- Job Number
- Description
- Levels
- Elevations
- Divisions

All of this should be set up before the job is started.

The recommended work flow in ACA looks like this:

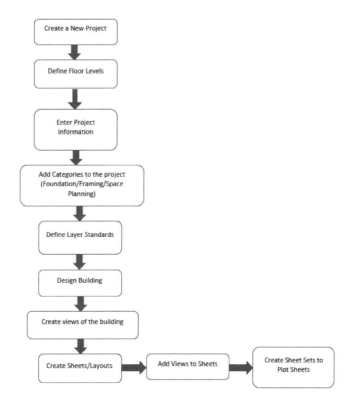

Basic Recommended Practices

- Use the Project Navigator to build your projects and manage.
- Start with project templates.
- Model in constructs. Use ACA objects (walls, doors, windows, stairs, curtainwalls, etc.).
- Dimension and annotate only in views files. Each view file should have at least one model space view.
- Sheet files should only have one layout.
- Your titleblock should be in your sheet template.
- Use fields for your sheet block annotation. The Project Navigator can populate those fields with project and sheet specific information.
- Drag model space views onto sheets.
- Use built in schedules.
- Use keynotes and tags.
- Use AEC dimension and AEC object types.
- Use grids.
- Let the layering key style build your layers. Avoid creating other layers outside of the ACA standard. Use the Project Navigator to manage your layer properties.
- Each view file should stand on its own without the need to coordinate annotation styles.
- Create your own styles but just a few per project.
- Build and use library and custom multi-view blocks for furniture, equipment, and factory components.
- Use the Styles Browser and the Styles Catalogs and Styles Library drawings to save time.
- Using tool palettes, especially project-based tool palettes, is a great way to manage and update content. You can create customized tool palettes to match the way you work.

After you have selected a project in the Project Browser, you use the Project Navigator to create and edit the actual building and documentation data. Here you create elements, constructs, model views, detail views, section views, and sheets, connecting them with one another.

You can define multi-story buildings using the Project Navigator. In the Navigator, you can specify the number of levels for the building. You can also use the Navigator to manage your views, sheets, and layer standards.

Note: Although project files and categories you create on the Project Navigator palette are shown as files and folders in File Explorer, you should not move, copy, delete, or rename project files from there. Such changes are not updated on the Project Navigator palette, and you could get an inconsistent view of your project data. Any changes you make to the project on the Project Navigator palette are managed and coordinated by the software. Also note that any changes you make on the Project Navigator palette (such as renaming, deleting, or changing the file's properties) cannot be undone using the AutoCAD UNDO command.

Because projects involve the use of multiple files, this can be confusing to keep track of when teaching a class or managing the files used for each lesson. To make it easier, I am going to create a zip file at the end of each lesson/chapter in the text. This file will serve as a snapshot of the textbook's project at different stages and help keep students (and instructors) on track as they gain proficiency in the software.

Exercise 1-10:
Using the Project Navigator and Project Browser

Drawing Name: new
Estimated Time: 20 minutes

This exercise reinforces the following skills:

- Project Browser
- Project Navigator
- Create levels
- Managing multi-story projects
- Archiving projects
- Closing projects

1. Start a new drawing.
2. Right click in the command window and select **Options**.
3. Select the **AEC Project Defaults** tab.
4. Set the AEC Project Location Search Path to the location where you are saving your files.

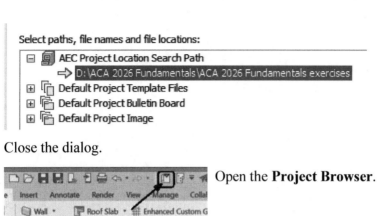

Close the dialog.

5. Open the **Project Browser**.

6. Select **New Project**.

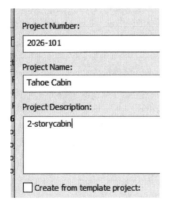

7. Type **2026-101** for the Project Number.

Type **Tahoe Cabin** as the Project Name.
Type **2-story cabin** for the Project Description.

Disable Create from template project.

Click **OK**.

ACA Overview

8.

   Notice that the Current Project is now the project you just defined.

   Notice that the project name is in bold under My Projects.

   Close the dialog.

9.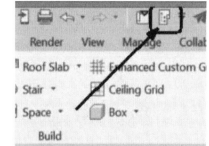

   The Project Navigator may already be open or may launch automatically.

   If it doesn't, select the **Project Navigator** tool from the Quick Access toolbar.

10.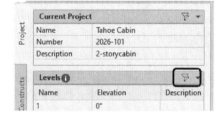

    On the Project tab:

    Click on **Create/Edit Levels**.

11.

    Rename the first level **Foundation**.
    Change the Floor Elevation to **-4'-0"**.
    Set the Floor to Floor Height to **4'-0"**.
    Set the ID to **0**.
    Set the Description to **Foundation**.

12.

    Click on **Add Level**.

13. Type **First Floor** for the Name.
    Set the Floor Elevation to **3'-0"**.
    Set the Floor to Floor Height to **10'-0"**.
    Set the ID to **1**.
    Set the Description to **First Floor.**

    Click **Add Level**.

14. Type **Second Floor** for the Name.
    Set the Floor Elevation to **13'-0"**.
    Set the Floor to Floor Height to **10'-0"**.
    Set the ID to **2**.
    Set the Description to **Second Floor.**

    Click **Add Level**..

15. Type **Roof** for the Name.
    Set the Floor Elevation to **23'-0"**.
    Set the Floor to Floor Height to **10'-0"**.
    Set the ID to **R**.
    Set the Description to **Roof.**

Name	Floor Elevation	Floor to Floor Height	ID	Description
Roof	23'-0"	10'-0"	R	Roof
Second Floor	13'-0"	10'-0"	2	Second Floor
First Floor	3'-0"	10'-0"	1	First Floor
Foundation	-4'-0"	7'-0"	0	Foundation

The Levels should appear as shown.

Click **OK**

16. 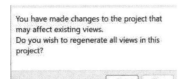 Click **Yes**.

ACA Overview

17. The levels are all listed.

18. Open the **Project Browser**.

19. Highlight the project name: **Tahoe Cabin**.

    Right click and select **Show in Windows Explorer**.

20. You can see where the project has been saved.
    Note that several subfolders were automatically created where the external files referenced by the project will be saved.

21. Highlight the project name: **Tahoe Cabin**.

    Right click and select **Archive**.

22.

    Click on the Files Table tab.

    You see that nine files have already been generated.

    Click on **Modify Archive Setup**.

23.

    Under Archive file folder, browse to where you want to back up your project files.

    Click **OK**.

24. Enter some notes regarding your first archive.

    Click **OK**.

25. Verify that the zip file is being saved in the correct location.
    Click **Save**.

26. Highlight the project name: **Tahoe Cabin**.

Right click and select **Close Current Project**.

27. 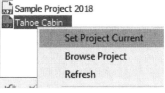 The dialog shows that no project is active. This is useful if you elect to work outside of a project and don't want your work saved to a project.

Exercise 1-11:
Modifying a Project's Properties

Drawing Name: none
Estimated Time: 5 minutes

This exercise reinforces the following skills:

- Project Browser

1. Close all open drawings.
Launch the Project Browser.

Highlight the Tahoe Cabin project.

Right click and select **Set Project Current**.

2. Right click on the Tahoe Cabin project.

Select **Project Properties.**

3. Expand the Templates section.

Set the Common Model/View Template to the *Aec Model (Imperial Ctb).dwt*.
Set the Sheet Template to *Arch D (24 x 36)*.

4. Expand the Project Browser section.

The htm file is the file that is displayed in the right pane of the Project Browser.
This is a great place to display project information for team members.
The project image is an image file. You can use your company logo, but the image must be a *.bmp file.
You can create a file in Microsoft Word and then save it as an htm file for use in the Project Browser.

5. Change the Bulletin Board to use the *Tahoe Cabin Project.htm* file.
Change the Project Image to use the *bbrown-logo.bmp* file.

6. Under File Check In Options,
Change the Maximum Backups to **3**.
Change Comments to **Yes**.

Click **OK**.

This will create a back-up file when files are checked out and checked in, so if you need to go back to previous version, you have a back-up to look at.

By setting Comments to Yes, any user who checks in the file can add comments as to what was changed.

ACA Overview

Notice that the right panel has updated with the htm that you uploaded.

Notice that the logo in the upper left has changed.

7. Right click on the Tahoe Cabin and select **Close Current Project**.

Close the Project Browser.

Exercise 1-12:
Using a Template to Create a Project

Drawing Name: new
Estimated Time: 30 minutes

This exercise reinforces the following skills:

- Project Browser
- Project Navigator
- Create levels
- Managing multi-story projects
- Archiving projects
- Closing projects

1. Open the **Project Browser**.

1-75

2. Select **New Project**.

3. Type **2026-102** for the Project Number.

   Type **Brown Medical Clinic** as the Project Name.
   Type **medical clinic** for the Project Description.

   Enable **Create from template project**.

   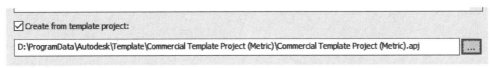

   Browse to the folder and select the *Commercial Template Project (Metric).apj* file.
   Click **Open**.

   Click **OK**.

   There will be a brief pause while ACA imports all the elements to be used in the project.

4. The Brown Medical Clinic shows as the active/current project.

Notice that the right pane and image are using the default values.

Close the Project Browser.

The Project Navigator should open.

5. On the Project tab:

Notice that it is a two-story building, with a site plan and a basement.

Current Project	
Name	Brown Medical Clinic
Number	2026-102
Description	medical clinic

Levels		
Name	Elevation	Description
R	7200.00	Roof
2	3600.00	Second Floor
1	0.00	First Floor
S	-150.00	Site Datum Level
B	-3600.00	Basement

6. 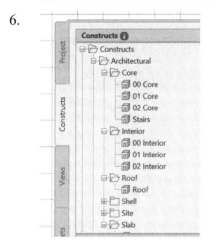 Open the Constructs tab.

Notice that categories and subcategories have already been predefined based on the selected template.

The template acts as an outline for the building project.

7. Under the Elements category, Locate the Typical Toilet Room.

   Right click and select **Open**.

8. A drawing is opened that consists of a single rectangle.

   The drawing is called Typical Toilet Room.

   This file basically acts as a placeholder where you can add toilet stalls, sinks, etc. which can then be placed in the building model as a block.

   Close the file without saving.

9. 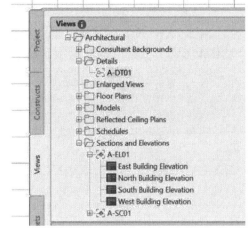 Click on the Views tab.

   Expand the Details folder.

   Expand the Sections and Elevations folder.

   The files listed below those folders are all drawings.

10. Open the Sheets tab.

    These are also drawings that are automatically generated using the designated title block in the project.

11. Open the **Project Browser**.

12. Highlight the project name: **Brown Medical Clinic**.

    Right click and select **Show in Windows Explorer**.

13. You can see where the project has been saved.
    Note that several subfolders were automatically created where the external files referenced by the project will be saved.

14. Highlight the project name: **Brown Medical Clinic**.

    Right click and select **Archive**.

15. Click on the Files Table tab.

    You see that over 100 files have already been generated.

    Click on **Modify Archive Setup**.

16.

    Under Archive file folder, browse to where you want to back up your project files.

    Click **OK**.

17.

    Enter some notes regarding your first archive.

    Click **OK**.

18. Verify that the zip file is being saved in the correct location.

    Click **Save**.

19. Highlight the project name: **Brown Medical Clinic**.

Right click and select **Close Current Project**.

Close the dialog box.

Layer Keys and Layer Keying

When you create an object, the layer key that is associated with the object automatically places that object on the layer to which it is mapped. Using layer keys to automatically place objects on predefined layers is called *layer keying*. Usually, you key objects to layers that conform to a layer standard. Each layer standard names layers according to a set of rules that you can modify.

Layer Key Styles

You can create different sets of layer keys, called layer key styles, that you can use to place objects on defined layers in your drawings. Each layer key style contains a set of layer keys. Both the AIA and BS1192 layer key styles contain layer keys and layer properties, including layer name, description, color, linetype, lineweight, plot style, and plot settings for all of the AEC objects. You can import the AIA and BS1192 layer standards and layer key styles that are provided with AutoCAD Architecture 2026 toolset from the *AecLayerStd.dwg* in the *C:\ProgramData\Autodesk\ACA <version>\enu\Layers* folder. You can modify these styles, if needed, or create new layer key styles. You can also create layer key styles from LY files.

Exercise 1-13:
Modifying the ACA Layer Keys

Drawing Name: new
Estimated Time: 10 minutes

This exercise reinforces the following skills:

- Project Browser
- Project Navigator
- Layer Keys

1. Start a new drawing.

2. 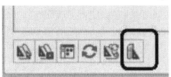 Open the Project tab.
   Note that the Current Project is set to the Brown Medical Clinic.

   Click on **Configure Project Standards**.

3. 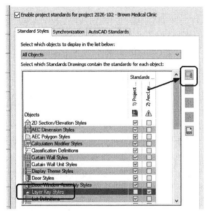 Highlight the Layer Key Styles.

   Click **Attach**.

4. 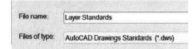 Locate the *Layer Standards.dws* file in the downloaded exercise files.

   Click **Open**.

5. 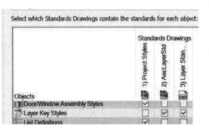 Click to enable the Layer Key Styles to use the Layer Standards.dws layer keys.

   Click **OK**.

ACA Overview

6.   *If you like, you can add a comment about the layer standards you are using.*

   Click **OK**.

7.   Open the **Layer Manager**.

8.   Click on **Layer Keys**.

9.   Highlight the Layer Key Style being used.

10. Click on the Keys tab.

   You can see the layer properties for each AEC object.

11. Review the Layer Key Styles used in your project.

   Click **OK**.

12. Close the Layer Manager.
    The changes that you made to the Brown Medical Clinic project will be included the next time we archive the project.

13. Close the Project Navigator.
    Close any open drawings.

Notes:

QUIZ 1

True or False

1. Doors, windows, and walls are inserted into the drawing as objects.
2. The Architectural Toolbars are loaded from the ACA Menu Group.
3. To set the template used by the QNEW tool, use Options.

4. If you start a New Drawing using the 'QNew' tool shown above, the Start-Up dialog will appear unless you assign a template.
5. Mass elements are used to create Mass Models.
6. The Layer Manager is used to organize, sort, and group layers.
7. Layer Standards are set using the Layer Manager.
8. You can assign materials to components in wall styles.

Multiple Choice
Select the best answer.

9. If you start a drawing using one of the standard templates, AutoCAD Architecture will automatically create _____ layouts.

    A. A work layout plus Model Space
    B. Four layouts, plus Model Space
    C. Ten layouts, plus Model Space
    D. Eleven layouts, plus Model Space

10. Options are set through:

    A. Options
    B. Desktop
    C. User Settings
    D. Template

11. The Display Manager controls:

    A. How AEC objects are displayed in the graphics window
    B. The number of viewports
    C. The number of layout tabs
    D. Layers

12. Mass Elements are created using the _____ Tool Palette.

    A. Massing
    B. Concept
    C. General Drafting
    D. Documentation

13. Wall Styles are created by:

    A. Highlighting a Wall on the Wall tab of the Tool Palette, right click and select Wall Styles
    B. Type **WallStyle** on the command line
    C. Go to **Format→Style Manager**
    D. All of the above

14. Visual Styles are used to:

    A. Determine which materials are used for rendering
    B. Controls which layers are visible
    C. Determines the display of edges, lighting, and shading in each viewport
    D. Determines the display of AEC elements in the Work layout tab

15. You can change the way AEC objects are displayed by using:

    A. Edit Object Display
    B. Edit Display Properties
    C. Edit Entity Properties
    D. Edit AEC Properties

16. The Styles Browser can be used for any of the following tasks: (select more than one)

    A. Search for object styles
    B. Import styles into your current drawing
    C. Place an element using a selected style from the browser
    D. Create new styles

17. The Project Browser may be used to:

    A. Create new projects
    B. Configure project settings and standards
    C. Select the Current Project
    D. All of the above

ANSWERS:

1) T; 2) T; 3) T; 4) F; 5) T; 6) T; 7) T; 8) T; 9) A; 10) A; 11) A; 12) A; 13) D; 14) C; 15) A; 16) A, B, and C (to create new styles you have to use the Styles Manager) 17) D

Lesson 2:
Foundations & Site Plans

Most architectural projects start with a site plan. The site plan indicates the property lines, the house location, a North symbol, any streets surrounding the property, topographical features, location of sewer, gas, and/or electrical lines (assuming they are below ground – above ground connections are not shown), and topographical features.

When laying out the floor plan for the house, many architects take into consideration the path of sun (to optimize natural light), street access (to locate the driveway), and any noise factors. AutoCAD Architecture includes the ability to perform sun studies on your models.

AutoCAD Architecture allows the user to simulate the natural path of the sun based on the longitude and latitude coordinates of the site, so you can test how natural light will affect various house orientations.

A site plan must include the following features:

- Length and bearing of each property line
- Location, outline, and size of buildings on the site
- Contour of the land
- Elevation of property corners and contour lines
- North symbol
- Trees, shrubs, streams, and other topological items
- Streets, sidewalks, driveways, and patios
- Location of utilities
- Easements and drainages (if any)
- Well, septic, sewage line, and underground cables
- Fences and retaining walls
- Lot number and/or address of the site
- Scale of the drawing

The site plan is drawn using information provided by the county/city and/or a licensed surveyor.

When drafting with pencil and vellum, the drafter will draw to a scale, such as $\frac{1}{8}" = 1'$, but with AutoCAD Architecture, you draw full-size and then set up your layout to the proper scale. This ensures that all items you draw will fit together properly. This also is important if you collaborate with outside firms. For example, if you want to send your files to a firm that does HVAC, you want their equipment to fit properly in your design. If everyone drafts 1:1 or full-size, then you can ensure there are no interferences or conflicts.

Linetypes

Architectural drafting requires a variety of custom linetypes in order to display specific features. The standard linetypes provided with AutoCAD Architecture are insufficient from an architectural point of view. You may find custom linetypes on Autodesk's website, www.cadalog.com, or any number of websites on the Internet. However, the ability to create linetypes as needed is an excellent skill for an architectural drafter.

It's a good idea to store any custom linetypes in a separate file. The standard file for storing linetypes is acad.lin. If you store any custom linetypes in acad.lin file, you will lose them the next time you upgrade your software.

Exercise 2-1:
Creating Custom Line Types

Drawing Name:	New
Estimated Time:	15 minutes

This exercise reinforces the following skills:

- Creation of linetypes
- Customization

A video of this lesson is available on my MossDesigns channel on Youtube at https://www.youtube.com/watch?v=gSCyFJm6pfY

1. Start a new drawing using **QNEW**.

   Launch the **Project Browser**.

2. Highlight the current/active project.

   Right click and select **Close Current Project**.

3. You should see No current project active in the dialog.

   Close the Project Browser.

4. Draw a property line.
   This property line was created as follows:
   Set ORTHO ON.
   Draw a horizontal line 100 units long.

   Use SNAP FROM to start the next line @30,0 distance from the previous line.
   You can also simply use object tracking to locate the next line.
   The short line is 60 units long.
   Use SNAP FROM to start the next line @30,0 distance from the previous line.
   The second short line is 60 units long.
   Use SNAP FROM to start the next line @30,0 distance from the previous line.
   Draw a second horizontal line 100 units long.

5. Activate the Express Tools ribbon.

   Select the **Tools** drop-down.
   Go to **Make Linetype**.

6. Browse to the folder where you are storing your work.

    Create a file name called *custom-linetypes.lin* and click **Save**.

Place all your custom linetypes in a single drawing file and then use the AutoCAD Design Center to help you locate and load the desired linetype.

7. When prompted for the linetype name, type property-line.
   When prompted for the linetype description, type property-line.
   Specify starting point for line definition; select the far left point of the line type.
   Specify ending point for line definition; select the far right point of the line type.
   When prompted to select the objects, start at the long line on the left and pick the line segments in order.
8. Type **linetype** to launch the Linetype Manager.

9. 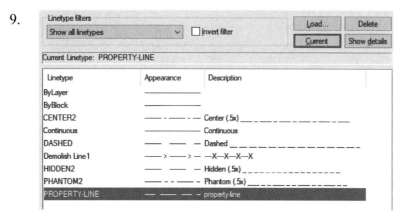 The linetype you created is listed.

   Highlight the PROPERTY-LINE linetype and select CURRENT.

   Click **OK**.

10. Draw some lines to see if they look OK. Make sure you make them long enough to see the dashes. If you don't see the dashes, adjust the linetype scale using Properties. Set the scale to 0.000125 or smaller.

11. ![] custom-linetypes   Locate the *custom-linetypes.lin* file you created.

    Open it using NotePad.

12. 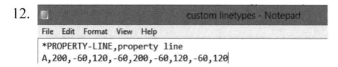 You see a description of the property-line.

13. Save as *ex2-1.dwg*.

Foundations & Site Plans

Exercise 2-2:
Creating New Layers

Drawing Name: New
Estimated Time: 20 minutes

This exercise reinforces the following skills:

- Design Center
- Layer Manager
- Creating New Layers
- Loading Linetypes

1. Start a new drawing using QNEW.

   Open ex2-1.dwg.

   You should see three drawing tabs:
   Start, ex2-1, and the new drawing

2. Activate the **View** ribbon and verify that the File Tabs is shaded.

3. Launch the Design Center.
   The Design Center is on the Insert ribbon in the Content section. It is also located in the drop-down under the Content Browser. You can also launch using Ctl+2.

4. Select the **Open Drawings** tab.

Browse to the *ex2-1.dwg* file.

Open the Linetypes folder.

Scroll to the **Property-line** linetype definition.

5. 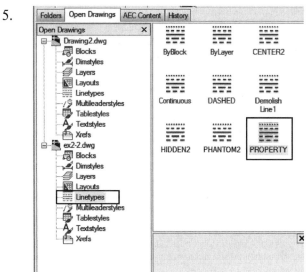 Highlight the PROPERTY-LINE linetype.

Drag and drop into your active window or simply drag it onto the open drawing listed.

This copies the property-line linetype into the drawing.

6. Close the Design Center.

7. Activate the **Layer Properties Manager** on the Home ribbon.

8. Note that several layers have already been created. The template automatically sets your Layer Standards to AIA.

9. Select the **New Layer from Standard** tool.

10.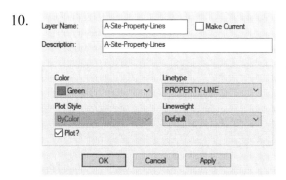

Under Layer Standard, select **Non Standard**.

Name the layer **A-Site-Property-Lines**.

Set the Color to **Green**.

Select the **Property-Line** linetype.

Set the Lineweight to **Default**.

Enable **Plot**.
Click **Apply** and **OK**.

11.

Create another layer by clicking the **New Layer from Standard** tool.

Name the layer **A-Contour-Line**.

Set the color to **42**.

Select the linetype pane for the new linetype.

Click **Other**.

12.

Enable **Show Linetypes in File**.

Highlight **DASHEDX2** and click **OK** to assign it to the selected layer name.

13.

Note that the linetype was assigned properly.

Set the Lineweight to **Default**.

Enable **Plot**.

Click **OK**.

14. Set the A-Site-Property-Line layer current.

    Highlight the layer name then select the green check mark to set current.

    You can also double left click to set the layer current.

15. Right click on the header bar and select **Maximize all columns** to see all the properties for each layer.

16. Use the X in the upper corner to close the Layer Manager.

17. Save as *ex2-2.dwg*.

Exercise 2-3:
Creating a Site Plan

Drawing Name: site_plan.dwg
Estimated Time: 30 minutes

This exercise reinforces the following skills:

- Use of ribbons
- Documentation Tools
- Elevation Marks
- Surveyors' Angles

1. Open *site_plan.dwg*.

2. Go to **Drawing Utilities→Drawing Setup**.

   This is located on the Application Menu panel.

3. Select the **Units** tab.
Set the Drawing Units to **Inches**.
Set up the Length Type to **Architectural**.
Set the Precision to ¼″.
Set the Angle Type to **Surveyors**.
Set the Precision to **N 0d00′ E**.

4. 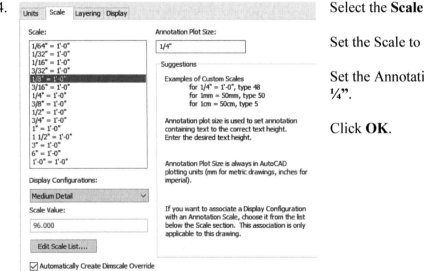 Select the **Scale** tab.

   Set the Scale to **1/8″ = 1′-0″**.

   Set the Annotation Plot Size to ¼″.

   Click **OK**.

5. When this dialog appears, select the first option. The drawing doesn't have any pre-existing elements, but this option ensures that everything is scaled correctly.

Foundations & Site Plans

6. On the Status bar: verify the scale is set to **1/8" = 1'-0"**.

You can set your units as desired and then enable **Save As Default** . Then, all future drawings will use your unit settings.

7. Draw the property line shown on the **A-Site-Property-Lines** layer.

   Select the Line tool.

8.
   Specify first point: 1',5'
   Specify next point: @186' 11" < s80de
   Specify next point: @75'<n30de
   Specify next point: @125'11"<n
   Specify next point: @250'<180

   This command sequence uses Surveyor's Units.

   You can use the TAB key to advance to the surveyor unit box.

2-11

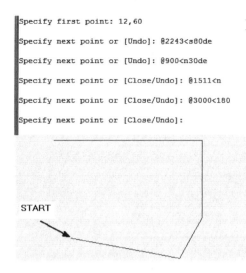

Metric data entry using centimeters:

If you double click the mouse wheel, the display will zoom to fit so you can see your figure.

Turn ORTHO off before creating the arc.

9. Draw an arc using **Start, End, Direction** to close the figure.

10. Select the bottom point as the Start point.
    Right click and select the End option.
    Select the top point at the End point.
    Click inside the figure to set the direction of the arc.

11. Set the **A-Contour-Line layer** current.

Foundations & Site Plans

12. **PTYPE** Type **PTYPE** to access the Point Style dialog.

You can also access the Point Style dialog by selecting Point Style on the Utilities panel of the Home ribbon.

13. Select the Point Style indicated.

Click **OK**.

14. *Use the **DIVIDE** command to place points as shown.*

You will not see the points until you set the point style.

15. **DIVIDE** Type **DIVIDE** to add points to the top horizontal line.

16. *DIVIDE Select object to divide:* Select the top horizontal line.

17. *DIVIDE Enter the number of segments or [Block]: 5* Type **5** to be divided into five equal segments. Click **ENTER**.

18. **Repeat DIVIDE / Recent Input** Right click and select **Repeat Divide**.
Add points to the bottom horizontal line.

19. *DIVIDE Select object to divide:* Select the BOTTOM horizontal line.

20. *DIVIDE Enter the number of segments or [Block]: 5* Type **4** to be divided into four equal segments. Click **ENTER**.

21. Right click and select **Repeat Divide**.
    Add points to the bottom horizontal line.

22. Select the right angled line.

23. Type **2** to be divided into two equal segments. Click **ENTER**.

24. Enable the **Node** OSNAP.

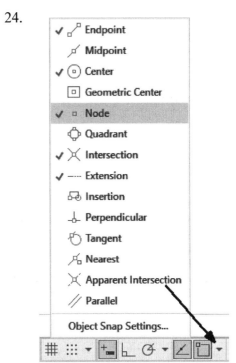

25. Draw contour lines using **Pline** and **NODE** Osnaps as shown.

    Be sure to place the contour lines on the contour line layer.

26. Type **qselect** on the *Command* line.

Foundations & Site Plans

27.

    Set the Object Type to **Point**.
    Set the Color = Equals **ByLayer**.

    Click **OK**.

28. All the points are selected.
    Right click and select **Basic Modify Tools→ Delete**.

29. Type UCSICON, OFF to turn off the UCS icon.

    When you start typing in the command line, you will see a list of commands.

    Use the up and down arrow keys on your keyboard to select the desired command.

30. Launch the **Layer Properties Manager** from the Home ribbon.

31. Select **New Layer from Standard**.

2-15

32. Click the button next to **Discipline Designator**.

33. Highlight **G** for General and click OK.

34. Click the button next to **Major**.

35. Highlight **Anno** for Annotation and click **OK**.

36. *Notice that you are building a layer name based on industry standards.*

   Click the button next to **Optional Minor 1**.

37. Scroll down and locate **Dims, Dimensions**.

Select and click **OK**.

38. *Notice that the software automatically fills in the correct color, linetype, and lineweight based on the standard.*

Enable **Make Current**.

Click **OK**.
The layer is created and set current.

Close the dialog.

39. Activate the **Design Tools** palette located under the Tools drop-down on the Home ribbon.

40. Right click on the gray bar on the palette to activate the short-cut menu.

Left click on **All Palettes** to enable the other palettes.

41. Activate the Annotation tab on the palette.

Locate the **Plan Elevation Label**, but it's not the type we need for a site plan.

Instead, we'll have to add an elevation label from the Design Center to the Tool Palette.

42.

    Type **Ctl+2** to launch the Design Center.
    Or:
    Activate the **Insert** ribbon.
    Select the **Design Center** tool under Content.
    Or:
    Type **DC**.

43.

    Select the **Folders** tab.

    Browse to the folder where you downloaded the exercises from the publisher.
    Locate Elevation Label_A.
    Highlight and drag and drop it onto the Annotation tool palette.

    Close the Design Center.

44.

    Right click on the **Elevation Label_A** tool.

45. Select **Properties**.

46. 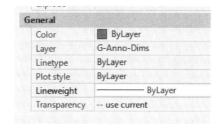 Scroll down to the General section.
Set the Color to **ByLayer.**
Set the Layer to **G-Anno-Dims**.
Set the Linetype, Plot Style, and Lineweight to **ByLayer.**

This means the element will use the properties set by the assigned layer.

Click **OK**.

47. 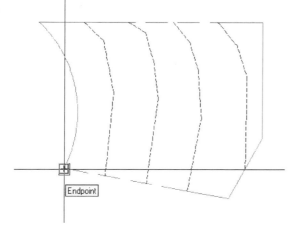 Select the Elevation Label on the Tool Palette.

Select the Endpoint shown.

48. Set the Elevation to **%%P 0″ [0.00]**.
    Set the Prefix to **EL**.
    Click **OK**.

    %%P is the code for the +/- symbol.

49. Zoom in to see the elevation label.

    Notice that the label is on the correct layer with the correct properties.

 You can use the **Zoom Object** tool to zoom in quickly.

    This is located on the View tab.

 The Elevation Label is automatically placed on the G-Anno-Dims layer.

    To verify this, just hover over the label and a small dialog will appear displaying information about the label.

50. Set the current layer to Layer **0** using the drop-down on the Home ribbon.

51. EL ±0.00″ Place an elevation label on the upper left vertex as shown.

Foundations & Site Plans

52. Place labels as shown.

    Notice that the label is on the correct layer with the correct properties.

53.

    To modify the value of an elevation label, double click the label to bring up the editor.

54. To change the toposurface to a 3D surface, select each line and modify the Z values to match the elevations.

55. *A quick way to modify properties is to use Quick Properties.*

Toggle Quick Properties on using the Status bar.

56. Select the CUI icon on the upper right of the Quick Properties dialog.

57. Highlight Line. Enable Start X, Start Y, and Start Z, and End X, End Y, and End Z. Enable Angle.

This adds those properties to the Quick Properties dialog.

Click **OK**.

58. Then select each line and change the start and end values of Z to match the elevation markers.

59. Use the ViewCube to inspect your toposurface and then return to a top view.

    Adjust points as needed to create an enclosed area. Use ID to check the point values of each end point.

    You can also type PLAN to return to a 2D view plan view.

60. Open the *fonts.dwg*. This is the file you created in a previous exercise.

61. Type **Ctl+2** to launch the Design Center.

62. Select the Open Drawings tab.

    Browse to the Textstyles folder under the fonts.dwg.

63. Drag and drop the **Text1** text style into the ex2-3 drawing.

    Close the Design Center.

64. Set **G-Anno-Dims** as the current Layer.

Length	186'-11"
Angle	S 80d0' E

    You can use Quick Properties to determine the length and angle of each line.

65. Set the Current Text Style to **TEXT1.**

66. Select the **Single Line** text tool from the Home ribbon.

67.

   Right click and select **Justify**.
   Set the Justification to **Center**.
   Select the midpoint of the line as the insertion point.
   Set the rotation angle to **–10** degrees.
   Use %%d to create the degree symbol.

68. To create the N 30 E… note, use the **TEXT** command.

   Use a rotation angle of 60 degrees.

When you are creating the text, it will preview horizontally. However, once you left click or hit ESCAPE to place it, it will automatically rotate to the correct position.

69. Create the **DUE NORTH 125′ 11″ [DUE NORTH 3840.48]** with a rotation angle of 90 degrees.

   Add the text shown on the top horizontal property line.

   DUE WEST 250′ 1/4″

70. Add the Chord note shown.
Rotation angle is 90 degrees.

71. 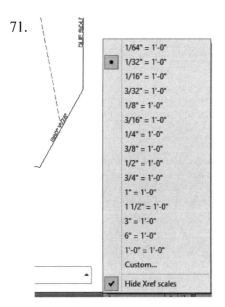 Adjust the scale to **1/32″ = 1′-0″** to see the property line labels.

72. Save the file as *ex2-3.dwg*.

Exercise 2-4:
Creating a Layer User Group

Drawing Name: layer_group.dwg
Estimated Time: 15 minutes

This exercise reinforces the following skills:

- Use of toolbars
- Layer Manager
- Layer User Group

A Layer User Group allows you to group your layers, so you can quickly freeze/thaw them, turn them ON/OFF, etc. *We can create a group of layers that are just used for the site plan and then freeze them when we don't need to see them.*

The difference between FREEZING a Layer and turning it OFF is that entities on FROZEN Layers are not included in REGENS. Speed up your processing time by FREEZING layers. You can draw on a layer that is turned OFF. You cannot draw on a layer that is FROZEN.

1. Open *layer_group.dwg*.

2. Select the **Layer Properties Manager** tool from the Home ribbon.

3. Highlight the word **All** in the Filters pane.

   Right click and select the **New Group Filter**.

4. 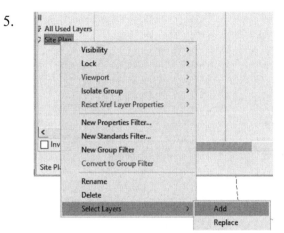 Name the group **Site Plan**.

5. 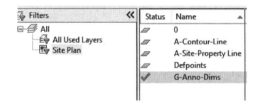 Highlight the Site Plan group. Right click and select **Select Layers → Add**.

6. Type **ALL** on the command line.
   This selects all the items in the drawing.
   Click **ENTER** to finish the selection.
   The layers are now listed in the Layer Manager under the Site Plan group.

   Close the Layer Manager.

7. We can use this group to quickly freeze, turn off, etc. the layers in the Site Plan group.

   Save the drawing as *ex2-4.dwg* and close.

Foundations & Site Plans

Layout Grids and Column Bubbles

Most architectural designers prefer to create a layout grid when placing structural members. The grid helps them manage the spacing of the framing and keeps the design organized. ACA comes with two tools to help with the placement of a grid: LAYOUTGRID and AECANNOGRIDBUBBLEADD.

Grids are used in floor plans to help architects and designers locate AEC elements, such as columns, walls, windows, and doors. The grid is one of the oldest architectural design tools – dating back to the Greeks. It is a useful tool for controlling the position of building elements. Grids may fill the entire design work area or just a small area.

In laying out wood framed buildings, a 16" or 24" grid is useful because that system relies on a stud spacing of 16" or 24".

In large projects, the layout design of different building sub-systems and services are usually assigned to different teams. By setting up an initial set of rules on how the grid is to be laid out, designers can proceed independently and use the grid to ensure that the elements will interact properly.

ACA comes with several grid tools.

The Enhanced Custom Grid allows you to place an entire grid using a dialog box to designate the bay spacing.

The Custom Grid Convert tool allows you to convert lines and arcs to grid lines. After the grid lines are placed, you have to manually edit the labels for each bubble.

The Column Grid tool allows you to place a rectangular grid with equal spacing between the grid lines.

Use the Enhanced Custom Grid tool if you want to use different spacing between grid lines or if you want to place radial grid lines.

Exercise 2-5:
Creating a 2D Layout Grid

Drawing Name: new
Estimated Time: 15 minutes

This exercise reinforces the following skills:

- Creating a Layout Grid
- Adding Column Bubbles

1. Left click on the + tab to add a new drawing.
   This tab uses whichever template is assigned in your options for New Drawings. You should not be in an active project for this exercise.

2. Open the **Design Tools** palette.

3. On the Design tab:

   Scroll down until you see the Column Grid tool.

   Click to select **Column Grid**.

   If you do not have the Column Grid tool on the tool palette, you can locate it on the Home ribbon on the drop-down under Enhanced Custom Grid.

   You can also type LAYOUTGRID *at the command prompt.*

4.

Set the X-Width to **20'-0"**.
Set the Y-Depth to **24'-0"**.

Set the X Axis Bay Size to **10'-0"**.

Set the Y Axis Bay Size to **8'-0"**.

5.

Set the Column Style to **None**.

Type **0,0** to place the grid at the Origin.
Click **ENTER** to accept a rotation angle of 0.
Left click to escape the command.

A 2D grid is placed.

6.

If you hover your mouse over the grid, you will see it has been placed on a new layer named **S-Grid**.

To change the color or linetype used by Layer S-Grid, use the Layer Manager.

7. Switch the tool palette to the Document palette.

   Right click on the palette bar and select **Document**.

8. On the Annotation tab:

   Locate the **Column Bubble** tool and select it.

   You can also type AECANNOGRIDBUBBLEADD at the command prompt.

   If you added the tool and modified it on the customized Structural tool palette, you can use the custom tool you created.

9. Left click at the bottom line of the grid.

   Change the Label to **A**.
   Enable **Apply at both ends of gridline**.
   Click **OK**.

10. *The grid bubble is placed.*

    Left click on the next horizontal grid line to place the next bubble.

11. *Notice that the Label auto-increments to B.*

    Click **OK**.

12. *The grid bubble is placed.*

    Left click on the next horizontal grid line to place the next bubble.

13. Click **OK**.

14. Left click on the top horizontal line.

    The Label auto-increments to D.

    Click **OK**.

15. Left click on the left vertical line of the grid.

    Change the Label to **1**.

    Click **OK**.

16. Click on the middle vertical line.

    The label auto-increments to 2.

    Click **OK**.

17. Click on the right vertical line.

    The label auto-increments to 3.

    Click **OK**.

    Click **ENTER** to exit the command.

18. If you hover over one of the column bubbles, you can see the bubbles are placed on S-Grid-Iden layer.

    Remember that Layer Key Styles control the layer properties of AEC elements.

19. Save as *ex2-5.dwg*.

Exercise 2-6:
Creating a Custom Grid Bubble

Drawing Name: AEC Annotation Symbols (Imperial).dwg
Estimated Time: 25 minutes

This exercise reinforces the following skills:

- Tool palette
- Block Editor
- Attributes

1. Browse to the location of the *AEC Annotation Symbols (Imperial).dwg* file.

   This file should be located in *ProgramData/Autodesk/Styles/Imperial*.

2. Open the file.

   Switch to **Model** space.

3. Locate the **Column Bubble** tool on the Annotation tool palette.

   Right click and select **Properties**.

4. Notice the drawing name that controls the block used.

   Click **OK**.

2-35

5. Switch to the Annotate ribbon.

   In the Text Style box, select the drop down and click on **Manage Text Styles**.

6. Click **New**.

7. Type **Comic Sans**.

   Click **OK**.

   If you prefer a different font, choose a different font.

8. Set the Font Name to **Comic Sans MS.**

   Click **Close**.

9. Click **Yes** to save your changes.

10. Switch to the Insert ribbon.

    Click **Edit Block**.

11. Locate the **BubbleDef** block.

    Click **OK**.

12. 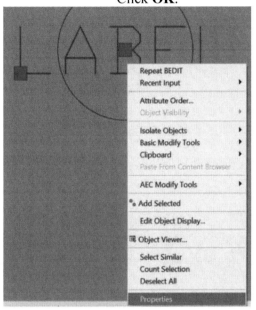 Select the attribute.
    This is the text.

    Right click and select **Properties**.

13. Change the Style to **Comic Sans**.

    Set the Height to **1"**.

14. 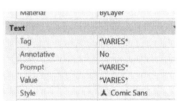 Change Annotative to **No**.

    Click **ESC** to release the selection.

15. *The attribute updates.*

    Click **Save Block** on the ribbon.

16. Click **Close Block Editor** on the ribbon.

17. 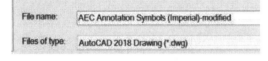 Save the drawing file in your exercise folder with a modified name.

18. Highlight the Column Bubble on the Tool Palette.

    Right click and select **Copy**.

19. 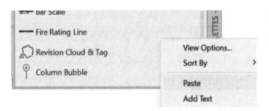 Right click and select **Paste** to add a copied column bubble.

20. 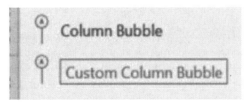 Rename the copied tool to **Custom Column Bubble**.

21. 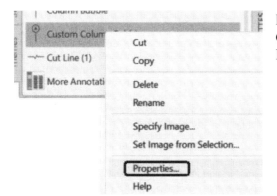 Right click on the **Custom Column Bubble** and select **Properties.**

22. Change the symbol location to the drawing where you stored the modified bubble.

    You may need to change the file type.

    Note the symbol used is the StandardGridBubble.

    Click **OK**.

23. Switch to the Insert ribbon.

    Select **Insert → BubbleDef** to insert the modified block.

    You may be prompted to redefine the block.

    Click to redefine.

24. 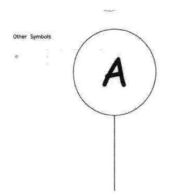 Place the symbol.

    Change the attribute to A.

    Add a line below the bubble.

25. 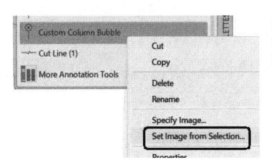 Right click on the **Custom Column Bubble** and select **Set Image from Selection.**

26. 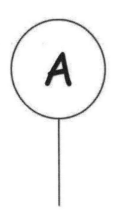 Select the bubble and line.

    Press ENTER to complete the selection.

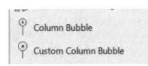 *The tool image updates.*

27. Save *as AEC Annotation Symbols (Imperial)-modified.dwg*.

Foundations & Site Plans

Exercise 2-7:
Insert Grid Lines

Drawing Name: 01 Column Grid.dwg
Estimated Time: 20 minutes

This exercise reinforces the following skills:

- Insert Drawing
- Project Navigator
- Constructs
- Column Grid
- Column Bubble
- Layer Manager

1. Start a new drawing.
2. Open the **Project Browser**.

3. Right click on the Brown Medical Clinic project. Select **Set Project Current**.

4. 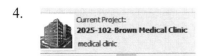 Verify that the Current Project is set to **Brown Medical Clinic**.

5. Close the Project Browser and the **Project Navigator** should launch.

6. Open the Projects tab.

   Click the **Edit** icon next to Levels.

2-41

7. 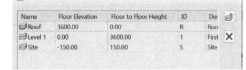 Delete the 02 Second floor level.
Delete the Basement Level.
Rename the levels as shown.
Adjust the Site level elevation to -150.
Adjust the Level 1 elevation to 0.00.
Adjust the Roof elevation to 3600.

8. Update the ID and Description columns to reflect the new information.

Click **OK**.

9. You have made changes to the project that may affect existing views.
Do you wish to regenerate all views in this project?

Click **Yes**.

10. 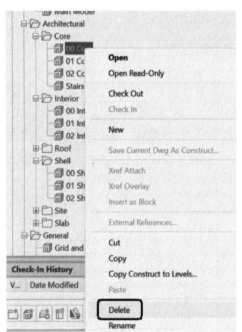 Open the Constructs tab.

Highlight **00 Core** construct.
Right click and select **Delete**.

11. Are you sure you want to delete the Construct 'Constructs\Architectural\Core\00 Core'?

Click **Yes**.

12. Delete the 02 and the Stairs constructs under Core.

13. 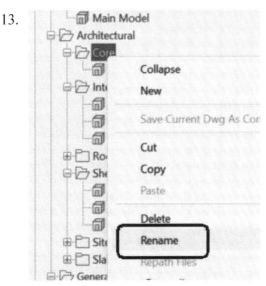 Highlight **Core**.
Right click and **Rename**.

14. Rename **Floor Plans**.

15. Click **Repath project now**.

16. Select the **Constructs** tab.

    Expand the Structural folder.
    Delete the 00 Column Grid under Grid.
    Click **Yes**.
    Delete the 02 Column Grid under Grid.
    Click **Yes**.

17. Locate the 01 Column Grid under Grid. Right click and select **Open**.

18. A drawing file opens.

    The file doesn't have anything in it.
    You may recall this project was created using a template. The template generated more than a hundred drawing files to act as placeholders.

    Notice the name of the drawing.

19. Set the View Scale to **1:1**.

20. 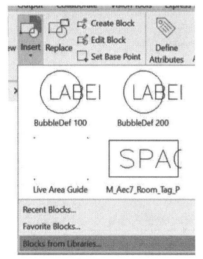 Go to the Insert ribbon.

    Select **Insert Blocks from Libraries**.

21. Select the Libraries tab.

    Browse to the Lesson 2 downloaded files.

    Locate the *medical clinic grids.dwg*.
    Click **Open**.

    Disable Insertion Point.

22. 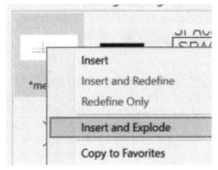 Right click on the drawing preview.

    Select **Insert and Explode**.

    Close the Blocks dialog.

23. 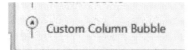 Open the Design Tools.
    Activate the Annotation palette.
    Locate the **Custom Column Bubble**.

24. Select the bottom horizontal grid line.

    Change the label to **A**.
    Change the Extension value to **2000**.
    Enable **Apply at both ends of gridline**.

    Click **OK**.

25. Label the horizontal Gridlines A-D.
Label the vertical gridlines 1-6.

You will need to zoom in to see the bubbles.

26. Select one of the column bubbles.
Right click and **Select Similar.**

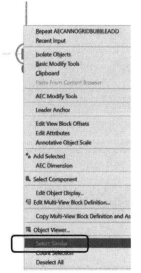

All the column bubbles will be selected.

Right click and select **Properties.**

27. Change the Scale to **254**.

Click **ESC** to release the selection.

28.

Use the grips to reposition the bubbles so they are positioned outside of the grid.

29. Switch to the Home ribbon.

Open the **Layer Manager**.

30. Change the properties for S-Grid to use the color 250 and DASHED linetype.
Change the properties for S-Grid-Iden to use the color Cyan and Continuous linetype.

Close the Layer Manager.

31. Save as *01 Column Grid.dwg and close.*

Foundations & Site Plans

Exercise 2-8:
Creating Constructs

Drawing Name: foundation floorplan – Tahoe Cabin.dwg
Estimated Time: 10 minutes

This exercise reinforces the following skills:

- Project Browser
- Project Navigator
- Constructs
- Adding an existing drawing to a project

1. Open *foundation floorplan – Tahoe Cabin.dwg*.

2. Open the Project Browser.

3. Set the **Tahoe Cabin** project current.

   Close the Project Browser.

4. Locate the **Project Navigator**.

   Verify the current project is the Tahoe Cabin.

2-47

5. 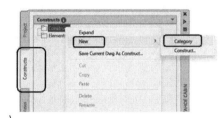 Select the Constructs tab.

   Highlight **Constructs**.
   Select **New→Category**.

6. 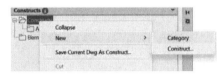 Type Architecture for the new category name.

7. 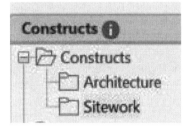 Highlight **Constructs**.
   Select **New→Category**.

8. 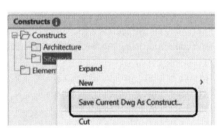 Name the new category **Sitework**.

9. Highlight the Sitework category.

   Right click and select **Save Current Dwg as Construct**.

   Notice that the name, description, and category are already filled in.

Foundations & Site Plans

10. Assign the drawing to the **Foundation** Division.

Click **OK**.

11. *The drawing is now added to the project as a construct.*

Exercise 2-9:
Convert Polylines to Column Grids

Drawing Name: foundation floorplan – Tahoe Cabin.dwg
Estimated Time: 10 minutes

This exercise reinforces the following skills:

- Convert Polylines to Colum Grids
- Add Column Bubbles

1. Open the **Project Navigator**.

2. Select the Constructs tab.
Locate the *foundation floorplan – Tahoe Cabin.dwg* under Sitework.
Right click and select **Open**.

3. Locate the **Custom Grid Convert** tool on the Home ribbon, located on the Build panel.

2-49

4.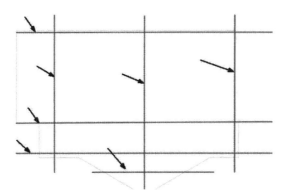

   Select the blue polylines.

   Click ENTER.

5.

   When prompted to place labels:
   Right click and select **No labels**.

6.

   When prompted to erase the linework:
   Right click and select **Yes**.

7.

   The Column Grid is placed.

   If you hover over the grid with the mouse, you will see the element and layer.

   Click **ESC** to release the column grid.

8.

   Launch the Design Tools if the palette is not available.

9. Right click on the Tool Palettes title bar.

   Switch to the **Document** Tool Palette.

10. Open the Annotation palette.

    Locate **the Custom Column Bubble**.

11. Label the horizontal grid lines **A-D**.

    Enable **Apply at both ends of gridline**.

12. Label the vertical grid lines **1-3**.

    Enable **Apply at both ends of gridline**.

    The bubbles will appear small because of the scale. If you adjust the view scale, the bubbles will look larger.

13. Save the file.

Slabs

Slabs are used to model floors and other flat surfaces. You start by defining a slab style which includes the components and materials which are used to construct the floor system.

You can create a floor slab by drawing a polyline and applying the style to the polyline or by selecting the slab tool and then drawing the boundary to be used by the slab.

Keynotes

Keynotes are used to standardize how materials are called out for architectural drawings. Most keynotes use a database. The database is created from the Construction Specifications Institute (CSI) Masterformat Numbers and Titles standard. ACA comes with several databases which can be used for keynoting or you can use your own custom database. The database ACA uses is in Microsoft Access format (*.mdb). If you wish to modify ACA's database, you will need Microsoft Access to edit the files.

Note: I had issues with my first installation of ACA 2026, where the software could not open any of the keynote databases. If this happens to you, uninstall and reinstall the software.

Exercise 2-10:
Creating Slab Styles

Drawing Name: foundation floorplan – Tahoe Cabin.dwg
Estimated Time: 30 minutes

This exercise reinforces the following skills:

- Creating Styles
- Display Properties
- Keynotes

1. Open the **Project Navigator**.

2. 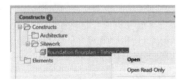 Select the Constructs tab.
Locate the *foundation floorplan – Tahoe Cabin.dwg* under Sitework.
Right click and select **Open**.

3. Activate the Manage ribbon.

   Select **Style Manager**.

4. Browse to the Slab Styles category.

   Highlight Slab Styles.

   Right click and select **New**.

5. On the General tab,

   change the Name to **Gravel Fill**.

6. Click **Select Keynote**.

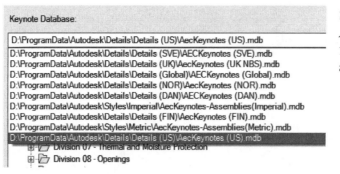

Select the *Details (US) AecKeynotes (US).mdb* file from the list of available databases.

7. Expand the *Division 31 – Earthwork* folder.

    Locate **31 23 00.B1**.

    Select and click **OK**.

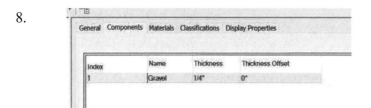

The keynote information is filled in.

8. Select the Components tab.

    Set the Name to **Gravel**.
    Set the Thickness to **¼"**.
    Set the Thickness Offset to **0"**.

9. Select the Materials tab.

    Select **New Material**.

10. 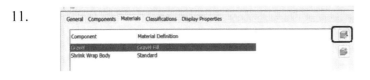 Type **Gravel Fill**.

    Click **OK**.

11. Highlight the **Gravel Fill** material definition.

    Select **Edit Material**.

12. Select the **Display Properties** tab.

    Click in the **Style Override** box or click the **Material Definition Override** icon.

13. Select the Hatching tab.

    Highlight all the hatches.

14. Click on the Pattern column.

    Set the Hatch Pattern type to **Predefined**.
    Set the Pattern Name to **GRAVEL**.

    Click **OK**.

    Close all the dialogs.

15. Save the file.

Exercise 2-11:
Creating a Gravel Fill

Drawing Name: foundation floorplan – Tahoe Cabin.dwg
Estimated Time: 5 minutes

This exercise reinforces the following skills:

- Creating a Slab

1. Open the **Project Navigator**.

2. 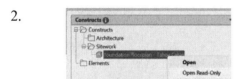 Select the Constructs tab.
   Locate the *foundation floorplan – Tahoe Cabin.dwg* under Sitework.
   Right click and select **Open**.

3. 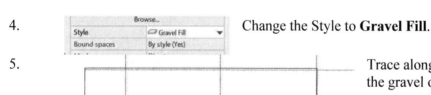 Go to the Home ribbon.

   Select the **Slab** tool.

4. Change the Style to **Gravel Fill**.

5. Trace along the elements on the gravel outline layer.

   Exit the command.

6. *If you hover over the slab with the mouse, you will see it was placed on Layer A-Slab and uses Style Name Gravel Fill.*

Save the file.

Structural Members

Architectural documentation for residential construction will always include plans (top views) of each floor of a building, showing features and structural information of the floor platform itself. Walls are located on the plan but not shown in structural detail.

Wall sections and details are used to show:

- the elements within walls (exterior siding, sheathing, block, brick or wood studs, insulation, air cavities, interior sheathing, trim)
- how walls relate to floors, ceilings, roofs, and eaves
- openings within the walls (doors/windows with their associated sills and headers)
- how walls relate to openings in floors (stairs).

Stick-framed (stud) walls usually have their framing patterns determined by the carpenters on site. Once window and door openings are located on the plan and stud spacing is specified by the designer (or the local building code), the specific arrangement of vertical members is usually left to the fabricators and not drafted, except where specific structural details require explanation.

The structural members in framed floors that have to hold themselves and/or other walls and floors up are usually drafted as framing plans. Designers must specify the size and spacing of joists or trusses, beams and columns. Plans show the orientation and relation of members, locate openings through the floor and show support information for openings and other specific conditions.

Autodesk AutoCAD Architecture includes a Structural Member Catalog that allows you to easily access industry-standard structural shapes. To create most standard column, brace, and beam styles, you can access the Structural Member Catalog, select a structural member shape, and create a style that contains the shape that you selected. The shape, similar to an AEC profile, is a 2D cross-section of a structural member. When you create a structural member with a style that you created from the Structural Member Catalog, you define the path to extrude the shape along. You can create your own structural shapes that you can add to existing structural members or use to create new structural members. The design rules in a structural member style allow you to add these custom shapes to a structural member, as well as create custom structural members from more than one shape.

All the columns, braces, and beams that you create are sub-types of a single Structural Member object type. The styles that you create for columns, braces, and beams have the same Structural Member Styles style type as well. When you change the display or style of a structural member, use the Structural Member object in the Display Manager and the Structural Member Styles style type in the Style Manager.

If you are operating with the AIA layering system as your current layer standard, when you create members or convert AutoCAD entities to structural members using the menu picks or toolbars, AutoCAD Architecture assigns the new members to layers: A-Cols, A-Cols-Brce or A-Beam, respectively. If Generic AutoCAD Architecture is your standard, the layers used are A_Columns, A_Beams and A_Braces. If your layer standard is Current Layer, new entities come in on the current layer, as in plain vanilla AutoCAD.

The Structural Member Catalog includes specifications for standard structural shapes. You can choose shapes from the Structural Member Catalog and generate styles for structural members that you create in your drawings.

A style that contains the catalog shape that you selected is created. You can view the style in the Style Manager, create a new structural member from the style, or apply the style to an existing member.
When you add a structural member to your drawing, the shape inside the style that you created defines the shape of the member. You define the length, justification, roll or rise, and start and end offsets of the structural member when you draw it.

You cannot use the following special characters in your style names:
- less-than and greater-than symbols (< >)
- forward slashes and backslashes (/ \)
- quotation marks (")
- colons (:)
- semicolons (;)
- question marks (?)
- commas (,)
- asterisks (*)
- vertical bars (|)
- equal signs (=)
- backquotes (`)

The left pane of the Structural Member Catalog contains a hierarchical tree view. Several industry standard catalogs are organized in the tree, first by imperial or metric units, and then by material.

	Open a catalog file - The default is the catalog that comes with ADT, but you can create your own custom catalog. The default catalog is located in the following directory path: \\Program Files\Autodesk AutoCAD Architecture R3\Catalogs\catalogs.
	Refresh Data
	Locate Catalog item based on an existing member – allows you to select a member in a drawing and then locates it in your catalog.
	Generate Member Style – allows you to create a style to be used.

Exercise 2-12:
Creating Member Styles

Drawing Name: member_styles.dwg
Estimated Time: 15 minutes

This exercise reinforces the following skills:

- Creating Member Styles
- Use of Structural Members tools

1. Open *member_styles.dwg*.

2. Activate the Manage ribbon.

   Go to **Style & Display → Structural Member Catalog**.

3. Browse to the **Imperial/Concrete/Cast in-place/Circular Columns** folder.

   Highlight the **14"** Diameter size.
   Right click and select **Generate Member Style.**

4. 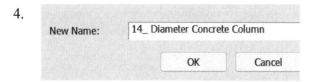 Change the Name to **14_Diamaeter Concrete Column.**

   Click **OK**.

5. Browse to the **Imperial/Timber/Lumber/Nominal Cut Lumber** folder.

2-60

6. In the lower right pane:

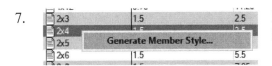 Locate the **2x4** shape designation.

7. Right click and select **Generate Member Style**.

8. 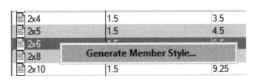 In the Structural Member Style dialog box, the name for your style automatically fills in.

   Click **OK**.

9. Locate the **2x6** shape designation.
   Right click and select **Generate Member Style**.

10. 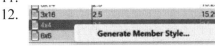 In the Structural Member Style dialog box, the name for your style is displayed.

    Click **OK**.

11.
12. Locate the **4x4** shape designation.
    Right click and select **Generate Member Style**.

13. In the Structural Member Style dialog box, the name for your style automatically fills in.

    Click **OK**.

14. Close the dialog.
    Save as *ex2-12.dwg*.

Exercise 2-13:
Creating Member Shapes

Drawing Name: member_shapes.dwg
Estimated Time: 10 minutes

This exercise reinforces the following skills:

- Structural Member Wizard

1. Open *member_shapes.dwg*.

2. Activate the **Manage** ribbon.

   Go to **Style & Display→Structural Member Wizard**.

3. Select the **Cut Lumber** category under Wood.

   Click **Next**.

4. Set the Section Width to **2"**.

   Set the Section Depth to **10"**.

   Click **Next**.

5. Enter the style name as **2x10**.

    Click **Finish**.

6. Save as *ex2-13.dwg*.

Exercise 2-14:
Copying Structural Member Styles

Drawing Name: foundation floorplan – Tahoe Cabin.dwg,
                       structural member styles.dwg
Estimated Time: 10 minutes

This exercise reinforces the following skills:

- Using the Styles Manager
- Copying Structural Member Styles

1.   Open the **Project Navigator**.

2. 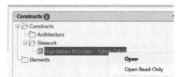 Select the Constructs tab.
    Locate the *foundation floorplan – Tahoe Cabin.dwg* under Sitework.
    Right click and select **Open**.

3.   Go to the Manage ribbon.

    Click on **Style Manager**.

4. Expand the **Structural Member Styles**.

   There is one style in the current drawing: Standard.

5. Open the *ex2-12.dwg* using the Open tool inside the Styles Manager.

   This is the drawing where you created several structural member styles from the catalog.

6. Browse to the Structural Member Styles category.

   You should see all the styles that you created.

7. Highlight the Structural Member Styles category.

   Right click and select **Copy**.

Foundations & Site Plans

8. Browse up to the foundation floorplan drawing.

Highlight the Structural Member Styles category.

Right click and select **Paste**.

9.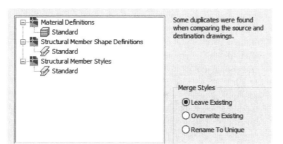

Enable **Leave Existing**.

Click **OK**.

10. *The structural members are now in the project's construct drawing.*

Close the Styles Manager.

Exercise 2-15:
Create Concrete Footings

Drawing Name: foundation floorplan – Tahoe Cabin.dwg
Estimated Time: 5 minutes

This exercise reinforces the following skills:

- Project Navigator
- External References
- Create Column

1. Open the Project Navigator.

2. Select the Constructs tab.
   Locate the *foundation floorplan – Tahoe Cabin.dwg* under Sitework.
   Right click and select **Open**.

3. Go to the Home ribbon.
   Go to **Tools→Design Tools**.

4. 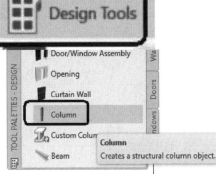 If necessary, switch to the Design Tool Palette.

   Select the **Column** tool.

5. Set the Style to **14_Diameter Concrete Column**.

   Set the Start Offset to **¼"**.

   Set the Logical Length to **5' 1"**.

   Place at Grid **B-1**.

   ESC out of the command.

6. Select the column.
   Open the Properties palette.

   Click **Anchor**.

7. The concrete will be embedded in the ground, so the elevation needs to be modified.

   Change the Z value to **-3'-0"**.

   Click **OK**.

8. Adjust the Logical Length to **5'-1"**, if needed.

9. Save the file.

Exercise 2-16:
Create Element

Drawing Name: foundation floorplan – Tahoe Cabin.dwg
Estimated Time: 15 minutes

This exercise reinforces the following skills:

- Project Navigator
- Add a Level
- Constructs
- Elements

1. Go to the Home ribbon.
   Go to **Tools→Design Tools**.

2. If necessary, switch to the Design Tool Palette.

   Select the **Column** tool.

3.

Set the Style to **4x4**.

Set the Start Offset to **0'-0"**.

Set the Logical Length to **2' 6"**.

Set Justify to **Baseline.**

Place at Grid **B-1** where the concrete column is located.

Escape out of the command.

4.

Switch to a 3D view.

Click on the word **[Top]** located at the upper left of the drawing window.

Select **SW Isometric** to switch to an isometric view.

5.

The post is placed inside the concrete column.

Select the **4x4 column**.

Right click and select **Properties** to open the Properties palette.

6. Click **Anchor**.

7. Change the Z value to **10**.
This centers the 4x4 column inside the concrete column.

   Click **OK**.

   Click **ESC** to release.

8. The 4x4 post should appear as shown.

9. 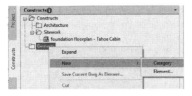 Open the Project Navigator.
Open the **Constructs** tab.
Highlight **Elements**.
Right click and select **New→Category**.

10. 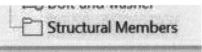 Name the Category **Structural Members**.

11. 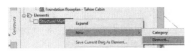 Highlight Structural Members.
Right click and select **New→Element**.

12.

    For Name, type **Concrete Column & 4x4**.
    For Description, type **Post with Footing**.
    Enable **Open in Drawing editor**.

    Click **OK**.

    The drawing opens, but it doesn't have anything in it.

13. Return to the foundation floorplan – Tahoe Cabin.dwg.

    Select the concrete column and 4x4.
    Right click and select **Clipboard→Copy with Basepoint**.

    Select the bottom center at Grid B-1.

14. Select the tab to switch to *the Concrete Column & 4x4* element drawing.

    Right click and select **Clipboard→Paste to Original Coordinates.**

15. *Because the column is anchored to the grid, the grid was automatically included in the selection.*

    Switch to a SW isometric view.

    Select the concrete column.

    Right click and select **Node Anchor→Release**.

16.

    Select the 4x4.

    Right click and select **Node Anchor→Release**.

    Select the grid and delete.

2-71

17. Move the columns to **0,0,0.**

    Save the drawing and close.

    Save the *foundation floorplan – Tahoe Cabin.dwg* and close.

Exercise 2-17:
Create Main Model

Drawing Name: ground floorplan – Tahoe Cabin.dwg
Estimated Time: 20 minutes

This exercise reinforces the following skills:

- Project Navigator
- Add a Level
- Constructs
- Elements
- External References

1. Open the Project Navigator.

2. Open the *ground floorplan – Tahoe Cabin.dwg.*

3. Open the Projects tab.

   Select the **Edit Levels** tool.

Foundations & Site Plans

4. 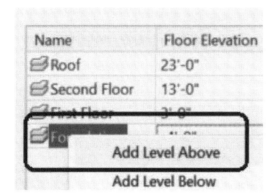 Highlight the Foundation Level.

   Right click and select **Add Level Above.**

5. Add a Ground Level at **0"**.

   Set the Floor to Floor Height at **3'-0"**

   Add the Description of **Ground Floor.**

   Verify that the other levels have retained the same floor elevations.
   Correct if needed.
   Click **OK.**

6. Click **Yes**.

7. Open *ground floorplan – Tahoe Cabin.dwg*.

8. 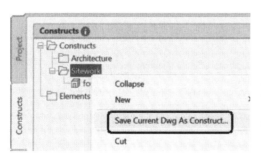 On the Project Navigator:

   Open the Constructs tab.

   Right click on Sitework.
   Select **Save Current Dwg As Construct**.

9. Enable the Ground Floor division.

   Click **OK**.

10. You see the new drawing has been added as a construct.

11. Start a new drawing.
    Save as **3D Model – Master.dwg**.

12. In the Project Navigator:

    Locate the **ground floorplan – Tahoe Cabin**.

    Hover over the file name.

    Note the file location for the file.

13. Type **xref** to open the External Reference Manager.

14. Select **Attach DWG**…

15.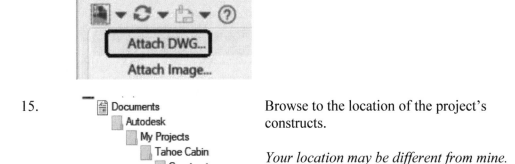

    Browse to the location of the project's constructs.

    Your location may be different from mine.

16. Select the *ground floorplan – Tahoe Cabin.dwg*.
Click **Open**.

Place at **0,0,0**.

Click **OK**.

17. Select **Attach DWG…**

18. Select the *foundation floorplan – Tahoe Cabin.dwg*.
Click **Open**.

Place at **0,0,-4'-0"**.

Click **OK**.

Close the Xref Manager dialog.

Switch to a SW Isometric view.

You can see the concrete column and the wooden post as well as the foundation slab.

19. In the Project Navigator:
Highlight **Constructs**.
Right click and select
New→Category.

20. Name the new construct – **3D**.

21. Verify that **3D Model – Master.dwg**. is the current/active window.

   Right click on the 3D construct and select **Save Current Dwg As Construct**.

22. Enable all the levels.

   Click **OK**.

23. Save and close all the drawings.
24. Start a new drawing.

   Close the current project.

Structural member geometry is created by a shape contained in the style of the structural member that is extruded along the axis of the member. Each shape can have different levels of detail in its geometry, allowing different displays of the structural member that the shape is defining. Each representation displays the structural shape in a different level of detail.

Foundations & Site Plans

High Detail Medium Detail

Low Detail Presentation

For example, you can use the Plan, Plan High Detail, and Plan Low Detail structural member representations to display a plan view of a structural member.

Most framing plans will use the Low Detail representation.

The Plan Low Detail display representation displays the member with simple lines and arcs. You can use this display representation to create a top view framing plan where you want a single line representation of a column. The Plan Low Detail display representation includes two display components, Beam Sketch and Brace Sketch. You can change the display properties of these components, such as layer, color, and linetype, to differentiate the display of beams and braces.

On the Other tab of the style override dialog box for this display representation, you can also add offsets between members to display them as you typically would in a top view framing plan. Note that the Use Member Offsets check box applies only to the start and end offsets. The Offset value below the check box applies only to structural braces, and allows you to offset them horizontally so that they are visible even when positioned directly underneath a beam.

Global Cut Plane

The global cut plane cuts all objects in a drawing at the same height. It is defined separately for each of the display configurations that can be applied to a drawing, so you can have, for example, one cut plane height for a regular plan view and another cut plane height for a Reflected view. The global cut plane determines what is displayed in the view.

The global cut plane is used on all objects that do not have an object-specific cut plane override.

The values for the display range are calculated relative to the WCS, not relative to the global cut plane height.

Think of the cut plane as the piece of paper your view sits on. The Display Above Range shows everything above the piece of paper up to that distance. The Display Below Range shows everything below the piece of paper up to that distance.

Exercise 2-18:
Defining a Low Detail Representation of a Framing Plan

Drawing Name: low_detail.dwg
Estimated Time: 10 minutes

This exercise reinforces the following skills:

- Detail Representations
- Global Cut Plane
- Layouts
- Use of Structural Members

1. Open *low_detail.dwg*.

Foundations & Site Plans

If you are not sure, verify that no projects are currently active.

The Model layout tab shows a basic frame.

There are three components in the model: a concrete slab, some posts and some beams.

2.

Open the **Framing Plan** Layout tab.

3. Go to the **Manage** ribbon.

Click **Style Manager**.

4. Locate the **10in Plywood Web Wood Joist** under Structural Member Styles.

5. Select the **Display Properties** tab.

Highlight **Plan Low Detail**.

Click **Style Overrides**.

6. Click the **Other** tab.

Disable **Use Member Offsets**.

Set the Start Offset to **6"**.
Set the End Offset to **-6"**.

Click **OK**.

Close the dialog.

2-79

7.

   On the status bar at the bottom of the display window:

   Change the Display Representation to **Low Detail**.

   The display updates.

   We still see the concrete slab. We only want to see the structural members and the column grid.

8. Select the **Global Cut Plane** tool on the Status Bar.

9. Change the Display Below Range to **1'-0"**.

   Set the Cut Height to **3' 6"**.

   Click **OK**.

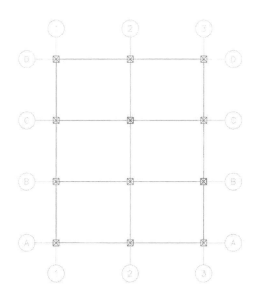

The concrete slab is no longer visible.

10. [−][SW Isometric][Realistic]   Switch back to the **Model** layout tab.

Use the controls in the upper left corner of the display window to change the display to SW Isometric and Realistic.

11.   Save as ex2-18.dwg.

Structural Member Tags

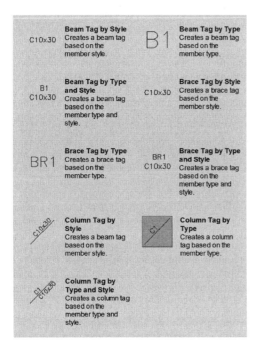

ACA comes with a selection of different tags that can be used with structural members.

Simply load or add the desired tag on to your tool palette and place as desired.

To place a tag, you must be in Model space.

Exercise 2-19:
Adding Tags to the Tool Palette

Drawing Name: structural member tags.dwg
Estimated Time: 15 minutes

This exercise reinforces the following skills:

- Detail Representations
- Tags
- Tool Palettes
- Content Browser

1. Open *structural member tags.dwg*.
   Close any open projects.
2. Open the **Framing Plan** layout tab.

3. Type **OPTIONS** to open the Options dialog.

   Go to the Profiles tab.

   Verify the **AutoCAD Architecture (US Imperial)** is the current profile.

   If not, set this profile current.

   Click **OK**.

4. Go to the Annotate ribbon.

   Launch the **Annotation Tools** palette.

5. Click the **Tags** tab.

   Scroll down and select **More Tag Tools**.

   This launches the Content Browser.

6. Locate the **Structural Tags**.

7. Click on **Structural Tags**.

8. Locate the **Beam Tag by Style** tool.

9. Hover over the tool and then select **Add to Tool Palette**.

10. *The tool will be added to the active tab on the tool palette.*

    Drag the tool above the Renumber Data Tool.

11. Locate the **Column Tag by Style** tool.

12. Hover over the tool and then select **Add to Tool Palette**.

13. The tag is added to the tool palette.

Drag below the Beam Tag by Style.

Close the Content Browser.

14. Highlight the Beam Tag by Style tool.

Right click and select **Properties**.

15.

Click in Tag location.

Browse to the Schedule Table (Imperial).dwg file that was included in the downloaded exercises to select it.

Click **OK**.

This means the tag will use the block that resides in this drawing.

16. Right click in an empty area of the tool palette.

    Select **Add Separator**.

17.

    Add Separator lines to help organize the tool palette.

    This makes it easier to locate your tools.

Save as *ex2-19.dwg*.

If tags don't link to the correct property set definitions, they can't extract information from the elements they tag.

The attribute value has to follow a specific format. For example, to extract the style information of an object, use the object name colon style; i.e. PROPERTYSETDEFINITIONNAME:PROPERTYNAME, DOOROBJECTS:STYLE, or STRUCTURALMEMBEROBJECTS:STYLE.

To see the property set definitions available go to the Style Manager. Expand the Documentation Objects and then the Property Set Definitions.

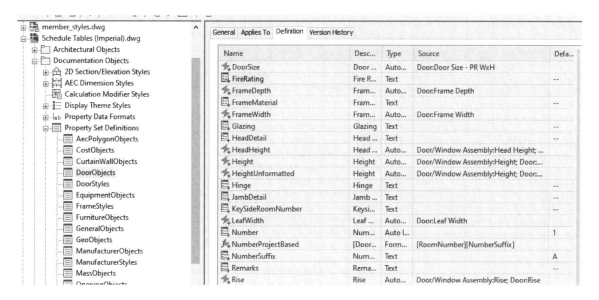

Exercise 2-20:
Adding Tags to Structural Members

Drawing Name: structural member tags.dwg
Estimated Time: 45 minutes

This exercise reinforces the following skills:

- Property Set Definitions
- Tags
- Tool Palettes
- Content Browser

1. Open *structural member tags.dwg*.
   Close any open projects.

2. Open the **Framing Plan** layout tab.

3. To place a tag you need to be in Model space.
   Double click inside the viewport to activate Model space.
   Select the **Beam Tag by Style** tool.
   Select the beam located at D1-D2.
   Click **ENTER** to place the tag

4.

Click **OK** when the Property Set Data dialog appears.
The tag is placed.

Exit the command.

5.

Select the Manage ribbon.

Select **Style Manager**.

6.

Locate the **10in Plywood Web Wood Joist**.

Right click and select **Rename**.

7.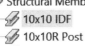

Rename **10x10 IDF**.

Click **OK** to close the Style Manager.

The tag updates.

Foundations & Site Plans

8. Use grips to reposition the tag above the beam.

You may need to turn off OSNAPS.

9. Select **the Beam Tag by Style** tool.
Select the beam located at D2-D3.
Click **a position above the beam**.
The property set data box will appear.
Click **OK**.
The tag is placed.

10. Right click and select **Multiple**.

11. Select all the horizontal beams.

Click **ENTER**.

2-89

12.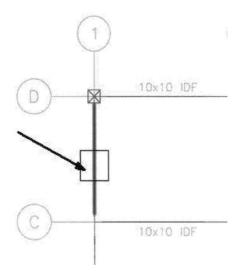

    The property set data dialog appears.

    Click **OK**.

    The beam tags are placed.

    You are still in the tag command.

13. Select the vertical beam located at C1-D1.

14. Click to place the tag to the left of the beam.

Click **OK** when the Property Set Data dialog appears.

ESC the command.

15. Rotate the tag so it is vertical using the ROTATE command.

Then ESC to release the selection.

16. Select the vertical tag.
Right click and select **Basic Modify Tools→Copy**.

17. 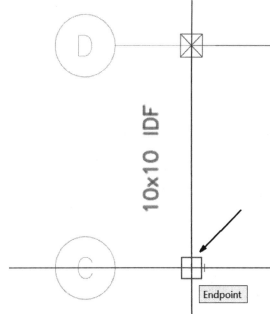 Select **C1** as the base point.

18. 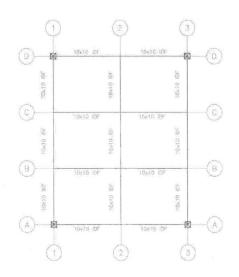 Select the grid intersections to place the remaining vertical tags.

19. Select the **Column Tag by Style** tool.

20.

Select the column post located at D1.

Click to position the tag to the side of the post located at D1.

21.

Click **OK**.

22.

The tag is placed.

Right click and select **Multiple**.

23. Select the remaining posts.

    Click **ENTER**.

24. Click **OK**.

25. Click **ENTER** to exit the command.

26. Select the Annotate ribbon.

    Select the **Linear Dimension** tool.

27. Place a horizontal dimension between grids 1 and 3, below the bubbles.

28. Select the dimension.

    Right click and select **Properties**.

29. In the Text Override field, type **2 @10' = <>**.

    The <> uses the default dimension.

    Click **ESC** to release the selection. *The dimension should update.*

30. Select the **Linear Dimension** tool.

31. Place a vertical dimension between grids A and D, to the right of the bubbles.

32. Select the dimension.

Right click and select **Recent Input→Properties**.

33. In the Text Override field, type **3 @8' = <>**.

Click **ESC** to release the selection.

34.

35. Switch to the **Model** layout tab.

36.

The linear dimensions are visible, but not the structural member tags.

You can control the appearance of the dimension using layer filter settings.

Save as *ex2-20.dwg*.

Exercise 2-21:
Adding Project Properties

Drawing Name: none
Estimated Time: 5 minutes

This exercise reinforces the following skills:

- Project Browser

1. 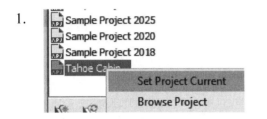 Bring up the Project Browser.

   Set the **Tahoe Cabin** project current.

2. Highlight the project name.

   Right click and select **Project Properties**.

3. 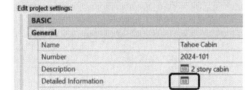 Click on **Detailed Information**.

4. Click **Add Category**.

5. Name the Category **Address**.

   Click **OK**.

6. Click **Add Detail**.

7. Type **Project Address**.

8. Fill in the address value.

9. Highlight **Unnamed** under the Unnamed category.

   Click **Delete**.

10. Highlight **Unnamed**.

    Click **Delete**.

11. Click **OK** twice to close the dialogs.

Exercise 2-22:
Creating a View in a Project

Drawing Name: First Floor Foundation – Tahoe Cabin.dwg
Estimated Time: 20 minutes

This exercise reinforces the following skills:

- Detail Representations
- Tags
- Properties
- Constructs
- Display Order

1. 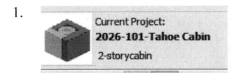 Launch the Project Browser.

   Make the **Tahoe Cabin** current.

   Close the Project Browser.

2. The Project Navigator opens.
   Open *First Floor Foundation – Tahoe Cabin.dwg*.

   This is one of the downloaded exercise files.

3. Highlight the Architecture Construct.
   Right click and select **Save Current Dwg As Construct**.

4.

Enable the **First Floor**.

Click **OK**.

5.

Go to the **Manage** ribbon.

Click **Style Manager**.

6.

Locate the **2x6** under Structural Member Styles.

7.

Select the **Display Properties** tab.

Highlight **Plan Low Detail**.

Click **Style Overrides**.

8. Click the **Other** tab.

Disable **Use Member Offsets**.

Set the Start Offset to **6"**.
Set the End Offset to **-6"**.

Click **OK**.
Close the dialog.
Close the Style Manager.

9.

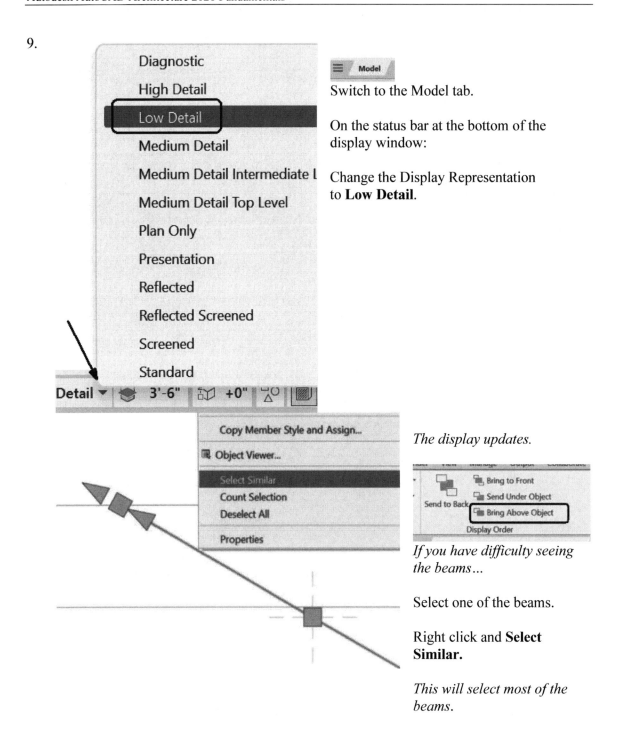

Switch to the Model tab.

On the status bar at the bottom of the display window:

Change the Display Representation to **Low Detail**.

The display updates.

If you have difficulty seeing the beams…

Select one of the beams.

Right click and **Select Similar.**

This will select most of the beams.

10. Window around the beams in the upper left corner of the grid.

11. 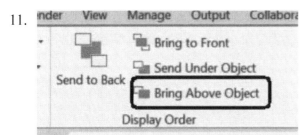 On the ribbon, **select Bring Above Object.**

12.

    The selected elements' visibility will be turned off momentarily.

    Select the Column Grid.

    Hit ENTER.

    Click ESC to release the selection.

13. Go to the Annotate ribbon.

    Launch the **Annotation Tools**.

14. Select the Tags palette.

    Select **the Beam Tag by Style** tool.

15. Select the beam located at D1-D2.
    Click **a position above the beam**.
    The property set data box will appear.
    Click **OK**.
    The tag is placed.

16. Right click and select **Multiple**.

17. Window around all the beams.

    Click **ENTER**.

18. The property set data dialog appears.

    Click **OK**.

    The beam tags are placed.

    You are still in the tag command.
    ESC out of the command.

19. *If you can't see the tags, use QSELECT to locate the tags selecting the multi-view block reference.*

    Type **QSELECT**.
    Select the **Multi-View Block Reference** from the object type list.

    Click **OK**.

20. Zoom into one tag.

    Release the selection set and select the one tag.

21. Right click and **Select Similar**.

    This will select all the beam tags.

22. Right click and select **Properties**.

23. Change the scale to **254**.

24. You should see all the beams and tags.

    Save the file.

Project Elements

Elements are blocks that can be used anywhere in a project. By adding elements to the Project Navigator, it is faster and easier to locate favorite building elements.

Exercise 2-23:
Adding an Element to a Project

Drawing Name: bolt and washer.dwg
Estimated Time: 5 minutes

This exercise reinforces the following skills:

- Project Navigator
- Elements

1. Open *bolt and washer.dwg*.
   Open the Project Navigator.

2. 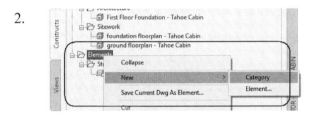 Open the **Constructs** tab.

   Right click on **Elements**.

   Select **New→ Category**.

3. 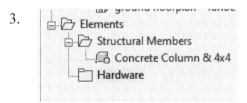 Rename the category **Hardware**.

4. Right click on **Hardware**.
   Select **Save Current Dwg As Element.**

5. Click **OK**.

Name	bolt and washer
Description	bolt and washer
Category	Elements\Hardware
File Name	bolt and washer

2-107

6. The drawing is now added as an element.

Close the drawing.
Close the Project Navigator.

Exercise 2-24:
Structural Detail

Drawing Name: column_detail.dwg
Estimated Time: 20 minutes

This exercise reinforces the following skills:

- Detailing
- Tool Palettes
- Reference Keynote
- Cut Line
- View Title
- Edit Attributes

1. Open the Project Browser.

   Set the **Tahoe Cabi**n Project Current.

   Close the browser.

2. Open *column_detail.dwg*.

3. Launch the Design Tools palette from the Home ribbon.

   Right click at the bottom of the tool palette to select the Detailing Tool palette.

   If you don't see the Document/Detailing/Visualization tool palettes, go to Options/Profiles. Switch to the Metric Profile of ACA and then switch back to the Imperial profile. This will reload all the tool palettes.

Foundations & Site Plans

4. Launch the **Detailing** Tool Palette.

   Select the **Basic** tab.

5. Draw a rectangle that is 2' long and 6" high.

6. Select **31- Earthwork**.

7. Select the rectangle to identify the boundary.
   Select inside the rectangle.

   The earthwork hatch is placed.

   Click **ENTER** to exit the command.

8. Select **03- Concrete**.

9. Set the Type to **Circular Columns**.
   Set the View to **Elevation**.

10. Set the Justification to **Center**.

2-109

11. Select the midpoint of the top of the rectangle.

    Draw the column so it is **5' 1"** high.

    Click **ENTER** to exit the command.

    Use the **QUICK MEASURE** tool to verify the dimensions of the column.

12.

    Select **06-Woods, Plastics & Composites**.

13.

    Select **4x4**.
    Set the View to **Elevation**.

14.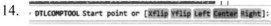

    Set the Justification to **Center**.

15.

    The post should be 2'-6" high and placed so it is 1'-1" embedded into the concrete column.

    If you have difficulty, draw a line at the start and end points, place the 4x4 and then delete the line.

Use the **QUICK MEASURE** tool to verify the dimensions and position of the 4x4 post.

16. 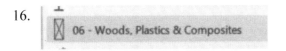 Select **06-Woods, Plastics & Composites**.

17. Select **2x6**.
Set the View to **Elevation**.

18. Set the Justification to **Right**.
19. Select a starting point using the upper left corner of the 4x4 post.

20. The 2x6 beam should be placed so it is on top of the 4x4 post.

You can center it on the post once it is placed.

21. Select **05-Metals**.

22. Set the Type to **CISC Angle Shapes**.
Set the Description to **L200x200x30**.
Set the View to **Section**.

23. A preview will appear to help you place the angle.

24. Use the MIRROR tool to mirror the angle to the other side.

    Or click Yflip on the command line and place a second angle.

25. Open the Project Navigator.

    Open the Constructs tab.

    Right click on **bolt and washer** under **Elements**.
    Select **Insert as Block**.

26. Enable **Insertion Point**.
Disable **Scale**.

Disable **Auto-Placement**.
Enable **Rotation**.
Enable **Repeat Placement**.

27. Highlight the drawing.
Right click and select **Insert**.

28. Select the midpoint of the left angle.

29. Rotate the block so the bolt is placed correctly.

30. Place a second block.

31. Place a third block.

    Use the ROTATE option on the command line to rotate the block or use the BLOCKS panel.

32. Place a fourth block.
    Use the ROTATE option on the command line to rotate the block or use the BLOCKS panel.

    Click ENTER to finish placing the bolts.

    Close the Blocks palette.

33. Select the **Hatch** tool from the Home ribbon.

34. Select the **AR-CONC** hatch pattern.

35. Pick inside the concrete column to place the hatch.

36. Select **Close Hatch Creation** from the ribbon to complete the hatch placement.

37. Select the **Hatch** tool from the Home ribbon.

38. Select the **WOOD_2** hatch pattern.

39. Pick inside the 4x4 post to place the hatch.

40. Select **Close Hatch Creation** from the ribbon to complete the hatch placement.

41. Select the **Hatch** tool from the Home ribbon.

42. Select the **ZIGZAG30** hatch pattern.

43. Pick inside the 2x6 beam to place the hatch.

44. Select **Close Hatch Creation** from the ribbon to complete the hatch placement.

45. Go to the Home ribbon.

    Launch the **DesignTools** palette.

46.

Switch to the Document Palette.
Open the Annotation tab.

Scroll down.
Select the **Cut Line** tool.

47.

To place the cut line, specify a starting point, and an end point. Then, specify the direction of the break/cut.

Select a point above the gravel fill.
Then a point below the gravel fill.
Then a point away from the gravel fill.

If the cut line doesn't work, bring up the Content Browser. Locate the Document Tool Catalog – Imperial. Search for the Cut Line tool. Right click and select Insert into Drawing.
This will fix the tool on the tool palette as well.

48.

The break line is placed.

You can use the grips to adjust the size of the zig-zag.

Place cut lines as shown.

49. Switch to the Annotate ribbon.
Select the Reference Keynote (Straight).

50. Select the 2x6 Beam.

51. 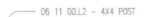 Select the top side of the beam.
Select a point for the landing.
Click ENTER to accept the default text width.

52. Add a keynote for the 4x4 post.
Add a keynote for the concrete column and the gravel fill.
Add a keynote for the angle.

Hint: If you set the FIELDDISPLAY to 0, the text will not be shaded.

53. To add a keynote for the bolt, press ENTER and then select the 05 05 23.B1 keynote to be placed.

54. The view should look similar to this.

55. Select the **Title (Number)** tool from the Annotate ribbon.

56. Place below the detail view.

    The view title is placed.

57. Select the View Number.
    Right click and select **Edit Attributes**.

58. Change the View Number to **5**.

    Click **OK**.

59. Select the View Title.
    Right click and select **Edit Attributes**.

60.

    Change the Scale to **1/8" = 1'-0"**.

    Change the Title to **W10X45 STEEL COLUMN w/4X10 NAILERS**.

    Click **OK**.

61.

    Add linear dimensions.
    Save as *ex2-24.dwg*.

Exercise 2-25:
Create a Foundation Deck Part 1

Drawing Name: foundation floorplan – Tahoe Cabin.dwg
Estimated Time: 20 minutes

This exercise reinforces the following skills:

- Detailing
- Tool Palettes
- Reference Keynote
- Cut Line
- View Title
- Edit Attributes

1. Open the Project Browser.

   Set the **Tahoe Cabi**n Project Current.

   Close the browser.

2. In the Project Navigator:

   Open the **foundation floorplan – Tahoe Cabin.**

3. 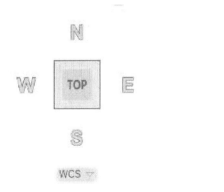 Adjust the Viewcube, so you are on a top view and oriented to the WCS.

   Check the bubbles on the grid to verify that the letters are oriented correctly.

4. Move the drawing so it is located near the UCS.

5.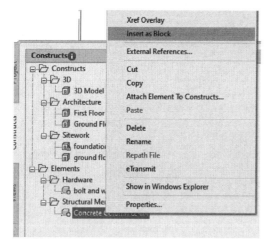

    In the Project Navigator:

    Locate the **Concrete Column & 4x4** element.

    Right click and select **Insert as Block**.

6.

    On the Blocks Palette:

    Enable **Insertion Point**.
    Enable **Repeat Placement**.

7.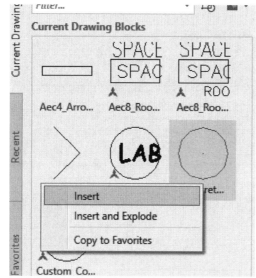

    On the Blocks Palette:

    Open the Current Drawing tab.

    Highlight the **Concrete Column & 4x4** block.

    Right click and select **Insert.**

8. Place columns at the grid intersections.

9. 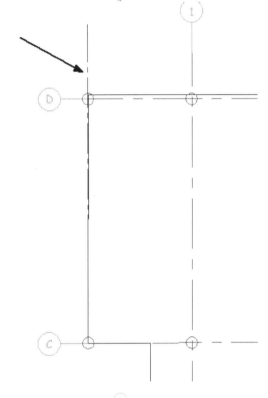 Switch the view back to a TOP view.

Draw a vertical line from the columns at the corners of Grid C and D to the left of Grid 1.

10. Select the Grid.

Right click and select **Add Grid Line**.

Select the vertical line.

Click ENTER.

Click ENTER to add label extension.
Click **Y** to erase the line.

11.

    Click on the bubble labeled 3.

    Right click and select **Properties**.

    Select **Attributes**.

12.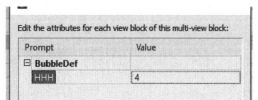

    Change the attribute to **4**.

    Click **OK**.

13.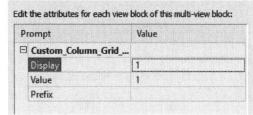

    For the new bubble:

    Add 1 to the Display and Value.

    Click **OK**.

14.

    Edit both the top and bottom bubbles.

    Each bubble is an independent block.

    Delete any columns that are not placed at grid intersections.

15. -][SW Isometric][2D Wireframe]

    Switch to a **SW Isometric** view.

16.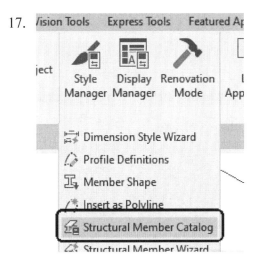

To check that the columns lowered, switch to a LEFT view.

Select one of the column blocks. Right click and **Select Similar** to select all the column elements.

Right click and select **Properties**.

Set Position Y to **-4' 5 13/16"**.

This lowers the columns so they are embedded in the earth.

Click **ESC** to release the selection.

17.

Go to the Manage ribbon.

Open the **Structural Member Catalog**.

18. Locate the 2x8 under Nominal Cut Lumber.

Right click and select **Generate Member Style**.

19. Click **OK**.

Close the dialog.

20. Open the **Style Manager**.

21. Locate the Structural Member Styles.

    Highlight the 2x8 style.

22. On the General tab:

    Click **Select Keynote**.

23. Locate the **06 11 00.G4 2x8 Joists**.

    Click **OK**.

    Click **OK** to close the dialog.

24. Save and close the file.

Exercise 2-26:
Create a Foundation Deck Part 2

Drawing Name: foundation floorplan – Tahoe Cabin.dwg
Estimated Time: 15 minutes

This exercise reinforces the following skills:

- Structural Members
- Slabs
- Style Manager
- Content Browser
- Properties

1.   Open the Project Browser.

   Set the **Tahoe Cabi**n Project Current.

   Close the browser.

2. 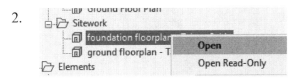   In the Project Navigator:

   Open the **foundation floorplan – Tahoe Cabin.**

3.   Switch to a **SW Isometric view**.

4. Open the Layer Manager.

   Create a new layer called **beam layout** and set it current.

   Close the Layer Manager.

5.   Draw lines from the midpoints of each 4x4 post to create a beam layout.

6. 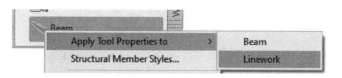 Locate the **Beam** tool on the Design palette and right click.

   Select **Apply Tool Properties to →Linework**.

7. Select the lines.

   Press **ENTER**.

8. Enable **Erase Layout Geometry**.

   Click **OK**.

9. On the Properties palette:

   Set the Style to **2x8**.
   Set the Roll to 0.00.

   Set the Justify to **Bottom Center**.

   Click **ESC** to release.

10. Change the view to **SW Isometric/Realistic.**

11. Inspect the deck.

12. Go to the Home ribbon.

    Launch the Content Browser.

13. Open the Design Tool Catalog – Imperial.

    Locate the **Wood Floor System** under Roof Slabs and Slabs.

14. Right click and select **Insert into Drawing**.

15. Trace the boundary outline of the floor slab using the joists.

    Use Properties to adjust the elevation of the floor slab to 3'-2 11/16".

16. Save and close the file.

Drape

The DRAPE command is used to create a 3D representation of a 2D sketch. You can use 2D polylines to create a toposurface. The DRAPE tool is located on the MASSING drop-down toolbar on the Home ribbon.

To access AutoCAD drawings of different locations, visit cadmapper.com/pro/home. Create a free account. Enter a location anywhere in the world. Select an area on the map and an AutoCAD dxf file will be created for you to download that you can use to create your topographic drawing.

You may need to clean up the drawing to create polylines. Use tools like PEDIT and OVERKILL to help in the clean up process.

Exercise 2-27:
Create Topography

Drawing Name: 3D Topography.dwg
Estimated Time: 40 minutes

This exercise reinforces the following skills:

- Drape
- Thicken
- Style Manager
- Mass Elements
- Extrude
- Surfaces
- Properties
- Convert to Mass Elements

1. Open the Project Browser.

   Set the **Tahoe Cabi**n Project Current.

   Close the browser.

You see a topo drawing.

2.

    Set the **S-Contour** layer current.

3.

    Select the **DRAPE** tool on the Home ribbon.

    Window around the polylines. Do not select the red boundary or points.

    Click **Yes** to erase the selected contours.

    Click **Yes** to generate a regular mesh.

    Select opposing corners of the red boundary as the corners for the mesh.

    Accept the default values of 30 for the X and Y directions for the mesh subdivisions.

    The more mesh subdivisions the finer the mesh.

    Set the base thickness to **10'**.

4. Switch to an isometric view to see your topography.

5. If you look at the Properties, you see it is a Mass Element.

6. Go to the Render ribbon.
Open the **Materials Browser**.

7. Search for **grass**.

   Add **Grass – St Augustine** to the document.

8. Search for **site**.

   Add **Dirt – Dark Borwn** to the document.

   Close the Materials Browser.

9. Go to the Manage ribbon.
Open the Style Manager.

Foundations & Site Plans

10. Locate the **Mass Element Styles** under Multi-Purpose Objects.

    Right click and select **New**.

11. Rename **Earth**.

12. Click on the Materials tab.
    Add a new Material.

13. Name the new material **Dirt**.

    Click **OK**.

14. Click **Edit Material**.

15. Click on Display Properties.
    Override the General display properties.
    Set the Render Material to **Dirt – Dark Brown**.
    Set the Mapping to **Same as Surface Hatch**.

16. Apply all the overrides to display representations.

    Click **OK**.

17. Click on the Mass Element Styles.
    Right click and select **New**.

18. Rename **Grass**.

19. Click on the Materials tab.
    Add a new Material.

20. Name the new material **Grass**.

    Click **OK**.

21. Click **Edit Material**.

22. Click on Display Properties.
    Override the General display properties.
    Set the Render Material to **Grass – St, Augustine.**
    Set the Mapping to **Same as Surface Hatch**.

23. Apply all the overrides to display representations.

    Click **OK**.

24. Close the Style Manager.

25. Select the mass element.
    Right click and select Properties.
    Change the Style to **Earth**.

26. Change the display to Realistic.

27. Switch to a TOP view.
    Move the element to the origin.
    Switch back to a SW Isometric view|2D Wireframe view.

Foundations & Site Plans

28. Switch to a LEFT view.
    Use POLYLINE to draw a polyline slightly below the surface of the mass element.

29. Switch to a SW Isometric view.

    Select the **Solids** ribbon.

    Click **Extrude**.

30. Select the polyline.

    You will be prompted for the height.

    Select the endpoint of the mass element.

31. Click on the extrusion.
    Right click and select **Properties**.

    You created a surface.

32. Select the **THICKEN** tool on the Solid Editing panel.

2-135

33. Select the surface.

    When prompted, give it a thickness of **3'**.

34. Select the thickened surface.
    Right click and select Properties.

    This is now a 3D Solid.

35. Select the 3D Solid.

    Select **Convert to Mass Elements** on the ribbon.

36.

    Type **Grass** for the Description.
    Enable **Convert to single Boolean mass element**.
    Enable **Erase layout geometry**.
    Click **OK**.

37. Right click and go to Properties.

    Change the Style to **Grass**.

    Click **ESC** to release the selection.

2-136

38. -][SW Isometric][Realistic]

    Change the display to **Realistic**.

    You see the two mass elements with the different materials assigned.

    Make the G-Mass layer current.
    Freeze the S-Boundary and S-Contour layers.

39. Go to the Project Navigator.

    Highlight the **Sitework** Construct category.
    Right click and select **Save Current DWG As Construct.**

40. Change the Name to **Topography**.
    Add a Description.
    Enable the **Foundation** level.
    Click **OK**.

41. Save and close.

Notes:

QUIZ 2

True or False

1. You must load a custom linetype before you can assign it to a layer.
2. The DIVIDE command divides a line or arc segment into smaller elements.
3. The Design Tools palette is used to access blocks and commands.
4. If you design a wall tool on the tool palette for a specific style wall, then whenever you add a wall using that design tool it will place a wall using that wall style.
5. Layer groups control which layers are displayed in the layer drop-down list.

Multiple Choice
Select the best answer.

6. If points are not visible in a view:

    A. Turn on the layer the points are placed on
    B. Bring up the Point Style dialog and set the Size Relative to Screen
    C. Change the Point Style used
    D. All of the above

7. The command to bring up the point style dialog is:

    A. PSTYLE
    B. PMODE
    C. PP
    D. STYLE

8. An easy way to change the units used in a drawing is to:

    A. Change the units on the status bar.
    B. Type UNITS
    C. Use the Drawing Setup dialog.
    D. B or C

9. To turn off the display of the USCICON:

    A. Type USCICON, OFF
    B. Type UCS, OFF
    C. Type UCSICON, 0
    D. Type UCS, 0

10. To add a Construct to a project, use the:

    A. Styles Manager
    B. Design Tools
    C. Project Browser
    D. Project Navigator

11. Slabs can be used to model: (select all that apply)

    A. Roofs
    B. Floors
    C. Ceilings
    D. Walls

12. A structural member is an object that can represent: (select all that apply)

    A. Beams
    B. Braces
    C. Columns
    D. Railings

13. To create styles for most *standard* beams, braces, and columns, you can use:

    A. Styles Manager
    B. Design Tools
    C. Structural Members Catalog
    D. Project Navigator

ANSWERS:
1) T; 2) F; 3) T; 4) T; 5) T; 6) D; 7) A; 8) D; 9) A; 10) D; 11) A, B, and C; 12) A, B, and C; 13) D

Lesson 3:
Floor Plans

AutoCAD Architecture comes with 3D content that you use to create your building model and to annotate your views. In ACA 2026, you may have difficulty locating and loading the various content, so this exercise is to help you set up ACA so you can move forward with your design.

The Content Browser lets you store, share, and exchange AutoCAD Architecture content, tools, and tool palettes. The Content Browser runs independently of the software, allowing you to exchange tools and tool palettes with other Autodesk applications.

The Content Browser is a library of tool catalogs containing tools, tool palettes, and tool packages. You can publish catalogs so that multiple users have access to standard tools for projects.

ACA comes with several tool catalogs. When you install ACA, you enable which catalogs you want installed with the software. By default, Imperial, Metric, and Global are enabled. The content is located in the path: C:\Program Files\Autodesk\ACA 2026\Tool Catalogs.

The floor plan is central to any architectural drawing.

A floor plan is a scaled diagram of a room or building viewed from above. The floor plan may depict an entire building, one floor of a building, or a single room. It may also include measurements, furniture, appliances, or anything else necessary to the purpose of the plan.

Floor plans are useful to help design furniture layout, wiring systems, and much more. They're also a valuable tool for real estate agents and leasing companies in helping sell or rent out a space.

If you are using Projects to organize your model, it is recommended that exterior walls are placed on Shell Constructs and interior walls are placed on Interior Constructs.

Exercise 3-1:
Creating a Floor Plan

Drawing Name: 01 Core.dwg
Estimated Time: 60 minutes

This exercise reinforces the following skills:

- Create Walls
- Wall Properties
- Wall Styles
- Style Manager
- Insert a PDF
- Insert Doors
- Insert Windows
- Materials
- Content Browser

1. Launch the US Metric version of ACA.

   *This ensures that all the content will be metric.
   You can also go to Options and switch to the AutoCAD Architecture Metric profile.*

2. Open the Project Browser.

3. Set the **Brown Medical Clinic** Current.

   The Brown Medical Clinic project was created using a metric project template. Placeholders were automatically generated.

   Close the Project Browser.
   The Project Navigator will automatically launch.

4.   Switch to the Constructs tab.

   Highlight **01 Core**.

   Right click and select **Open**.

5.   *There is a rectangle in the drawing acting as a placeholder.*

   Select the rectangle.

   Right click and select **Open Xref**.

   The external reference is an element called Typical Toilet Room.

   Close the drawing.

6. Switch to the Insert ribbon.

   Select **PDF Import**.

7. Locate the *medical clinic – first floor.pdf*.

   Click **Open**.

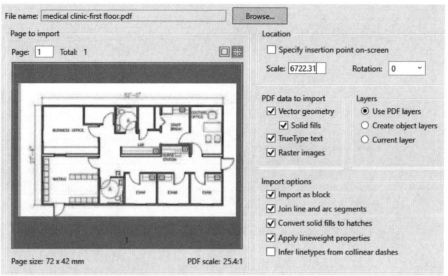

8. Disable **Specify insertion point**.
This will insert the PDF at 0,0,0
Change the Scale to **6722.31**:
Enable **Raster Images**.
Enable **Import as block**.
Enable **Convert solid fills to hatches**.
Enable **Apply lineweight properties**.

Click **OK**.

9. Set the View Scale to **1:1**.

10. Launch the **Content Browser** from the Home ribbon.

Floor Plans

11. Locate the **Design Tool Catalog -Metric**.

12. 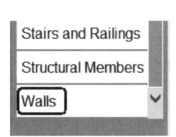 Scroll down and select **Walls**.

13. Select **Brick**.

14. 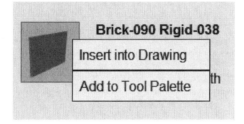 Locate the **Brick-090 Rigid-038 Air-050 Brick-090**.

    Right click and select **Insert into Drawing**.

    Exit the WALLADD command.

15. Go to the Render ribbon.

    Select **Materials Browser**.

16. 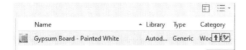 Locate the **Gypsum Board**.

    The material exists in the library, but not in the active drawing.

3-5

17. *Import into the current drawing.*

    Highlight the gypsum material. Right click and select **Add to →Document Materials.**

    The gypsum material is now copied to the active document/drawing

18. Highlight the Gypsum Board material that is in the document. Right click and select **Duplicate**.

19. Rename the copied Gypsum Board material:
    Gypsum Board - Painted Sage Green.

    Double click on the material to edit.

20. Change the Color to **RGB 171,171,155**.

    I use the ColorPicker website to help you determine the RGB values of paint colors.

21. Right click on the image and select **Edit Image**.

22. Click on the Source file name.
Select the image file located in the Lesson 3 download files named *SW 6178 Clary Sage*.
Close the dialog.

23. The appearance has been edited.

Close the Materials Editor.

Close the Materials Browser.

24. Go to the Manage ribbon.

Launch the **Style Manager**.

25. Browse to **Wall Styles** under Architectural Objects.
You will see the wall style you just imported.

26. Create a copy of the Brick-090 wall style.
Paste under Wall Styles.
Rename the copied style: **Brick-090 Rigid-038 Air-050 Gypsum Wall Board**.

27. Change the Description.

28. Select the Components tab.

Set up the layers as shown.

The Brick Veneer should be on the exterior.

29. Select the Materials tab.

    Click on **New Material**.

30. Name the new material **Finishes.Gypsum Board.Painted**.

    Click **OK**.

31. Edit the Gypsum Wall Board.

32. Select the **Display Properties** tab.

    Click on **Style Override**.

33. Set the Plan Linework color to **Green** on the Line/Color/Linetype tab.

34. Set the Hatching to **PLAST** on the Hatching tab.

35. Set the Render Material to the **Gypsum Wall Board Sage Green** on the Other tab.

    Click **OK** to close all the dialog boxes.

Floor Plans

36. If the Properties palette is closed:

    Go to the Home ribbon and launch **Properties** from the Tools drop-down.

37. Select the **Wall** tool from the Home ribbon.

38. Set the Style to **Brick-090 Gypsum Wall Board**.
    Set the Base Height to **4000**.

39. Turn ORTHO ON.

    Draw the four walls that are the outline of the building.

    The horizontal walls are 15850 mm long.
    The vertical walls are 8230 mm long.

40. Launch the **Content Browser** from the Home ribbon.

3-9

41. Locate the **Design Tool Catalog -Metric**.

42. Locate the **Doors** category.

43. 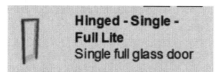 Locate the **Hinged – Single – Full Lite** door.

44. 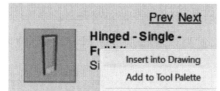 Right click and select **Insert into Drawing**.

45. 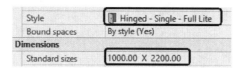 Set the Door Style to **Hinged – Single – Full Lite**
Set the Standard size to **1000 x 2200.**

46. Set Position along wall to **Offset/Center**.

47. Place in the locations shown – where the exterior doors are located on the pdf.

48. If required, select the placed door. Use the arrows to flip the door so it is oriented correctly.

    You can use the rectangular center grip to adjust the door's location.

49.

    Return to the Design Tool Catalog – Metric.

    Select the **Windows** category.

50.

    Locate **the Casement – Single Casement window**.

    Right click and select **Insert into Drawing.**

51. *The window command is active.*

    Set the size to **900.00 x 2000.00**.

52.

    Place a window using the PDF as your guide.

    Place the additional windows.

    Click ENTER to exit the command.

53. You can use the arrows to orient the windows correctly.

    The arrows should be located on the exterior side of the windows. You can use the middle grip to position the window.

    You can use the end grips to resize the window.

54. The PDF should be placed on the PDF_Images layer.

    Freeze this layer.

55. Switch to a 3D view.

    Save the *01 Core.dwg* and close.

Exercise 3-2:
Adding Interior Walls

Drawing Name: 01 Core.dwg
Estimated Time: 20 minutes

This exercise reinforces the following skills:

- Create Walls
- Insert Doors
- Content Browser

1. Open the Project Browser.

2. 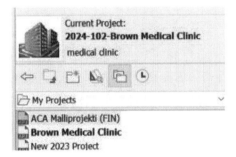 Set the **Brown Medical Clinic** Current.

   The Brown Medical Clinic project was created using a metric project template. Placeholders were automatically generated.

3. Switch to the Constructs tab.

   Highlight **01 Core**.

   Right click and select **Open**.

4. Switch the view to Top.
   Thaw the PDF_Images layer so you can see the PDF.

   Turn off OSNAPS and use running OSNAPS to place the interior walls.

5. Launch the **Content Browser** from the Home ribbon.

6. Locate the **Design Tool Catalog -Metric**.

7. Scroll down and select **Walls**.

8. 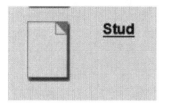 Select the **Stud** category.

9. 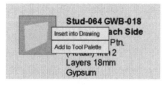 Locate the **Stud-064 GWB-018 2 Layers Each Side**.
Right click and select **Insert into Drawing**.

Floor Plans

10. 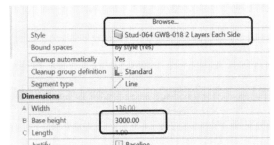 Verify that the Style is set correctly.
Set the Base Height to **3000**.
Set Justify to **Center**.

11. Trace over the PDF to place just the interior walls.

12. You can freeze and thaw the PDF_Images to review your work.

    Lock the PDF_Images layer to ensure that the PDF is not moved or accidentally deleted.

13. Launch the **Content Browser** from the Home ribbon.

14. Locate the **Design Tool Catalog -Metric**.

15. Locate the **Doors** category.

16. 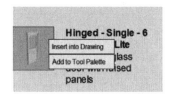 Locate the **Hinged – Single – - 6 Panel - Half Lite** door.
Right click and select **Insert into Drawing**.

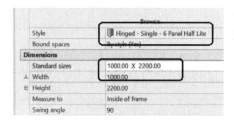 Set the Standard size to **1000 x 2200**.

17. Use the grips and flip arrows to adjust the orientation, position, and size of the doors to match the PDF layout.

Floor Plans

18. Locate the **Design Tool Catalog -Metric**.

19. Locate the **Doors** category.

20. Locate the **Bifold – Single Louver** door.
Right click and select **Insert into Drawing**.

21. Set the Standard size to **700 x 2200**.

    Place in the Staff Break room.

22. Locate the **Design Tool Catalog -Metric**.

23. Locate the **Doors** category.

3-17

24. Locate the **Hinged - Single** door. Right click and select **Insert into Drawing**.

25. Set the Standard size to **950 x 2200**.

    Place in the two bathrooms.

    If you accidentally placed a different door style in the bathrooms, select the door and use Properties to change the door style.

26. Save and close the file.

- ➢ If you draw a wall and the materials composing the wall are on the wrong side, you can reverse the direction of the wall. Simply select the wall, right click and select the Reverse option from the menu.

- ➢ To add a wall style to a drawing, you can import it or simply create the wall using the Design Tools.

- ➢ Many architects use external drawing references to organize their projects. That way, teams of architects can concentrate just on their portions of a building. External references also use fewer system resources.

- ➢ You can convert lines, arcs, circles, or polylines to walls. If you have created a floor plan in AutoCAD and want to convert it to 3D, open the floor plan drawing inside of AutoCAD Architecture. Use the Convert to Walls tool to transform your floor plan into walls.

Floor Plans

> To create a freestanding door, click the ENTER key when prompted to pick a wall. You can then use the grips on the door entity to move and place the door wherever you like.

> To move a door along a wall, use Door→Reposition→Along Wall. Use the OSNAP From option to locate a door a specific distance from an adjoining wall.

Exercise 3-3:
Place a Grid

Drawing Name: new
Estimated Time: 10 minutes

This exercise reinforces the following skills:

- Place a grid
- Create a new Construct

1. Launch the US Metric version of ACA.

   This ensures that all the content will be metric.

2.   Launch the Project Navigator.
   On the Constructs tab:
   Highlight **Constructs**.
   Right click and select
   New→Category.

3-19

3. Name the new category **General**.

4. Highlight **General**.
Right click and select
New→Construct.

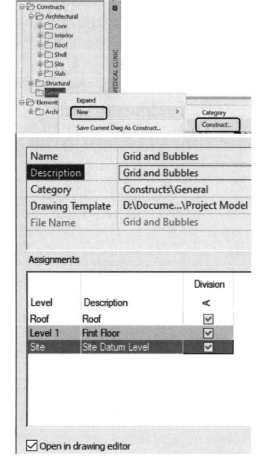

5. Change the Name to **Grid and Bubbles**.
In Description, type **Grid and Bubbles**.
Enable all the **Levels**.
Enable **Open in drawing editor**.

Click **OK**.

6. Set the Scale to **1:1**.

Floor Plans

7. Toggle off the Grid and Snap to Grid.

8. Click on **Enhanced Custom Grid** on the Home ribbon.

9. Select the **Bottom** tab.
Type in the following values:

3635
1357
1410
786
1143
1518
536
2571
2895

10. Switch to the Left tab.
Type in the following values:

2270
393
1463
874
1231
483
1617

3-21

11. *There is a preview window which shows the grids.*
Click **OK** to place the grid.

12. Type **0,0** as the insertion point.
Click **ENTER** to accept the rotation angle of 0.
The grid is placed.

13. Select one of the column bubbles.
Right click and **Select Similar**.

14. Change the Scale to **125** in the Properties palette.

    Click ESC to release the selection.

15. The grid updates.

    You can select the overlapping column bubbles and move them to a new position.

    Save and close the file.

Floor Plans

Exercise 3-4:
Combining Constructs

Drawing Name: Main Model.dwg
Estimated Time: 15 minutes

This exercise reinforces the following skills:

- Add Constructs to a 3D model
- Create a new Construct
- Visual Styles

1. Launch the US Metric version of ACA.

   This ensures that all the content will be metric.

2. Launch the Project Navigator.
   On the Constructs tab:
   Highlight **Constructs**.
   Right click and select **New→Category**.

3. Name the new category **3D**.

4. Highlight **3D**.
   Right click and select **New→Construct**.

3-23

5.

   Change the Name to **Main Model**.
   In Description, type **Main Model**.
   Enable all the **Levels**.
   Enable Open in drawing editor.

   Click **OK**.

6.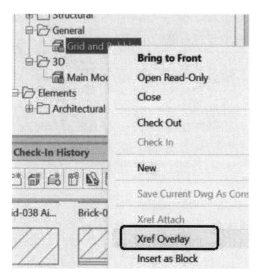

   Highlight the **Grid and Bubbles** construct.
   Right click and select **Xref Overlay**.

   The Grid and Bubbles drawing is placed in the Main Model drawing.

Floor Plans

7. Highlight the **01 Core** construct.

   Right click and select **Xref Overlay**.

8. If necessary, reposition the 01 Core construct so it is aligned with the grid layout.

9. 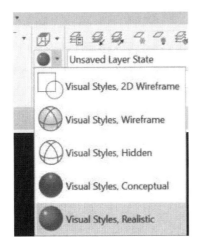 Switch to an isometric view.

10. Set the Visual Style to Realistic.

    Orbit around the model.

    Check for any other errors and correct as needed.

11. Save and close the drawing.

3-25

Exercise 3-5:
Create a Floor Plan Reprised

Drawing Name: new
Estimated Time: 30 minutes

This exercise reinforces the following skills:

- Import PDF
- Levels
- Copy and Paste Wall Style
- Style Browser
- Walls
- Doors
- Windows

1.   Launch the ACA English (US Imperial) software.

   You can also go to Options/Profiles and set the (US Imperial) profile current.

2.

   Set the **Tahoe Cabin** project current.

   Close the Project Browser.

3. Start a new drawing.

   Toggle off the Grid and Snap to Grid.

4. Open the Project Navigator. Select the **Project** tab.

   Click on **Edit Levels**.

5. Change the Ground Floor Level Floor to Floor Height to **8'-0"**.

   Notice that all the other levels adjust.

   Click **OK**.

6. Click **Yes**.

7. Go to the **Insert** ribbon.

   Click **PDF Import.**

8. Locate the *tahoe-basement-floor-plan.pdf* in the downloaded files.

   Click **Open**.

9. Disable **Specify insertion point**.
   This will insert the PDF at 0,0,0
   Set the Scale to **55**.
   This scales the PDF to the correct imperial measurements.
   Enable **Raster Images**.
   Enable **Import as block**.
   Enable **Convert solid fills to hatches**.
   Enable **Apply lineweight properties**.
   Click **OK**.

10. Place the PDF on the PDF_Images layer and lock the layer.

11. Go to the Project Navigator.

    Open the **Constructs** tab.

    Right click on the **Architecture** category.
    Select **Save Current Dwg As Construct**.

Floor Plans

12. Name the drawing **Ground Floor Plan**.
    Add the description.
    Enable the **Ground Floor** Division.

    Click **OK**.

13. Go to the Manage ribbon.

    Open the **Styles Manager**.

14. Open the *wall styles.dwg* in the downloaded exercise files.

    Locate the **Stud-4 Rigid-1.5 Air- 1 Log** wall style.

    Copy and paste into the Ground Floor Plan drawing.

15. You should see the new wall style in the Ground Floor Plan under the Wall Styles category.

Close the Style Manager.

16. Set ORTHO ON.

Go to the Home ribbon.

Select the **Wall** tool.

17. 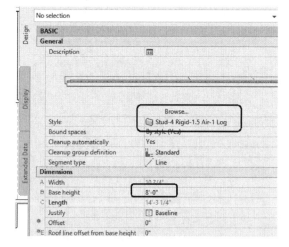 On the Properties palette:

Set the Style to **Stud-4 Rigid-1.5 Air-1 Log**.

Set the Base height to **8'-0"**.

Set Justify to **Center.**

18. Trace around the exterior of the building using the PDF as the guide.

Check that walls are oriented correctly with the arrow on the outside of the building.

19. Go to the Home ribbon and open the **Styles Browser**.

20. Locate the **Stud -3.5 GWB-0.625 2 Layers Each Side** wall style.

21. Right click on the wall tool and select **Add object**.

22. Add the interior walls.
DO NOT PLACE ANGLED WALLS.

Use TRIM, EXTEND, and ALIGN to clean up walls as needed.

23. 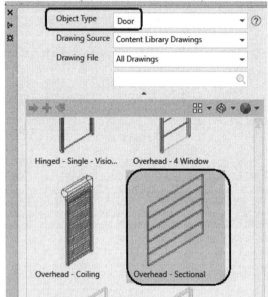 Open the Style Browser.

Set the Object Type to Door.

Locate the **Overhead – Sectional door**.

24. Right click on the door tool and select **Add object**.

25. Set the Width to **15'-8"**.

Set the Height to **7' 8"**.

Floor Plans

26. Place on garage wall.

27. Locate the **Hinged – Single** door in the Styles Browser.

Right click and select **Add object**.

28. Set the Size to 2'-6" x 6'-8".

Style	Hinged - Single
Bound spaces	By style (Yes)
Dimensions	
Standard sizes	2'-6" X 6'-8"
A Width	2'-6"
B Height	6'-8"
Measure to	Inside of frame
Swing angle	90

3-33

29.

Place four doors as shown.

Use the arrows to flip the door's orientation as needed. Use the grips to resize the doors as needed.

30.

Locate the **Bifold – Double - Louver** door in the Styles Browser.

Right click and select **Add object**.

31.

Set the Width to **4'10"** in the Properties palette.

Set the Height to **6'-8"**.

Floor Plans

32. Place in the furnace room.

33. Change the Object Type to **Window** in the Styles Browser.

Locate the **Casement** window.

Right click and select **Add object**.

34. Change the Width to **5'6"**.

Change the Height to **4'-0"**.

35. Add the windows in the two locations indicated.

Check that the windows are oriented with the exterior arrow outside the building.

36. Save and close the drawing.

3-35

Curtain Walls

Curtain walls provide a grid or framework for inserting objects such as windows and doors. Curtain walls have many similarities to standard walls, such as baseline, roof line, and floor line, and they allow for interferences. You can insert doors, windows, and door/window assemblies into a curtain wall, just like standard walls, but the insertion process is different.

Curtain Wall Grids

Curtain walls are made up of one or more grids. Each grid in a curtain wall has either a horizontal division or a vertical division, but you can nest the grids to create a variety of patterns from simple to complex.

Elements of Grids

Grids are the foundation of curtain walls, curtain wall units, and door/window assemblies. Every grid has four element types:

- **Divisions:** Define the direction of the grid (horizontal or vertical) and the number of cells
- **Cell Infills:** Contain another grid, a panel infill, or an object such as a window or a door
- **Frames:** Define the edge around the outside of the primary grid and nested grids
- **Mullions:** Define the edges between the cells

Note: Division is an abstract element, in contrast to the other three element types that represent physical elements of the curtain wall.

Each element type is assigned a default definition that describes what elements of that type look like.

Element type	Default definitions
Divisions	Primary horizontal grid with a fixed cell dimension of 13' and secondary vertical grid with a fixed cell dimension of 3'
Cell Infills	Cells containing simple panels 2" thick
Frames	Left, right, top, and bottom outer edges of grid 3" wide and 3" deep
Mullions	Edges between cells 1" wide and 3" deep

Floor Plans

Exercise 3-6:
Place a Curtain Wall

Drawing Name: Ground Floor Plan
Estimated Time: 15 minutes

This exercise reinforces the following skills:

- Place a curtain wall
- External References
- Steering Wheel
- Views
- UCS

1. Launch the ACA English (US Imperial) software.

2.

   Set the **Tahoe Cabin** project current.

   Close the Project Browser.

3.

   Go to the Constructs tab on the Project Navigator.

   Open **3D Model-Master**.

3-37

4. On the Project Navigator:

   Open the **Constructs** tab.

   Highlight **Ground Floor Plan**.

   Right click and select **Xref Overlay**.

5. Zoom out.

   The Ground Floor Plan was inserted at 0,0.

   The other Xrefs are located far apart.

6. Shift the xrefs so they are aligned at the 0,0 location.

7. Type **XREF** to bring up the XREF Manager.

   Change all the XREFs to Overlays.

   If you see this dialog, enable **Do not show me this message again** and click **Close**.

Floor Plans

8. Highlight the ground floorplan XREF.

Right click and select **XREF Type→Overlay**.

9. Highlight the foundation floorplan-Tahoe Cabin XREF.

Right click and select **XREF Type→Overlay**.

Close the XREF Manager.

10. On the Home ribbon:
Switch to a **SW Isometric view**.

11. Rotate around.

You will see the Ground Floor level inserted at the correct elevation.

3-39

12. Select the Ground Floor Plan XREF.

    On the ribbon, select **Edit Reference In-Place**.

13. Click **OK**.

14. Switch to a **Top** view.

Floor Plans

15.

Under the Viewcube, select **WCS** to use the World UCS.

You will see the UCSICON adjust.

16.

Freeze the **0PDF_Images** layer.

17.

Select the **Curtain Wall** tool on the Home ribbon.

18.

Set the Base Height to **28'-0"**.

3-41

19. Draw two angled lines to place the curtain wall.

    ESC out of the Curtain Wall tool.

20. On the Home ribbon: Switch to a **SW Isometric view**.

21. Press the SHIFT key and the middle mouse button to orbit around the model and inspect the curtain wall.

22. Switch the View ribbon.

    Launch the **Full Navigation** Steering Wheel.

23. Use the different tools on the steering wheel to view the model.

    When you are done, click the X located in the upper right corner of the steering wheel to close.

24.

Select **Save Changes** on the ribbon.
Click **OK**.

25.

Save the *3D Model_Master.dwg*.

Exercise 3-7:
Create a Second Floor Plan

Drawing Name: new
Estimated Time: 30 minutes

This exercise reinforces the following skills:

- PDF Import
- Walls
- Doors
- Windows
- Properties

1. Launch the ACA English (US Imperial) software.

2.

   Set the **Tahoe Cabin** project current.

   Close the Project Browser.

3.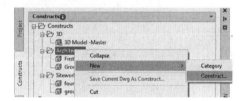

   In the Project Navigator:

   Open the Constructs tab.

   Highlight the **Architecture** category:

   Right click and select **New→Construct**.

4.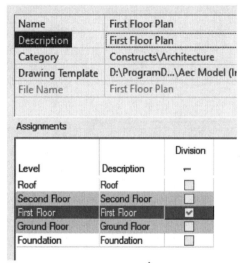

   Assign **First Floor Plan** to the Name.
   Assign **First Floor Plan** to Description.
   Enable the **First Floor** Division.

   Enable **Open in drawing editor.**

   Click **OK.**

5.

   Toggle off the Grid and Snap to Grid.

Floor Plans

6. Go to the **Insert** ribbon.

   Click **PDF Import.**

7. Locate the *tahoe-main-floor-plan.pdf* in the downloaded files.

   Click **Open**.

8. Disable **Specify insertion point**. *This will insert the PDF at 0,0,0* Set the Scale to **60**. *This scales the PDF to the correct imperial measurements.* Enable **Raster Images**. Enable **Import as block**. Enable **Convert solid fills to hatches**. Enable **Apply lineweight properties**.
   Click **OK**.

9. Place the PDF on the **PDF_Images** layer and lock the layer.

10. Go to the Manage ribbon.

    Open the **Style Manager**.

3-45

11. Click Open.

    Browse to the **Architecture** category under Constructs.

12. Open the *Ground Floor Plan.dwg*.

13. Highlight **Wall Styles** in the Ground Floor Drawing, Right click and select **Copy**.

    Paste into the *First Floorplan.dwg*.

14. Enable **Leave Existing**.

    Click **OK**.

15. Highlight **Door Styles** in the Ground Floor Drawing, Right click and select **Copy**.

    Paste into the *First Floorplan.dwg*.

Floor Plans

16. Enable **Leave Existing**.

    Click **OK**.

17. Copy and Paste the **Casement** Window Style from the Ground Floorplan into the First Floor Plan.

    Close the Style Manager.

18. Launch the Layer Manager.

    Create layer named **exterior walls.**

    Make that layer current.

19. Close the Layer Manager. Toggle ORTHO ON.

    Trace the exterior outline of the building using lines.

    Do not place lines where the curtain wall is located. Those are the two angled walls.

20. Locate the **Wall** tool on the Design Tool Palette.

    Right click and select **Apply Tool Properties to →Linework**.

21. Select the lines that were placed.

    You can window around the lines to select them.

    Click **ENTER**.

22. 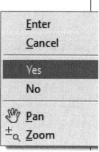 Right click and select **Yes** to erase the lines.

23. The walls should still be selected.

    On the Properties palette:

    Change the Style to **Stud-4-1.5 Air – 1 Log**.

    Click **ESC** to release the selection.

24. Go around the walls and flip the orientation so that the exterior is oriented correctly.

Floor Plans

25. Select the Wall tool from the Home ribbon.

26.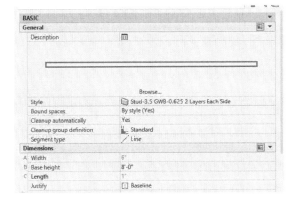

    On the Properties palette:

    Set the **Style to Stud-3.5 GWB-0.625 2 Layers Each Side**.

    Add the interior walls, tracing over the PDF.

27.

    [−][SW Isometric][Hidden]

    Change the view to **SW Isometric/Hidden** to inspect the floor plan.

28. [−][Top][Hidden]   Return to a **Top** view.

29.

    Add casement windows at the locations shown.

    All the windows are 5'6" x 4'-0" except for the bathroom window.

    The bathroom window is 3' x 4'.

3-49

30. Add single hinged doors in the locations shown.

    The master closet door is 2'-0" x 6'8".
    The other doors are 2'6" x 6' 8".

31. Add a 4'-6" x 6'-8" bifold closet door at the entrance.

32. Save and close the drawing.

Exercise 3-8:
Use the Style Browser to Add Doors

Drawing Name: First Floor Plan
Estimated Time: 10 minutes

This exercise reinforces the following skills:

- Doors
- Properties
- Styles Browser

1.   Launch the ACA English (US Imperial) software.

2.

Set the **Tahoe Cabin** project current.

Close the Project Browser.

3.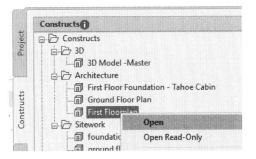

In the Project Navigator:

Open the Constructs tab.

Highlight the **First Floor Plan** under the **Architecture** category:

Right click and select **Open**.

4.

Launch the **Styles Browser** from the Home ribbon.

5.

Set the Object Type to Door.

Locate the **Slding – Double- Full Lite** door.

3-51

6.

Right click and select **Import styles**.

This adds the door style to the open drawing.

Close the Styles Browser.

7.

Add a sliding door that is 5' 10 7/8" x 6' 10 11/16" in the dining room and master bedroom as shown.

8. Save and close the file.

Exercise 3-9:
Create a Door and Window Assembly

Drawing Name: new
Estimated Time: 30 minutes

This exercise reinforces the following skills:

- Doors
- Properties
- Styles Browser
- Style Manager
- Door/Window Assembly

1. Launch the ACA English (US Imperial) software.

Floor Plans

2.

   Set the **Tahoe Cabin** project current.

   Close the Project Browser.

3.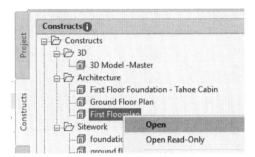

   In the Project Navigator:

   Open the Constructs tab.

   Highlight the **First Floor Plan** under the **Architecture** category:

   Right click and select **Open**.

4.

   Launch the **Styles Browser.**

5.

   Set the Object Type to **Door.**

   Locate the **Hinged - Single – 6 Panel – Half Lite.**

   Right click and select **Import styles.**

6. Set the Object Type to Door/Window Assembly.

   In the search field, type Hinged Single.

   Locate the **Hinged Single 3- 0x6-8 + Sidelights 2-0x6-0 (R)** ·

   Right click and select **Add object**.

7. Place the door at the entrance.

8. [−][NW Isometric][Hidden]   Change the view to NW Isometric/Hidden.

9. You see the door window assembly that was just placed.

   Select the sidelights.

10. With the sidelights selected,

    Click **Edit** under Division on the ribbon.

    Click on the left window sidelight.

11. Select the – grip at the bottom of the window.

    Click **Finish** on the ribbon.

12. Click **Save**.

13. Go to the Manage ribbon.

    Open the Style Manager.
    Locate the **Hinged Single 3- 0x6-8 + Sidelights 2-0x6-0 (R).**
    Copy and Paste to create a duplicate.

14. Highlight the copied door/window assembly style.
    Right click and select **Rename**.

15. Rename the assembly: **Hinged Single 3-0x6-8 + Left Sidelight 2-0x6-0**

16. Select the Design Rules tab.

    Click the New Nested Grid and change to New Cell Assignment. Set the Element to Default Infill.

17. Set the cell location to the **Start**.

18. Click **Divisions**.

    Set the Division Type to **Fixed Number of Cells**.
    Set the Number of Cells to **2**.

    There will be the door and a single sidelight.

    Click **OK** to close the Style Manager.

19. Switch back to a Top view.

    Select the door/window assembly and assign the new style with the single sidelight.

    Change the Width to **5'0"**.

    If you see a warning icon, shift the position of the door window assembly slightly and it should resolve.

Floor Plans

20.

    [−][NW Isometric][Realistic]

    Change the view to NW Isometric/Realistic.

    Select the door.

21.

    On the Properties palette:

    Change the door style to **Hinged – Single – 6 Panel Half Light.**

    Click **ESC** to release the selection.

22.

    Orbit around to inspect the door.

23.

    Return to the Style Manager.

    Highlight the **Hinged Single 3-0x6-8 + Left Sidelight 2-0x6-0.**

    On the Design Rules tab:

    Set the Default Division.
    Set the Division Type to Fixed Cell Dimension.

3-57

24. Set the Cell Dimension to 4'-0".

   This will be the door width.

   Enable **Auto-Adjust Cells**.
   Set Cell Adjustment to **Shrink**.

   This will decrease the width of the sidelight.

25. Set the Default Cell Assignment to the Hinged – Single – 6 Panel – Half Lite.

   Click **OK**.

26. Save and close file.

Floor Plans

Exercise 3-10:
Add an Overlay

Drawing Name: 3D Model - Master
Estimated Time: 10 minutes

This exercise reinforces the following skills:

- Project Navigator
- XREF
- UCS
- Project Navigator

1. Launch the ACA English (US Imperial) software.

2.   Set the **Tahoe Cabin** project current.

   Close the Project Browser.

3. 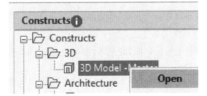 In the Project Navigator:

   Open the Constructs tab.

   Highlight the **3D Model – Master** under the **3D** category:

   Right click and select **Open**.

4.   Highlight the First Floor Plan construct.
   Right click and select **Xref Overlay**.

3-59

5. It is placed in the model.

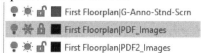

Freeze the First Floorplan|PDF Images layer, so you can see the model.

6. [−][Left][Hidden (Fast)]   Switch to a **LEFT| Hidden** display.

7. Type **UCS, View**.

This changes the UCS to an XY display.

8. Use DIST to measure the distance from the bottom of the concrete columns to the top of the foundation.

This will be the elevation for the ground floor. The foundation is inserted at -4'. So, the ground floor should be located 4' below the distance measured.

9. Bring up the Project Navigator.

Go to the Project tab.

Click on **Edit Levels**.

10. Set the Ground Floor Elevation to **3' 11 ¾"**.

The other elevations should update.

Click **OK**.

Floor Plans

11. Click **Yes**.

   You have made changes to the project that may affect existing views.
   Do you wish to regenerate all views in this project?

12. Use MOVE to place the XREFs so they are aligned on top of each other.

13. Switch to a SE Isometric view.

14. 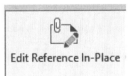 Use the MOVE tool to adjust the position of the first floor.

   Some of the exterior walls need to be adjusted to match the ground floor.

15. Select the first floor.

   Click **Edit Reference In-Place** on the ribbon.

16. Click **OK**.

3-61

17. When you are done with the adjustments, click Save Changes on the ribbon.

18. Click **OK**.

19. Orbit around the model to verify the walls are aligned.

Save and close the file.

Exercise 3-11:
Create a Third Floor Plan

Drawing Name: new
Estimated Time: 30 minutes

This exercise reinforces the following skills:

- Project Navigator
- Insert PDF
- Styles Manager
- Styles Browser
- Walls
- Doors
- Windows
- Properties

1. Launch the ACA English (US Imperial) software.

2.

Set the **Tahoe Cabin** project current.

Close the Project Browser.

3.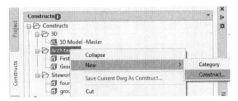

In the Project Navigator:

Open the Constructs tab.

Highlight the **Architecture** category:

Right click and select **New→Construct**.

4.

Assign **Second Floor Plan** to the Name.
Assign **Second Floor Plan** to Description.
Enable the **Second Floor** Division.

Enable **Open in drawing editor.**

Click **OK.**

5.

Toggle off the Grid and Snap to Grid.

6. Go to the **Insert** ribbon.

   Click **PDF Import.**

7. Locate the *tahoe-second-floor-plan.pdf* in the downloaded files.

   Click **Open**.

8. Disable **Specify insertion point**.
   This will insert the PDF at 0,0,0
   Set the Scale to **56**.
   This scales the PDF to the correct imperial measurements.
   Enable **Raster Images**.
   Enable **Import as block**.
   Enable **Convert solid fills to hatches.**
   Enable **Apply lineweight properties**.
   　Click **OK**.

9. Place the PDF on the **PDF_Images** layer and lock the layer.

10. Go to the Manage ribbon.

    Open the **Style Manager**.

Floor Plans

11. The Ground Floor Plan.dwg should still be listed as an open drawing.

12. If the Ground Floor Plan.dwg isn't listed, click **Open**.

    Browse to the **Architecture** category under Constructs.

13. Open the *Ground Floor Plan.dwg*.

14. Highlight **Wall Styles** in the Ground Floor Drawing,
    Right click and select **Copy**.

    Paste into the *Second Floorplan.dwg*.

15. Enable **Leave Existing**.

    Click **OK**.

16. Highlight Door Styles in the *Ground Floor* Drawing,
    Right click and select **Copy**.

    Paste into the Second Floorplan.dwg.

17. Enable **Leave Existing**.

    Click **OK**.

3-65

18. 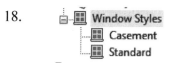 Copy and Paste the **Casement Window** Style from the Ground Floorplan into the Second Floor Plan.

19. Close the Style Manager.

20. Launch the Layer Manager.
    Create a layer named **exterior walls**.
    Make that layer current.
    Close the Layer Manager.

21. Turn ORTHO ON.

    Trace the exterior outline of the building using lines.

    Do not place lines where the curtain wall is located. Those are the two angled walls.

22. Locate the **Wall** tool on the Design Tool Palette.

    Right click and select **Apply Tool Properties to →Linework.**

23. Select the lines that were placed.

    Click **ENTER**.

24. Right click and select **Yes** to erase the lines.

25. The Properties palette should appear.

    Change the Wall Style to **Stud-4 Rigid-1.5 Air – 1 Log**.

    Click **ESC** to release the selection.

26. Verify that all the walls are oriented with the exterior side on the outside of the building.

To change the orientation, just click on the arrow.

27. Place a 5'6" x 4'-0" Casement window in the two locations indicated.

28. Change the Global Cut Plane to **5'-0"**.

If you don't change the cut plane, you won't see the next set of windows that are placed.

29. Place four casement windows in the location shown.

These windows should be 2'-0" x 3'0".

Verify that they are oriented correctly.

30. Place a 5'-0" x 4'-0" casement window in the location indicated.

31. Launch the **Styles Browser** from the Home ribbon.

32. 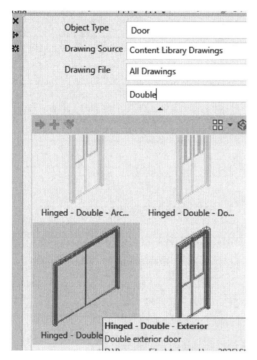 Set the Object Type to Door.

    Locate the **Hinged – Double – Exterior** door.

Floor Plans

33. Right click and select **Add object**.

34. Set the size to **5'-0" x 6'8"**.

35. Place in the two locations indicated.

36. Save and close the file.

Exercise 3-12:
Add Interior Walls and Doors

Drawing Name: Second Floor Plan.dwg
Estimated Time: 15 minutes

This exercise reinforces the following skills:

- Project Navigator
- Walls
- Doors
- Properties

1. Launch the ACA English (US Imperial) software.

2. Set the **Tahoe Cabin** project current.

   Close the Project Browser.

3. 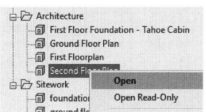 In the Project Navigator:

   Open the Constructs tab.

   Highlight the **Architecture** category:

   Right click on the Second Floor Plan and select **Open**.

Floor Plans

4. Select the **Wall** tool from the Home ribbon.

5. The Style should be set to **Stud-3.5 GWB-0.625 2 Layers Each Side.**

   This is an interior wall style.

6. Place interior walls as indicated.

7. Select the **Door** tool from the Home ribbon.

8. On the Properties palette:

   Set the Style to **Hinged – Single**.

   Set the Size to **2'-6" x 6'-8"**.

9. Place doors in locations indicated.

   Use Properties to adjust the size of the doors to match the PDF.
   Use arrows to orient the doors properly.

10. Save and close the file.

Exercise 3-13:
Add Overlay - Reprised

Drawing Name: 3D Model - Master.dwg
Estimated Time: 15 minutes

This exercise reinforces the following skills:

- Project Navigator
- XREF

1. Launch the ACA English (US Imperial) software.

2.

   Set the **Tahoe Cabin** project current.

   Close the Project Browser.

3. 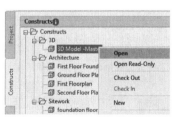 In the Project Navigator:
   Highlight the **3D Model – Master**.
   Right click and select **Open**.

4. Locate the **Second Floor Plan** in the Project Navigator.

   Right click and select **Xref Overlay**.

5. Locate the **Second Floor Plan|PDF Image** layer in the layer drop-down list.
Freeze the layer.

6. Use the MOVE tool to adjust the XREF position to align one of the building corner's with the existing model.

7. Select the Second Floor XREF.

   Select **Edit Reference In-Place.**

8. Click **OK**.

9. Adjust the exterior walls so they are aligned with the first level.

   Tip: Use FILLET with Radius 0 to clean up the wall corners.

   When all edits are completed, select **Save Changes** on the ribbon.

10. Switch to a **Realistic** display.

    Save and close.

Exercise 3-14:
Add an Opening to a Wall

Drawing Name: 01 Core.dwg
Estimated Time: 10 minutes

This exercise reinforces the following skills:

- Add an opening to a wall

1. Launch the US Metric version of ACA.

   This ensures that all the content will be metric.

   You can also use Options→Profiles to switch to the Metric Profile.

2. Open the **Project Browser**.

3. 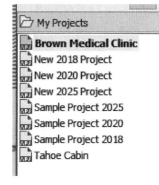 Set the **Brown Medical Clinic** Current.

   The Brown Medical Clinic project was created using a metric project template. Placeholders were automatically generated.

   Close the Project Browser.

4. The Project Navigator should open.

   Switch to the Constructs tab.

   Highlight **01 Core** under Floor Plans.

   Right click and select **Open**.

5. Thaw the PDF_Images layer.

6. Switch to an Isometric view.

   Select the wall located between the business office and the waiting area.

7. Select **Opening** on the ribbon.

8. Place the opening so it aligns with the opening shown in the PDF.

9. Click on the bottom arrow grip to raise the height of the opening.

10. The opening should be adjusted to look like a window between the rooms.

11. Save and close the drawing.

Notes:

QUIZ 3

True or False

1. When you insert a PDF into a drawing, it cannot be converted to AutoCAD elements, like lines or text.

2. When you insert an image, it cannot be converted to AutoCAD elements, like lines or text.

3. The direction you place walls – clockwise or counter-clockwise – determines which side of the wall is oriented as exterior.

4. Curtain walls can only be linear, not arcs, in AutoCAD Architecture.

5. Grids can only be lines, not arcs, in AutoCAD Architecture.

6. To re-orient a door, use the Rotate command.

7. You can set cut planes for individual objects (such as windows), an object style (such as walls) or as the system default.

Multiple Choice

8. To change the hatch display of wall components in a wall style:

    A. Modify the wall style
    B. Change the visual style
    C. Change the display style
    D. Switch to a plan\top view

9. This tool on the status bar:

    A. Sets the elevation of the active level
    B. Controls the default cut plane of the view and the display range
    C. Sets the distance between levels
    D. Sets the elevation of the active plane

10. To assign a material to a door:

    A. Modify the door component by editing the door style
    B. Drag and drop the material from the Material Browser onto a door
    C. Use the Display Manager
    D. Define a new Visual Style

11. You want to create a wall that shows a specific paint color. Put the steps in the correct order.

    A. Place a wall.
    B. Open the Styles Manager.
    C. Import the desired material into the current drawing.
    D. Use the Materials Browser to locate a similar material.
    E. Duplicate the Material and redefine it with the correct color specification.
    F. Create a new wall style.
    G. Assign the desired material to a wall component.
    H. Set the Render material for the wall component to the desired material definition.

12. You want to place a door style that is not available on the Design Tools palette. You open the Design Tool Catalog and search for the desired door style. You locate the desired door style. Now what?

    A. Select the Door tool on the Home ribbon and use the Properties palette to select the desired door style.
    B. Add the Door Style from the Design Tool Catalog to the Design Tools palette.
    C. Right click on the desired door style in the catalog and select Insert into Drawing.
    D. Right click on the desired door style in the catalog and select Add to Styles Manager.

13. You select on a window that was placed in the model. The arrows can be used to:

    A. Change the window location/position.
    B. Change the window orientation.
    C. Change the window size.
    D. Change the window opening.

ANSWERS:

1) F; 2) T; 3) T; 4) F; 5) F; 6) F; 7) T; 8) A; 9) B; 10) A; 11) D, E, C, B, F, G, H, A; 12) C; 13) B

Lesson 4:
Space Planning

A residential structure is divided into three basic areas:

- Bedrooms: Used for sleeping and privacy
- Common Areas: Used for gathering and entertainment, such as family rooms and living rooms, and dining area
- Service Areas: Used to perform functions, such as the kitchen, laundry room, garage, and storage areas

When drawing your floor plan, you need to verify that enough space is provided to allow placement of items, such as beds, tables, entertainment equipment, cars, stoves, bathtubs, lavatories, etc.

AutoCAD Architecture comes with Design Content to allow designers to place furniture to test their space.

Exercise 4-1:
Creating AEC Content

Drawing Name: New
Estimated Time: 30 minutes

This lesson reinforces the following skills:

- Design Center
- AEC Content
- Content Browser
- Tool Palettes
- Customization

1. Launch the ACA English (US Imperial) software.

2. Set the **Tahoe Cabin** project current.

3. 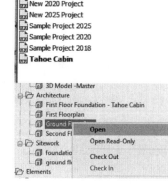 Open the **Ground Floor Plan**.

4. Launch the **Design Tools** from the Home ribbon.

5. Launch the **Content Browser** from the Home ribbon.

Space Planning

6. 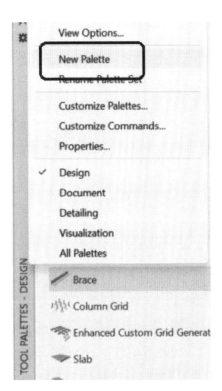 Right click on the Design Palette. Select **New Palette**.

7. 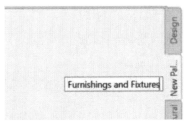 Rename the **Palette Furnishings and Fixtures**.

8. Locate the **Design Tool -Catalog – Imperial**.

   We will be adding elements from the catalogs to the palettes. Feel free to select any elements you think might be useful to your work.

9. Browse to the Residential folder.

10. Add a Dryer, Washer, and Water Heater to the palette.

    - Dryer 28x26
    - Washer 30x26
    - Water Heater - 24in

11. Design Tool Catalog - Imperial
    Catalog Top < Equipment < Office

    Browse to the Office folder.

12. Add a Copier and Water Cooler to the palette.

    - Copier - Large
    - Water Cooler

13. Design Tool Catalog - Imperial
    Catalog Top < Equipment < Food Service < Refrigerator

    Browse to the Refrigerator folder.

14. Add a Refrigerator to the palette.

    - Top-Bot 31x28

15. Catalog Top < General < People

    Browse to the People folder.

16. Add the Person to the palette.

    - Person

17. Design Tool Catalog - Imperial
    Catalog Top < Mechanical < Plumbing Fixtures < Lavatory

    Browse to the Lavatory folder.

18. Add the Vanity to the palette.

    - Vanity
      Plumbing: Lavatory:
      Vanity w/ Lav [15400]

4-4

Space Planning

19.	Design Tool Catalog - Imperial Catalog Top < Mechanical < Plumbing Fixtures < Toilet	Browse to the Toilet folder.
20.	Tank 2 Plumbing: Toilet: Tank flush, floor mount WC [15400]	Add Tank 2 to the palette.
21.	Design Tool Catalog - Imperial Catalog Top < Mechanical < Plumbing Fixtures < Shower	Browse to the Shower folder.
22.	Tank 2 HC Shower - Left HC Shower - Right	Add the Left and Right HC Shower elements to the palette.
23.	Design Tool Catalog - Imperial Catalog Top < Mechanical < Plumbing Fixtures < Bath	Browse to the Bath folder.
24.	HC Shower - Right Tub 30x48 Tub 30x54	Add a couple of tubs to the palette.
25.	Design Tool Catalog - Imperial Catalog Top < Furnishing < Furniture < Table	Browse to the Table folder.
26.	Night 18x18 Coffee Table Conf 12ft - 12 Seat	Add a Night table, a Coffee Table, and a Conference table to the palette.
27.	Design Tool Catalog - Imperial Catalog Top < Furnishing < Furniture < Bed	Browse to the Bed folder.

28.		Add a King, Hospital and Queen Bed to the palette.
29.		Browse to the Desk folder.
30.		Add a desk to the palette.
31.		Browse to the Chair folder.
32.		Select several chairs to add to the palette.
33.		Browse to the Sofa folder.

Space Planning

34. Add the modular sofa elements to the palette.

These will give you the most flexibility in placing a sofa.

35. Browse to the Unit Kitchens folder.

36. Add the Medium Kitchen to the palette.

37. Locate a vehicle to place in the garage.

38.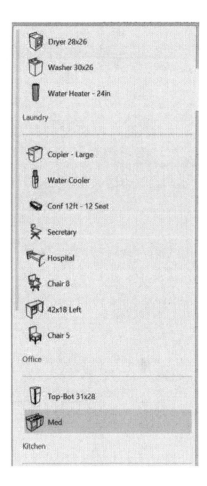

Add separators and text to organize the palette.

This will make it easier to locate the desired elements.

39.

Go to the Insert ribbon.

Launch the Design Center.

Space Planning

40. You can drag and drop content from the Design Center onto the tool palette.

    Open the **AEC Content** tab.

    Locate the Vanity Unit in the Basin folder under Metric/Design/Bathroom and place on the tool palette.

41.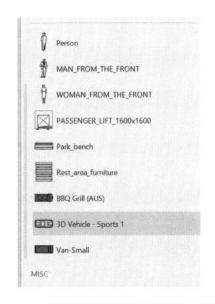

    Browse through the Design Center and add any desired elements to the tool palette.

42. *There are several drawings in the downloaded files that also can be added to the tool palette.*

    Select the Folders tab on the Design Center. Browse to the folder where you downloaded the files from the publisher.

    Drag and drop onto the tool palette.

43. Save and close.

Exercise 4-2:
Inserting AEC Content

Drawing Name: Ground Floor Plan.dwg
Estimated Time: 15 minutes

This lesson reinforces the following skills:

- Inserting blocks

1. Launch the ACA English (US Imperial) software.

2. Set the **Tahoe Cabin** project current.

3. Launch the Project Navigator.

   Open the **Ground Floor Plan** construct drawing.

4. Place the Water Heater and Furnace in the closet.

   To place just drag and drop from the tool palette to the desired location.

5. When dragging and dropping, set Specify rotation on screen to **Yes** to allow the block to rotate.

Space Planning

6. Drag and drop a vehicle into the garage.

7. Place a vanity and toilet in the bathroom.

8. Place a coffee table and sofa in the rec room.

9. Go to the Insert ribbon.

   Click **Insert→Blocks from Libraries**.

10. Click to **Browse**.

11. 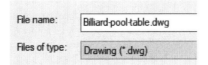 Browse to the downloaded exercise files and locate the *Billiard-pool-table.dwg*.

    Click **Open.**

12. Under Options:

    Enable **Insertion Point**.
    Enable **Rotation**.

13. Highlight the file name.

    Right click and select **Insert**.

14. Place in the rec room.

    Select the block and place on the **I-Furn** layer.

15. Freeze the PDF_Image layer.

    Switch to an isometric view.

    Orbit around to inspect the floor plan.

16. Save and close the file.

Space Planning

Exercise 4-3:
Inserting AEC Content - Reprised

Drawing Name: First Floorplan.dwg
Estimated Time: 15 minutes

This lesson reinforces the following skills:

- Inserting blocks

1. Launch the ACA English (US Imperial) software.

2.   Set the **Tahoe Cabin** project current.

3. 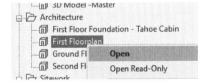 The Project Navigator opens.

   Open the **First Floor Plan** construct drawing.

4. Switch to a **Top View**.

4-13

5. Switch to a **2D Wireframe** display.

6. 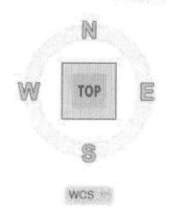 Verify that the UCS is set to **WCS**.

7.   The imported PDF shows the rough location of the bedroom furniture and the bathroom fixtures.

   If you do not see the PDF, thaw the **PDF_Images** layer.

8. Place the washer and dryer in the utility room.

   Set rotation on screen to **Yes**.

Location		
Specify rotation on screen	Yes
Rotation	0.00
Elevation	0"

Space Planning

9. Place a dining table and chairs in the dining room.

10. Add a queen bed and night stand in the Master Bedroom.

11. Add a loveseat, sofa, coffee table and end table to the living room.

12. Add a toilet and vanity to the bathroom.

13. Add a toilet, tub, toilet and two vanities to the master bath.

14. Your drawing should look similar to this.

    Save your work.

Exercise 4-4:
Inserting AEC Content – Second Floor

Drawing Name: Second Floor Plan.dwg
Estimated Time: 15 minutes

This lesson reinforces the following skills:

- Inserting blocks

1. Launch the ACA English (US Imperial) software.

Space Planning

2. 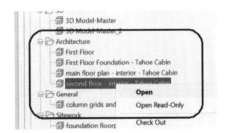 Launch the Project Navigator.

Open the **Second Floor Plan** construct drawing.

3. Switch to a **Top View**.

4. 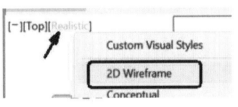 Switch to a **2D Wireframe** display.

5. Verify that the UCS is set to **WCS**.

6. The imported PDF shows the rough location of the bedroom furniture and the bathroom fixtures.

If you do not see the PDF, thaw the **PDF_Images** layer.

7. Use the elements placed on the Furnishing & Fixtures tool palette to populate the floor plan.

   Freeze the PDF-Image layer.

8. Switch to a 3D view.

   Change the display to Realistic.

   Orbit the model and verify how things appear.

9. Save and close.

The Space Planning process is not just to ensure that the rooms can hold the necessary equipment but also requires the drafter to think about plumbing, wiring, and HVAC requirements based on where and how items are placed.

As an additional exercise, place towel bars, soap dishes and other items in the bathrooms.

Space Planning

Exercise 4-5:
Designing a Kitchen

Drawing Name: main floor plan – interior – Tahoe Cabin
Estimated Time: 45 minutes

Common areas are the Living Room, Dining Room, and Family Room.

This lesson reinforces the following skills:

- Insert blocks
- Extrudes
- Boolean Operations – Subtract
- Materials
- Groups

1.   Launch the ACA English (US Imperial) software.

2.

   Set the **Tahoe Cabin** project current.

3.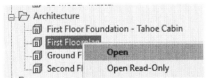

   Launch the Project Navigator.

   Open the **First Floor Plan** construct drawing.

4. Switch to a **Top View**.

5. 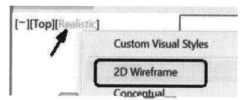 Switch to a **2D Wireframe** display.

6. Verify that the UCS is set to **WCS**.

7. 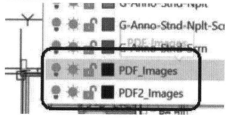 The imported PDF shows the rough location of the bedroom furniture and the bathroom fixtures.

8. If you do not see the PDF, thaw the **PDF_Images** layer.

9.

When organizing the kitchen, you will need to place base and wall cabinets.

Use the layout shown to place the kitchen elements.

You may find it helpful to create a tool palette for casework and add the blocks that you will be using to create the kitchen layout.

In the downloaded files, I have created a file called kitchen blocks.dwg.

This drawing has the entire kitchen laid out.

You can copy and paste it into your floor plan or add the blocks to the tool palette and try to recreate it on your own.

10.

    Switch to a 3D view to inspect the kitchen layout.

    The base cabinets do not have countertops.

    You will have to create the countertops for the base cabinets.

11.

    Create a layer called **countertops** and set it current.

Space Planning

12.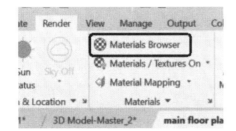
Switch to the Render ribbon.

Launch the **Materials Browser**.

13.
Locate the material you want to use for the countertops.

I selected **Granite – Gray Speckled**.

Add it to the document.

14.
Switch back to a top view.
Set the WCS as current.
Turn off the PDF_Images layer.

Zoom into the lower left corner of the kitchen area.

Draw a rectangle aligned to the cabinet outline.

15. Type **EXTRUDE**.
Select the rectangle.
Press ENTER.
Set the Height to ¼".

16. Select the 3D Solid that was just created.
On the Properties palette:
Assign the **Granite – Gray Speckled** material.

4-23

17. Switch to a 3D view.

    You see the countertop on the floor instead of on top of the cabinet.

18. Use MOVE to move the countertop on top of the cabinet.

19. Switch to the Realistic Visual Style to see what the countertop looks like.

    We want to group the cabinet with the countertop, so they move together.

20. Type **GROUP**.

    Right click and select **Name**.

21. Type **36-in-cabinet-w-countertop**.

    Note you need the dashes between the words or the entire name will not be used.

Space Planning

22.

Select the cabinet and the countertop.

They are now grouped together.
Switch back to a top view.
Set the WCS as current.
Set the Visual Style to Wireframe.

We will create a countertop for the corner area.

23.

Select the **Polyline** tool.

24.

Draw a polygon aligned to the cabinet outlines.

Type **EXTRUDE**.
Select the polygon.
Press ENTER.
Set the Height to ¼".

25.

Select the 3D Solid that was just created.
On the Properties palette:
Assign the **Granite – Gray Speckled** material.

4-25

26. Switch to a 3D view.

You see the countertop on the floor instead of on top of the cabinet.

27. Use the MOVE tool to move the countertop to the top of the cabinets.

28. 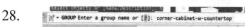 Group the countertop with the cabinets it sits on.
Name the group **Corner-cabinet-w-countertop**.

29. When you hover over the group, you should see the three cabinets and the countertop highlight.

30. Switch back to a top view.
Set the **WCS** as current.
Set the Visual Style to **Wireframe**.

We will create a countertop for the sink and cabinet next the refrigerator.

Space Planning

31. Select the **Polyline** tool.

32. Draw a polygon aligned to the cabinet outlines.

33. Type **EXTRUDE**.
    Select the outside polygon.
    Select the sink cutout
    Press ENTER.
    Set the Height to ¼".

34. Select the 3D Solid that was just created.
    On the Properties palette:
    Assign the **Granite – Gray Speckled** material.

35. Switch to a 3D view.

    You see the countertop on the floor instead of on top of the cabinet.

    Use the MOVE tool to move the countertop to the top of the cabinets.

36.

Position the sink so it is sitting on top of the countertop.

37.

Switch back to a top view.
Set the **WCS** as current.
Set the Visual Style to **Wireframe**.

We will create a cutout for the sink in the countertop.

38.

Select the **Polyline** tool.

39.

Draw a second polygon outlining the sink.
Add a 1" radius to the corners.
This will be the sink cutout in the countertop.

40. Type **EXTRUDE**.
Select the sink cutout.
Press ENTER.
Set the Height to ¼".

41.

Switch to a 3D view.

You should see two 3d Solids – one for the countertop and one for the sink opening.

Verify that they are lying on top of each other.

42.

Type **SUBTRACT**.

Select the countertop.
Press ENTER.
Select the sink cutout.

Press ENTER.

43.

Switch to a Realistic Visual Style.

You now see the sink on top of the countertop placed properly.

44.

Create a group of the counter top, the sink, and the two cabinets.

45. Switch back to a top view.
Set the **WCS** as current.
Set the Visual Style to **Wireframe**.

We will create a countertop for the kitchen island.

46. Select the **Polyline** tool.

47. Draw a rectangle.

    Extend one side of the rectangle down to create a sitting area for the stools.

48. Type **EXTRUDE**.
    Select the rectangle.
    Press ENTER.
    Set the Height to ¼".

49. Select the 3D Solid that was just created.
    On the Properties palette:
    Assign the **Granite – Gray Speckled** material.

50. Move the countertop to the top of the kitchen island.

Space Planning

51. Orbit around the 3D view to inspect your work and check for any errors.

52. Create a group for the kitchen island.
53. Save the file.

Tips & Tricks

If the drawing preview in the Design Center is displayed as 2D, then it is a 2D drawing.

Extra:

Add towel bars, plants, mirrors, and other accessories to the floor plan using blocks from the design center or downloaded from the internet.

Exercise 4-6:
Modifying an Element

Drawing Name: 01 Core.dwg
Estimated Time: 15 minutes

This exercise reinforces the following skills:

- Content Browser
- External References

1. Launch the US Metric version of ACA.

   This ensures that all the content will be metric.

   You can also use Options→Profiles to switch to the Metric profile.

2. Open the Project Browser.

Space Planning

3. Set the **Brown Medical Clinic** Current.

   The Brown Medical Clinic project was created using a metric project template. Placeholders were automatically generated.

4. Open the Project Navigator.

   Switch to the Constructs tab.

   Highlight **01 Core**.

   Right click and select **Open**.

5. Set the View Scale to **1:1**.

6. Select the cyan rectangle element that represents the Typical Toilet Room.
   Click **Edit Reference In-Place** on the ribbon.

7. Click **OK.**

4-33

8. 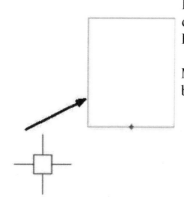 Locate the rectangle that is designated as the Typical Toilet Room.

   Move it to overlay the top bathroom.

9. Scale the outline so it is inside the bathroom area.

10. If you hover over the polyline outline, you will see that it is on a layer designated as NO PLOT.

11. Thaw the PDF Images layer.

Space Planning

12. Launch the Design Tools palette. Select the FF + E tab.

Locate the 3D Toilet – Flush Valve.

Drag and drop the toilet into the bathroom area.

Use the PDF to guide you in the placement of the toilet.

13. Launch the Content Browser.

You can use Ctl+4 as a shortcut key to launch the Content Browser.

14. Open the Design Tool Catalog – Metric.

    Locate the **Vanity Unit**.

15. Right click and select **Insert into Drawing**.

16. Place in the bathroom.

    Right click and select ENTER to exit the command.

17. Click **Save Changes** on the ribbon.

Space Planning

18. Click **OK**.

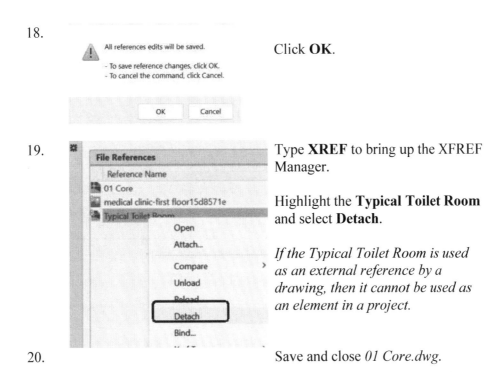

19. Type **XREF** to bring up the XFREF Manager.

    Highlight the **Typical Toilet Room** and select **Detach**.

    If the Typical Toilet Room is used as an external reference by a drawing, then it cannot be used as an element in a project.

20. Save and close *01 Core.dwg*.

Exercise 4-7:
Inserting an Element

Drawing Name: Main Model.dwg
Estimated Time: 30 minutes

This exercise reinforces the following skills:

- Content Browser
- External References
- Elements

1. Launch the US Metric version of ACA.

   This ensures that all the content will be metric.

4-37

2. Open the Project Browser.

3. 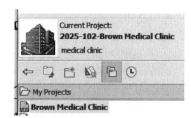 Set the **Brown Medical Clinic** Current.

   The Brown Medical Clinic project was created using a metric project template. Placeholders were automatically generated.

4. 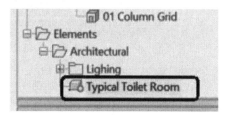 Open the Project Navigator.

   Switch to the Constructs tab.

   Highlight **Typical Toilet Room** under Elements.

   Right click and select **Open**.

5. The magenta object represents the current basepoint.

   Delete it.

6. Open the Insert ribbon.

   Select **Set Base Point**.

7. Select the lower left corner of the polyline.

   Save the drawing and close.

8. 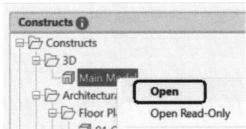 Launch the Project Navigator.

   Switch to the Constructs tab.

   Highlight **Main Model** under 3D.

   Right click and select **Open**.

9. Set the View Scale to **1:1**.

10. Thaw the **01 Core|PDF_Images** layer.

11. Look under Interior Constructs.
    Delete 00 Interior and 02 Interior.

12. Click **Yes**.

13. 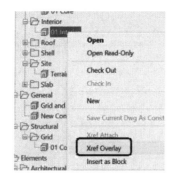 Highlight 01 Interior.

    Right click and select **Xref Overlay**.

14. Type **QS** for Quick Select.
    Set Object Type to **External Reference**.
    Highlight **Name**.
    Set Operator to **Equals**.
    Set Value to **01 Interior**.
    Click **OK**.

15. 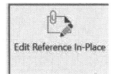 Click **Edit Reference In-Place** on the ribbon.

16. Click **OK**.

17. 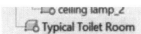 Locate the Typical Toilet Room under Elements.

    Right click and select **Insert As Block**.

Space Planning

18.   Open the Libraries tab.

Browse to the location where you are storing your project files.

19. Locate the *Typical Toilet Room.dwg*.

Enable **Insertion Point**.

20. 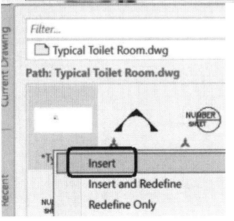 Right click on the block and select **Insert**.

21. The bathroom comes in at a very large scale.

    This will happen if the view scale was not set correctly.

    Move the bathroom into the correct location on the floor plan.

22. Select the block.
    Right click and select **Basic Modify Tools→Scale**.

23. Click the lower left corner as the base point.

24. Right click and select **Reference**.

25. For the reference length, select the two end points of the bottom horizontal line of the block.

26. For the new length, click the inside face of the right-side wall of the bathroom.

27. Select the block.
Right click and select **Properties**.

Note the scale value.
The scale value may be slightly different from the value shown.

You can use this for other insertions.

28. Locate the Typical Toilet Room under Elements.

    Right click and select **Insert As Block**.

29. Open the Libraries tab.

    Locate the *Typical Toilet Room.dwg*.

    Enable **Insertion Point**.
    Set the Scale to **the value noted earlier**, if needed.
    Enable **Rotation**.
    Enable **Auto-Placement**.

Space Planning

30. Right click on the block and select **Insert**.

31. Rotate and position the element inside the lower bathroom.

32. Go to the Insert ribbon.

    Launch the Design Center.

33. Open the AEC Content tab.

    Browse to the Site/Parking category.

    Locate the **Symbol-ADA**.

4-45

34. Right click and select **Insert**.

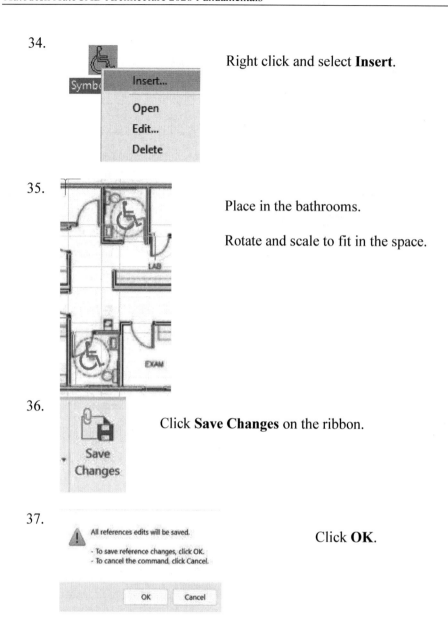

35. Place in the bathrooms.

    Rotate and scale to fit in the space.

36. Click **Save Changes** on the ribbon.

37. Click **OK**.

38. Save and close the *Main Model.dwg*.

Extra: Using what you have learned, edit the 01 Interior construct to include the furniture shown in the PDF. Can you create casework in the business office, lab, and nurse station areas?

I have included blocks and textures in the exercise files to help you plan the interior floor plan for the medical clinic. Can you add the 01 Interior as an Xref Overlay so the bathroom fixtures are included?

Notes:

QUIZ 4

True or False

1. Custom content can be located in any subdirectory and still function properly.
2. The sole purpose of the Space Planning process is to arrange furniture in a floor plan.
3. The Design Center only has 3D objects stored in the Content area because ADT is strictly a 3D software.
4. Appliances are automatically placed on the APPLIANCE layer.
5. When you place a wall cabinet, it is automatically placed at the specified height.
6. You can create tools on a tool palette by dragging and dropping the objects from the Design Center onto the palette.

Multiple Choice

7. A residential structure is divided into:

    A. Four basic areas
    B. Three basic areas
    C. Two basic areas
    D. One basic area

8. Kitchen cabinets are located in the _____ subfolder.

    A. Casework
    B. Cabinets
    C. Bookcases
    D. Furniture

9. Select the area type that is NOT part of a private residence:

    A. Bedrooms
    B. Common Areas
    C. Service Areas
    D. Public Areas

10. To set the layer properties of a tool on a tool palette:

    A. Use the Layer Manager
    B. Select the tool, right click and select Properties
    C. Launch the Properties dialog
    D. All of the above

11. Vehicles placed from the Design Center are automatically placed on this layer:
    A. A-Site-Vhcl
    B. A-Vhcl
    C. C-Site Vhcl
    D. None of the above

12. To combine elements so that they act as a single object, use this command:
    A. GROUP
    B. SUBTRACT
    C. ADD
    D. INCLUDE

13. To create a 3DSolid, use this command:
    A. SOLID
    B. EXTRUDE
    C. MASS
    D. 3DSOLID

ANSWERS:

1) T; 2) F; 3) F; 4) F; 5) T; 6) T; 7) B; 8) A; 9) D; 10) B; 11) C; 12) A; 13) B

Lesson 5:
Roofs

Roofs can be created with single or double slopes, with or without gable ends, and with or without overhangs. Once you input all your roof settings, you simply pick the points around the perimeter of the building to define your roof outline. If you make an error, you can easily modify or redefine your roof.

You need to pick three points before the roof will begin to preview in your graphics window. There is no limit to the number of points to select to define the perimeter.

To create a gable roof, uncheck the gable box in the Roof dialog. Pick the two end points for the sloped portion of the roof. Turn on the Gable box. Pick the end point for the gable side. Turn off the Gable box. Pick the end point for the sloped side. Turn the Gable box on. Pick the viewport and then Click ENTER. A Gable cannot be defined with more than three consecutive edges.

Roofs can be created using two methods: ROOFADD places a roof based on points selected or ROOFCONVERT which converts a closed polyline or closed walls to develop a roof.

- ➢ If you opt to use ROOFCONVERT and use existing closed walls, be sure that the walls are intersecting properly. If your walls are not properly cleaned up with each other, the roof conversion is unpredictable.
- ➢ The Plate Height of a roof should be set equal to the Wall Height.
- ➢ You can create a gable on a roof by gripping any ridgeline point and stretching it past the roof edge. You cannot make a gable into a hip using grips.

Shape – Select the Shape option on the command line by typing 'S.'	Single Slope – Extends a roof plane at an angle from the Plate Height.	*(end elevation view: slope, overhang)*
	Double Slope – Includes a single slope and adds another slope, which begins at the intersection of the first slope and the height specified for the first slope.	*(end elevation view: upper slope, lower slope, overhang, upper height)*
Gable – Select the Gable option on the command line by typing 'G.'	If this is enabled, turns off the slope of the roof place. To create a gable edge, select Gable prior to identifying the first corner of the gable end. Turn off gable to continue to create the roof.	*(gable roof end)*
Plate Height – Set the Plate Height on the command line by typing 'PH.'	Specify the top plate from which the roof plane is projected. The height is relative to the XY plane with a Z coordinate of 0.	
Rise – Set the Rise on the command line by typing 'PR.'	Sets the angle of the roof based on a run value of 12.	A rise value of 5 creates a 5/12 roof, which forms a slope angle of 22.62 degrees.
Slope – Set the Slope on the command line by typing 'PS.'	Angle of the roof rise from the horizontal.	If slope angles are entered, then the rise will automatically be calculated.

Upper Height – Set the Upper Height on the command line by typing 'UH.'	This is only available if a Double Slope roof is being created. This is the height where the second slope will start.	
Rise (upper) – Set the Upper Rise on the command line by typing 'UR.'	This is only available if a Double Slope roof is being created. This is the slope angle for the second slope.	A rise value of 5 creates a 5/12 roof, which forms a slope angle of 22.62 degrees.
Slope (upper) – Set the Upper Slope on the command line by typing 'US.'	This is only available if a Double Slope roof is being created. Defines the slope angle for the second slope.	If an upper rise value is set, this is automatically calculated.
Overhang – To enable on the command line, type 'O.' To set the value of the Overhang, type 'V.'	If enabled, extends the roofline down from the plate height by the value set.	

	The Floating Viewer opens a viewer window displaying a preview of the roof.
	The match button allows you to select an existing roof to match its properties.
	The properties button opens the Roof Properties dialog.
	The Undo button allows you to undo the last roof operation. You can step back as many operations as you like up to the start.
	Opens the Roof Help file.

Exercise 5-1:
Creating a Roof using Existing Walls

Drawing Name: roofs1.dwg
Estimated Time: 10 minutes

This exercise reinforces the following skills:

- Roof
- Roof Properties
- Visual Styles

1. Open *roofs1.dwg*.

2.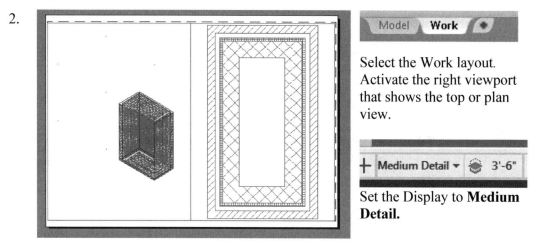

   Select the Work layout. Activate the right viewport that shows the top or plan view.

   Set the Display to **Medium Detail.**

3.   Select the **Roof** tool from the Home ribbon.

Roofs

4. Expand the Dimensions section on the Properties palette.
Set the Thickness to **10″ [254.00 mm]**.
Set the Shape to **Single slope**.
Set the Overhang to **1′-0″ [609.6 mm]**.

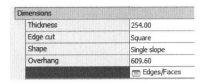

5. Expand the Lower Slope section.
Set the Plate height to **10′-0″ [3000 mm]**.

The plate height determines the level where the roof rests.

6. Set the Rise to **1′-0″ [100 mm]**.

7. Pick the corners indicated to place the roof.
Click **Enter**.

5-5

8. Activate the left 3D viewport.

9. Activate the View ribbon.

   Select the **Shades of Gray** under Visual Styles.

10. Save as *ex5-1.dwg*.

    In order to edit a roof, you have to convert it to Roof Slabs.

Roof Slabs

A roof slab is a single face of a roof. Roof slab elements differ from roof elements in that each roof slab is independent of other roof slabs. When you use multiple roof slabs to model a roof, you have more flexibility as you can control the shape and appearance of each slab or section of the roof.

While roof slabs are independent, they can interact. You can use one roof slab as a trim or extend boundary. You can miter roof slabs together. You can cut holes in roof slabs and add or subtract mass elements.

You can use grips to modify the shapes of roof slabs. You can use basic modify tools, like move or rotate, to reposition roof slabs.

Layer States

Layer states are used to save configurations of layer properties and their state (ON/OFF/FROZEN/LOCKED). For example, you can set a layer to be a different color depending on the state. Instead of constantly resetting which layers are on or off, you can save your settings in layer states and apply them to layouts.

Layer States are saved in the drawing. To share them across drawings, you need to export them. Each layer state has its own LAS file. To export a layer state, select it in the Layer States Manager and choose Export.

To import a layer state, open the Layer States Manager and click the Import tool. Then select the *.las file you wish to import.

You can save layer states in your drawing template.

Exercise 5-2:
Create Layer Filters and Layer States

Drawing Name: 3D Model-Master.dwg
Estimated Time: 30 minutes

This exercise reinforces the following skills:

- Layers
- Layer Filters
- Layer States

1. Launch the Project Browser.
   Set the **Tahoe Cabin project** current.

   Close the Project Browser.

2. 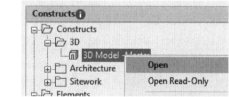 Open the Project Navigator.

   Open the *3D Model-Master.dwg*.

3. Go to Options→Profiles.

   Set the Current Profile to **US Imperial**.

   Close Options.

4. Set the View to **Top/2D Wireframe**.

Roofs

5. Set the UCS to **WCS**.

6. Launch the **Layer Manager**.

7. 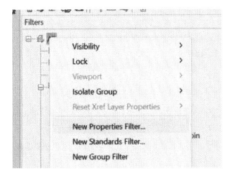 Highlight All.

   Right click and select **New Properties Filter**.

8. Name the Filter:
   PDF Inserts.
   Under Name:
   Type ***PDF***.

   All the layers with PDF in the name are displayed.

   Press **OK**.

9. Freeze all the PDF layers.

5-9

10. Highlight All.

    Right click and select **New Properties Filter**.

11. Name the Filter:
    Space Planning.
    Under Name:
    Type ***Furn***.
    Plum
    Fix
    case
    count
    appl

    All the layers that meet the filter are displayed.

    Press **OK**.

12. 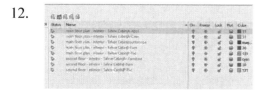 Freeze all the space planning layers.

13. Select the **Layer States Manager**.

14. Select **New**.

15. 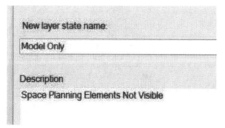 Type **Model Only** for the layer state name.

    In the Description field:
    Type **Space Planning Elements Not Visible**.

    Click **OK**.

16. Click **Close**.

17. There are a few elements in the model that need to be included in the Layer Properties filter.

    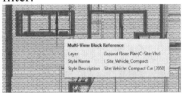

    The vehicle is on the C-Site-Vhcl layer.

    The other elements are on layer 0 and need to be moved to the correct layers.

    Your model may be different depending on what blocks you inserted. The next few steps walk you through how to modify the file so that all the space planning elements are controlled by the filter. If you don't have any stray elements, you can skip these steps.

18. Highlight the Space Planning filter in the Layer Manager.

    Right click and select **Properties**.

19. 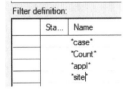 Add ***site*** to the list of names.

    Click **OK**.

20. 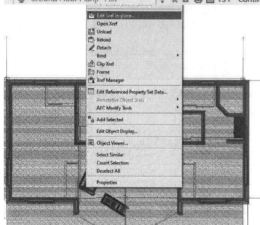 Freeze the **C-Site-Vhcl** layer.

21. Select the furniture that is visible.

    Right click and select **Edit Xref in-place**.

22. Click **OK**.

23. *The xref that is being edited will show the layers as 0*.*

    Select the furniture and move to the **0I-Furn** layer that is frozen.

Roofs

24. Click **Close.**

25. Move the vanities to the **0P-Fixt** layer.

26. Click **Close.**

27. Click **Save Changes** on the ribbon.

28. Click **OK**.

29.

    You can see the Layer State now in the drop-down list on the Layers panel.

    Close the Layer Manager.

30. Save and close *3D Model-Master.dwg*.

5-13

Exercise 5-3:
Roof Slabs

Drawing Name: 3D Model-Master.dwg , roof_slabs – Tahoe Cabin.dwg
Estimated Time: 15 minutes

This exercise reinforces the following skills:

- AddRoof
- Project Navigator
- Convert to Roof Slabs
- Modify Roof Lines
- Trim Roof Slabs
- Roof Properties

1. Launch the Project Browser.
   Set the **Tahoe Cabin project** current.

2. Open *roof_slabs- Tahoe Cabin.dwg*.

3. 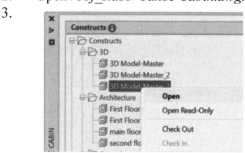 Launch the Project Navigator.

   Open the *3D Model-Master.dwg*.

   You may need to redefine the path of your external references.

4. Switch to the *roof_slabs- Tahoe Cabin.dwg*.

Roofs

5.

   Open the Project Navigator.

   Right click on **Architecture**.

   Select **Save Current Dwg As Construct**.

6.

   Enable **Roof**.

   Click **OK**.

7. Switch back to the *3D Model-Master.dwg* tab.

8.

   Highlight the Construct: *roof_slabs- Tahoe Cabin.dwg*.

   Right click and select **Xref Overlay**.

9.

   Switch to an isometric view.

   The roof slabs construct has some polylines.

   Select it and move it into the correct position.

5-15

It should sit right on top of the building.

Select the roof slabs construct.
Right click.

10. Select **Open Reference** from the ribbon.

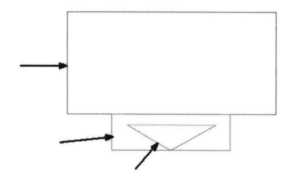

There are three polygons in the drawing:
A large rectangle, a small rectangle and a triangle.

These will be used to create three different roofs.

11. Select the **Roof** tool from the Home ribbon.

Roofs

12.

Open the Properties palette.

Set the Overhang to **0"**.
Set the Slope to **60**.

13.

Select the four corners on main building to place a roof.

Click ENTER to complete the command.

14.

Click on the roof to select.

Select the grip indicated in red and shift the vertex so it overlies the midpoint on the left.

This eliminates the slope on the left side of the roof.

The roof now looks like this.

5-17

15.

    Select the grip indicated in red and shift the vertex so it overlies the midpoint on the right.

    This eliminates the slope on the right side of the roof.

16.

    Release the grips and the roof should appear as shown.

17.

    Switch to a 3D view so you can see what the roof looks like.

    Notice that the roof is elevated above the polylines.

18.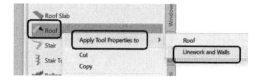

    Return to a top view.

    Launch the Design Tools.

    Right click on the **Roof** tool and select **Apply Tool Properties to Linework and Walls**.

    Select the cyan triangle.

    When prompted to erase linework, select No.

Roofs

19.

    The roof is created.

    Change the Slope to **45** on the Properties palette.

20.

    Select the center grip of the triangular roof.
    Place that grip on the middle top grip.

    Click ESC to release the selection.

    The roof should look like this.

21.

    `[−][Left][2D Wireframe]`

    Switch to a LEFT view.

    Move the A-frame roof on the left down to the polyline.

    Your roofs should look like this.

22.

Switch to a SW Isometric view.

23. Select the two roofs.

Select **Convert** on the ribbon.

This converts the roofs to roof slabs.

24.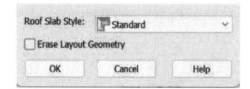

Disable **Erase Layout Geometry.**

Click **OK**.

Click **ESC** to release the selection.

25. Select the left rectangular side of the smaller roof.

Select **Extend** on the ribbon.

26. 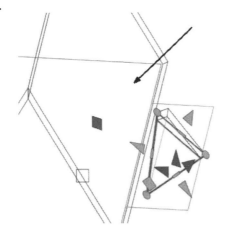 You are prompted to select a boundary to extend to.

Select the A-frame slab closest to the small roof.

27. Select the top edge of the slab to extend. Select the bottom edge of the slab to extend.

 I switched to a Shaded view so you can see what the extended roof looks like.

28.

    [−][Top][2D Wireframe]

    Switch to a **Top View/2D Wireframe**.

29.

    Select the right small roof slab and delete it.

30.

    Select the remaining small roof slab.

    Right click and select **Basic Modify Tools→Mirror**.

31.

    Mirror to the other side.

Roofs

32.

Switch to an Isometric view so you can see the roof.

33.

Set layer 0 Current.

Freeze the following layers:

A-Roof
Roof outline
roof outline_1
Roof outline_2
Roof outline_3

34. Save the file and close.

35.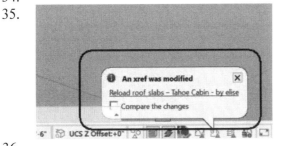

Disable **Compare the changes**.

Click **Reload roof slabs – Tahoe cabin** to see the changes.

36. Save and close the *3D Model-Master.dwg* file.

5-23

Exercise 5-4:
Attach Walls to Roofs

Drawing Name: 3D Model-Master_3
Estimated Time: 15 minutes

This exercise reinforces the following skills:

- Attach walls to roofs
- Modify Roof Line

1. Launch the Project Browser.
Set the **Tahoe Cabin project** current.

2. Launch the Project Navigator.

Open the *3D Model-Master.dwg*.

3. Select the exterior wall of the second floor.

5-24

Roofs

4. 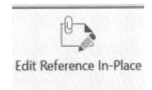 Select **Edit Reference In-Place** from the ribbon.

5. Select **OK**.

6. Select the wall.

On the ribbon: select **Modify Roof Line**.

7. 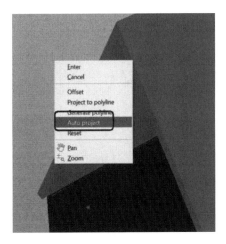 Right click and select Auto project.

Select the roof.

Click **ENTER**.

Click ESC to release your selection.

5-25

The wall adjusts to meet the roof.

Orbit around to the other side of the building model.

8.

Select the wall.

On the ribbon: select **Modify Roof Line**.

9.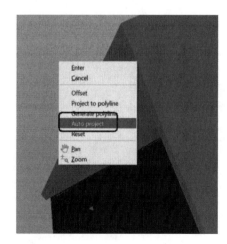

Right click and select Auto project.

Select the roof.

Click **ENTER.**

Click ESC to release the selection.

10. *The wall now meets the roof.*

 Orbit the model around to inspect the walls and roof.

11. Select **Save Changes** on the ribbon.

12. Click **OK**.

13. Save and close the file.

Rendering Materials in ACA

Materials represent substances such as steel, concrete, cotton and glass. They can be applied to a 3D model to give the objects a realistic appearance. Materials are useful for illustrating plans, sections, elevations and renderings in the design process. Materials also provide a way to manage the display properties of object styles.

The use of materials allows you to more realistically display objects. You need to define the display of a material such as brick or glass only once in the drawing or the drawing template and then assign it to the component of an object where you want the material to display. You typically assign materials to components in the style of an object such as the brick in a wall style. Then whenever you add a wall of that style to your drawing, the brick of that wall displays consistently. Defining materials in an object style can provide control for the display of objects across the whole project. When the characteristics of a material change, you change them just once in the material definition and all objects that use that material are updated. With the Material tool you can apply a material to a single instance of the object.

You can take advantage of Visual Styles, Rendering Materials, Lights, and Cameras in AutoCAD® Architecture. Materials provide the ability to assign surface hatches to objects. Surface hatches can be displayed in model, elevation, and section views. This is helpful to clearly illustrate sections and elevations.

Exercise 5-5:
Creating Materials

Drawing Name: 3D Model-Master.dwg
Estimated Time: 30 minutes

This exercise reinforces the following skills:

- Design Palette
- Materials
- Style Manager

1. 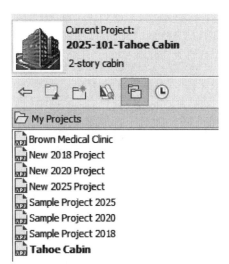 Launch the Project Browser.
   Set the **Tahoe Cabin project** current.

2. Launch the Project Navigator.

   Open the *3D Model-Master.dwg*.

Roofs

3. Select the roof.

On the ribbon:
Select **Edit Reference In-Place**.

4. Click **OK**.

5. [−][SW Isometric][Hidden] Switch to an **SW Isometric Hidden** view.

6. Launch the Design Tools.

7. 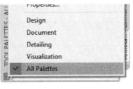 Right click on the title bar of the Design Tools and enable **All Palettes**.

8. Right click on the tabs of the Design Tools and enable **Materials**.

5-29

9. 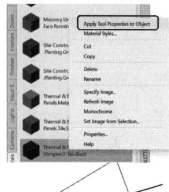 Locate the **Asphalt Shingles** material.

10. Right click on the **Asphalt Shingles.**

    Select **Apply Tool Properties to Object.**

11. Select the roof.

    You are prompted if you are modifying the style or just the object.

    Click ENTER to modify the object.

    The roof material updates.

Roofs

12. Type **MATERIALS**.

    This brings up ACA's Materials Browser.

13. Type **plywood** in the search field.

14. Highlight the **Formwork – Wood Plywood**.

    Right click and select **Add to→Active Tool Palette**.

15. 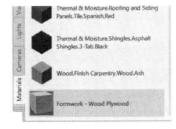 The material appears at the bottom of the Materials palette.

16. 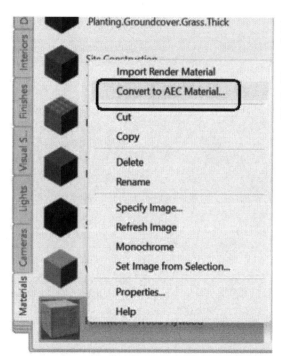 Highlight the **Formwork – Wood Plywood.**

    Right click and select **Convert to AEC Material.**

17. Set the AEC Material to use as a Template to **Standard.**

    Click **OK**.

18. Click **Close**.

    Save the drawing file.

19. Type **rubber** in the search field in the Materials Browser.

Roofs

20. Highlight the **Rubber-Black**.

    Right click and select **Add to→Active Tool Palette**.

21. The material appears at the bottom of the Materials palette.

22. 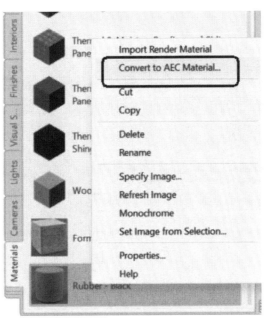 Highlight the **Rubber - Black**.

    Right click and select **Convert to AEC Material**.

23. Set the AEC Material to use as a Template to **Insulation**.

    Change the New AEC Material Name to **Membrane – Black**.

    Click **OK**.

24. Click **Close**.

Save the drawing file.

Close the Materials Browser.

25. Switch to the Manage ribbon.

Launch the **Style Manager**.

26. In the active drawing:

Expand **Multi-Purpose Objects**.

Expand **Material Definitions**.

27. The materials that were added to the tool palette are available in the Style Manager.

Close the Style Manager.

28. Select **Save Changes** on the ribbon.

29. Click **OK**.

30. Save and close the **3D Model – Master** file.

Exercise 5-6:
Roof Slab Styles

Drawing Name: 3D Model-Master.dwg
Estimated Time: 10 minutes

This exercise reinforces the following skills:

- Roof Slab Styles
- Design Palette
- Materials
- Style Manager

1. 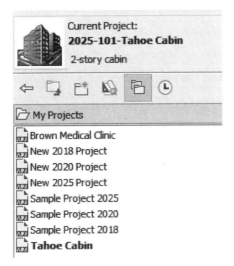 Launch the Project Browser.
Set the **Tahoe Cabin project** current.

2. 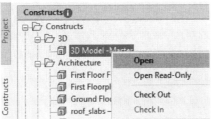 Launch the Project Navigator.

Open the *3D Model-Master.dwg*.

3. Select the roof.

On the ribbon:
Select **Edit Reference In-Place**.

4. Click **OK**.

5. [–][SW Isometric][Hidden]   Switch to an **SW Isometric Hidden** view.

6. Activate the Manage ribbon.

Select the **Style Manager**.

7. Locate the Roof Slab Styles under Architectural Objects.

There are two Standard styles.
The 0Standard style is used by the external reference.

8. Right click on the Roof Slab Style and select **New**.

9. Rename the style **Asphalt Shingles**.

10. Define three components:
    - Asphalt Shingles with a thickness of ½" and Thickness Offset of 0.
    - Membrane with a Thickness of 1/8" and Thickness offset of ½".
    - Plywood Sheathing with a thickness of ¼" and Thickness offset of 5/8".

11. *Use the lower preview window to check the placement of each component.*

12. Switch to the Materials tab.

    Highlight the **Asphalt Shingles** component.

    Select the Asphalt Shingles material from the drop-down list.

    This material was added to the drawing when it was applied to the rood slab.

13. Highlight the **Membrane** component.

    Select the **Rubber - Black** material from the drop-down list.

14. Highlight the **Plywood Sheathing** component.

    Select the **Formwork – Wood Plywood** material from the drop-down list.

    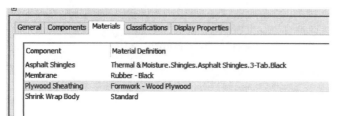 *The assigned materials should look like this.*

    Click **OK**.
    Close the Style Manager.

15. Select one of the roof slabs. Right click and **Select Similar** so that all roof slabs are selected.

16. 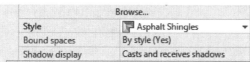 On the Properties palette:

    Set the Style to **Asphalt Shingles.**

    Click **ESC** to release the selection.

17. Select **Save Changes** on the ribbon.

Roofs

18. Click **OK**.

19. Save and close the file.

Extra:

Open the ACA Metric Application.
Set the Brown Medical Clinic project current.
Open the Main Model.dwg.
Open the internal external reference and move blocks onto the correct layers.
Edit Blocks to place elements onto the correct layers.
Create a Layer filter and Layer State to control the visibility of the furniture and the fixtures.

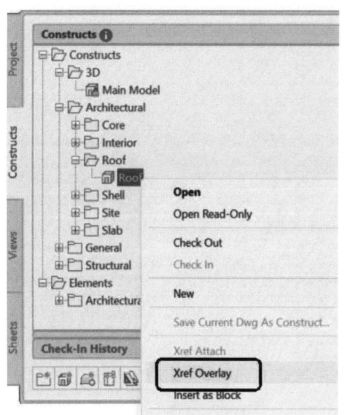

Add the roof construct to the Main Model as an Xref Overlay.
Edit the Roof external reference in-place.
Hint: Use QSELECT to select an external reference using the Name "Roof".
Add a roof.

Create a roof slab style using Spanish tiles.
Convert the roof to roof slabs.
Assign the Spanish Tile roof style to the roof slabs.

Freeze the A-Roof layer.

Notes:

QUIZ 5

True or False

1. Roof slabs are a single face of a roof, not an entire roof.
2. The thickness of a roof slab can be modified for an individual element without affecting the roof slab style.
3. If you change the slope of a roof slab, it rotates around the slope pivot point.
4. Once you place a roof or roof slab, it cannot be modified.
5. You can use the TRIM and EXTEND tools to modify roof slabs.

Multiple Choice

6. Materials are displayed when the view setting is: (select all that apply)

    A. Wireframe
    B. Shaded
    C. Hidden
    D. Rendered

7. Roof slab styles control the following properties: (select all that apply)

    A. Slab Thickness
    B. Slab Elevation
    C. Physical components (concrete, metal, membrane)
    D. Materials

8. Identify the tool shown.

    A. Add Roof
    B. Add Roof Slab
    C. Add Gable
    D. Modify Roof

9. To change the elevation of a slab:

    A. Modify the slab style.
    B. Use Properties to change the Elevation.
    C. Set layer properties.
    D. All of the above.

10. Roof slabs can be created: (select all that apply)
    A. Independently (from scratch)
    B. From Existing Roofs
    C. From Walls
    D. From Polylines

ANSWERS:

1) T; 2) T; 3) T; 4) F; 5) T; 6) A, B, D; 7) A, C, D; 8) B; 9) B; 10) A, B, C, D

Lesson 6:
Floors, Ceilings and Spaces

Slabs are used to model floors and other flat surfaces. You start by defining a slab style which includes the components and materials which are used to construct the floor system.

You can create a floor slab by drawing a polyline and applying the style to the polyline or by selecting the slab tool and then drawing the boundary to be used by the slab.

Ceiling grids can be used to define drop ceilings.

You can also use spaces to define floors and ceilings. You can use the Space/Zone Manager to apply different styles to floors and ceilings.

There are two reasons why you want to include floors and ceilings in your building model. 1) for your construction documentation and 2) for any renderings.

Exercise 6-1:
Creating Slab Styles

Drawing Name: slab_styles.dwg
Estimated Time: 30 minutes

This exercise reinforces the following skills:

- Creating Styles
- Copying Styles
- Renaming Styles
- Use of Materials

1. Close any current projects.

    Open the ACA Imperial software.

2. Open the *slab_styles.dwg*.

3. Activate the Manage ribbon.

    Select **Style Manager**.

4. Browse to the Slab Styles category.

    Highlight Slab Styles.

    Right click and select **New**.

Floors, Ceilings, and Spaces

5. Rename **Carpet**.

6. Create three components:
   - Carpet
   - Plywood
   - Wood Joist

   Set the Carpet at 1/8" and ¼" Thickness Offset.
   Set the Plywood at ¼" and 0" Thickness Offset.
   Set the Wood Joist at 2" and -2" Thickness Offset.

7. Use the preview window to verify that the thicknesses and offsets are correct.

8. Create new materials for each of the components.

   I have pre-loaded several materials in the exercise files. Some of the materials use image files that are part of the exercise files.

9. Edit the carpet material definition to use the **Berber – Pattern 2** render material.

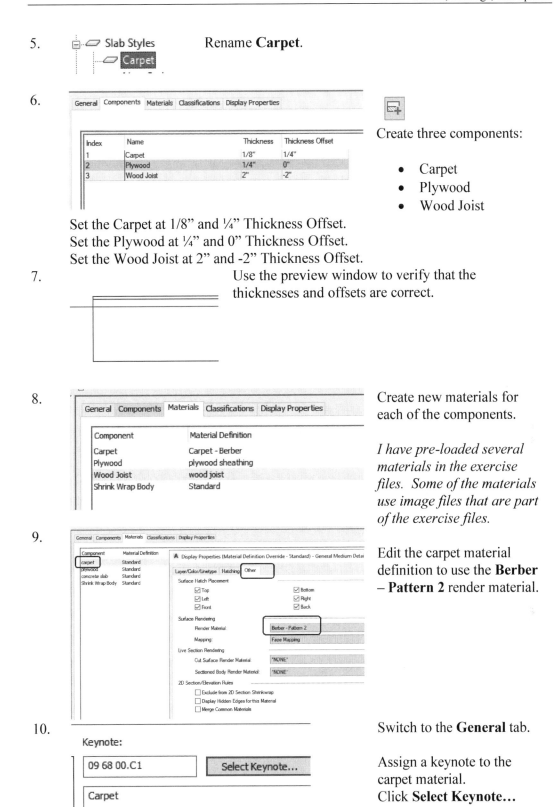

10. Switch to the **General** tab.

    Assign a keynote to the carpet material.
    Click **Select Keynote…**

6-3

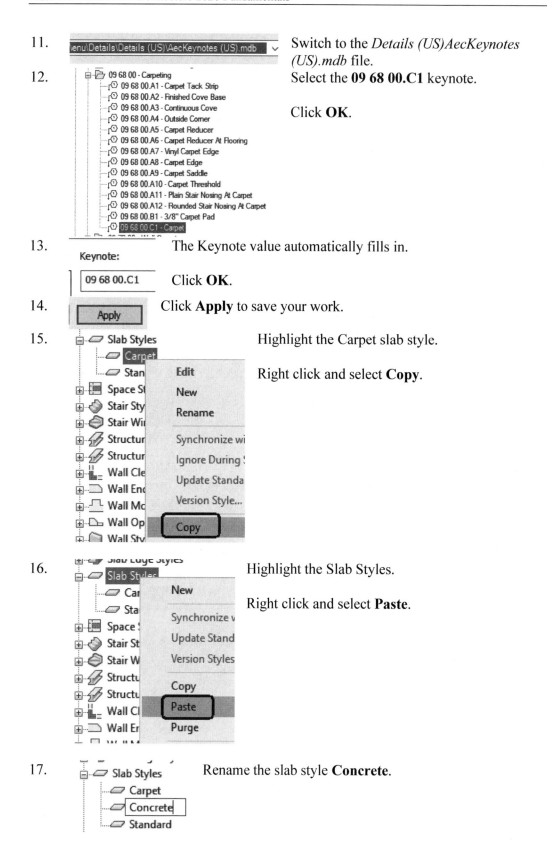

11. Switch to the *Details (US)AecKeynotes (US).mdb* file.
12. Select the **09 68 00.C1** keynote.

    Click **OK**.

13. The Keynote value automatically fills in.

    Click **OK**.

14. Click **Apply** to save your work.
15. Highlight the Carpet slab style.

    Right click and select **Copy**.

16. Highlight the Slab Styles.

    Right click and select **Paste**.

17. Rename the slab style **Concrete**.

Floors, Ceilings, and Spaces

18. Switch to the Components tab.

    Highlight the carpet component.
    Select **Remove**.
    Highlight the plywood component.
    Select **Remove**.

    There should be one component named Concrete that is 6" thick.

19. Select the Materials tab.

    Assign the **in-place concrete** material to the component.

20. Click **Apply** to save your work.

21. Highlight the Carpet slab style.

    Right click and select **Copy**.

22.

    Highlight the Slab Styles.

    Right click and select **Paste**.

6-5

23. Rename **Oak Floor**.

24. Switch to the Components tab.

    Change the name of the carpet component to **oak flooring.**

25. Click **Apply**.
    Verify that the carpet component is still the top component for the carpet slab style.

26. Verify that the oak flooring component is the top component for the oak floor slab style.

27. Switch to the Materials tab for the oak floor.

    Highlight the oak flooring.
    Select **Edit Material**.

28. Assign **White Oak** as the Render Material.

    Click **OK**.

29. Click **Apply** to save your work.

30. Highlight the Slab Styles category.
Right click and select **New**.

31. Rename **Stucco Ceiling**.

32. Make the first component Stucco 7/8" thick with a Thickness Offset of -7/8".

33. Add a component.
Name it plywood sheathing 1/8" thick with a Thickness Offset of 0".

34. Add a component.
Name it wood joists 2" thick with a Thickness Offset of 1/8".

35. Switch to the Materials tab.

Apply the correct materials for the components:

- Stucco
- Plywood sheathing
- Wood joist

Hint: The Materials are in alphabetical order in the drop-down list.

Click **Apply** to save your changes.

36. 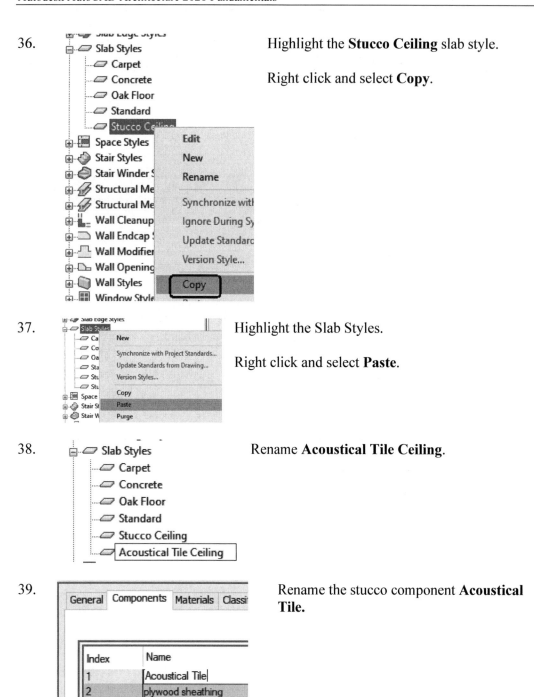 Highlight the **Stucco Ceiling** slab style.

    Right click and select **Copy**.

37. Highlight the Slab Styles.

    Right click and select **Paste**.

38. Rename **Acoustical Tile Ceiling**.

39. Rename the stucco component **Acoustical Tile.**

40. 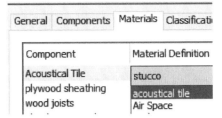 Switch to the Materials tab.

Select the **acoustical tile** material from the drop-down list.

41. 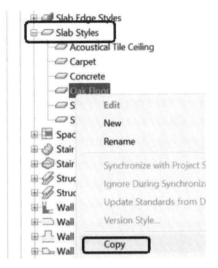 Highlight the **Oak Floor** slab style.

Right click and select **Copy**.

42. Highlight the Slab Styles.

Right click and select **Paste**.

43. Rename **TimberTech Decking - Mahogany**.

44. 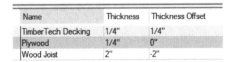 Rename the oak flooring component **TimberTech Decking.**

Change the Thickness to ¼"

45. 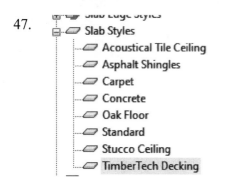 Switch to the Materials tab.
Assign the **TimberTech Decking – Mahogany** material to the TimberTech Decking component.

46. Click **Apply** to save your work.

47. You should have the following slab styles defined:

    - Acoustical Tile Ceiling
    - Asphalt Shingles
    - Carpet
    - Concrete
    - Oak Floor
    - Standard
    - Stucco Ceiling
    - TimberTech Decking

    Click **OK** to close the dialog.

48. Save as *slab_styles_2.dwg*.
    Close the file.

Exercise 6-2:
Create Slab from Linework

Drawing Name: 3D Model-Master.dwg, deck outline.dwg
Estimated Time: 30 minutes

This exercise reinforces the following skills:

- Creating Slabs
- Project Navigator
- External References
- Constructs
- Polylines
- Style Manager
- Properties

1. Set the **Tahoe Cabin** project current.

2. Open *3D Model_Master.dwg*.

3. Open *deck outline.dwg*.
   In the Project Navigator:
   Go to the Constructs tab.
   Highlight the Architecture category.
   Right click and select **Save Current Dwg As Construct**.

4. Enable **First Floor**.

   Click **OK**.

5. 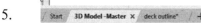 Switch to the **3D Model-Master** drawing tab.

6. In the Project Navigator:

   Highlight the deck outline construct.

   Right click and select **Xref Overlay**.

7.

   Switch to a Top view and zoom out.

   The model and the xref are far apart.

   Move the deck outline to the correct location on the model.

8. Switch to a 3D view.

   Adjust the position of the deck outline.

9. Select the deck outline external reference. Right click and select **Properties**.

   Modify the Z property to match the Z value of the first floor.

10. Switch to the **Deck Outline** drawing tab.

11.
    Click the Home ribbon.

    Launch the **Design Tools**.

12. Locate the Slab tool.

    Right click and select **Apply Tool Properties to →Linework and Walls.**

13. Select the deck outline polyline.

    Click **ENTER**.

14. Select **No**.

15. Select **Direct**.

16. Set the Justification to **Top**.

17. Select the midpoint of the top of the boundary as the pivot point for the slab.

    The slab will be horizontal, so it doesn't really need a pivot point.

18. Open the Manage ribbon.

    Launch the **Style Manager**.

19. Open the *slab_styles_2.dwg* file.

20. Locate the **TimberTech Decking** slab style.

    Copy and paste into the deck outline.dwg.

21. Close the Style Manager.

22. Select the slab.
    Right click and select **Properties**.

    Set the slab style to **TimberTech-Decking**.

    Note that the slope is set to 0.0.

23. Save and close the *deck outline.dwg*.

24. Click to **Reload** the xref.

You won't see any changes unless you reload the xref.

25. Switch to an isometric view to inspect your slab floor.

Set the view style to **Realistic.**

26. Save as *3D Model-Master.dwg*.

Views

Typically, you create view drawings and model space views after you have defined levels, divisions, and the basic constructs. For example, you could create the following series of views for individual floors: First Floor Plan, Second Floor Plan, Basement Plan, Roof Plan. You could also create a series of views based on plan type, such as: Plan View, Model View, Reflected View. Another approach could be by function; for example: Walls, Framing, Furniture. Only constructs can be referenced into a view drawing. To see elements in a view, they must be referenced by a construct.

After the structure of the building project is defined, and constructs are assigned to levels and divisions, you can start to create view drawings. A view drawing references a number of constructs to present a specific view of the building project. To create a view drawing, you first decide which portion of the building you wish to look at and which type of view to generate. You could, for example, create a first-floor reflected ceiling plan or a second-floor framing plan, or create a composite view of all floors in the building. View drawings automatically reference the appropriate constructs according to their level/division assignments within the building. For example, to create a floor plan of the west wing of the second floor, you would create a view that references all constructs assigned to the second floor and the west wing. This would also include a curtain wall spanning the first through fifth floors.

Types of View Drawings

There are three different types of view drawings in the Drawing Management feature of the Project Navigator:

- **General view drawing**: A general view drawing contains referenced constructs from the project, representing a specific view on the building model. General view drawings are based on the general view template defined in the project settings.

  You can reference a view drawing in a sheet. When you reference the view drawing into a sheet, a sheet view is created that contains the view drawing reference.

- **Detail view drawing**: A detail view drawing contains one or more model space views that show a defined portion of the detail drawing in the level of detail you specify. A model space view containing a detail can be associated with a callout. Detail view drawings are based on the detail view template defined in the project settings.

- **Section/Elevation view drawing**: A section/elevation view drawing contains one or more model space views, each showing a defined portion of the section/elevation view drawing. A model space view containing a section or elevation can be associated with a callout. Section/Elevation view drawings are based on the section/elevation view template defined in the project settings.

Model Space Views

A model space view is a portion of a view drawing that may be displayed in its own paper space viewport on a sheet. Model space views are an evolution of the Named Views concept of AutoCAD. Unlike Named Views, a model space view has a defined boundary. When a model space view is placed onto a sheet, a sheet view is created. A view drawing can contain any number of model space views.

Floors, Ceilings, and Spaces

Exercise 6-3:
Create View Categories and Views

Drawing Name: First Floor Plan.dwg
Estimated Time: 20 minutes

This exercise reinforces the following skills:

- Views
- Project Navigator
- Layer Filters
- Layer Properties
- Style Manager
- Slab Styles

1. 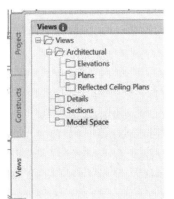 *The Tahoe Cabin Project should be active.*

   Launch the Project Navigator.

   Select the Views tab.

   Create additional view categories.
   Under Architectural:
   Elevations
   Plans
   Reflected Ceiling Plans
   Under Views:
   Details
   Sections
   Model Space

2. 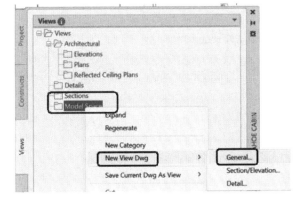 Highlight the **Model Space** category.

   Right click and select **New View Dwg→General**.

6-17

3. Type **First Floor** in the Name field.
Click in the Description field and type **First Floor**.
Enable. **Open in drawing editor**.

Click **Next**.

4. Select the **First Floor** level.

Click **Next**.

5. Disable the 3D category.
Disable the Sitework category.
Under Architecture:
Disable deck outline.
Disable First Floor Foundation – Tahoe cabin.
Enable **First Floor Plan**
Click **Finish**.

Only one drawing should be checked.

6. Set the view scale to **1'-0" = 1'-0"**.

7. Launch the **Layer Manager**.

8. Highlight All.

Right click and select **New Properties Filter**.

9. Name the Filter: **PDF Inserts**.
Under Name:
Type ***PDF***.

All the layers with PDF in the name are displayed.

Press **OK**.

10. Freeze all the PDF layers.

11. Highlight **All**.

Right click and select **New Properties Filter**.

12.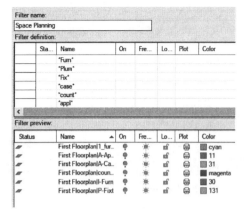

Name the Filter: **Space Planning**.
Under Name:
Type ***Furn***.
Plum
Fix
case
count
appl

All the layers that meet the filter are displayed.

Press **OK**.

13.

Freeze all the space planning layers.

14.

Select the **Layer States Manager**.

15.

Select **New**.

16.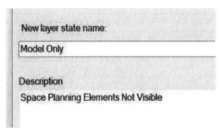

Type **Model Only** for the layer state name.

In the Description field:
Type **Space Planning Elements Not Visible**.

Click **OK**.

17.

Click **Close**.

18. You can see the Layer State now in the drop-down list on the Layers panel.

    Close the Layer Manager.

    You see the view updates with just the floor plan.

19. Switch to the Manage ribbon.
    Open the **Style Manager**.

20.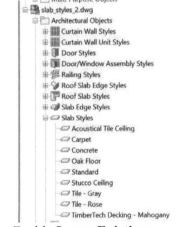

    Open the *slab_styles_2.dwg*.

    You should see several slab styles.

    Copy and paste the slab styles into the *First Floor.dwg*.

21. Enable **Leave Existing**.

    Click **OK**.

    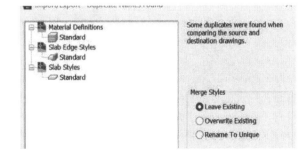

22. The slab styles are now available in the First Floor.dwg.

    Close the Style Manager.

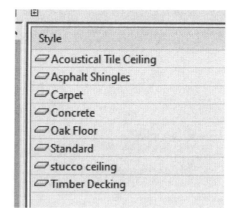

23. Save and close the *First Floor.dwg*.

Exercise 6-4:
Create Slab from Boundary

Drawing Name: First Floor.dwg
Estimated Time: 10 minutes

This exercise reinforces the following skills:

- Saved Views
- View Cut Height
- Create Slab

1.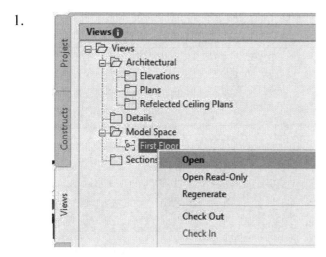

   Go to the Views tab of the Project Navigator.

   Right click on the **First Floor** view.

   Select **Open**.

Floors, Ceilings, and Spaces

2. Launch the Layer Manager.

   Right click on the **PDF Inserts** filter.

   Select **Visibility→Thawed**.

   The PDF is now visible.

3. Zoom into the Master Bedroom area.

4. *Change the Cut Height to adjust the view depth.*

   Set the Value to **3'-0"**.

5. Set the Display Above Range to **10'-0"**.
   Set the Cut Height to **3'**.
   Set the Display Below Range to **0"**.

   Click **OK**.

6. Select the **Slab** tool from the Home ribbon.

    We will add a carpet slab to this room.

7. Set the Style to **Carpet**.

8. *You are going to trace the boundary for the floor to be placed.*

    Start at the upper left corner of the room.

    Trace around the room.

    At the last segment, right click and select **Close**.

    Click ENTER when the boundary is completed.

9. Switch to an isometric view and inspect the floor you just placed in the bedroom area.

10.

Add an oak floor slab to the kitchen and dining room area.

11.

Place slabs in the remaining rooms using appropriate slab styles.

Save and close the file.

Exercise 6-5:
Create a Reflected Ceiling Plan View

Drawing Name: First Floor RCP.dwg
Estimated Time: 25 minutes

This exercise reinforces the following skills:

- Views
- Project Navigator
- Layer Filters
- Layer States
- Style Manager
- Slab Styles

1. *The Tahoe Cabin Project should be active.*

   Launch the Project Navigator.

   Select the Views tab.

2. 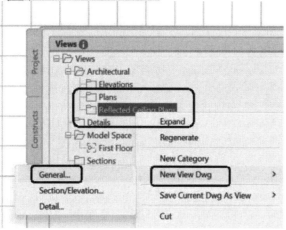 Highlight the **Reflected Ceiling Plans** category.

   Right click and select **New View Dwg→General**.

Floors, Ceilings, and Spaces

3. Type **First Floor RCP** in the Name field.
   Click in the Description field and type **First Floor RCP**.
   Enable **Open in drawing editor**.

   Click **Next**.

4. Select the **First Floor** level.

   Click **Next**.

5. Disable the 3D category.
   Disable the Sitework category.
   Under Architecture:
   Disable deck outline.
   Disable First Floor Foundation – Tahoe cabin.
   Enable **First Floor Plan**.
   Click **Finish**.

   Only one file should be checked.

6. Set the view scale to **1'-0" = 1'-0"**.

7. Open the **First Floor** view.

6-27

8. 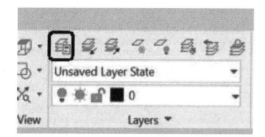 Launch the **Layer Manager**.

9. Click the **Save** icon.

10. Browse to your work folder.
    Name the file *layer filters*.
    Click **Save**.

11. Open the **Layer States Manager**.

12. 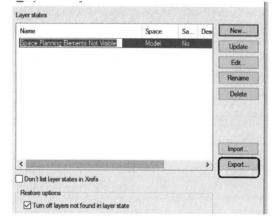 Highlight the **Space Planning Elements Not Visible** Layer State.

    Click **Export**.

13. 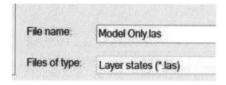 Browse to your work folder.
    Name the file ***Model Only.las***.
    Click **Save**.

14. Close all the dialogs.
    Save and Close the *First Floor.dwg*.
    Set the *First Floor RCP.dwg* active.

15. Launch the **Layer Manager**.

16. Select **Load Filter Groups**.

17. Click **Yes**.

    Open the layer filters file that was saved.

18. 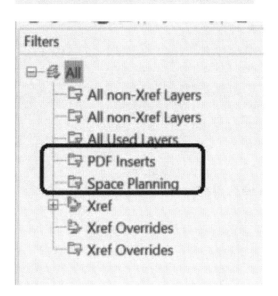 *The layer filters are now available in this drawing.*

    Open the **Layer States Manager**.

19. Click **Import**.

20. 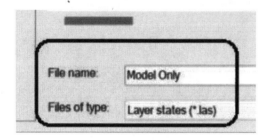 Set the Files of type: to ***.las**.

    Select the *Model Only* file.

    Click **Open**.

21. The layers states in C:\ACA 2024 Fundamentals\ACA 2024 Fundamentals exercises\ACA 2024 exercises reorganized\Lesson 06\completed exercises\Model Only.las were successfully imported. Do you want to restore any layer states?

    Click **Restore states**.

    Close the Layer Manager.

22. Switch to the Manage ribbon.
    Open the **Style Manager**.

Floors, Ceilings, and Spaces

23. Open the *slab_styles_2.dwg*.

    You should see several slab styles.

    Copy and paste the slab styles into the *First Floor RCP.dwg*.

24. Enable **Leave Existing**.

    Click **OK**.

25. *The slab styles are now available in the First Floor RCP.dwg.*

    Close the Style Manager.

26. Save and close the *First Floor RCP.dwg*.

Exercise 6-6:
Levels and Elevations

Drawing Name: 3D Model-Master.dwg
Estimated Time: 20 minutes

This exercise reinforces the following skills:

- Levels
- Elevations
- Project Navigator
- External References
- Blocks
- Properties

1. Set the **Tahoe Cabin** project current.

2. Open *3D Model_Master.dwg*.

3. [−][Front][2D Wireframe]   Switch to a **Front|2D Wireframe** view.

Floors, Ceilings, and Spaces

4. Verify that all the levels align well.

If they don't adjust the insertion points for the Y-values, follow the guidance below. Your values may be different.

5. Select the foundation floor plan xref.

   Right click and select Properties.

   Change the Insertion Point Y value to **-4'-1/16"**.

6. Select the Ground Floor Plan xref.

   Right click and select Properties.

   Change the Insertion Point Z value to **-2' 8-15/16"**.

7. Select the First Floorplan xref.

   Right click and select Properties.

   Change the Insertion Point Z value to **-10'-8 15/16"**.

8. Select the Second Floor Plan xref.

   Right click and select Properties.

   Change the Insertion Point Z value to **-20'-8 15/16"**.

9. Select the roof slabs – Tahoe Cabin xref.

   Right click and select Properties.

   Change the Insertion Point Z value to **-28'**.

10. Open the Project Navigator.
Open the Project tab.
Click **Edit** on the Levels bar.

11. Adjust the values of the Floor Elevations.

    Verify the Floor to Floor Heights.

    Click **OK**.

12. Click **Yes**.

13. Switch to a **Top|2D Wireframe** view.

14. Open the Home ribbon.

    Select the **Elevation Line** tool.

15. Turn ORTHO ON.

    Draw a line below the model.

Floors, Ceilings, and Spaces

16. Pick a point to the right of the model.

Click **OK**.

An elevation view of the model is placed.

17. Type **WBLOCK** to create an external drawing.
18. Window around the elevation view.
19. Select the top left endpoint of the foundation as the Base Point.

20. Enable **Delete** from drawing.

    Save to your exercise folder.

    Name **South Elevation – Tahoe Cabin**.

    Set the Insert units to **Inches**.

    Click **OK**.

21. Hover over the elevation line that was placed.

    Note that it is on the A-Elev-Line layer.
    Turn off the layer filter and restore the layer list.

    Freeze that layer and A-Elev-Iden.

22. Save and close **3D Model-Master.dwg**.

ACA's Coordinate System

The **UCS** is the User Coordinate System. You can modify the UCS for any drawing or view to shift the coordinate system to match your model. Elements are drawn on the XY plane, so you want to be aware of how the XY plane is oriented. **WCS** is the World Coordinate System.

The UCS defines:

- The *XY* plane, also called the *work plane* or construction plane, on which objects are created and modified
- The horizontal and vertical directions used for features like Ortho mode, polar tracking, and object snap tracking
- The alignment and angle of the grid, hatch patterns, text, and dimension objects
- The origin and orientation for coordinate entry and absolute reference angles

All objects in a drawing are defined by their coordinates in the World Coordinate System (WCS), a permanently fixed Cartesian coordinate system. The UCS is initially coincident with the WCS in new drawings. The squares in the lower-left corners of each of the icons indicates that the UCS icon is currently coincident with the WCS.

You can create Named UCS, so you can quickly switch from one user coordinate system to another as you move around a model. This is helpful if you want to insert elements at different elevations. For example, you could create a UCS for each level of a building model and save them. As you move from level to level, activate the required UCS so that elements are modified and created correctly.

Exercise 6-7:
Create an Elevation View

Drawing Name: South Elevation Tahoe Cabin.dwg
Estimated Time: 20 minutes

This exercise reinforces the following skills:

- Elevations
- Project Navigator
- Blocks
- ID
- Views

1. Set the **Tahoe Cabin** project current.

2. Open *South Elevation Tahoe Cabin.dwg*.

3. Go to the View ribbon.

   Select **UCS Origin** to designate a new 0,0,0 coordinate in the drawing.

4. Select the top endpoint of the foundation as the origin.

Floors, Ceilings, and Spaces

5. Go to the Home ribbon.

Select **ID Point** from the Utilities panel.

6. Select the bottom endpoint of the concrete column.

The Y-value is displayed as -7'-11 3/4".

7. Set **A-Elev** as the current layer.

8. Set the Scale to **1" = 1'-0"**.

9. Go to the Insert ribbon.

Select **Insert →Blocks from Libraries**.

10. Locate the *elevation tag.dwg* in the downloaded exercise files.

6-39

11. Enable **Insertion Point**.

    Set the Uniform Scale to **4**.

12. Right click on the drawing name.

    Select **Insert**.

13. 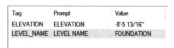 Fill in the information for the attributes.

    Click **OK**.

14. Repeat to place the next elevation tag.

Your drawing should look like this.

15. 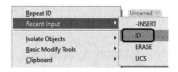 Right click to select **Recent Input→ ID**.

16. Select the bottom endpoint of the first floor.

17. Set the ELEVATION to **7'-11 1/2"**.
    Set the LEVEL NAME to **FIRST FLOOR**.

    Click **OK**.

18. Right click to select **Recent Input→ ID.**

    Select the bottom endpoint of the second floor.

19. Set the ELEVATION to **17'-10 1/2"**.
    Set the LEVEL NAME to **SECOND FLOOR**.

    Click **OK**.

20. Right click to select **Recent Input→ ID.**

    Select the bottom endpoint of the roof.

21. Set the ELEVATION to **28'-3 1/2"**.
    Set the LEVEL NAME to **ROOF**.

    Click **OK**.

The drawing should appear as shown.

Your elevation values may be slightly different from mine.

22.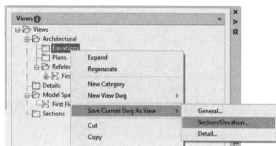

Open the Project Navigator.

Open the Views tab.

Highlight **Elevations** under Architectural.
Right click and select **Save Current Dwg As View→Section/Elevation**.

23. Click **Next**.

24.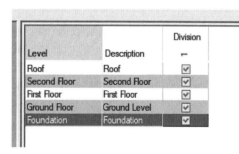

Enable all the Divisions.

Click **Next.**

25. 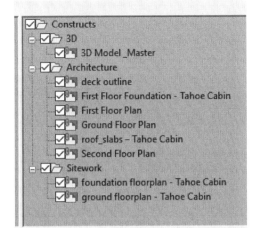 Click Finish.

26. Save and close the file.

Ceiling Grids

Grids are AEC objects on which you can anchor other objects, such as columns, and constrain their locations. Grids are useful in the design and documentation phases of a project. A ceiling grid allows you to mount light fixtures to a ceiling.

The Design Tools palette contains tools which quickly place ceiling grids with a specific ceiling grid style and other predefined properties. You can use the default settings of the tool, or you can change its properties. You can also use ceiling grid tools to convert linework to ceiling grids and to apply the settings of a ceiling grid tool to existing ceiling grids.

You can change existing ceiling grids in different ways. You can change the overall dimensions of the grid, the number and position of grid lines, and the location of the grid within the drawing. You can also specify a clipping boundary for the grid and use that to mask the grid or insert a hole into the grid.

Exercise 6-8:
Create Ceiling Grid

Drawing Name: First Floor - RCP
Estimated Time: 25 minutes

This exercise reinforces the following skills:

- Named Views
- Ceiling Grid
- Properties
- Set Boundary

1. 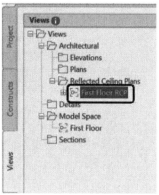 Open the **First Floor RCP** view.

2. Switch to the Home ribbon.
   Select **Ceiling Grid**.

3. Select the inside corner of the bedroom.

   Click **ENTER** to accept the default rotation of 0.00.

   Click **ESC** to exit the command.

Floors, Ceilings, and Spaces

4. Switch to an isometric view.
The ceiling grid was placed at the 0 elevation.

   Select the ceiling grid.

5. Right click and select **Properties.**

6. Change the Elevation to **8' 0"**.

   The ceiling grid position will adjust.
   Click **ESC** to release the selection.

7. Switch back to the **top** view.

   Select the **Rectangle** tool from the Draw panel on the Home ribbon.

8. Place a rectangle in the bedroom.

6-45

9.

    Select the rectangle.

    Set the Global Width to **1"**
    Set the Elevation to **8'-0"**.
    Change the color to **Red.**

    This just makes it a little easier to see.

    Click **ESC** to release the selection.

10.

    Switch to the isometric view.

    Turn ON the **A-Clng-Grid** layer.

11.

    Move the ceiling grid so that it is located inside the bedroom.

12. Enable **Lineweight**.
    Enable **Selection Cycling**.
13.

    Select the ceiling grid.

14. Select **Set Boundary** from the Clipping panel.

    Note: You won't see this tool unless the ceiling grid is selected.

15. *The Selection Cycling dialog should list the polyline that is the rectangle.*

    Click on the Polyline in the list to select.

16. *The ceiling grid boundary is modified to fit inside the room.*

    Click ESC to exit the command.

17. Switch back to a top view.

18. Change the Display Configuration to **Reflected.**

    Select the polyline and change the color to Bylayer.

    The polyline should be on the A-Clng-Grid layer.

19. Save and close *First Floor RCP.dwg*.

Lighting

When there are no lights in a scene, the scene is rendered with default lighting. Default lighting is derived from one or two distant light sources that follow the viewpoint as you orbit around the model. All faces in the model are illuminated so that they are visually discernible. You can adjust the exposure of the rendered image, but you do not need to create or place lights yourself.

When you place user-defined lights or enable sunlight, you can optionally disable default lighting. Default lighting is set per viewport, and it is recommended to disable default lighting when user-defined lights are placed in a scene.

Light fixtures are placed for three reasons – 1) for rendering 2) to create lighting fixture schedules, so the construction documents can detail which light fixtures are placed where; and 3) for electrical wiring drawings.

Exercise 6-9:
Add Lights to Ceiling Grid

Drawing Name: First Floor RCP.dwg
Estimated Time: 10 minutes

This exercise reinforces the following skills:

- ❑ Reflected Ceiling Plan Display
- ❑ Viewports
- ❑ Design Center
- ❑ Insert Block

1. 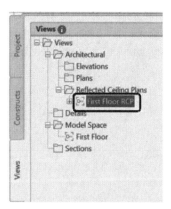   Open the **First Floor RCP** view.

Floors, Ceilings, and Spaces

2. On the status bar:

   Notice that the Display Configuration is set to **Reflected.**

3. Switch to the Insert ribbon.

   Launch the **Design Center**.

4. Switch to the **AEC Content** tab.

   Browse to *Imperial/Design/Electrical/Lighting/Fluorescent.*

5. Locate the **2x2** lighting.

6. Select and right click.

   Select **Insert**.

7. Select the ceiling grid when prompted to select the layout node.

   Then select the grid intersection to use to place the lighting fixture.

8. Move the cursor over and select another location for the lighting fixture.

9. Place four lighting fixtures.

   Click **ESC** to exit the command.

10. Switch to an isometric view.

    The lighting fixtures are displayed in the ceiling grid.

    Save and close *First Floor RCP.dwg*.

Spaces

Spaces are 2-dimensional or 3-dimensional style-based architectural objects that contain spatial information about a building, including floor area, wall area, volume, surface information, and more. Spaces can be used for organizing schedules, such as statements of probable construction cost, energy requirements and analysis, leasing documents, operating costs and fixtures, and lists of furniture and equipment.

Spaces can have a number of different data types attached to them:

- Geometric data belonging to the space: This is data inherent to the space like its height or width. This data can be displayed in the Properties palette or used in schedule tables and space tags.
- Modified and calculated data derived from the space: this is data derived from the geometric data by applying calculation modifier styles, boundary offset calculation formulas, or formula properties. Schedule properties exist for values created by calculation modifiers, boundary offsets, and formulas, so that they can be displayed in the Properties palette and used in a schedule table, too.
- Data generated by a geometric decomposition of the space area.
- Space surface properties: Data attached to the surfaces of a space.
- User-defined information sets: you can define any set of relevant property set data for spaces, like for example, floor finish, ceiling material etc. This data can be displayed in the Properties palette and used in schedule tables and space tags.

Exercise 6-10:
Add a Space

Drawing Name: First Floor.dwg
Estimated Time: 5 minutes

This exercise reinforces the following skills:

- Named Views
- Space

1. 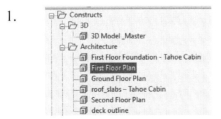 Open the **First Floor Plan** construct.

2. It should appear like this.

3. On the Home ribbon:

   Click **Manage Layer States** from the drop-down Layers control.

4. Click **Import.**

5. 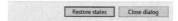 Import the **Model** layer state file into the drawing.

6. Click **Restore states**.

7. 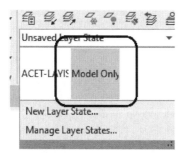 Set the **Model Only** Layer state active.

Floors, Ceilings, and Spaces

8. Switch to a Top view.

Select the **Space** tool from the Build panel on the Home ribbon.

9. Click on **Height**.

10. Set the Ceiling Height to **8'-2"**.

11. Draw a rectangle in the master bedroom by selecting the opposing corners.

Click **ESC** to exit the command.

12. Switch to an isometric view so you can see the space.

You may need to click on the space to be able to see it.

13. Rotate the view so you can see the underside of the space and the model.

Save and close *First Floor.dwg*.

6-53

Ceilings and Floors

You can use the Space/Zone Manager to modify the style that is applied to the floor or ceiling of a space. This will automatically update in any existing schedules.

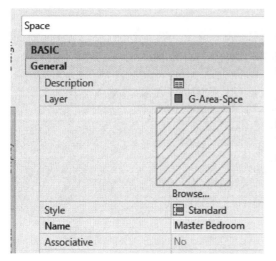

It helps if you name the space assigned to each room before you start applying different styles to ensure that you apply the correct styles to each space.

You can create space styles that use specific floor and ceiling materials to make it more efficient when defining your spaces.

Exercise 6-11:
Add a Ceiling and Floor to a Space

Drawing Name: First Floor Plan .dwg
Estimated Time: 10 minutes

This exercise reinforces the following skills:

- Add Slab
- Slab Styles
- Properties

1. Open the **First Floorplan** construct.

2. -][SW Isometric][Hidden]   Switch to a **SW Isometric** view.

Floors, Ceilings, and Spaces

3. Switch to the Manage ribbon.
   Open the **Style Manager**.

4. Open the *slab_styles_2.dwg*.

   You should see several slab styles.

   Copy and paste the slab styles into the *First Floor Plan.dwg*.

5. Enable **Leave Existing**.

   Click **OK.**

6. *The slab styles are now available in the First Floorplan.dwg.*

   Close the Style Manager.

7. Launch the **Design Tools**.

6-55

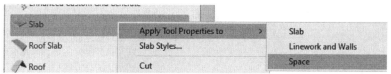

8. Locate the Slab tool.
   Right click and select **Apply Tool Properties to→ Space**.

9. Select the space that is located in the master bedroom.

   Click **ENTER** to complete selection.

10. Enable **Convert Ceiling to Slab**.
    Enable **Convert Floor to Slab**.

    Click **OK**.

11. *The two slabs appear.*

    Click **ESC** to release the selection.

12. Switch to a **2D Wireframe** display.

13. Select the ceiling slab.

14. Set the Style to **Stucco Ceiling**.

    Click **ESC** to release the selection.

15. Orbit the view so you can select the floor slab.

16. 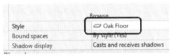 Set the Style to **Oak Floor**.

    Click **ESC** to release the selection.

17. Save and close *First Floor Plan.dwg*.

Exercise 6-12:
Add a Lighting Fixture to a Ceiling

Drawing Name: First Floor Plan.dwg
Estimated Time: 5 minutes

This exercise reinforces the following skills:

- Inserting Blocks
- Properties

1. Open the **First Floor Plan** construct.

2. [-][Top][Realistic]   Set the view to **Top|Realistic**.

3. Switch to the Insert ribbon.

   Select **Insert →Blocks from Libraries**.

4. Select **Browse Block Libraries** from the drop-down list.

Floors, Ceilings, and Spaces

5. Locate the *ceiling_fan.dwg* file located in the downloaded exercises.

   Click **Open**.

6. 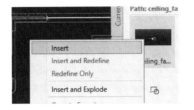 Highlight the file.

   Right click and select **Insert**.

7. Place in the center of the master bedroom.

8. Select the fan and set the Position Z to **7'-4"**.

   It took me some trial and error to figure out the correct Z value to place the fan.

9. Switch to an isometric 2D Wireframe view to inspect the placement of the ceiling fan.

10. Save and close the file.

Stairs

Stairs are AEC objects that use flights of treads and risers to accommodate vertical circulation. Stairs also interact with railing objects. You can control the style of the stair, the shape of the landing, the type of treads, and the height and width of the stair run. By default, ACA will comply with standard business codes regarding the width of the tread and riser height. An error will display if you attempt to enter values that violate those standards.

You can modify the edges of stairs so that they are not parallel, and ACA allows curved stairs.

Landings can also be non-rectangular. Stairs allow the use of nearly arbitrary profiles for the edges of flights and landings. In addition, railings and stringers can be anchored to stairs and can follow the edges of flights and landings. You can create custom stairs from linework or profiles to model different conditions as well.

Materials can be assigned to a stair. These materials are displayed in the Realistic visual style, or when rendered. Materials have specific settings for the physical components of a stair, such as risers, nosing, and treads. You can include the material properties in any schedules.

Stair styles allow you to predefine materials for the stair. A stair style allows you to specify the dimensions, landing extensions, components, and display properties of the stair.

You can create a stair tool from any stair style. You can drag the style from the Style Manager onto a tool palette. You can then specify default settings for any stair created from the tool.

Floors, Ceilings, and Spaces

Exercise 6-13:
Placing a Stair

Drawing Name: 3D Model-Master.dwg
Estimated Time: 20 minutes

This exercise reinforces the following skills:

- Stair
- Project Navigator
- Constructs
- External References
- Slabs
- Slab Styles
- Stairs

1. 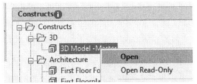 Open *3D Model-Master.dwg* on the Constructs tab of the Project Navigator.

   Switch to a **SW Isometric|Hidden** view display.

2. Select the first floor.

   Select **Edit Reference In-Place** from the ribbon.

   TIP: *You can hover over the xref to select it or use Properties to verify that you selected the correct xref.*

3. Click **OK**.

6-61

4. Set the view to **Top 2D Wireframe**.

[-][Top][2D Wireframe]

5. Go to the Manage ribbon.

Open the Style Manager.

6.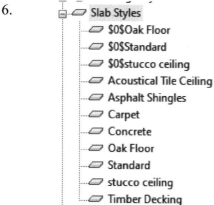

Copy and Paste the slab styles from the *slab styles2.dwg* into the 3D Model – Master.dwg.

7.

Enable **Leave Existing.**

Click **OK.**

Close the Style Manager.

8.

Thaw the **First Floorplan|PDF Images** layer.

This will allow you to see where stairs should be placed.

Floors, Ceilings, and Spaces

9. Freeze all the roof slabs layers.

    EXTRA: *Create a Property Filter for roof and roof slabs.*

10. Draw a rectangle at the top of the building.

11. Launch the **Design Tools**.

    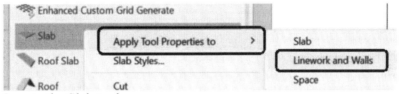

12. Locate the Slab tool.
    Right click and select **Apply Tool Properties to→ Linework and Walls**.
13. Select the rectangle.
    Click ENTER.
14. Click **Yes** to erase the layout geometry.

15. Click ENTER to accept **Projected**.
16. Set the Base Height to **10'-8-15/16"**.
17. Set the Justification to **Bottom**.

6-63

18. Set the top midpoint as the pivot point.

19. Set the Style to **TimberTech Decking**.

    Click **ESC** to release the selection.

20. Select the **Stair** tool on the Home ribbon.

21. On the Properties palette:

    Set the Shape to **Multi-landing**.
    Set the Vertical Orientation to **Down**.

    Set the Width to **7'-6"**.
    Set the Height to **7'-8-1/2"**.
    Set Justify to **Center**.
    Set Flight Length to **Tread Length**.
    Set Calculation Rules to **Tread.**

Floors, Ceilings, and Spaces

22.

Select a point above the building model and draw the stairs straight up.

When seven risers are displayed, click to start the landing.

Type **4'-0"** for the landing width.

Move the cursor to the left.

When all the risers are shown, click to end the stair run.

Click ENTER to exit the command.
You can move them next to the deck after the stairs are placed.

23.

Switch to a 3D view to inspect the stairs.

Switch to a left view.

24.

Adjust the position of the stairs so they meet the floor slab for the deck.

The bottom of the stairs will be aligned to the bottom of the garage door.

Save changes to the XREF.

25.

Switch to an isometric view to inspect the stairs and verify they are placed correctly.

Tip: *Restore the Model Only layer state to see the full model.*

26. Save and close the file.

Railings

Railings are objects that interact with stairs and other objects. You can add railings to existing stairs, or you can create freestanding railings.

Railings can have guardrails, handrails, posts, balusters, and one or more bottom rails. Additionally, you can add custom blocks to railings.

A railing style can control the properties for all railings that use that style, rather than changing properties for each railing in the drawing. Various styles exist in the templates for common railing configurations, such as guardrail pipe, handrail grip, and handrail round.
Within the railing style, you can specify the rail locations and height, post locations and intervals, components and profiles, extensions, material assignments, and display properties of the railing.

Exercise 6-14:
Placing a Railing on a Stair

Drawing Name: 3D Model-Master.dwg
Estimated Time: 5 minutes

This exercise reinforces the following skills:

- railing

1. Select the **First Floor Plan** XREF.
Select **Edit Reference In-Place** from the ribbon.

    Click **OK** when the Reference Edit dialog appears.

    Set the view to **Top 2D Wireframe**.

    [−][Top][2D Wireframe]

2. Zoom into the stairs at the top of the building.
Switch to the Home ribbon.

    Select the **Railing** tool.

3. Click **Attach**.

4. Click **Stair**.

5. Select the left side of the stairs.
Select the right side of the stairs.

    Click **ENTER** to complete the stair command.

    Railings should be visible on the left and right side of the stairs.

6. Set the view to **NE Isometric Hidden**.

   [−][NE Isometric][Hidden]

   Inspect the railing placed on the stair.

7. Click **Save Changes** on the ribbon.

   Save and close the 3D Model-Master file.

Exercise 6-15:
Placing a Railing on Slab

Drawing Name: 3D Model-Master.dwg
Estimated Time: 5 minutes

This exercise reinforces the following skills:

- railing

1.

   You should be working in the Tahoe Cabin project.
   Open the 3D Model Master construct.

   Select the **First Floor Plan** xref.

   You can use Properties to verify that you selected the correct Xref.

   Select **Edit Reference In-Place** from the ribbon.

2.

   Click **OK**.
   Set the view to **Top 2D Wireframe**.

   [–][Top][2D Wireframe]

   Zoom into the deck at the top of the building.

3.

   Sketch a path for the railing following the outer edge of the deck using a polyline.

Floors, Ceilings, and Spaces

Draw two polylines because there should be one railing on the left and one on the right.

4.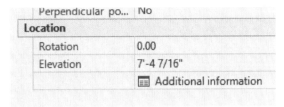

   Select the two polylines.

   Set the Elevation to **7'-4-7/16"** on the Properties palette.

   Click **ESC** to release the selection.

   This is the elevation of the decking.

5. Launch the Design Tools.
6.

   Select the **Railing** tool on the Design Tools palette.
   Right click and select **Apply Tool Properties to →Polyline.**

7. [image of command line]

   Select the two polylines.

   Click **YES** to erase the polylines.

8. Click ESC to release the selection.
9.

   Set the view to **NE Isometric Hidden**.

   Inspect the railing placed on the deck.

10.

    Switch to a left view to verify that everything is placed correctly.

11. Click **Save Changes** on the ribbon to save the changes to the xref.

   Save and close the 3D Model-Master file.

Exercise 6-16:
Create Named Views

Drawing Name: First Floor Plan.dwg
Estimated Time: 15 minutes

This exercise reinforces the following skills:

- Named Views
- View Manager

1. 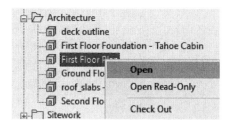 In the Project Navigator:

   Open the Constructs tab.
   Open First Floor Plan.dwg

2. Set the view to **Top 2D Wireframe**.

   Thaw the PDF Images layer.

Floors, Ceilings, and Spaces

3. Switch to the View ribbon.

   On the View list drop-down:

   Select View Manager.

4. Click **New**.

5. Type **Kitchen** for the view name.
   Enable **Define window**.

   Window around the kitchen area.

   Click **OK**.

6. The named view is listed.

   Click **New.**

6-73

7. Type **Dining Room** for the view name.
Enable **Define window**.

   Window around the dining room area.

   Click **OK**.

8. Click **New.**

9. Type **Entry Foyer** for the view name.
Enable **Define window**.

   Window around the foyer area.

   Click **OK**.

10. Click **New.**

11.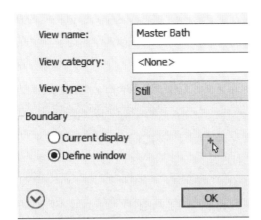

Type **Master Bath** for the view name.
Enable **Define window**.

Window around the bathroom area.

Click **OK**.

12.

Click **New.**

13.

Type **Master Bedroom** for the view name.
Enable **Define window**.

Window around the bedroom area.

Click **OK**.

14.

Click **New.**

15.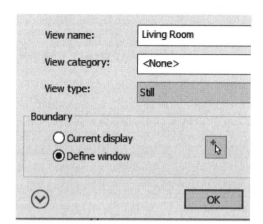

Type **Living Room** for the view name.
Enable **Define window**.

Window around the bedroom area.

Click **OK**.

16.

Highlight the **Kitchen** named view.

Click **Set Current.**

Click **Apply**.

17.

The view should zoom into the kitchen area.

Click **OK** on the View Manager dialog.

18. The Named Views are listed in the views list.

    Click on each named view to see what is displayed.

    Named views provide an easy way to navigate around your drawing.

19. Save and close the drawing file.

Exercise 6-17:
Placing a Stair with a Landing

Drawing Name: First Floor Plan.dwg
Estimated Time: 15 minutes

This exercise reinforces the following skills:

- Stair
- Project Navigator
- Constructs
- External References
- Stairs
- Railings

1. In the Project Navigator:

   Open the Constructs tab.
   Open First Floor Plan.dwg

2. Set the view to **Top 2D Wireframe**.

   [−][Top][2D Wireframe]

   Switch to the View ribbon.

   Activate the **Entry Foyer** named view.

6-77

3.

It can be easier to create stairs outside of the building model and then move them into the correct location.

Set the elevation to **First Floor: 11'-3/4"**.

The view should show the Foyer area. The PDF layer can be thawed so that you can see where to locate the stairs.

4.

Select the **Stair** tool on the Home ribbon.

5.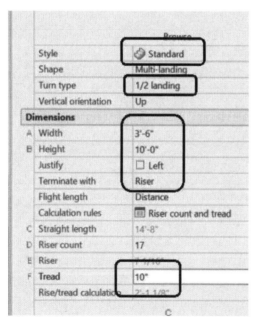

On the Properties palette:

Set the Shape to **Multi-Landing**.
Set the Turn type to **1/2 landing.**
Set the Vertical orientation to **Up.**
Set the Width to **3'-6"**.
Set the Height to **10'-0"**.
Set Justify to **Left**.
Set the Tread to **10"**.

6.

Start at the left endpoint of the stairs closest to the door.

The second point should be at the end of the first flight.

7.

Select a point to indicate the start of the second flight.

Drag the mouse straight down until all the treads are used. Click to complete the stairs. Click ENTER.

8.
Location	
Rotation	0.00
Elevation	0"

Select the stairs.
On the Properties palette:

Set the Elevation to **0"**.

9.

Use the grips on the stairs to adjust the location of the treads.

10. Switch to different view orientations to adjust the position of the stairs.

    This is a Front|2D Wireframe view.

11. This is a Right|2D Wireframe.

12. Switch back to a Top view.

    Select the **Railing** tool from the Home ribbon.

    Select **Attach**.
    Select **Flight**.

Floors, Ceilings, and Spaces

13.

    Select the outside of the stair to place the railing.

    Click **ENTER**.

    Repeat to add to the second flight.

14.

    To adjust the position of the railing, select the railing.
    Right click and select **Properties.**

    Click on **Anchor**.

15.

    You can set the Justification to Right/Left/Center.

    You can also adjust how far from the edge the railing is offset into the stairs.

    Adjust to the desired settings.
    Click **OK**.

16. Switch to an isometric view to inspect the railings.

    Save the model and close.

6-81

Exercise 6-18:
Create a Stair and Railing Style

Drawing Name: First Floor Plan.dwg
Estimated Time: 45 minutes

This exercise reinforces the following skills:

- Stair
- Style Browser
- Materials
- Style Manager
- Railings

1. 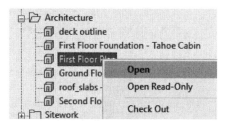 Open Construct: *First Floor Plan.dwg*

2. Go to the Home ribbon.

   Under Tools:

   Select **Styles Browser**.

3. Under Object Type:

Select **Stair**.

4. Locate the Wood-Saddle stair.

Right click and select **Import styles**.

 A green check is displayed next to the style.

A green check indicates the style exists in the active drawing.

5. Select **Railing** under Object Type.

6. 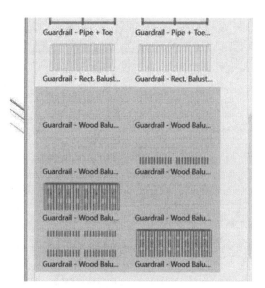 Hold down the CTL key and select all the Guardrail – Wood Baluster styles.

   Right click and select **Import styles**.

    Green checks indicate the styles now are available in the active drawing.

7. Close the Style Browser.

8. Go to the Render ribbon.

   Click **Materials Browser**.

Floors, Ceilings, and Spaces

9. Search for the **red oak** material.

10. Highlight the **red oak** material.

    Click the up arrow to import the material into the active document.

11. Close the Materials Browser.

12. Go to the Home ribbon.

    Launch the **Content Browser**.

13. Open the **Design Tool Catalog – Imperial**.

14. Browse to the Railings category.

Locate the **Handrail – Grip** profile.

Right click and select **Insert into Drawing**.

15. Close the Content Browser.

16. Go to the Manage ribbon.

Select **Style Manager**.

17. 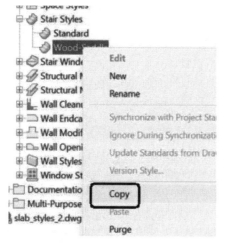 Open the 3D Model Master.dwg.

Locate the **Wood-Saddle** stair style.

Right click and select **Copy**.

18. 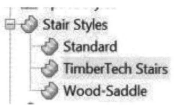 Rename the copy **TimberTech Stairs**.

19. Paste the copied style into the 3D Model-Master.dwg.

Floors, Ceilings, and Spaces

20. Select the Materials tab.

    Assign the TimberTech material to all the components.

    Click **Apply**.

21. Go to the *First Floor Plan.dwg*.

    Repeat for the TimberTech Stairs style in that drawing.

    Locate the **Wood-Saddle** stair style.

    Create a copy and paste.

22. Rename the copy **Oak**.

23. Create a new material named **Red Oak**.

24. Edit the Material.
    Assign it the **Red Oak – Natural** material.

6-87

25. 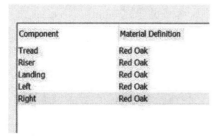 Assign all the components the Red Oak material.

    Click **Apply**.

26. Locate the Railing Styles.

27. 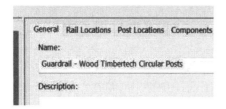 Rename the first railing style to:

    Guardrail – Wood Timbertech Circular Posts.

28. Select the Post Locations tab.

    Set the value for E to **6"**.

29. Select the Components tab.

    Change the Profile Name to ***circular*** for all the components.

Floors, Ceilings, and Spaces

30. Select the Materials tab.

    Assign the **TimberTech** material to all the components.

    Click **Apply**.

31. Rename the 02 railing style to:

    Guardrail – Wood Red Oak

32.

    Select the Rail Locations tab.
    Disable **Guardrail**.
    Enable **Handrail**.
    Enable **Bottomrail**.

33. Select the Components tab.

    Set the Handrail to **HR_GRIP**.
    Set the Bottomrail to **Rectangular**.
    Set the remaining components to **Baluster 01**.

34.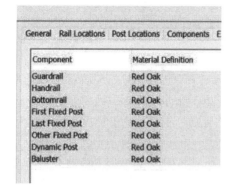

    Select the Materials tab.

    Set all the Components to **Red Oak**.

    Click **Apply**.

    Click **OK** to close the Styles Manager.

35.

    Freeze the PDF Images layer.

    Select the railings at the front of the building model.

    Each railing needs to be assigned individually.

    Select one railing, change the properties, then go to the next railing.

36.

    On the Properties palette:
    Assign the TimberTech railing style to the selected railings.

    Click ESC to release the selection.

37.

    Select the stairs and assign the TimberTech Stairs style.

    Click ESC to release the selection.

38.

    [−][Custom View][Realistic]

    Change the display to Realistic to see how the new styles appear.

Floors, Ceilings, and Spaces

39. For the stair in the entry way:

Set the Style to **Oak**.

40. Select the railing on the entry stairs.
Set the Style to **Guardrail – Wood Red Oak.**
Repeat for the second railing/

Save and close the file.

Exercise 6-19:
Add Slabs to the Second Floor Plan

Drawing Name: Second Floor Plan.dwg
Estimated Time: 30 minutes

This exercise reinforces the following skills:

- Layers
- Slabs
- Materials
- Style Browser
- Display Properties

1. Open Construct:
Second Floor Plan.dwg

2. Switch to a **Top|2D Wireframe** view.

Open the Layers Manager.

Thaw the **PDF Images** layer.

Close the Layers Manager.

6-91

3.

You may find it helpful to create a layer for your floor outlines with a width of 0.50.

This will make it easy to select and identify. I set it to DO NOT PLOT.

Draw a rectangle in Bedroom #2.

4.

Draw a rectangle in the bathroom.

Draw a rectangle in Bedroom #3.

Use a polyline to trace the outline of the Loft area.

5.

Launch the **Design Tools** from the Home ribbon.

6.

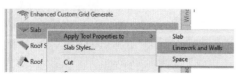

Locate the Slab tool.

Right click and select **Apply Tool Properties to→Linework and Walls.**

Floors, Ceilings, and Spaces

7. Select the rectangles and polyline that was placed.

Click **ENTER**.

8. 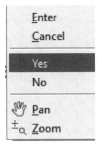 Right click and select **Yes** to erase the layout geometry.

9. Right click and select **Projected**.

10. Set the Base Height to **0'-0"**.

11. Set the Justification to **Bottom.**

Select a point on each slab edge to act as a pivot point.

Click ENTER.

Click ESC to release the selection.

12. Open the *slab_styles_2.dwg*
13. Go to the Render ribbon.
Launch the **Materials Browser**.

6-93

14. Highlight the Ceramic category.

    Import some of the ceramic tile materials into the *slab_styles_2.dwg*.

15. Close the Materials Browser.

16. Go to the Manage ribbon.

    Launch the **Style Manager**.

17. Locate the slab_styles_2.dwg.

    Browse to the **Material Definitions** category under Multi-Purpose Objects.
    Right click and select **New**.

18. Name the new material **Finishes.Floor.Mosaic Gray Tile**.

19. Select the **Display Properties** tab.
    Click in the Style Override box.

    Select the **Other** tab.

    Assign the **Mosaic Gray** render Material.
    Set the Mapping to **Same as Surface Hatch**.

    Click **OK**.

20. Override the Style and repeat for all the Display Representations.

Click **Apply** and **OK**.

21. In the slab styles 2.dwg, launch the **Styles Browser**.

Set the Object Type to **Slab**. Locate the **Wood Floor System**.

Highlight and select **Import Styles**.

Close the Styles Browser.

22. Relaunch the **Style Manager** from the Manage ribbon.
23. 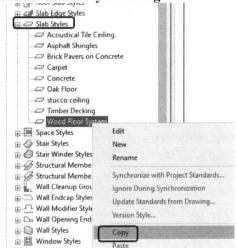 Highlight the **Wood Floor System** slab style in the slab_styles_2.dwg file.

Create a copy.

Paste a new copy.

24. 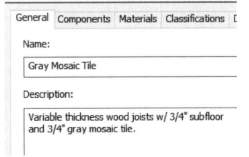 Rename the copy **Gray Mosaic Tile**.

Modify the description.

25.		Open the Components tab.
		Change the wood floor name to **Gray Mosaic Tile**.
26.		Open the Materials tab.
		Assign the Finishes.Floor.Mosaic Gray Tile to the Gray Mosaic Tile component.
		Click **Apply**.
27.	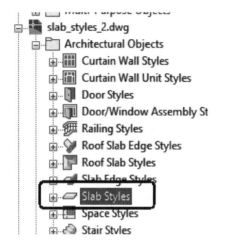	Copy and Paste the **Slab Styles** from *slab_styles2.dwg* into *Second Floor Plan.dwg*.
28.		Enable **Leave Existing.**
		Click **OK**.

29. Continue working in the Style Manager. Open the *First Floor Plan.dwg*.

30.

Locate the Railing Styles.

Copy and Paste the **Railing Styles** from *First Floorplan.dwg* into *Second Floor Plan.dwg*.

Floors, Ceilings, and Spaces

31. 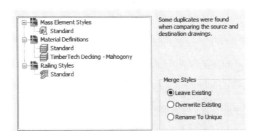 Enable **Leave Existing.**

    Click **OK**.

    Close the Style Manager.

    Save and Close the *slab styles 2.dwg.*

32. Select the slabs in the bedrooms and loft.

33. 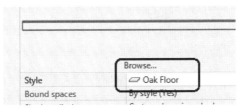 Right click and select **Properties**.

    Set the Style to **Oak Floor.**

    Click **ESC** to release the selection.

34. Select the bathroom slab.

    Set the Style to **Gray Mosaic Tile.**

    Click **ESC** to release the selection.

35. Switch to an isometric view.

    Set the Display Style to Realistic.

    Orbit around to inspect the floor slabs.

36. Save and close the file.

Exercise 6-20:
Add Balconies

Drawing Name: Second Floor Plan.dwg
Estimated Time: 20 minutes

This exercise reinforces the following skills:

- Railings
- Slabs
- Materials
- Style Browser
- Design Tool Palette

1. Open Construct:
   Second Floor Plan.dwg

2. Switch to a **Top|2D Wireframe** view.

   Open the Layers Manager.

   Thaw the **PDF Images** layer.

3. Close the Layers Manager.
   Draw two rectangles where the balconies are located.

4. Launch the **Design Tools** from the Home ribbon.

Floors, Ceilings, and Spaces

5. 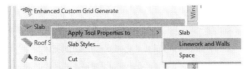 Locate the **Slab** tool.

Right click and select **Apply Tool Properties to→Linework and Walls.**

6. Select the two rectangles.

7. 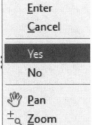 Right click and select **Yes** to erase the layout geometry.

8. Right click and select **Projected**.

9. Set the Base Height to **0'-0"**.

10. Set the Justification to **Bottom.**

Select a point on each slab edge to act as a pivot point.

Click ENTER.

11. Change the Style to **Timber Decking**.

Click **ESC** to release the selection.

12. Use POLYLINE to sketch the location for the railing on each balcony.

6-99

13. 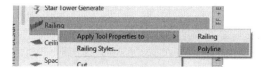 On the Design Tools Palette:

    Locate the **Railing** tool.
    Right click and select **Apply Tool Properties to→Polyline.**

14. Select the two polylines and click **ENTER**.
15. Right click and select **Yes** to erase the layout geometry.

16. Set the Style to **Guardrail – Timbertech Circular Posts**.

    Click **ESC** to release the selection.

17. Select the PDF Image.

    Click **Freeze layer** on the ribbon.

    Click **ENTER**.

18. Switch to an isometric realistic view.

    Save and close the file.

Exercise 6-21:
Add a Hole to a Slab

Drawing Name: 3D Model-Master.dwg
Estimated Time: 20 minutes

This exercise reinforces the following skills:

- Modifying External References
- Add a Hole to a Slab

1.

   Open Construct:
   3D Model-Master.dwg

   Take a minute to orbit around your model and appreciate how far you have come!

2.

   Open the Layers Manager.

   Highlight the **Roof & Roof Slabs** property filter.

   Freeze all the layers listed.

3.

   Expand the Xref category.

   Highlight the foundation floorplan – Tahoe Cabin xref.

   Freeze all the layers.

4.

Highlight the **Ground Floor Plan** xref.

Freeze all the layers.

Highlight **All**.

Whatever filter is highlighted is the list that will appear in the layer drop-down list.

Close the Layers Manager.

5.

Select the slab on the second floor.

You can use Properties to verify that you selected the second floor.

6.

On the ribbon:

Select **Edit Reference In-Place**.

7. Click **OK**.

Floors, Ceilings, and Spaces

8. Select the slab in the loft area.

9. Use the grip to extend the slab past the stairs.

   Click **ESC** to release.

10. Switch to a **Top|2D Wireframe** view.

11. Draw a rectangle around the second/top flight of stairs.

12.

Switch back to a 3D view.

Orient the view so you see the floor slab on the second level, the rectangle and the interior stairs.

13.

Select the floor slab.

On the ribbon:

Select **Hole→Add**.

Select the rectangle.
Click **ENTER**.

Click **Yes** to erase the layout geometry.

A hole is created in the floor slab.

14.

Switch to a Realistic display.

You can now see the upper flight of stairs.

15. Select the floor slab.

Use the grip to extend the slab edge to allow more space for the slab.

Click ESC to release the selection.

6-104

16. Extend the slab edge to be aligned with the inside face of the exterior walls.

    Use the grip to edit.

17. Extend the slab to allow you to adjust the bedroom door's location.

    Use the middle grip to move the bedroom door to be in front of the stairs.

18. Adjust the closet walls so they don't interfere with the entrance into the bedroom.

    Adjust the doors shown.

19. −][Top][2D Wireframe]

    Switch to a **Top|2D Wireframe** view.

    Draw a polyline to be used for the railing on the loft slab.

    Use the elevation value of the slab for the rail.

20. On the Design Tools palette:

    Select **Railing**.
    Right click and **Apply Tool Properties to →Polyline.**

21.

    Select the two polylines.
    Click **ENTER**.
    Right click and select YES to erase the polylines.

    Click ESC to release the selection.

22.

    Go to the Manage ribbon.

    Launch the **Style Manager**.

23.

    Open the *First Floor Plan.dwg*.

    Locate the **Guardrail – Wood Red Oak** railing style.

    Copy and paste into the *3D Model-Master.dwg*.

    Close the Style Manager.

24.

    Add a rail next to the stair opening.

25.

    Select the rails in the loft area.

    Assign them to the **Guardrail – Wood Red Oak** railing style.

    Change the elevation to the same as the slab.

    Click **ESC** to release.

26.   Select **Save Changes** on the ribbon to save the changes to the external reference.

27. Click **OK**.

Save and close the file.

Extra:

Add a ceiling to the second level. Add a chandelier to the foyer area. I have included two chandelier drawings in the exercise folder for you to choose from. When you place the chandelier, be sure you place it qt the ceiling height.

Use the Style Manager to copy styles into the Ground Floor Plan.

Open the Ground Floor Plan.dwg. Add stairs. Apply the oak stair style. Create a railing style that is just a handrail and use the handrail on the stairs.

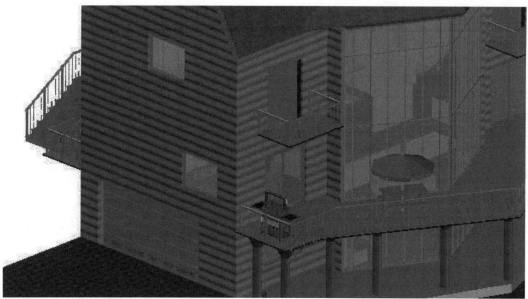

Place a paved driveway and patio with columns to support the first floor deck. Add a picnic table, BBQ, lounge chairs and other items. You can locate columns on the Style Browser.

Add floor slabs and ceiling to the ground floor plan.

Switch to the ACA Metric application.
Open the Core 01 Construct for the Brown Medical Clinic.
Add floor slabs and ceiling slabs.
Add a ceiling grid.
Add lighting.

QUIZ 6

True or False

1. You can create a floor or ceiling slab by converting a space.
2. Once you place a ceiling grid, it can't be modified.
3. When you place a lighting fixture on a ceiling grid, you cannot snap to the grid.
4. Railings are automatically placed on both sides of a selected stair.
5. You can assign materials to different components of a railing.

Multiple Choice

6. Slabs can be used to model: (select all that apply)

    A. Roofs
    B. Floors
    C. Ceilings
    D. Walls

7. Ceiling grids can be created using: (select all that apply)

    A. Linework
    B. Walls
    C. Roof Slabs
    D. Arcs

8. Space Styles: (select all that apply)

    A. Control the hatching displayed
    B. Control the name displayed when spaces are tagged
    C. Cannot be modified
    D. Have materials assigned

9. Railings can have the following: (select all that apply)

    A. Guardrails
    B. Handrails
    C. Posts
    D. Balusters

10. The first point selected when placing a set of stairs is:

   A. The foot/bottom of the stairs
   B. The head/top of the stairs
   C. The center point of the stairs
   D. Depends on the property settings

11. The Styles Browser can be used to:

   A. Create styles
   B. Modify existing styles
   C. Import styles into the current drawing
   D. Delete styles

ANSWERS:

1) T; 2) F; 3) F; 4) F; 5) T; 6) D; 7) A, B, C; 8) A, B; 9) A, B, C, D; 10) A; 11) C

Lesson 7:
Curtain Walls

Curtain walls provide a grid or framework for inserting objects such as windows and doors. Curtain walls have many similarities to standard walls, such as baseline, roof line, and floor line, and they allow for interferences. You can insert doors, windows, and door/window assemblies into a curtain wall, just like standard walls, but the insertion process is different.

Grids are the foundation of curtain walls, curtain wall units, and door/window assemblies.

Every grid has four element types:

- Divisions
- Cell Infills
- Frames
- Mullions

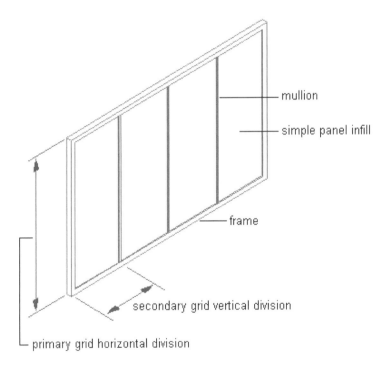

You can assign different materials to the mullions and panel infills. However, any materials need to be loaded into the document BEFORE it can be assigned.

Curtain walls can be defined using a curtain wall style. Curtain Wall Units can be inserted into a curtain wall as an infill panel. This would be considered a *nested grid*.

Curtain wall styles cannot be inserted into curtain wall units.

Curtain walls and curtain wall units are defined using the Design Rules.

Divisions establish the grids. Horizontal or vertical elements within a curtain wall.

Infills are the elements placed between the grids. Normally, this is a simple glass panel, but you could also have alternating types of colored glass, or insert granite material in some infills or some other material.

Frames are the boundaries around each grid.

Mullions are normally aluminum, but can be steel, wood or fiberglass. They are the materials that hold the glass or other infills in place. Most mullions are between 2" and 6" (5-15 cm) in width and 4" to 10" (10-25 cm) in depth. You can customize the size and profiles of the mullions in your curtain wall style.

Divisions determine how the grid is divided, based on the width and height of the curtain wall.

If you select a horizontal division with a cell dimension of 8', there will be a grid line every 8' in the horizontal direction.

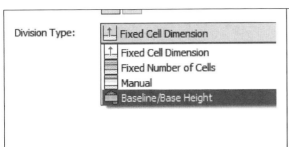	Division Type defines how ACA calculates how to divide up the curtain wall. A Fixed Cell Dimension will use the value you set. Let's say the curtain wall is 20' high and you set a horizontal division using a fixed cell dimension of 8'. The bottom and middle cell divisions would be 8', but the top cell division would only be 4'.

Fixed number of cells: the curtain wall will have three divisions (rows) no matter how tall the curtain wall is.

Manual: The first row will be the set value, the second row will be the set value, etc. The top row will equal or be less than the set value for that row.

Baseline/BaseHeight: Controls what happens if the wall is adjusted for a stepped baseline or gabled rooflines.

The Primary Grid uses a horizontal division.

The Division Type is set to Fixed Cell Dimension of 6'-8".

This means the rows are 6'8" high.

The top row may be less than 6'8" high depending on the curtain wall height.

The Secondary Grid has a Vertical Division with a width of 4'-0".

The columns may be less than 4'-0" depending on the length of the curtain wall.

By default, each cell of the grid is filled with a Simple Panel. This is a clear glass panel.

You can control the alignment or placement of the glass so it is centered in the curtain wall or at a specific distance from the center/front/back.

You also can control how thick the material of the infill is.

(Default Frame settings)	Frames are placed around the border of the curtain wall. You can download additional frame profiles from the Content Browser.
(Default Mullion settings)	Mullions are placed at each grid between the cells. You can use any closed polyline as a profile for a mullion or frame.

Once you understand what each component is, it is a bit less confusing to read the table shown.

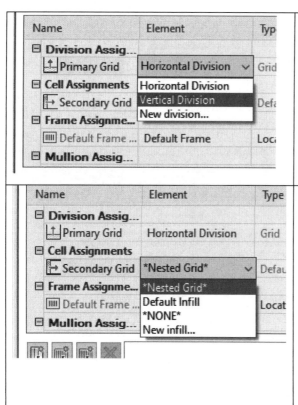

	The Primary grid may be set to the use either rows or columns.
	The secondary grid can use whichever orientation is not selected for the primary grid. If the Primary is set to Horizontal (rows), then the secondary is set to Vertical (columns) or vice versa. The secondary grid can use the same infill as the primary or a different infill. Or you can assign different infills to specific cells. You can also assign a Nested Grid. A nested grid allows you to divide the secondary grid.

Exercise 7-1:
Creating a Curtain Wall Style

Drawing Name: Ground Floor Plan.dwg
Estimated Time: 90 minutes

This exercise reinforces the following skills:

- Curtain Wall Styles
- Style Manager

1. 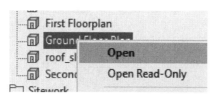   *You should be in the Tahoe Cabin project.*

   Open Construct:
   Ground Floor Plan.dwg

Curtain Walls

2. Go to the Manage ribbon.

   Open the **Style Manager**.

3. 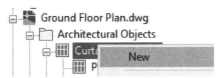 Locate the Curtain Walls category.
   Right click and select **New**.

4. Rename **Stucco Panel**.

5. Click on the Design Rules tab.

   Highlight the **Primary Grid**.

   Right click and select **Rename**.

6. Rename to **MainOverall**.
   Set the Element to **Horizontal**.

7. Set the Division Type to **Manual**.

   Click **Add Gridline**.

8. Set the Gridline Offset to **8'-0"** from **Grid Top**.

   This creates a row 8'-0" from the top of the curtain wall.

7-7

9. Move into the right panel.
Highlight the **Secondary Grid** under Division Assignment.

Right click and select **Rename**.

10. Rename **Main Columns.**

11. Set the Division Type to **Manual**.

Click **Add Gridline**.

12. Add four gridlines as shown.

If you sketch this out, you would get an idea of how the curtain wall definition currently looks.

Curtain Walls

13. Highlight **Divisions.**

    Click **New** Division.

14. Name the new division **FloorToFloor.**
    Set it to **Horizontal.**
    Set the Division Type to **Fixed Cell Dimension.**

15. Set the Cell Dimension to **12'-0".**
    Enable **Auto-Adjust Cells**.

    Set the Cell Adjustment to **Grow**.
    Enable the **bottom** row.

16. Highlight **Divisions.**

    Click **New** Division.

17. Name the new division **One Floor Division.**
Set it to **Horizontal.**
Set the Division Type to **Manual.**

18. Add two grid lines as shown.

19. Highlight **Divisions.**

    Click **New** Division.

20. Name the new division **LeftWindow.**
Set it to **Vertical.**
Set the Division Type to **Fixed Cell Dimension**

21. Set the Cell Dimension to **5'-0".**

    Enable **Auto-Adjust Cells**.

    Set the Cell Adjustment to **Shrink**.
    Enable the **End** column.

    Enable **Maintain at least half of cell dimension.**

Curtain Walls

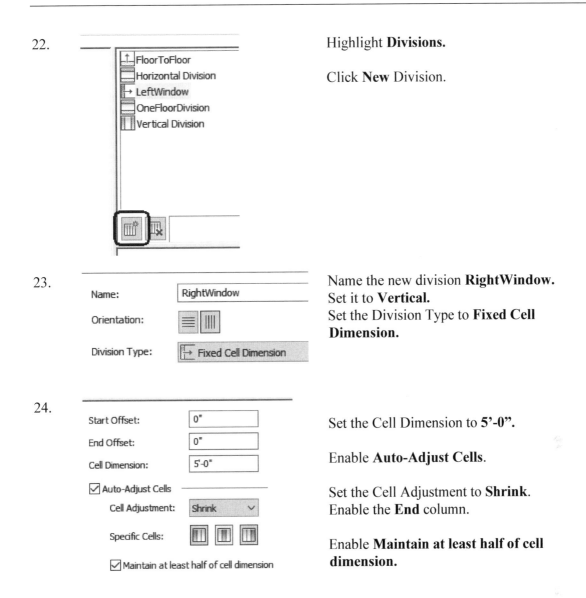

22. Highlight **Divisions.**

    Click **New** Division.

23. Name the new division **RightWindow.**
    Set it to **Vertical.**
    Set the Division Type to **Fixed Cell Dimension.**

24. Set the Cell Dimension to **5'-0".**

    Enable **Auto-Adjust Cells**.

    Set the Cell Adjustment to **Shrink.**
    Enable the **End** column.

    Enable **Maintain at least half of cell dimension.**

7-11

25. Highlight **Divisions.**

Click **New** Division.

26. Name the new division **Center 15 Foot.**
Set it to **Vertical**.
Set the Division Type to **Fixed Cell Dimension**.

27. Set the Cell Dimension to **15'-0"**.

Enable **Auto-Adjust Cells**.

Set the Cell Adjustment to **Shrink**.
Enable the **End** column.

Enable **Maintain at least half of cell dimension.**

28. Highlight **Divisions.**

    Click **New** Division.

29. Name the new division **Center Window.**
    Set it to **Vertical.**
    Set the Division Type to **Fixed Cell Dimension**

30. Set the Cell Dimension to **5'-0".**

    Enable **Auto-Adjust Cells**.

    Set the Cell Adjustment to **Shrink**.
    Enable the **Start** column.

    Click **Apply** to save your work.

31. Highlight **Infills.**

    Click **New.**

    We will be defining four new infill types.

32. Set the Name to **Column**.
Set Infill Type to **Simple Panel**.
Set Alignment to **Center**.
Set Offset to **0"**.
Set Panel Thickness to **2'-0"**.

33. Highlight **Infills**.

    Click **New**.

34. Set the Name to **Parapet**.
Set Infill Type to **Simple Panel**.
Set Alignment to **Back**.
Set Offset to **3"**.
Set Panel Thickness to **1'-6"**.

35. Highlight **Infills**.

    Click **New**.

36. Set the Name to **Stucco**.
Set Infill Type to **Simple Panel**.
Set Alignment to **Center**.
Set Offset to **-1"**.
Set Panel Thickness to **6 1/2"**.

37. Highlight **Infills**.

    Click **New**.

38. Set the Name to **Clear Glass**.
    Set Infill Type to **Simple Panel**.
    Set Alignment to **Center**.
    Set Offset to **0"**.
    Set Panel Thickness to **1/2"**.

    Did you notice that the names automatically sorted alphabetically?

39. Highlight **Mullions**.

    Click **New**.

40. Set the Name to **Standard Mullion**.
    Set the Width to **2"**.
    Set the Depth to **6"**.

41. Highlight **Mullions**.

    Click **New**.

42. Set the Name to **Butt Glazing**.
    Set the Width to **1/2"**.
    Set the Depth to **1/2"**.

43. Highlight **Mullions**.

    Click **New**.

44. Set the Name to **Stucco Joint**.
    Set the Width to **1/2"**.
    Set the Depth to **5"**.

Curtain Walls

45. Highlight **Mullions**.

    Click **New**.

46. 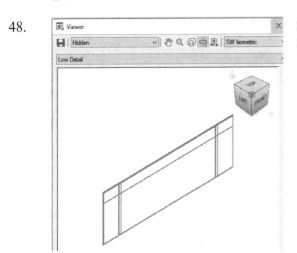 Set the Name to **Stucco Reveal**.
    Set the Width to **1"**.
    Set the Depth to **5"**.

    Click **Apply** to save your work so far.

47. Click the **Floating Viewer** at the bottom left of the Style Manager.

48. Set the view display to Hidden.
    Set the view orientation to SW Isometric.

    You can see how the curtain wall is currently defined.

49. Highlight the Primary Grid – which is now called MainOverall.

    Click **New Cell Assignment**.

7-17

50. 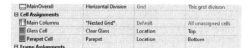 Create two cell assignments.
There should be a total of three cell assignments available.
Set the Default Cell Assignment to **Nested Grid**.
Set the second Cell Assignment to **Clear Glass**.
Set the Location to **Top**.

Set the third Cell Assignment to **Parapet**.
Set the Location to **Bottom.**
Rename the Cell Assignments.

51. Scroll down to the **Frame Assignments**.
Click in the **Used In** column.

Disable all the frame edges.

Click **OK**.

Frame Assignments should display as *NONE*.

52. Highlight the secondary grid.
This should be named **Main Columns**.

Add five more cell elements.

53. Assign Elements to the Cells.
The second, third, and fifth cell assignments should be nested grids.
The second and fourth should be columns.

54. 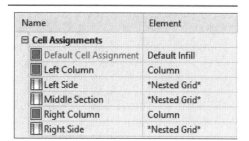 The Cell Assignments should be named:
- Left Column
- Left Side
- Middle Section
- Right Column
- Right Side

Curtain Walls

55.

    Left Side, Middle Section, and Right Side should be assigned Nested Grids.

    Once they are assigned as nested grids, you will see the new nested grids listed under Main Columns.

56. Change the Left Column Type to **Index**.
    Change the Left Column Used In to **2**.
    Change the Left Side Type to **Location**.
    Change the Left Column Used In to **Start**.
    Change the Middle Section Type to **Location**.
    Change the Middle Section Used In to **Middle**.
    Change the Right Column Type to **Index**.
    Change the Right Column Used In to **4**.
    Change the Right Side Type to **Location**.
    Change the Right Side Used In to **End**.

57. Scroll down and set the Default Mullion Assignment to **Standard Mullion**.

58.

    Look at the viewer to see how the curtain wall appears.

59. Highlight the **Left Side** Division.

    Click **New**.

7-19

60. Set the new cell to use a Nested Grid.

    Name the New Cell Assignment **OneFloor.**

61. Set LeftSide to use the **FloorToFloor** Element.

    Set the Cell Assignment to **OneFloor.**

62. Scroll down and set the Mullion Assignment to **Stucco Joint.**

63. Highlight OneFloor.

    Set the OneFloor Element to **OneFloorDivision**.

64. With OneFloor highlighted:

    Select **New Cell Assignment**.
    Change the Element to **Nested Grid.**

65. Set the top Cell Assignment to **Clear Glass.**
    It will change from Nested Grid to Default Cell Assignment.
    Rename the nested grid cell to **Left Windows.**
    Set the Location to **Middle**.

Curtain Walls

66. Select **New Cell Assignment**.
Rename the new cell **Stucco Infill**.

67. Set the Element for Stucco Infill to **Stucco**.
Set the Location to **Bottom, Top**.

68. Scroll down and set the Mullion Assignment to **Standard Mullion**.

69. 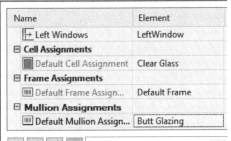 Highlight **Left Windows.**
Set the Element to **LeftWindow.**

    Set the Element for the Cell Assignment to **Clear Glass.**
    Set the Mullion Assignment to **Butt Glazing.**

70. Go to the Preview window.

    The left side of the curtain wall has been defined.

7-21

71.

Highlight the **Right Side** Division.
Set the Element for the Right Side to **FloorToFloor.**
Assign the Element for the Default Cell Assignment to **Nested Grid**.
Change the name for the cell assignment to **Right Floor.**

72.

Set the Mullion Assignment to **Stucco Joint.**

73.

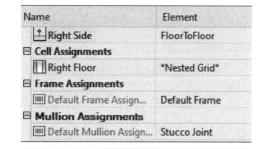

Highlight the **Right Floor** Division.
Set the Element for the Right Floor Division to **OneFloorDivision**.
Set the Default Cell Assignment to **Clear Glass**.
Add two cell assignments.

74.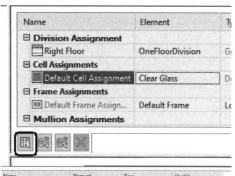

Set one of the new cell assignments to Nested Grid.
Then rename to **Right Window**.
Set the Location for Right Window to **Middle.**
Set the other new cell assignment to use **Stucco** for the Element.
Rename to **Stucco Infill**.
Set the Location to **Bottom, Top**.
Set the Mullion Assignment to **Standard Mullion.**

75.

Curtain Walls

76.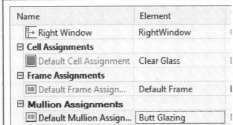

Highlight **Right Window.**
Set the Element to **RightWindow.**

Set the Element for the Cell Assignment to **Clear Glass.**
Set the Mullion Assignment to **Butt Glazing.**

Click **Apply** to save.

77.

Go to the Preview window to see that the right side of the curtain wall has updated.

78.

Highlight the **Middle Section** Division.
Set the Element for Middle Section to **Center 15 Foot.**
Set the Default Cell Assignment to **Nested Grid.**
Add two new cell assignments.

79.

Rename the cell assignment that is used in all unassigned cells to **15 Foot Middle.**
Rename one of the cell assignments **Right Side of Middle.**
Set the Location for Right Side of Middle to **End.**
Rename one of the cell assignments **Left Side of Middle.**
Set the Location for Left Side of Middle to **Start.**

All the cell assignments should be set to **Nested Grid.**

7-23

80. 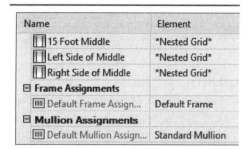 Set the Mullion Assignment to **Standard Mullion.**

81. 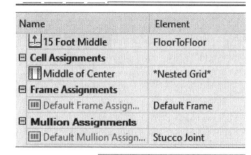 Highlight the 15 Foot Middle Division.
Set the Element to **FloorToFloor.**
Change the Default Cell Assignment to **Nested Grid.**
Rename the Cell Assignment to **Middle of Center.**
Set the Mullion Assignment to **Stucco Joint.**

82. Highlight the **Middle of Center** Division.
Set the Element to **OneFloorDivision.**
Set the Element for the Default Cell Assignment to **Clear Glass.**
Add two more Cell Assignments.

83. Set one of the new Cell Assignments to **Nested Grid.**
Rename it to **Middle Window.**
Set the Location to **Middle.**
Set the element for the second cell assignment to **Stucco.**
Rename to **Stucco Infill.**
Set the Location to **Bottom, Top.**
Set the Mullion Assignment to **Stucco Reveal.**

84. 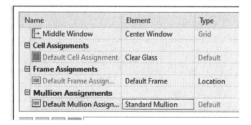 Highlight the **Middle Window** Division.
Set the Element to **Center Window.**
Set the Default Cell Assignment to **Clear Glass.**
Set the Mullion Assignment to **Standard Mullion.**

85.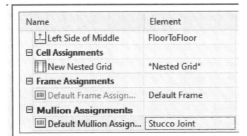

Highlight the **Left Side of Middle** Division.
Set the Element to **FloorToFloor.**
Change the Default Cell Assignment to **Nested Grid.**
Set the Mullion Assignment to **Stucco Joint.**

86.

Rename the nested grid division to **Left Side Middle.**
Highlight the **Left Side Middle** Division.
Set the Element to **OneFloorDivision.**
Set the Element for the Default Cell Assignment to **Clear Glass**.
Add two more Cell Assignments.

87.

Set one of the new Cell Assignments to **Nested Grid**.
Rename it to **Middle Left Window**.
Set the Location to **Middle**.
Set the element for the second cell assignment to **Stucco**.
Rename to **Stucco Infill.**
Set the Location to **Bottom, Top.**
Set the Mullion Assignment to **Standard Mullion.**

88.

Highlight the **Middle Left Window** Division.
Set the Element to **LeftWindow.**
Set the Default Cell Assignment to **Clear Glass.**
Set the Mullion Assignment to **Standard Mullion.**

89.

Click Apply to save your work.

Go to the Preview window.
There is one more section to be defined.
This is the Right Side of Middle.

90.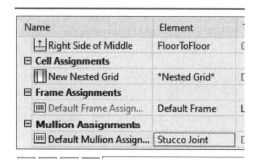

Highlight the **Right Side of Middle** Division.
Set the Element to **FloorToFloor**.
Change the Default Cell Assignment to **Nested Grid**.
Set the Mullion Assignment to **Stucco Joint**.

91.

Rename the nested grid division to **Right Side Middle**.
Highlight the **Right Side Middle** Division.
Set the Element to **OneFloorDivision**.
Set the Element for the Default Cell Assignment to **Clear Glass**.
Add two more Cell Assignments.

92. Set one of the new Cell Assignments to **Nested Grid**.
Rename it to **Middle Right Window**.
Set the Location to **Middle**.
Set the element for the second cell assignment to **Stucco**.
Rename to **Stucco Infill**.
Set the Location to **Bottom, Top**.
Set the Mullion Assignment to **Standard Mullion**.

Curtain Walls

93.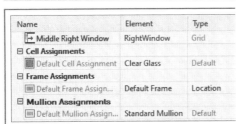

Highlight the **Middle Right Window** Division.
Set the Element to **RightWindow**.
Set the Default Cell Assignment to **Clear Glass**.
Set the Mullion Assignment to **Standard Mullion**.

94.

Click **Apply** to save your work.

Go to the Preview window.

95.

Click the **Materials** tab.

We need to create new materials for the different components we defined.

96. Open the *First Floor Plan.dwg*.

Highlight **Material Definitions**.
Right click and select **Copy**.

Paste into the **Ground Floor Plan.dwg**.

7-27

97. Enable **Leave Existing**.

    Click **OK**.

98. 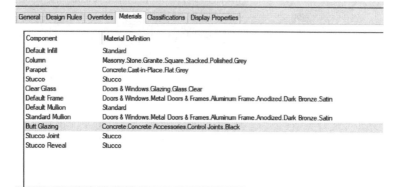 Assign the copied materials to the different components.

    Click **Apply**.

99. Return to the Preview window.

    Change the display to **Realistic**.

    Close the Style Manager.

100. Save and close the *Ground Floor Plan.dwg*.

Curtain Walls

Exercise 7-2:
Create a Custom Profile

Drawing Name: Ground Floor Plan.dwg
Estimated Time: 10 minutes

This exercise reinforces the following skills:

- Polylines
- Profiles
- Style Manager

1. 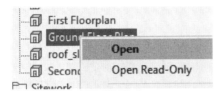 Open Construct:
   Ground Floor Plan.dwg

2. [–][Top][2D Wireframe]   Switch to a **Top|2D Wireframe** view.

3. Draw the polyline shown.

   Dimensions are for reference only.

   If you prefer, you can use lines and an arc and then use PEDIT and JOIN to convert to a polyline.

4. Select the polyline.

   Right click and select **Convert to→Profile Definition.**

   Profiles can be used for mullions and frames on windows, doors, and curtain walls.

7-29

5. Select **Centroid** as the insertion point.

6. Select **New**.

7. 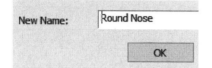 Type **Round Nose** for the Name.

   Click **OK**.

8. Erase the polyline and any dimensions.
9. Go to the Manage ribbon.

   Open the **Style Manager**.

10. 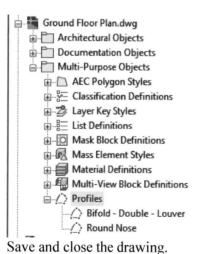 Expand **Multi-Purpose Objects**.

    Open the **Profiles** Category.

    The custom profile is listed.

    Close the Style Manager.

11. Save and close the drawing.

Curtain Walls

Exercise 7-3:
Add a Door to a Curtain Wall

Drawing Name: Ground Floor Plan.dwg
Estimated Time: 30 minutes

This exercise reinforces the following skills:

- Curtain Wall Styles
- Doors
- Style Manager
- Merge Cells
- Override Cell Assignment

1. Open Construct:
   Ground Floor Plan.dwg

2. Go to the Home ribbon.

   Launch the **Content Browser**.

3. Locate the **Hinged – Double Full Lite** door.

4. Right click and select **Insert into Drawing**.

   Click **ESC** to exit the command.

7-31

5. Go to the Manage ribbon.

   Open the **Style Manager**.

6. Locate the **Hinged – Double – Full Lite** door.

   Create a copy.
   Paste into the Door Styles.

7. Change the Name to:
   Hinged - Double - Full Lite Curtain Wall.

   Modify the Description.

   Description: Double full glass door used in Curtain Wall

8. Open the Dimensions tab.

   Change the Glass Thickness to **3/4"**.

   Exterior doors use thicker glass.

   Frame:
   - A - Width: 2"
   - B - Depth: 5"
   - Auto-Adjust to Width of Wall ✓

   Stop:
   - C - Width: 3/4"
   - D - Depth: 2"

   E - Door Thickness: 1 3/4"
   Glass Thickness: 3/4"

9. Open the Standard Sizes tab.

   Add two standard sizes:
   - 5' x 6'-8"
   - 6' x 6'-8"

10. 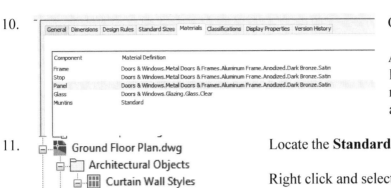 Open the Materials tab.

    Assign the Dark Bronze,Satin Aluminum material to the frame, stop, and panel.

11. Locate the **Standard** Curtain Wall Style.

    Right click and select **Copy**.
    Right click and select **Paste**.

12. Rename the copied style to **Tahoe Cabin**.

13. Open the Design Rules tab.

    Set the Primary Grid to a **Vertical Division**.
    Set the Division Type to **Fixed Cell Dimension**.
    Set the Cell Dimension to **3'-0"**.
    Enable **Auto-Adjust.**
    Set the Cell Adjustment to **Shrink.**

14. 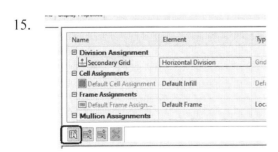 Highlight Divisions.
    Highlight Horizontal Division.
    Set the Division Type to **Fixed Cell Dimension**.
    Set the Cell Dimension to **6'-8"**.
    Enable **Auto-Adjust.**
    Set the Cell Adjustment to **Shrink.**

15. Highlight the **Secondary Grid**.
    Set the Secondary Grid to a **Horizontal Division**.

    Click **New** Cell Assignment.

16.   Name the new Cell Assignment **Bottom Row**.
    Set the Element to **Clear Glass.**
    Set the Location to **Bottom**.
    Set the Default Cell Assignment to **Clear Glass**.
    Set the Frame Location to **Left, Right, Top, Bottom**.

17.   Scroll down and set the Default Mullion Assignment to use the **Round Nose** profile.

    Enable **Use Profile**.
    Select **Round Nose** from the drop-down list.
    Set the Width to 1 ¼"
    Set the Depth to 1 ¼".

18.   Use the Preview Window to inspect the design.

19.   Highlight Infills.

    Click **New**.

Curtain Walls

20. Name the new infill: **Curtain Wall Double Door.**
Set Infill Type to **Style.**
Highlight the Hinged **Double – Full Light Curtain Wall** door style.
Set Alignment to **Center.**
Click **Apply.**

21. Open the Materials tab.

Assign the **Aluminum Frame** material to the Frame and Mullion.

Click **Apply** and **OK**.

22. Switch to an isometric view.

Select the two curtain walls.

Assign the **Tahoe Cabin** style to the curtain walls.

23. Select the right curtain wall.
Right click and select **Infill→Show Markers**.

24. Select the curtain wall.
Right click and select **Infill→Merge**.

25. Select the second cell from the right on the bottom row when prompted for Cell A.

Select the third cell from the right on the bottom row when prompted for Cell B.

The two cells are combined or merged.

26. Select the curtain wall.
Right click and select **Infill→Override Assignment.**

27. Select the merged cell to be replaced.
Click **ENTER.**
Select the **Curtain Wall Double Door** from the drop-down list.

Enable **Bottom** to remove the frame from the bottom of the door.
Click **OK.**

A door replaced the cell.

28. Select the curtain wall.
Right click and select **Infill→Hide Markers**.

29. Switch to a Realistic display.

30. Switch to a Top view and select the curtain wall door to verify that it is oriented correctly.

Close and save the file.

Extra:

Open the Brown Medical Clinic project. *Remember to work in the Metric version of ACA!*

Modify the 01 Core construct so there is a curtain wall in the lobby area.

Create a curtain wall door style.
Create a curtain wall style for the medical clinic.
Modify the curtain wall to add a door.

QUIZ 7

True or False

1. Curtain walls, curtain wall units and door/window assemblies all use the same type of dialog to define their styles.
2. There must be a slab to host the curtain wall.
3. Curtain walls can only be rectangular.
4. You can convert a 2D Layout Grid to a Curtain Wall.
5. Curtain walls must have a frame around all the edges or the pieces will fall out.

Multiple Choice

6. To place a door in a curtain wall:

    A. Select an infill panel, right click and select Override Assignment
    B. Create an infill panel that uses a door
    C. Use the DOORADD tool
    D. Create a curtain wall style with a nested grid and assign a door to one of the cells

7. To create a profile, the shape must be:

    A. 2D
    B. A closed polyline
    C. 3D
    D. A shape

8. In order to assign materials to the components of a curtain wall:

    A. The materials should already be loaded into the active document
    B. The materials can be created "on the fly"
    C. Copy and paste the materials from one drawing to another
    D. Place the curtain wall on the correct layer

9. Location refers to:

    A. The placement of the curtain wall
    B. The placement of the curtain wall frame
    C. The placement of the nested grid
    D. The placement of the Primary Grid

10. Which of the following is NOT a Division Type:

    A. Fixed Cell Dimension
    B. Fixed Number of Cells
    C. Vertical
    D. Manual

11. Curtain wall infills can be: (pick two)

    A. Nested Grids
    B. Simple Panels
    C. Frames
    D. Mullions

12. To merge two cells in a curtain wall:

    A. Select the curtain wall, right click and select Infill→Show Markers.
    B. Select the curtain wall, right click and select Infill→Merge.
    C. Select the curtain wall, right click and select Infill→Override Assignment.
    D. Modify the curtain wall style in the Style Manager.

ANSWERS:

1) T; 2) F; 3) F; 4) T; 5) F; 6) A; 7) B; 8) A; 9) B; 10) C; 11) A & B 12) B

Lesson 8:
Views, Schedules, and Legends

Before we can create our construction drawings, we need to create layouts or views to present the design. AutoCAD Architecture is similar to AutoCAD in that the user can work in Model and Paper Space. Model Space is where we create the 3D model of our house. Paper Space is where we create or set up various views that can be used in our construction drawings. In each view, we can control what we see by turning off layers, zooming, panning, etc.

To understand paper space and model space, imagine a cardboard box. Inside the cardboard box is Model Space. This is where your 3D model is located. On each side of the cardboard box, tear out a small rectangular window. The windows are your viewports. You can look through the viewports to see your model. To reach inside the window so you can move your model around or modify it, you double-click inside the viewport. If your hand is not reaching through any of the windows and you are just looking from the outside, then you are in Paper Space or Layout mode.

You can create an elevation in your current drawing by first drawing an elevation line and mark, and then creating a 2D or 3D elevation based on that line. You can control the size and shape of the elevation that is generated. Unless you explode the elevation that you create, the elevation remains linked to the building model that you used to create it. Because of this link between the elevation and the building model, any changes to the building model can be made in the elevation as well.

When you create a 2D elevation, the elevation is created with hidden and overlapping lines removed. You can edit the 2D elevation that you created by changing its display properties. The 2D Section/Elevation style allows you to add your own display components to the display representation of the elevation and create rules that assign different parts of the elevation to different display components. You can control the visibility, layer, color, linetype, lineweight, and linetype scale of each component. You can also use the line work editing commands to assign individual lines in your 2D elevation to display components and merge geometry into your 2D elevation.

After you create a 2D elevation, you can use the AutoCAD BHATCH and AutoCAD DIMLINEAR commands to hatch and dimension the 2D elevation.

AutoCAD Architecture comes with standard title block templates. They are located in the Templates subdirectory under *Program Data \ Autodesk\ ACA 2026 \enu \Template*.

Many companies will place their templates on the network so all users can access the same templates. In order to make this work properly, set the Options so that the templates folder is pointed to the correct path.

You use the Project Navigator to create additional drawing files with the desired views for your model. The views are created on the Views tab of the Project Navigator. You then create a sheet set which gathers together all the necessary drawing files that are pertinent to your project.

Previously, you would use external references, which would be external drawing files that would be linked to a master drawing. You would then create several layout sheets in your master drawing that would show the various views. Some users placed all their data in a single drawing and then used layers to organize the data.

This shift in the way of organizing your drawings will mean that you need to have a better understanding of how to manage all the drawings. It also means you can leverage the drawings so you can reuse the same drawing in more than one sheet set.

You can create five different types of views using the Project Navigator:

- Model Space View – a portion that is displayed in its own viewport. This view can have a distinct name, display configuration, description, layer snapshot and drawing scale.
- Detail View – displays a small section of the model, i.e. a wall section, plumbing, or foundation. This type of view is usually associated with a callout. It can be placed in your current active drawing or in a new drawing.
- Section View – displays a building section, usually an interior view. This type of view is usually associated with a callout. It can be placed in your current active drawing or in a new drawing.
- Elevation View – displays a building elevation, usually an exterior view. This type of view is usually associated with a callout. It can be placed in your current active drawing or in a new drawing.
- Sheet View – this type of view is created when a model space view is dropped onto a layout sheet.

Note: Some classes have difficulty using the Project Navigator because they do not use the same workstation each class or the drawings are stored on a network server. In those cases, the links can be lost and the students get frustrated trying to get the correct results.

I have created an archive file at the end of each lesson to help students keep up. Simply select the zipped archive file for the previous lesson you will be doing, extract it, redefine the paths to the different external references and go from there.

When creating elevation and section views as new drawings to be added as views to the Project Navigator, several of the views were not generated correctly. This is a bug in the software and not user error. If this happens to you, add the view in the current drawing and then use WBLOCK to create the external view drawing, then add it to the Project Navigator as a view.

Views, Schedules and Legends

As we start building our layout sheets and views, we will be adding schedule tags to identify different building elements.

Schedule tags can be project-based or standard tags. Schedule tags are linked to a property in a property set. When you anchor or tag a building element, the value of the property displays in the tag. The value displayed depends on which property is defined by the attribute used by the schedule tag. ACA comes with several pre-defined schedule tags, but you will probably want to create your own custom tags to display the desired property data.

Property sets are specified using property set definitions. A property set definition is a documentation object that is tracked with an object or object style. Each property has a name, description, data type, data format, and default value.

To access the property sets, open the Style Manager. Highlight the building element you wish to define and then select the Property Sets button. You can add custom property sets in addition to using the default property sets included in each element style.

To determine what properties are available for your schedules, select the element to be included in the schedule, right click and select Properties.

Tags and schedules use project information. If you do not have a current project defined, you may see some error messages when you tag elements.

A Property Set Definition defines the bits of data that we want to be able to show in a schedule. In the schedule table style definition, these properties can become columns. When the properties are attached to an object, the schedule table that is based on that schedule table style will display those bits of data.

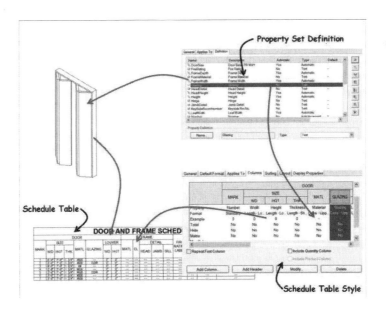

Elevation Views

Elevations of the building models are created by using the Elevation tool on the Annotate ribbon. You first draw an elevation line and mark to indicate the direction of the elevation, selecting the scope/depth of the view, and then placing a 2D or 3D elevation based on the elevation line. You can control the size and shape of any elevation that you create. If you modify the building model, you can update the elevation view so it shows the changes. 2D elevations are created with hidden and overlapping lines removed. You can control the display of 2D elevations by modifying or creating elevation styles and modifying the display properties of the 2D elevation.

We can also create live 3D sections to see the model interiors.

Exercise 8-1:
Creating a 3D Section View

Drawing Name: 3D Model-Master.dwg
Estimated Time: 15 minutes

This exercise reinforces the following skills:

- ❑ Creating an Elevation View
- ❑ Enable and Disable Live Section
- ❑ Project Navigator

1.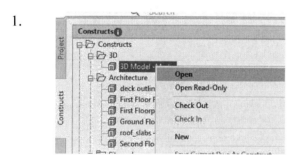

   The Tahoe Cabin project should be current.

   Open *3D Model-Master.dwg*.

Views, Schedules and Legends

2. 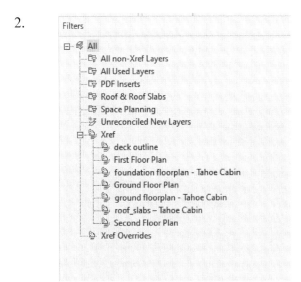 Launch the Layer Properties Manager.

Expand the Xref category.

You will see a list of all the Xrefs in the drawing.

3. 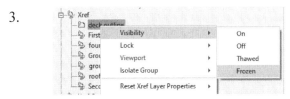 Highlight **deck outline**.
Right click and select
Visibility→Frozen.

Repeat for **foundation floorplan** and **Ground Floor Plan.**

The only thawed xref should be First Floor Plan, Second Floor Plan, and roof slabs.

4. Click **Layer States Manager**.

5. Click **New**.

6.

Enter a new layer state name and description.

Click **OK.**

Click **Close.**

7. Switch to a Top|2D Wireframe view.

Zoom into the 3D model.

8-5

8. Go to the Home Ribbon.

   Select the **Elevation Line** tool.

9. Place the elevation marker to the left of the stairs and orient towards the stairs.

   Click to the right of the building model.

10. Click a place in the drawing to place the elevation.

    A 2D elevation is created.

    The elevation shows the first floor, the second floor, and the roof.

Views, Schedules and Legends

11. Type **WBLOCK**.

Select a point on the elevation view to be used as the insertion point.
Window around the entire elevation view.
Enable **Delete from drawing.**
Browse to the folder where you want to save the drawing.
Name the drawing *First Floor Stairs.dwg.*

Click **OK**.

12. Select the section line.

13. Click **Enable Live Section** on the ribbon.

14. Switch to a **SW Isometric|Hidden** view.

8-7

15. You see a 3D view of the interior stairs.

16.

    -][Top][2D Wireframe]

    Return to a Top|2D Wireframe view.

    Select the elevation line.

    Select **Disable Live Section**.

17. Open the *First Floor Stairs.dwg*.

    This is the block drawing created earlier.

18. Set the Scale to **1' = 1'-0"**.

Views, Schedules and Legends

19. Go to the Insert ribbon.

Select **Insert→Blocks from Libraries**.

20. 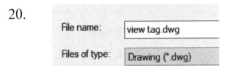 Locate the *view tag.dwg*.

This is a downloaded file from the publisher.

Click **Open**.

21. Enable **Insertion Point.**

22. Right click on the drawing name and select **Insert**.

Click to place below the view.

23. Type in the drawing view scale: **1'-0" = 1'-0"**.
Type the View Title: **First Floor Stairs.**
Type a View Number: **1**.

Click **OK**.

The view label is placed.

8-9

24.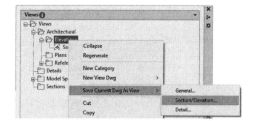

    Go to the Project Navigator.

    Select the Views tab.

    Right click on the **Elevations** category and select **Save Current Dwg As View→Section/Elevation**.

25.

    Click **Next**.

26.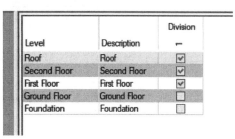

    Enable the **First Floor**.
    Enable the **Second Floor**.
    Enable **Roof**.

    Click **Next**.

    Click **Finish**.

27.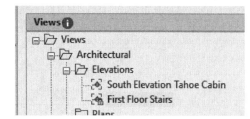

    A view of the stairs is created.

    Save and close all the drawings.

Views, Schedules and Legends

Exercise 8-2:
Creating a Detail View

Drawing Name: column detail.dwg
Estimated Time: 5 minutes

This exercise reinforces the following skills:

- Creating a DetailView
- Project Navigator

1.

   The current project should be the Tahoe Cabin.

   Open *column detail.dwg*.

   This is in the downloaded exercises.

2.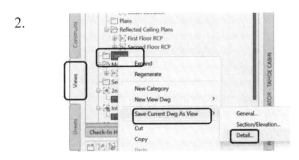

   Go to the Project Navigator.
   Open the Views tab.
   Highlight **Details**.
   Right click and select **Save Current Dwg As View→Detail**.

3.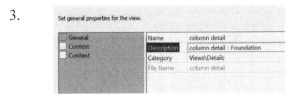

   Type **column detail** for the Name.
   Type **column detail – Foundation** for the description.
   Click **Next**.

4.

   This is a detail view, so do not select any of the levels.

   Click **Next**.

8-11

5. 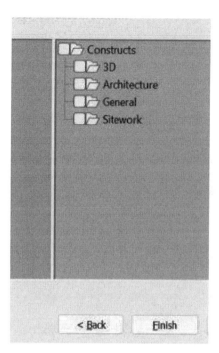 Do not select any of the constructs.

   Click **Finish**.

6. 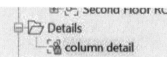 The view is now listed under the Details category.

   Save and close all drawings.

Wall Sections

Most building documents include section cuts for each wall style used in the building model. The section cut shows the walls from the roof down through the foundation. Imagine if you could cut through a house like a cake and take a look at a cross section of the layers, that's what a wall section is. It shows the structure of the wall with specific indication of materials and measurements. It doesn't show every wall, it is just a general guide for the builder and the county planning office, so they understand how the structure is designed.

If you define the components for each wall style with the proper assigned materials, you can detail the walls in your model easily.

Exercise 8-3:
Creating a Wall Section

Drawing Name: First Floor Plan.dwg
Estimated Time: 30 minutes

This exercise reinforces the following skills:

- Wall Section
- Views

1. 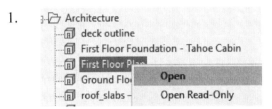 *The current project should be the Tahoe Cabin.*

   Open **First Floor Plan** from the Constructs tab on the Project Navigator.

2. Activate the **Annotate** ribbon.

   Turn **ORTHO** ON.
   Select the **Section (Sheet Tail)** tool.

3. Draw the section through the north wall.

   Select a point below the wall.
   Select a point above the wall.
   Right click and select ENTER.
   Left click to the right of the section line to indicate the section depth.

   If the block is small, check the properties and verify that the scale is set to 1.

8-13

4. Type Exterior Wall Section in the View Name field.

   Enable Generate Section/Elevation.

   Enable Place Title mark.
   Set the Scale to 1/8" = 1'-0".

   Click **New View Drawing**.

5.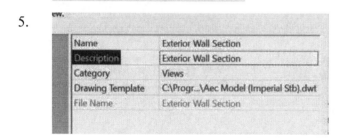

   Type **Exterior Wall Section** for the Name.
   Type **Exterior Wall Section** for the description.
   Click **Next**.

6. Enable **First Floor**.

   Click **Next**.

7. Enable **First Floorplan**.

   Click **Finish**.

   Click outside the building model to create the view.

Views, Schedules and Legends

8.

   Go to the Project Navigator.

   Open the Views tab.

   Drag the **Exterior Wall Section** to the Sections category.

9. Click **Repath project now.**

10.

    Highlight the **Exterior Wall Section**.
    Right click and select **Open.**

11. Double click on the view title for the wall section to bring up the attribute editor.

    Type **1/8" = 1'-0"** for the SCALE.

    The title is already filled in.

    Click ESC to release and update.

12.

    Select the View title bubble.

    Type **S1.1** for the NUMBER.
    Click **OK**.

    Click **ESC** to release and update.

13. If you go to the Style Manager for the drawing and check the wall style, you can verify the components used in the wall.

14. Open the Annotate ribbon.

    Select **Reference Keynote (Straight).**

    There will be a pause while ACA launches the keynote database.

15. Select the exterior side of the wall.

16. Type **timber** in the search field.

    Click **Filter.**

17. Highlight the 12x12 keynote.

    Click **OK**.

18. Select the exterior of the wall.

    Click to place the keynote.

    Click **ENTER**.

    The keynote is placed.

Views, Schedules and Legends

19. Select **Reference Keynote (Straight)** from the ribbon.

20.

    Select the top of the wall section.

    Search for **air**.

    Select the **07 26 00.A5** keynote.

    Click **OK**.

21.

    Click to select the top of the wall.

    Click **ENTER**.

    The second keynote is placed.

22. Select **Reference Keynote (Straight)** from the ribbon.

23.

    Select the top of the wall section.

    Search for **insulation**.

    Select the **07 21 00.B3** keynote.

    Click **OK**.

8-17

24. Click to select the top of the wall.

    Click **ENTER.**

    The keynote is placed.

25. Select **Reference Keynote (Straight)** from the ribbon.

26. 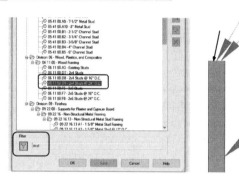 Select the top of the wall.

    Search for **stud**.

    Select the **06 11 00.D9** keynote.

    Click **OK.**

27. Click to select the top of the wall.

    Click **ENTER.**

    The keynote is placed.

28. Select **Reference Keynote (Straight)** from the ribbon.

Views, Schedules and Legends

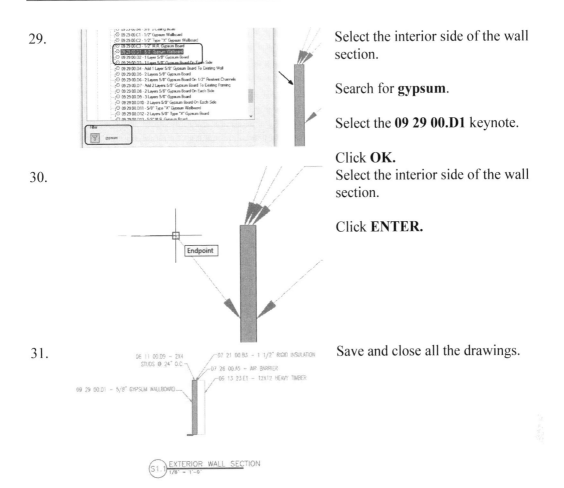

29. Select the interior side of the wall section.

    Search for **gypsum**.

    Select the **09 29 00.D1** keynote.

    Click **OK**.

30. Select the interior side of the wall section.

    Click **ENTER**.

31. Save and close all the drawings.

EXTRA: Create a section view for the interior wall.

EXTRA: If you created a section view of the interior wall, add keynotes to that section view.

Exercise 8-4:
Add Keynote Legend

Drawing Name: Exterior Wall Section.dwg
Estimated Time: 15 minutes

This exercise reinforces the following skills:

- Keynote Legend
- Keynote display
- View Manager

1. *You are working in the Tahoe Cabin project.*

   Open *the Exterior Wall Section.dwg.*

2. 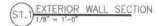 Activate the Model layout tab.

Notice the keynote numbers and text.

3. Switch to the Annotate ribbon.

   Locate the **Reference Keynote Display** tool and select it.

Views, Schedules and Legends

4.

    Enable **Reference Keynote – Key only**.

    Enable **Uppercase**.

    Click **OK**.

    The keynotes update to display keys only.

5.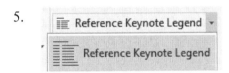

    Select the **Reference Keynote Legend** tool from the Keynotes panel on the Annotate tab.

6.

    You will be prompted for the keynotes to be included in the legend.

    Window around to select all the keynotes.

    Click ENTER to complete the selection.

8-21

7. 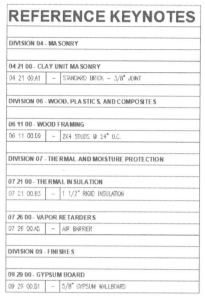 Click to place the keynote legend.

   There will be a slight pause before the legend is placed while ACA compiles the data.

8. Switch to the View ribbon.

   Launch the **View Manager**.

9. Click **New**.

10. Type **Exterior Wall Keynotes Legend**.

    Enable **Define Window**.

    Click the window icon.

    Window around the keynotes legend.

    Click **ENTER**.

    Click **OK**.

11.

    The new named view is listed.

    You can see a preview in the preview window.

12. Look in the Project Navigator.

    The two named views are listed under the drawing.

13. Save the drawing and close.

Extra: *Create a keynotes legend in the interior wall section drawing. Create a named view for the legend.*

Section Views

Section views show a view of a structure or building as though it has been sliced in half or along an imaginary plane. This is useful because it gives a view through spaces and can reveal the relationships between different parts of the building which may not be apparent on the plan views. Plan views are also a type of section view, but they cut through the building on a horizontal plane instead of a vertical plane.

Exercise 8-5:
Create a Section View

Drawing Name: First Floor Plan.dwg
Estimated Time: 20 minutes

This exercise reinforces the following skills:

- Sections
- Elevations
- WBLOCK
- View Manager
- Layers
- Layer States

1. 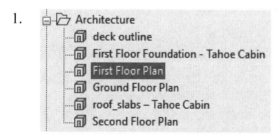 *The Tahoe Cabin is the current project.*

   In the Project Navigator:
   Open the Constructs tab.
   Highlight *First Floor Plan.dwg*.
   Right click and select **Open**.

2. Open the Layer Manager.

   Thaw the furniture, appliance, countertops, casework, etc. layers.

Views, Schedules and Legends

You should see all the furniture and kitchen equipment.

3. Launch the **Layer States Manager**.

4. Click **New**.

5. Name the Layer State **Space Planning.**

   Enter a description, if desired.

   Click **OK**.

6. Click **Close**.
   Close the Layer Manager.

7. You should see two saved layer states in the layer states drop-down list.

   Model Only shows only the walls, windows, and doors.

   Space Planning shows the furniture, casework, etc.

8. 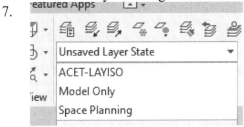 Open the Annotate ribbon.

   Set the Display to **Top|Hidden**.
   Turn **ORTHO** ON.

   Select the **Section (Sheet Tail)** tool on the Callouts panel.

8-25

9. Draw a horizontal line through the kitchen as shown.

   Click **ENTER**.

10. Select a point outside the building and above the kitchen area to define the view extents.

11. Name the View **Kitchen Elevation – North Wall**.
    Enable **Generate Section/Elevation**.
    Enable **Place Titlemark**.
    Set the Scale to **1/2″ = 1′-0″**.

    Click **Current Drawing**.

    Place the view in the current drawing to the left of the building.

    The view is created.
    It doesn't look correct.

    Select the view.

12. Select **Regenerate** on the ribbon.

Views, Schedules and Legends

13.

Highlight **Model High Detail**.

Enable **Replace Existing.**

Click **OK**.

14.

The view will regenerate.

Click ESC to release the selection.

You can use the elevation view to adjust the window size and position. Go back to the plan view and select the window. Go to the window properties to change the window size. Use GRIPS to adjust the window location.

15.

Double click on the View Number.

Change to **S1.3**.

Click **OK**.

16.

Double click on the View Title.
Change to **Kitchen- North Wall**.
Change the Scale to: **Scale: 1/2" = 1'-0"**.
Click **OK**.

17.

Switch to the View ribbon.

Launch the **View Manager**.

8-27

18. *The Kitchen Elevation view is listed.*

    Click **OK**.

19. Type **WBLOCK** to create a new view drawing.

20.

    Select the lower left point of the view as the base point.
    Window around the view to select it, include the view title.
    Name the file **S1.3 – Kitchen North Wall**.
    Click Save.
    Click OK.

21. Save and Close the First Floor Plan file.
22. Open the file *S1.3 Kitchen North Wall.dwg*
23.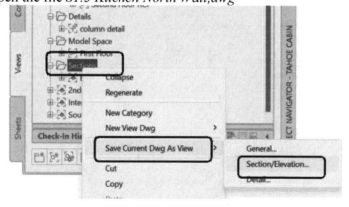

    In the Project Navigator:
    Highlight the **Sections** category on the Views tab.
    Select **Save Current Dwg As View→Section/Elevation**.

24. Click **Next**.

Name	S1.3 – Kitchen North Wall.
Description	S1.3 – Kitchen North Wall.
Category	Views\Sections
File Name	S1.3 – Kitchen North Wall.

Views, Schedules and Legends

25. Do not select any of the levels.

    Click **Next**.

26. Click **Finish**.

27. Save and close all open files.

To create an elevation view with different visual styles, create a camera view.

Exercise 8-6:
Add a Door Elevation

Drawing Name: First Floor Plan.dwg
Estimated Time: 15 minutes

This exercise reinforces the following skills:

- Elevations
- View Titles
- View Manager
- Named Views

1. *The Tahoe Cabin project is active.*

   Open the Project Navigator.

   Select the **Constructs** tab.

   Highlight **First Floor Plan.**

   Right click and select **Open**.

2. 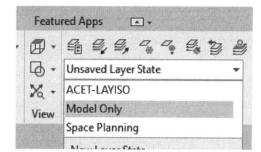 Restore the **Model Only** layer state.

3. Zoom into the laundry room area.

   We will create an elevation for the interior door frame.

4. 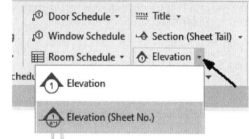 Activate the Annotate ribbon.

   Select the **Elevation (Sheet No)** tool.

5. Left click to the left of the door to place the elevation marker.

   Orient the marker so it is pointing toward the door.

Views, Schedules and Legends

6. Name the view **Single Interior Door**.
Enable **Generate Section/Elevation**.
Enable **Place Titlemark**.
Set the Scale to **1/2" = 1'-0"**.

Click **New View Drawing**.

7. 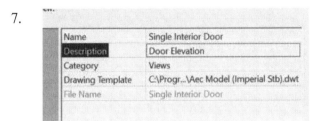 Type **Single Interior Door** for the Name.
Type **Door Elevation** for the Description.

Click **Next**.

8. 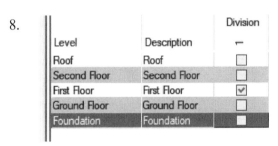 Enable **First Floor**.

Click **Next**.

9. Enable **First Floor Plan**.

Click **Finish.**

10.

Draw a rectangle around the door to define the scope of the elevation.

Left click in the drawing to generate the elevation view.

11.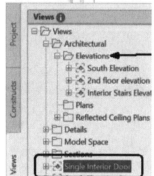

Open the Project Navigator.
Open the **Views** tab.
Locate the **Single Interior Door** Elevation.

Move the view into the Elevations category.

Click **Repath the Project Now**.

12.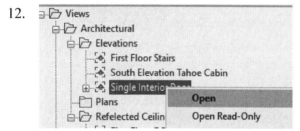

Highlight the **Single Interior Door** Elevation.
Right click and select **Open**.

13.

Open the View ribbon.
Select the **Single Interior Door** named view to zoom into the viewer.

Views, Schedules and Legends

14. The view updates.

15. 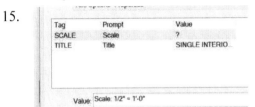 Double click on the title attribute.

Change the Scale to ½" = 1'-0".

Click **OK.**

16. 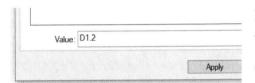 Double click on the view number attribute.

Change the View Number to **D1.2**.

This is what the view should look like.

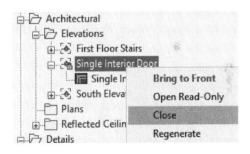

Highlight the open drawing in the Project Navigator.
Right click and select **Close.**
When prompted to save, click **Yes.**
Save and close all the open drawings.

8-33

Callouts

Callouts are typically used to reference drawing details. For example, builders will often reference a door or window call-out which provides information on how to frame and install the door or window. Most architectural firms have a detail library they use to create these callouts as they are the same across building projects.

Exercise 8-7:
Add a Callout

Drawing Name: Single Interior Door.dwg
Estimated Time: 30 minutes

This exercise reinforces the following skills:

- Callouts
- Viewports
- Detail Elements
- Layouts
- Hatching

1. 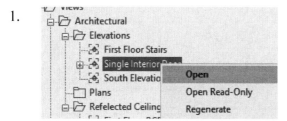 *The Tahoe Cabin is the current project.*

   Open the Project Navigator.

   Select the Views tab.

   Highlight **Single Interior Door**.

   Right click and select **Open**.

2. Open the View ribbon.
   Select the **Single Interior Door** named view to zoom to the view.

Views, Schedules and Legends

3. Activate the Annotate ribbon.

   Turn ORTHO **ON**.

   Locate and select the **Detail Boundary (Rectangle)** tool on the Detail drop-down list on the Callouts panel.

4. Draw a small rectangle to designate the callout location around the top of the door.

   Hint: Turn off OSNAPs to make it easier to place the rectangle.

   Select the midpoint of the left side of the rectangle for the start point leader line.
   Left click to the side of the callout to place the label.

   Click **ENTER** or right click to accept.

5. Type **Head Detail – Interior Door** in the View Name field.

   Enable **Generate Section/Elevation**.

   Enable **Place Titlemark**.

   Set the Scale to **1″ = 1′-0″**.

   Click on the **Current Drawing** button.

6. Place the view to the right of the elevation.

7. Select the View title bubble.

   Type **HD1** for the NUMBER.

   Click **OK.**

8-35

8. 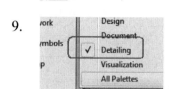 Launch the **Design Tools** from the Home ribbon.

9. 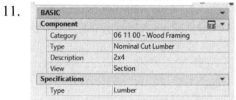 Right click on the Tool palette's bar.

   Enable the **Detailing** palette.

10. Select the **06- Woods, Plastics % Composites** detail tool on the Basic tab.

11. Select 2x4 from the Description list on the Properties palette.

12. Right click and select Rotate to rotate the detail.

13. Place the stud in the upper door frame location.

14. Select the stud detail.

    Right click and select Properties.
    Change the X scale to **1.3**.
    Change the Y scale to **3.5**.

    The stud size will adjust to fit the frame.

    To get those values, I took the desired dimension 12" and divided it by the current dimension 3.5 to get 3.5. I took the desired dimension of 2.0 and divided it by the current dimension of 1.5 to get 1.3. To determine the dimensions, simply measure the current length and width and the desired length and width.

15. Copy and place the stud to the other side of the door.

16. Activate the Home ribbon.
    Create a layer called A-Detl-Wide.
    Assign it the color BLUE and linetype CONTINUOUS.

17. 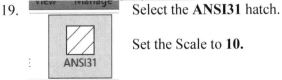 Set the layer **A-Detl-Wide** current.
    Draw a rectangle in the header area.

18. Select the **Hatch** tool.

19. Select the **ANSI31** hatch.

    Set the Scale to **10.**

20. Place a hatch inside the rectangle.

21. Select **Close Hatch Creation** on the ribbon.

22. Activate the Annotate ribbon.

    Select the **Text (Straight Leader)** tool.

23. Select the left side of the stud as the start for the leader.

    Click **ENTER** when prompted to Set the text width.

24. Text should read:

    ADD RETURN ON FRAME WHERE DRYWALL FINISH IS REQUIRED

25. Select the text.
    Right click and select **Add Leader**.

26. Add a second leader to the other side of the door frame.

    Click **ESC** to release the selection.

27. Hover over the leader that was just placed.

    Notice that it is on the **G-Anno-Note** layer. *This layer was created automatically when you placed the leader.*

28. Select the Linear Dimension tool on the Annotate ribbon.

29. Place a dimension in the opening.

    Your dimension might be different.

30. Select the dimension.
    Right click and select **Properties**.

    Modify the text override field to read:

    THROAT OPENING = PARTITION WIDTH + 1/8" MIN.

31. Freeze the **G-Elev** layer.

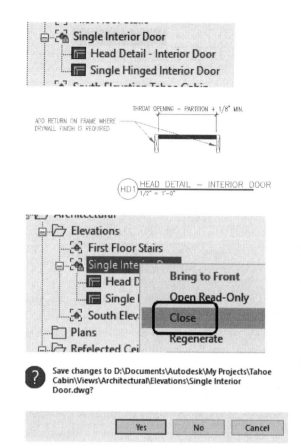

Go to the Project Navigator.
Notice that there are now two views available under the Single Interior Door.

This is what the view should look like.

Go to the Project Navigator.
Right click on the Single Interior Door view.
Select **Close**.

Click **Yes**.

Schedule Tags

Schedule tags are symbols that connect building objects with lines of data in a schedule table. Schedule tags display data about the objects to which they are attached. There are schedule tag tools with predefined properties provided with the software on the Scheduling tool palette in the Document tool palette set and in the Documentation Tool Catalog in the Content Browser. You can import schedule tags from the Content Browser to add them to your palette.

You can also create custom schedule tags to display specific property set data for objects in the building. After you create a schedule tag, you can drag it to any tool palette to create a schedule tag tool.

Exercise 8-8:
Adding Door Tags

Drawing Name: First Floor Plan.dwg
Estimated Time: 15 minutes

This exercise reinforces the following skills:

- Tags

1.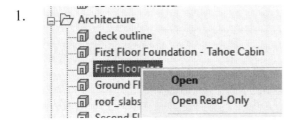

   The Tahoe Cabin is the current project.

   In the Project Navigator:
   Open the Constructs tab.
   Highlight *First Floor Plan.dwg*.
   Right click and select **Open**.

2. Add a new **Layout**.

3.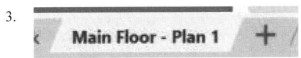

   Rename the Layout **Main Floor – Plan 1**.

4. Right click on the layout tab.

   Select **Page Setup Manager**.

5. Click **New**.

6. Type **ARCH B PDF** for the new page setup name.

   Click **OK**.

7. Set the Printer to **Adobe PDF**.
   Set the Paper Size to **ARCH B**.
   Set the Scale to **1'-0" = 1'-.0"**.
   Click **OK**.

Views, Schedules and Legends

8.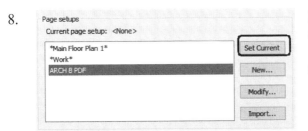
   Highlight **ARCH B PDF**.
   Click **Set Current**.

   Click **Close.**

9.
   Create a new layer called **Viewport**.
   Set the layer to use the color **Cyan**.
   Set it to **NO PLOT**.

10.
    Open the Main Floor Plan 1 layout.

    Place the viewport on the viewport layer.
    Resize the viewport to fit the sheet.
    Set the Scale to 1'-0" = 1'-0".
    Set the Annotation Scale to 1'-0" = 1'-0".
    Set the Visual Style to **2D Wireframe.**
    Adjust the view inside the viewport so that you see the entire floor plan.
    Lock the display so that the floor plan doesn't move around.

    Release the viewport.

11. Double click inside the viewport to activate model space.
12. Activate the Annotate ribbon.
    Select the **Door Tag** tool.

13.
14.
    Select a door.

    Click ENTER to center the tag on the door.

8-43

15. Click **OK**.

Some students may be concerned because they see the Error getting value next to the Room Number field.

If you tag the spaces with a room tag assigning a number, you will not see that error.

16. Right click and select **Multiple**.
    Window around the entire building.

    All the doors will be selected.

    Click **ENTER**.

17. Click **No**.

18. Click **OK**.

Views, Schedules and Legends

19. All the doors are tagged.

    If the door tags don't show the correct numbers, try closing the software and then re-opening it.

    If the door tags are very small, verify that they have the 1'-0" = 1'0" annotative object scale added to them.

20. Select a Door.
    Right click and Select **Properties**.

    Select the Extended Data tab.

    The Number that will appear in the door tag is shown.
    You can edit the value here.

21. 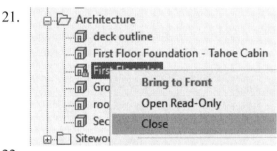 Highlight **First Floor Plan** in the Project Navigator.
    Right click and select **Close**.

22. Click **Yes**.

Extra: Tag all the windows in the building.

Create a layer for the curtain wall outline. The curtain wall resides on the Ground Floor.
Place a couple of lines or polylines to indicate the curtain wall.

Create a layer state for Model Only with Tags and update the Model Only layer state to have the tag layers frozen.

Hint: The door tags are on A-Door-Iden layer and the window tags are on A-Glaz-Iden layer.

Schedule Styles

A schedule table style specifies the properties that can be included in a table for a specific element type. The style controls the table formatting, such as text styles, columns, and headers. To use a schedule table style, it must be defined inside the building drawing file. If you copy a schedule table style from one drawing to another using the Style Manager, any data format and property set definitions are also copied.

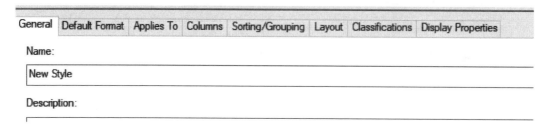

When you create a new Schedule Table Style, there are eight tabs that control the table definition.

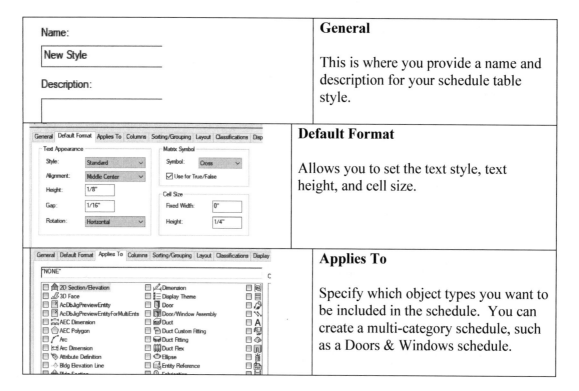

	General This is where you provide a name and description for your schedule table style.
	Default Format Allows you to set the text style, text height, and cell size.
	Applies To Specify which object types you want to be included in the schedule. You can create a multi-category schedule, such as a Doors & Windows schedule.

Views, Schedules and Legends

Columns

Select which property set definitions to be included in the schedule. You can determine the order of the columns as well as the data format and use formulas.

Sorting/Grouping

Specify the sort order or use filters to control which elements are included in the schedule. This tab also allows you to group elements and create sub-totals on counts.

Layout

Specify the title of the schedule and the text style to be applied to the title, column headers, and data cells.

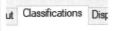

Classifications

Assign a group of named properties to different object types. They can be used to control how objects are displayed and grouped.

Display Properties

Controls the visibility and color of different components of the schedule table.

Exercise 8-9:
Create a Door Schedule

Drawing Name: First Floor Plan.dwg
Estimated Time: 15 minutes

This exercise reinforces the following skills:

- Schedules
- Named Views
- Layouts

1. 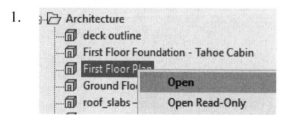 *The Tahoe Cabin is the current project.*

   In the Project Navigator:
   Open the Constructs tab.
   Highlight *First Floor Plan.dwg*.
   Right click and select **Open**.

2. Activate the **Model** layout tab.

3. Activate the Annotate ribbon.

   Select the **Door Schedule** tool.

4. Window around the building model.

   ACA will automatically filter out any non-door entities and collect only doors.

   Click **ENTER**.

5. Left click to place the schedule in the drawing window.

   Click **ENTER**.

Views, Schedules and Legends

6. *A ? will appear for any doors that are missing tags. So, if you see a ? in the list go back to the model and see which doors are missing tags.*

Once you add door tags, you need to update the schedule. Select the schedule, right click and select Update Schedule Table.

7.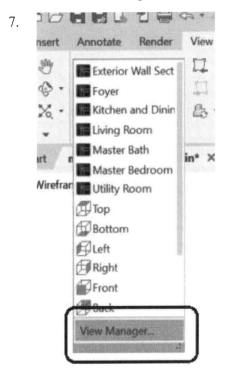

   Go to the View ribbon.

   Launch the **View Manager**.

8.

   Select **New**.

9. Name the view **Door Schedule 1**.
Click **Define Window** and window around the door schedule.

Click **OK**.

10. *The door schedule now is included in the list of named views.*

Click **OK**.

11. Add a new **Layout**.

12. Rename the Layout **Main Floor – Door Schedule 1**.

Open the layout.

13. Move the viewport to the Viewport layer.

14. 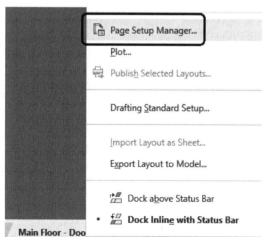 Right click on the layout.

Select **Page Setup Manager**.

15. Set **ARCH B PDF** as the Current page setup.

16. Double click inside the viewport. Restore the door schedule named view.

17. Select the viewport.
Right click and select **Properties**.

Change the Annotation scale to **6" = 1'-0"**.
Change the Standard scale to **6" = 1'-0"**.
Set the Display locked to **Yes.**

Release the selection.

18. 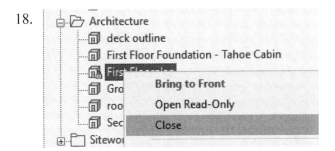 Highlight **First Floor Plan** in the Project Navigator.

Right click and select **Close**.

19. 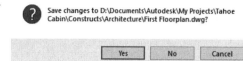 Click **Yes**.

Exercise 8-10:
Create a Door Schedule Style

Drawing Name: First Floor Plan.dwg
Estimated Time: 30 minutes

This exercise reinforces the following skills:

- Schedules
- Style Manager
- Text Styles
- Update Schedule

1. 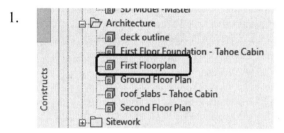 *The Tahoe Cabin is the current project.*

   In the Project Navigator:
   Open the Constructs tab.
   Highlight *First Floorplan.dwg*.
   Right click and select **Open**.

2. ![Model] Activate the **Model** layout tab.

3. Activate the View ribbon.

   Restore the **Door Schedule 1** view.

Views, Schedules and Legends

4. Select the door schedule.

   Right click and select **Copy Schedule Table Style and Assign…**.

   This will create a new style that you can modify.

5. Select the **General** tab.

   Rename **Custom Door Schedule**.

6. Select the **Columns** tab.

7. Highlight Louver, WD, and HGT.

8. Click **Delete**.

9. You will be asked to confirm the deletion.

   Click **OK**.

10. Highlight the columns under Hardware.

    Click **Delete**.

11. Click **OK**.

12. Highlight **MARK**.

    Click the **Add Column** button.

13.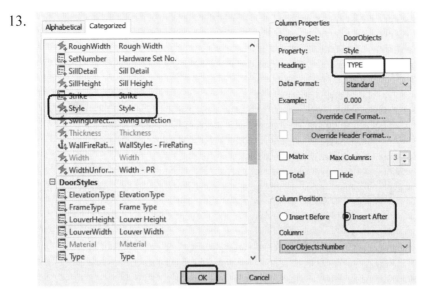

Scroll down until you see Style.

Highlight **Style**.

Confirm that the Column Position will be inserted after the DoorObjects: Number.

Change the Heading to **TYPE**.

Click **OK**.

14.

The new column is now inserted.

15. Select the Layout tab.

Change the Table Title to **DOOR SCHEDULE**.

16. Activate the Columns tab.

Highlight the **WD** column.

Select **Modify**.

8-55

17. Change the Heading to **WIDTH**.

    Click **OK**.

18. Highlight the **HGT** column.

    Select **Modify**.

19. Change the Heading to **HEIGHT**.

    Click **OK**.

20. Delete the THK column.

21. Click **OK**.

22. Click **OK** to close the dialog.

23. The schedule updates.

    If there are question marks in the schedule, that indicates doors which remain untagged.

24. 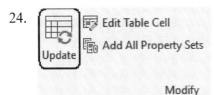 Select the schedule.
Select **Update** from the ribbon.
Click **ESC** to release the selection.

25. Activate the Home ribbon.

Select the **Text Style** tool on the Annotation panel.

26. Notice there are text styles set up for schedules.
Highlight each one to see their settings.

27. Highlight **Schedule-Data.**
Set the Font Name to **Arial Narrow**.
Enable **Annotative**.
Click **Apply**.

28. 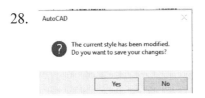 If this dialog appears, Click **Yes**.

29. Highlight Schedule-Header.
Set the Font Name to **Arial**.
Set the Font Style to **Bold**.
Enable **Annotative**.

Click **Apply**.

30. Highlight Schedule-Title.
Set the Font Name to **Arial**.
Set the Font Style to **Bold**.
Enable **Annotative**.

Click **Apply** and **Close**.

Note that the schedule automatically updates.

31. Highlight **First Floor plan** in the Project Navigator.

Right click and select **Close**.

32. Click **Yes**.

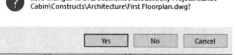

Legends

Component legends are used to display symbols that represent model components, such as doors and windows. Some architectural firms may already have tables with these symbols pre-defined. In which case, you can simply add them to your drawing as an external reference or as a block. However, if you want to generate your own legends using the components in your ACA model, you do have the tools to do that as well.

Exercise 8-11:
Create Door Symbols for a Legend

Drawing Name: First Floor Plan.dwg
Estimated Time: 20 minutes

This exercise reinforces the following skills:

- Doors
- Images
- Object Viewers

1. 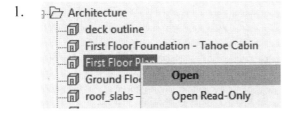 The Tahoe Cabin is the current project.

   In the Project Navigator:
   Open the Constructs tab.
   Highlight *First Floor Plan.dwg*.
   Right click and select **Open**.

2. *Before you save the door images, it will make the doors easier to see if you assign a new color to the A-Door and A-Glaz layers.*

   Launch the Layer Manager.
   Search for the **A-Door** layer. Assign a darker color.
   Search for the **A-Glaz** layer. Assign a darker color.
   Close the Layer Manager.

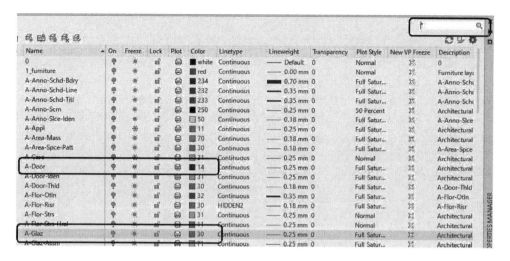

3. Type **REGEN** to see the new color assignments.
4. Select one of the windows.

   Right click and select **Edit Window Style.**

5. Open the Display Properties tab.

   We want to override the display in Plan, Plan High Detail, Plan Low Detail, and Sill Plan display representations.

6. Assign Color 130 to replace any light colored layers.

   Click **OK.**

7.   Set the Display Configuration to **Medium Detail**.

   Hover over the interior door in the laundry room.

   Note that it is a Single hinged door.

Views, Schedules and Legends

8.

    Select the interior door in the laundry room.

    Right click and select **Object Viewer**.

9. Use the arrows above the view cube to rotate the view so the door appears to be horizontal.

10.

    Set the Display to **Hidden**.
    Select the **Save** button in the upper left.

11.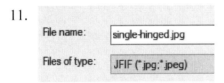

    Browse to your work folder.

    Type **single-hinged** for the file name.

    Click **Save**.
    Close the Object Viewer.

12. Hover over the closet door.

    Note that it is a Bifold Double door.

13.

    Select the closet door.

    Right click and select **Object Viewer**.

8-61

14. Use the arrows above the view cube to rotate the view so the door appears to be horizontal.

15. Set the Display to **Hidden**.

    Select the **Save** button in the upper left.

16. Browse to your work folder.

    Type **Bifold-Double** for the file name.

    Click **Save**.
    Close the Object Viewer.

17.

    Select the door and the sidelight window at the entrance.

18. 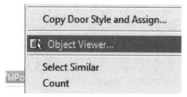 Right click and select **Object Viewer**.

19.

    The door should appear correctly.

    If not, use the arrows over the Viewcube to orient it correctly.

Views, Schedules and Legends

20. Set the Display to **Hidden**.

Select the **Save** button in the upper left.

21. Browse to your work folder.

Type **Door w Sidelight** for the file name.

Click **Save**.
Close the Object Viewer.

22. 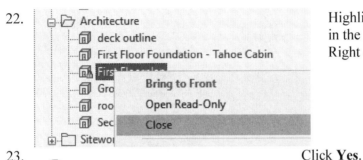 Highlight **First Floor Plan** in the Project Navigator.
Right click and select **Close**.

23. Click **Yes**.

Exercise 8-12:
Convert Images to Blocks

Drawing Name: First Floor Plan.dwg
Estimated Time: 20 minutes

This exercise reinforces the following skills:

- Images
- Blocks
- Attach

1. 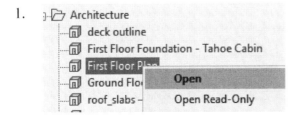 *The Tahoe Cabin is the current project.*

In the Project Navigator:
Open the Constructs tab.
Highlight *First Floor Plan*.
Right click and select **Open**.

8-63

2. Activate the Insert ribbon.

   Select **Attach**.

3. Locate the **Bifold-Double** image file.
   Click **Open**.

4. Enable **Specify Insertion point**.
   Disable **Scale**.
   Disable **Rotation**.

   Click **OK**.

5. Left click to place in the display window.
   Select **Create Block** from the Insert ribbon.

6.

   Type **bifold-double** for the Name.

   Select a corner of the image as the base point.
   Select the image.
   Enable **Delete**.
   Enable **Scale Uniformly**.
   Disable **Allow Exploding**.
   Click **OK**.

7. Select **Attach**.

8.

   Locate the **Door w Sidelight** image file.
   Click **Open**.

Views, Schedules and Legends

9.
Enable **Specify Insertion point**.
Disable **Scale**.
Disable **Rotation**.

Click **OK**.

Left click to place in the display window.

10. Select **Create Block** from the Insert ribbon.

11.
Type **Door w Sidelight** for the Name.

Select a corner of the image as the base point.
Select the image.
Enable **Delete.**
Enable **Scale Uniformly**.
Disable **Allow Exploding**.

Click **OK**.

12. Select **Attach**.

13. Locate the **single-hinged** image file.
Click **Open**.

14. Enable **Specify Insertion point**.
Disable **Scale**.
Disable **Rotation**.

Click **OK**.

Left click to place in the display window.

15. Select **Create Block** from the Insert ribbon.

8-65

16. Type **Single-Hinged** for the Name.

    Select a corner of the image as the base point.
    Select the image.
    Enable **Delete**.
    Enable **Scale Uniformly**.
    Disable **Allow Exploding**.

    Click **OK**.

17. Highlight **First Floor Plan** in the Project Navigator.

    Right click and select **Close**.

18. Click **Yes**.

Views, Schedules and Legends

Exercise 8-13:
Create a Door Legend

Drawing Name: First Floor Plan.dwg
Estimated Time: 20 minutes

This exercise reinforces the following skills:

- Legends
- Tables
- Blocks
- Text Styles
- Viewports
- Layouts

1.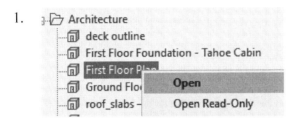

    The Tahoe Cabin is the current project.

    In the Project Navigator:

    Open the Constructs tab.

    Highlight *First Floor Plan*.
    Right click and select **Open**.

2.

    In order for the blocks to appear properly, you need to re-path all the image files.

    Bring up the XREF Manager and verify that all the images are loaded into the drawing properly.
    If not, assign the images to the correct file location.

    Close the XREF Manager.

3.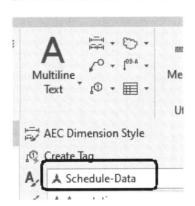

    On the Home ribbon:

    Set **Schedule-Data** as the active text style.

8-67

4. Activate the Home ribbon.

   Select the **Table** tool located in the drop-down on the Annotation panel.

5.
   Set the Columns to **2**.
   Set the Data rows to **4**.

   Click **OK**.

6. Left click to place the table next to the door schedule.

   Type **DOOR LEGEND** as the table header.

7. Highlight the second row, first cell.
   Right click and select **Insert Block**.

8. Select **bifold-double** from the drop-down list.
Enable **Auto-fit**.
Set the Overall cell alignment to **Middle Center**.
Click **OK**.

Hint: Start typing the block name and the drop-down list will take you to that name.

9. The image appears in the cell.

To turn off the IMAGEFRAME, type IMAGEFRAME, 0.

10. Type **Bifold Double** in the second cell, second row.

Change the text height to **1/4"**.

Adjust the width of the columns.

11. Highlight the third row, first cell.
Select **Insert Block** from the ribbon.

12. Select **Door w Sidelight** from the drop-down list.
Enable **Auto-fit**.
Set the Overall cell alignment to **Middle Center**.
Click **OK**.

13. The image appears in the cell.

14. Type **Door w Sidelight** in the second cell, third row.

Change the text height to **1/4"**.

15. Select the cell and set the Alignment to **Middle Center.**

16. Highlight the fourth row, first cell.
Right click and select **Insert Block**.

17. Select **Single-Hinged** from the drop-down list.
Set the Scale to **1.**
Set the Overall cell alignment to **Middle Center**.
Click **OK**.

Hint: If you start typing the block name, the list will scroll to the name.

18. The image appears in the cell.

19. 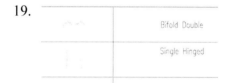 Type **Single-Hinged** in the second cell, fourth row.

Change the text height to **1/4"**.

Views, Schedules and Legends

20.

DOOR LEGEND
Bifold-Double
Single-Hinged
Door w Sidelight

Place the table on the **A-Anno-Schd-Bdry** layer.

Type IMAGEFRAME and then 0 to turn off the border around the images.

21. Go to the View ribbon.

Launch the **View Manager**.

22. Select **New**.

23. Type **Door Legend** in the View name field.
Enable **Define window**.

Window around the legend table.
Click **ENTER**.
Click **OK**.
Close the View Manager.

24. Activate the View ribbon.

Double click on the **Door Legend** view.

The display in the viewport updates with the door legend.

8-71

25. Add a viewport to the Main Floor Door Schedule 1 layout.

Place the door legend in the viewport.

Lock the viewport display.

26. 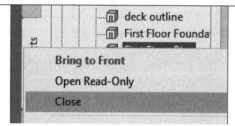 Highlight **First Floor Plan** in the Project Navigator.
Right click and select **Close**.

27.
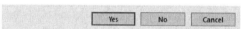 Click **Yes**.

Views, Schedules and Legends

Exercise 8-14:
Creating a Custom Imperial Multi-Leader

Drawing Name: Leader Symbols (Imperial).dwg
Estimated Time: 40 minutes

This exercise reinforces the following skills:

- Tool palette
- Multi-Leader Styles
- Content Browser
- Tool Properties
- Text Styles
- Attributes
- Block Editor

1. 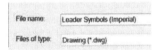 Open the *Leader Symbols (Imperial).dwg*.

   This file is available in the downloads.

2. On the Home ribbon:

   Locate the Annotation panel.

   In the drop-down, select **Manage Multileader Styles**.

8-73

3. Select **New**.

4. Type **Detail Callout** in the New style name field.

   Select **Standard** under Start with.
   Enable **Annotative.**

   Click **Continue**.

5. 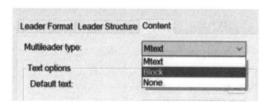 On the Leader Format tab:
   Set the Type to Straight.
   Set the Arrowhead Symbol to **Open**.
   Set the Size to **3/8"**.

6. Select the Content tab.

   Under Multileader type:

   Select **Block**.

7. Set the Source block to **Detail Callout**.

   Set the Scale to **1"**.

   Click **OK**.

8.

    The new multi-leader style is now listed.

    Click **Close**.

9. Save your drawing, but do not close it.

    This saves the style you just created.

10. Go to the Annotate ribbon.

    Launch the **Annotation Tools** palette.

11.

    Select the **Callouts** tab.

12. Go to the Home ribbon.

    Open the **Content Browser**.

13. Locate and left click to open the **Documentation Tool Catalog – Imperial**.

14. Click on the **Leaders** category.

Views, Schedules and Legends

15. 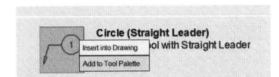 Locate the **Circle (Straight Leader)** tool.

Highlight and right click **to Add to Tool Palette**.

16. The tool should be added to the **Document/Callouts** tool palette.

Move it to a good location on the palette.

Highlight the **Circle (Straight Leader)** tool.

Right click and select **Copy.**

17. Move the cursor to a blank area on the palette.

Right click and select **Paste.**

18. Rename the copied tool **Detail Callout**.

8-77

19. Click **Settings** on the tool palette.

20. Select **View Options**.

21. Set the View Style to **Icon with text**.

    Click **OK**.

22. 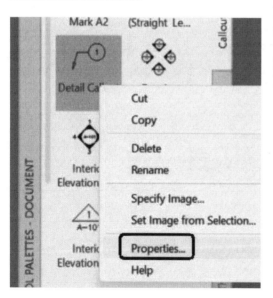 Highlight the **Detail Callout** tool.

    Right click and select **Properties**.

23. *Notice that the tool uses blocks located in the Leader Symbols (Imperial).dwg that you modified earlier.*

24. 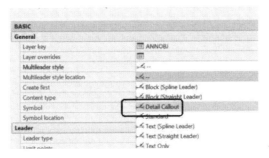 Select the **Detail Callout** style from the drop down list.

    This style will only appear if you saved the file earlier.

    If you did a SAVEAS to a new location, browse to the correct file.

25. Set the Symbol to **_DetailCallout**.

26. Set the **Attribute Style to As defined by tag**.

27. 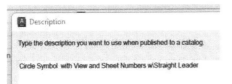 Change the Description to indicate the multileader style correctly.

    Click **OK**.

    Note that the preview icon is not correct.

28. 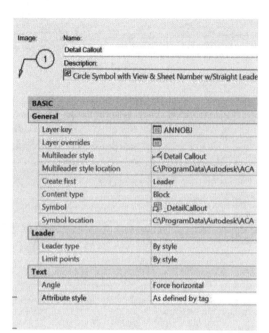 Review the Properties panel to ensure that everything looks correct.

    Click **OK** to close the Properties dialog.

29. Return to the **Leader Symbols (Imperial).dwg** file.

    Verify that you are in the **Model** space tab.

30. Click on the Detail Callout tool to place a detail callout in the drawing.

    Click to select the start and end point for the leader.

    Enter in a View Number and Sheet Number when the attribute dialog appears.

    Click **OK**.
    The multileader is placed.

    Select the multileader.
    Right click and select **Properties**.
    Set the Scale for the block to **1.0**.
    Click ESC to release the selection.

Views, Schedules and Legends

31.

Switch to the Annotate ribbon.

In the Text Style box, select the drop down and click on **Manage Text Styles**.

32.

Click **New**.

33.

Type **Comic Sans**.

Click **OK**.

If you prefer a different font, choose a different font.

34.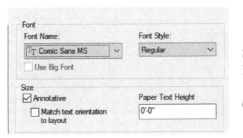

Set the Font Name to **Comic Sans MS.**

Click **Close**.

35.

Click **Yes** to save your changes.

36. Switch to the Insert ribbon.

    Click **Edit Block**.

37. Highlight the **_DetailCallout** block.

    Click **OK**.

38. Set the view scale to **1'-0":1'-0"**.

39. 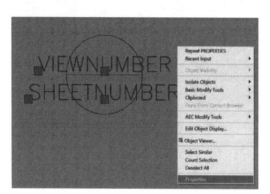 Select the two attributes. *This is the text.*

    Right click and select **Properties**.

40. 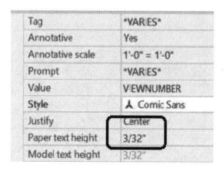 Change the Style to **Comic Sans**.

    Change the Paper text height to **3/32"**.

Views, Schedules and Legends

41.

    The attributes update.
    Adjust the position of the attributes.

    Click **Save Block** on the ribbon.

42.

    Click **Close Block Editor** on the ribbon.

    The multileader updates.

    Select the multi-leader and change the color to ByBlock using Properties.

    Click ESC to release the selection.

43.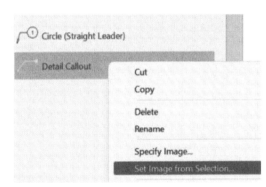

    Highlight the Detail Callout on the tool palette.

    Right click and select **Set Image from Selection**.

44.

    Select the multileader and press ENTER.

    The icon on the tool palette updates.

45. Save and close *Leader Symbols (Imperial).dwg*.

Extra: Repeat the exercise using the Leader Symbols(metric).dwg.

Exercise 8-15:
Create a Framing Plan View

Drawing Name: new
Estimated Time: 30 minutes

This exercise reinforces the following skills:

- Project Browser
- Project Navigator
- Drawing Utilities
- Insert Image
- Insert Hyperlink

1. 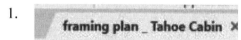 *The Tahoe Cabin is the current project.*

   Start a new drawing.
   Name it *framing plan – Tahoe Cabin.dwg*.

2. Go to the Application menu.

   Select **Drawing Utilities→Drawing Setup**.

3. Open the Display tab.

Highlight **Structural Member** in the Object Type list.
Highlight **Plan Low Detail**.
Set the Drawing Default Display Configuration to **Plan Low Detail**.
Enable **When used as an Xref Overlay, use this drawing's default display** configuration initially.

Click **OK**.

4. Open the Project Navigator.
Go to the Constructs tab.
Expand the Sitework category.

Highlight the **foundation floorplan – Tahoe Cabin**.
Right click and select **Xref Overlay**.

5. Highlight the **ground floorplan -Tahoe Cabin**.
Right click and select **Xref Overlay**.

6. Look under the Architecture category.

Highlight the **first floor foundation - Tahoe Cabin**.
Right click and select **Xref Overlay**.

7. Position the xrefs so they are overlaying each other.

8.

Name	Elevation	Description
Roof	31'-11 3/4"	Roof
Second Floor	21'-11 3/4"	Second Floor
First Floor	11'-11 3/4"	First Floor
Ground Floor	3'-11 3/4"	Ground Floor
Foundation	-4'-0"	Foundation

Open the Project tab of the Project Navigator.

Note the elevation of each level.

9. Switch to a **Front** view.

10. Open the View ribbon.

Set the Coordinates to use a Front view.

Notice that the UCS in the view flipped.

11.

Geometry	
Insertion point X	-950'-1 15/32"
Insertion point Y	3'-11 3/4"
Insertion point Z	-106'-11 7/8"
Scale X	1.00000
Scale Y	1.00000
Scale Z	1.00000

Select the **ground floorplan -Tahoe Cabin overlay**.

Hint: Use QSELECT to select the XREF by name.

Right click and select **Properties**.
Set the Insertion point Y to **3'-11 3/4"**.
Click **ESC** to release the selection.

12.

Select the **First Floor Foundation -Tahoe Cabin overlay**.
Right click and select **Properties**.
Set the Insertion point Y to **3'-11 3/4"**.
Click **ESC** to release the selection.

13.

Go to the View ribbon.

Launch the View Manager.

Save the Current View as a **Front-Elevation.**

Notice that the UCS setting is saved with the view.

Click **OK.**

14. Freeze the following layers:

- Deck outline
- Gravel outline
- Grids
- S-Grid
- S-Grid-Iden
- G-Elev
- G-Elev-Iden
- G-Elev-Line
- A-Slab

15.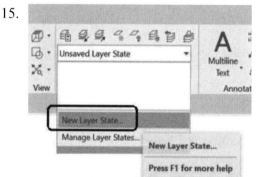

On the Home ribbon:

Select **New Layer State**.

16. Type **framing plan**.

Click **OK**.

17. Switch to a **Top|2D Wireframe** view.

18. 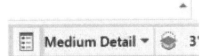 Set the Display Configuration to **Medium Detail**.

19. Open the Document tool palette.

    Select the **Callouts** tab.

    Select the **Detail Callout** tool.

20. Place the callout.
    Start the leader at the column located at the upper right of the layout.
    Change the attributes as shown.
    The View Number should be **5.**
    The sheet number should be **SD-2.1**.

21.

    Change the scale of the block to **1**.

22. Go to the View ribbon.
    Open the View Manager.

    Create a Named View called **Framing Plan**.

    Click **OK** to close.

23.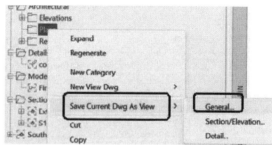

Go to the Views tab of the Project Navigator.
Highlight the Plans category.

Right click and select **Save Current Dwg As View→General**.

24.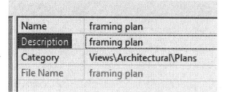

Type **framing plan** for the Name and Description.

Click **Next**.

25.

Enable **Ground Level** and **Foundation**.
Click **Next**.

26.

Disable the **3D** category.
Uncheck the Topography drawing.

Click **Finish**.

27.

The Named View is listed under the drawing.

28.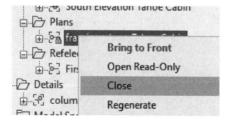

Highlight **framing plan – Tahoe Cabin** in the Project Navigator.
Right click and select **Close**.

29. Save and close all drawings.

Extra:

1) Create additional elevation and section views for the kitchen, the second bathroom, the exterior elevations, and windows.

2) Add the new views to layouts.

3) Add window tags to all the windows.

4) Create a window schedule.

5) Create a window legend.

6) Create a detail view for window framing.

7) Create a callout to the window framing detail view.

8) Create a section elevation view of an interior wall.

9) Add keynotes to the interior wall section elevation view.

Notes:

QUIZ 8

True or False

1. You can create a view drawing by selecting constructs from the Project Navigator palette and using them as external references in a View drawing.

2. A construct drawing can be used as a view drawing.

3. View drawings are usually created after you have defined the project's levels and basic construct drawings.

4. In order to create a schedule, you need to add schedule tags to the objects to be included in the schedule first.

5. Property set definitions must be attached to an object or style before they can be added to a schedule.

Multiple Choice

6. The three types of views that can be created in a project are:

    A. General
    B. Architectural
    C. Detail
    D. Section/Elevation
    E. Floor Plan
    F. Reflected Ceiling Plan

7. To display the external references for a view drawing:

    A. Highlight the view drawing in the Project Navigator, right click and click External References
    B. Open the view drawing, bring up the XREF Manager
    C. Launch the Layers Properties Manager, highlight XREFs
    D. Go to the View ribbon, click on XREFs

8. Space Styles: (select all that apply)

    A. Control the hatching displayed
    B. Control the name displayed when spaces are tagged
    C. Cannot be modified
    D. Have materials assigned

9. When placing a wall tag:

    A. Tags are positioned relative to the midpoint of a wall
    B. Tags are positioned relative to the end of a wall
    C. Tags are positioned relative to the center of a wall
    D. Tags are positioned based on user input

10. When placing a space tag:

    A. Tags are positioned based on user input
    B. Tags are hidden behind the space hatch and need to have the display order changed
    C. Tags are positioned relative to the center of the geometric extents of the space
    D. Tags are positioned above the space hatch

ANSWERS:

1) T; 2) F; 3) T; 4) F; 5) T; 6) B, C, and D; 7) A; 8) A, B; C, and D 9) A; 10) C;

Lesson 9
Rooms & Sheets

Layouts

Layouts act as the sheets for your documentation set. You name the layouts, add views to the layouts, add text and dimensions, and any other relevant annotation.

You place one or more viewports on a layout. The area outside the viewport is called *paper space*. Normally, paper space is used to add a title block and possibly notes. Views are created in model space for any schedules, elevations, plans, etc. These are then added to the layout. The viewport controls the scale and display of the model elements inside the viewport.

You can access one or more layouts from the tabs located at the bottom-left corner of the drawing area to the right of the Model tab. You can use multiple layout tabs to display details of the various components of your model at several scales and on different sheet sizes.

If the view does not generate properly for you, use the Current Drawing option, then use WBLOCK to create a new drawing using the view.

Exercise 9-1:
Creating a View Drawing

Drawing Name: new
Estimated Time: 10 minutes

This exercise reinforces the following skills:

- Project Browser
- Project Navigator
- Layers

1. Open the Revit (Metric) Application.

   You can also switch to the Metric profile using Options.

2. 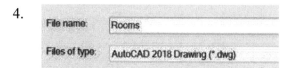 Launch the Project Browser.

    Set the **Brown Medical Clinic** as the current project.

    Close the Project Browser.

    The Project Navigator will launch.

    Ignore the Project Navigator for now.

3. Start a new drawing.

4.   Save as *Rooms.dwg*.

5.   Right click on the **01 Core** construct. Select **Xref Overlay**.

    Double click the mouse wheel to **Zoom Extents**.

6. Select the **Freeze Layer** tool on the Home ribbon.

7.

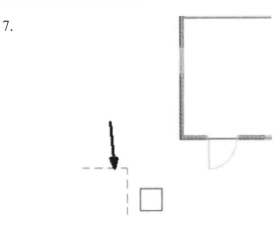

Select the grid lines indicated located at the lower left of the drawing.

8.

Set the Display Representation to **Low Detail**.
Set the Level to **Level 1:0.00**.

9.

[−][Top][Hidden (Fast)]

Set the display to **Top|Hidden**.

Go to the View ribbon.

Launch the **View Manager**.

10.

Create a Named View of the top plan view of the building.

Click **OK**.

11. Click **OK**.

12. Set the Display Configuration to **Medium Detail**.

13. 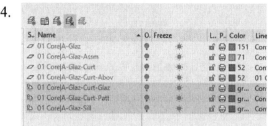 Launch the Layer Properties Manager.
Do a search for layers with the word **Door**.
Change the layer color to **Blue**.

14. Do a search for layers with the word **Glaz**.
Change the layer color to **Green**.

This changes the layer colors in the host drawing only – not in the external reference files.

15. Freeze the PDF_Images layer.

16. Freeze the Ceiling light layer.

You only need to do this if you did one of the extra exercises which had you place ceilings and lights.

Close the Layer Properties Manager.

The view should look similar to this.

A curtain wall was added as an extra exercise in Lesson 7.

17. 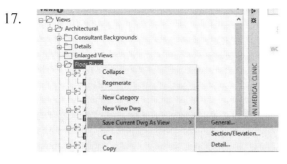 Open the Project Navigator.
Open the Views tab.

Highlight the Floor Plans category.

Right click and select **Save Current Dwg As View →General.**

18. Name the View **A-FP01-Rooms**.

Click **Next.**

19. Enable **First Floor**.

Click **Next.**

20. 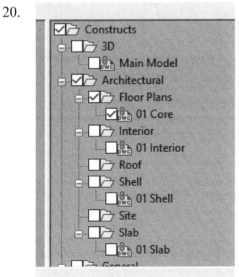 Enable **Floor Plans**.

Click **Finish.**

21. Locate **A-FP01-Rooms** in the Project Navigator.

Right click and select **Close**.

22. Click **Yes**.

Extra: Can you create and save a new layer state called Rooms?

Space Styles

Depending on the scope of the drawing, you may want to create different space styles to represent different types of spaces, such as different room types in an office building. Many projects require a minimum square footage for specific spaces – such as the size of bedrooms, closets, or common areas – based on building code. Additionally, by placing spaces in a building, you can look at the traffic flow from one space to another and determine if the building has a good flow pattern.

You can use styles for controlling the following aspects of spaces:

- Boundary offsets: You can specify the distance that a space's net, usable, and gross boundaries will be offset from its base boundary. Each boundary has its own display components that you can set according to your needs.
- Name lists: You can select a list of allowed names for spaces of a particular style. This helps you to maintain consistent naming schemes across a building project.
- Target dimensions: You can define a target area, length, and width for spaces inserted with a specific style. This is helpful when you have upper and lower space limits for a type of room that you want to insert.
- Displaying different space types: You can draw construction spaces, demolition spaces, and traffic spaces with different display properties. For example, you might draw all construction areas in green and hatched, and the traffic areas in blue with a solid fill.
- Displaying different decomposition methods: You can specify how spaces are decomposed (trapezoid or triangular). If you are not working with space decomposition extensively, you will probably set it up in the drawing default.

Space Styles are created, modified, or deleted inside the Style Manager.

Rooms and Sheets

In order to place a space, the room needs to be a closed boundary. Walls, doors, and windows are normally identified as boundary objects. Roofs and roof slabs are not normally considered valid boundary objects. You can set the Boundary Space property for an element in the Styles Manager.

Type AECSPACEDISPLAYBOUNDSPACES-PROPERTY to add the Bound Space property to the Properties palette for objects. You can then select an object and see the Bound spaces property listed. This will help you determine if the object can be used as a boundary when generating a space.

Exercise 9-2:
Adding Spaces

Drawing Name: A-FP01-Rooms.dwg
Estimated Time: 20 minutes

This exercise reinforces the following skills:

- Layouts
- Spaces

1.

   Open the Project Navigator.

   Open *A-FP01-Rooms.dwg*.

2.

   Go to the Manage ribbon.

   Launch the Style Manager.

3. 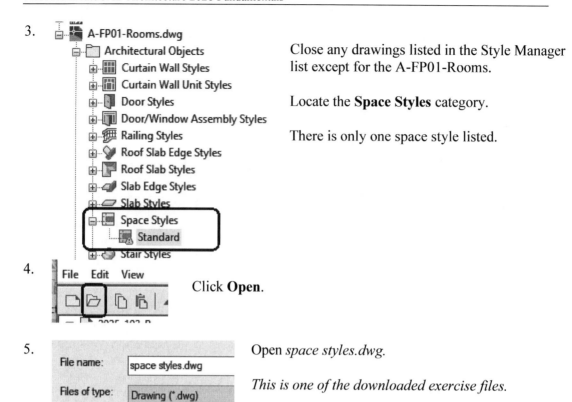 Close any drawings listed in the Style Manager list except for the A-FP01-Rooms.

Locate the **Space Styles** category.

There is only one space style listed.

4. Click **Open**.

5. Open *space styles.dwg*.

This is one of the downloaded exercise files.

Rooms and Sheets

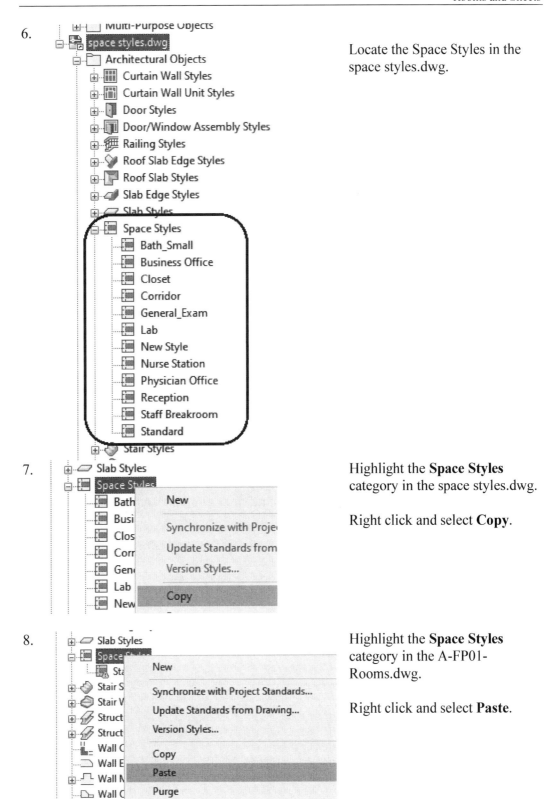

6. Locate the Space Styles in the space styles.dwg.

7. Highlight the **Space Styles** category in the space styles.dwg.

   Right click and select **Copy**.

8. Highlight the **Space Styles** category in the A-FP01-Rooms.dwg.

   Right click and select **Paste**.

9. 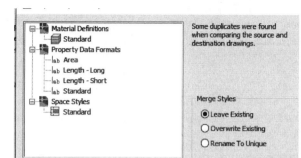 Enable **Leave Existing**.

   Click **OK**.

10. 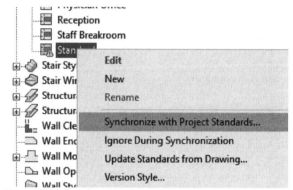 If you see a warning error on the Standard space style, right click and select **Synchronize with Project Standards**.

11. Highlight the Standard space style.
    Click **OK**.

    The warning symbol will disappear.

    Close the Style Manager.

12. Select the **Space** tool from the Home ribbon on the Build panel.

13. Click **Create type** in the command prompt window.
    Set the type to **Rectangle**.

14. Select the three corners of the Lobby area.

15. On the Properties palette, select the **Lobby** space style.
    Type **Waiting Room** in the Name list.

16. If you hover over the space, you should see a tool tip with the space style name.

17. Select the **Space** tool from the Home ribbon on the Build panel.

18. On the Properties palette, select the **Business Office** space style.
Change the Name to **Office** using the drop-down list.

Left click inside the upper left room to place the space.

Click **ESC** to exit the command.

19. If you hover over the space, you should see a tool tip with the space style name.

HINT: You need to hover over one of the boundaries to see the tool tip.

20. Select the **Generate Space** tool from the Home ribbon on the Build panel.

21. On the Properties palette, select the **Physician Office** space style.
Change the Name to **Office** using the drop-down list.

Left click inside the upper right room to place the space.

Click **ESC** to exit the command.

22. If you hover over the space, you should see a tool tip with the space style name.

23. Select the **Generate Space** tool from the Home ribbon on the Build panel.

24. On the Properties palette, select the **Bath Small** space style.

    Change the Name to **Bath**.

25. Left click inside the two rooms indicated to place the space.

    Click **ESC** to exit the command.

26. If you hover over the space, you should see a tool tip with the space style name.

27. Select the **Generate Space** tool from the Home ribbon on the Build panel.

Rooms and Sheets

28. On the Properties palette, select the **General_Exam** space style.

    Change the Name to **General Exam** using the drop-down list.

29. Left click inside the three rooms indicated to place the spaces.

    Click **ESC** to exit the command.

30. If you hover over the space, you should see a tool tip with the space style name.

31. Select the **Generate Space** tool from the Home ribbon on the Build panel.

32. On the Properties palette, select the **Closet** space style.

    Change the Name to **Closet** using the drop-down list.

33. Left click inside the room indicated to place the space.

    Click **ESC** to exit the command.

9-13

34. If you hover over the space, you should see a tool tip with the space style name.

    You may need to zoom in because the closet space is small.

35. Select the **Polyline** tool from the Home ribbon.

36. Trace around the area indicated with the red line.

    This is the space boundary.

    The corridor space fills in areas that are designated for other uses. This will be corrected in the next exercise.

Rooms and Sheets

37. On the Home ribbon:

    Launch the **Design Tools** palette.

38. Right click on **Space Generate**.

    Select **Apply Tool Properties to → Linework and AEC Objects**.

39. Select the polyline.

    Set the Cut Plane Height to **1400**.

    Enable **Erase Layout Geometry**. Click **OK.**

40. On the Properties palette, select the **Corridor** space style.

    Change the Name to **Corridor** using the drop-down list.

41. Trace the area shown in yellow to create the corridor space.

42. Assign the remaining two enclosed rooms as office spaces.

43. 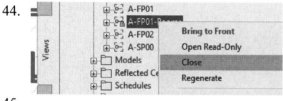 Change the Display Configuration to **Low Detail**.

44. 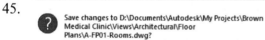 Open the Project Navigator.

    Highlight **A-FP-01-Rooms**.
    Select **Close**.

45. Click **Yes**.

If you don't see the hatch or fill patterns on your spaces, verify that A-Area-Spce-Patt layer is ON and THAWED.

You can edit the appearance of your spaces, by selecting a space, right click and select Edit Space Style.

Exercise 9-3:
Modifying Spaces

Drawing Name: A-FP01-Rooms.dwg
Estimated Time: 10 minutes

This exercise reinforces the following skills:

- Spaces
- Divide Space

1. 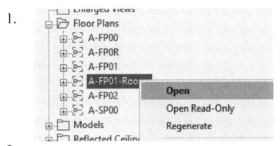 Open the Project Navigator.

   Locate **A-FP01-Rooms**.
   Right click and select **Open**.

2. Select the **Corridor** space.

3. On the Space contextual ribbon, select **Divide Space**.

4. Verify that the **A-Area-Spce** layer is current.

9-17

5. Turn ORTHO ON.
   Draw polylines to designate the staff break room area.

6. Draw polylines to designate the lab area.

7. Draw polylines to designate the Nurse Station area.

   Verify that the polylines are placed on the A-Area-Spc layer.

8.

Select the Staff Breakroom area space.

Right click and select **Properties**.

Change the Style to **Staff Breakroom**.
Change the Name to **Staff Breakroom.**

Click **ESC** to release the selection.

9.   Select the lab area space.

Right click and select **Properties**.

Change the Style to **Lab**.
Change the Name to **Lab**.

Click **ESC** to release the selection.

10.

    Select the Nurse Station area space.

    Right click and select **Properties**.

    Change the Style to **Nurse Station**.
    Change the Name to **Nurse**.

    Click **ESC** to release the selection.

    If the corridor space doesn't divide properly, place a polyline and use the Apply Tool Properties method to create the corridor.

11.

    Inspect the floor plan to verify that all spaces have been placed.

    Note that different space styles use different hatch patterns and colors.

    If your spaces don't display with different hatch patterns and colors, verify that the display override is checked for that display style.

12.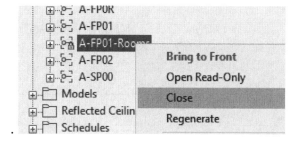

    Open the Project Navigator.

    Highlight **A-FP01-Rooms**.
    Right click and select **Close**.

13. Save changes to D:\Documents\Autodesk\My Projects\Brown Medical Clinic\Views\Architectural\Floor Plans\A-FP01-Rooms.dwg?   Click **Yes**.

[Yes] [No] [Cancel]

Property Set Definitions

Property set definitions are used to assign properties to AEC objects. These properties can then be used in tags and schedules.

Exercise 9-4:
Adding Room Tags

Drawing Name: A-FP01-Rooms.dwg
Estimated Time: 15 minutes

This exercise reinforces the following skills:

- Spaces
- Property Set Definitions
- Style Manager
- Property Set Formats
- Attributes
- Add/Delete Scales
- Tags
- Palettes
- Blocks

1. *The current project is the Brown Medical Clinic.*

   Open the Project Navigator.
   Locate **A-FP01-Rooms**.

   Right click and select **Open**.

2. Right click on the Design Tool Palette to switch to the Document tools palette.

   Click on the Tags tab.

   Locate the **Room Tag**.

   Place on the top left space in the drawing.

   Click **ENTER** to accept placing in the center of the space.

3. The available properties will display.

   Click **OK**.

   Right click to select **Multiple**.

4. Window around the building.
   All spaces are automatically selected.
   Click **ENTER** to complete the selection.

   Click **No**.

5. Click **OK**.

   Click ENTER to exit the command.

6. The tags are placed, but they may be too small or too large.

   Select one of the tags.
   Right click and **Select Similar**.
   This will select all placed tags.

Rooms and Sheets

7. 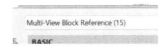 Right click and select **Properties**.

Select **Multi-View Block Reference** from the drop-down list.
Change the Scale to **0.50** (or to a value that makes sense to you).

Click **ESC** to release the selection.

8. You can modify the displayed names by selecting the space.

Don't select the tag. The tag gets the information from the space properties.

Right click and select **Properties**.
Then modify the Name.

9. Modify the names the way you would like them to appear.

10. Highlight **A-FP01-Rooms** in the Project Navigator. Right click and select **Close**.

9-23

11. 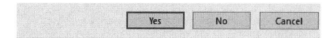 Click **Yes**.

Exercise 9-5:
Create a Custom Room Tag

Drawing Name: schedule tags_metric.dwg
Estimated Time: 15 minutes

This exercise reinforces the following skills:

- Spaces
- Property Set Definitions
- Style Manager
- Property Set Formats
- Attributes
- Tags

1. 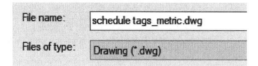 Open schedule tags_metric.dwg.

   This is downloaded from the publisher's website as part of the exercise files.

2. Switch to the Manage ribbon.

   Click on **Style Manager**.

Rooms and Sheets

3. Expand the **Documentation Objects** folder.

   Expand **Property Set Definitions**.

   Click on **SpaceObjects**.

   Select the **Definition** tab.

4. Click on **Add Automatic Property Set Definitions**.

5. Click on the Alphabetical tab.

   Enable **Base Area**.

6. Enable **Length**.

9-25

7. Enable **Name** and **Style**.

8. Enable **Width**.

9. Click **OK**.

   You can see a list of properties which will be applied to space objects.

   Click **Apply** to save your changes.

10. *Set the Format for the Property Set Definitions.*

    Highlight BaseArea.

    In the Format column: use the drop-down list to select **Area**.

11.

Set BaseArea to **Area**.
Set Length to **Length – Short**.
Set Width to **Length – Short**.
Click **Apply**.

12.

Locate the **Property Data Formats** category.

Right click and select **Synchronize with Project Standards.**

This will not be available if it is not needed.

13.

Click **OK.**

14. Expand the **Property Data Formats** category.

15. Highlight **Area** in the list.

    Click on the **Formatting** tab.

    Set the Precision to **0.0**.

    Verify that the other fields are set correctly.

16. Verify that the Suffix is set to **M2**.

    Click **Apply**.

17. Highlight Length – Short.

    Set the Precision to **0**.

    Click **Apply**.

18. Highlight **Property Data Formats**.
    Right click and select **New**.

19. Rename to **Case-Sentence**.

20. Set the Case to **Sentence**.

21. 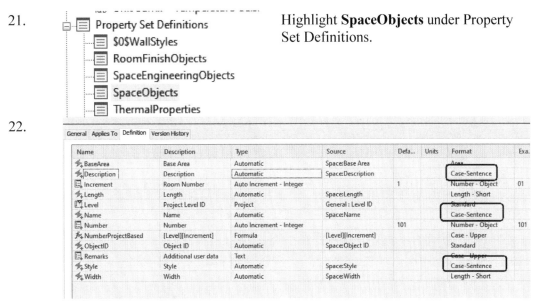 Highlight **SpaceObjects** under Property Set Definitions.

22. In the Format column:

    Set Description to **Case – Sentence**.
    Set Name to **Case – Sentence**.
    Set Style to **Case – Sentence**.

23. Click **OK** to close the Style Manager.

24. Set layer **0** current.

25. Switch to the Insert ribbon.

    Click **Define Attributes**.

26.

In the Tag field:
Type **SPACEOBJECTS:STYLE**.
In the Prompt field:
Type **Style**.
In the Default field:
Type **Lobby**.
Set the Justification to **Center**.
Set the Text style to **RomanS**.
Disable **Annotative**.
Set the Text height to **300.**
Enable **Specify on-screen** for the insertion point.
Click **OK**.

27. Click to place the attribute in the drawing.

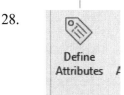

Zoom into the attribute.

28.

Click **Define Attributes**.

*You can also right click and select **Repeat ATTDEF**.*

29.

In the Tag field:
Type **SPACEOBJECTS:BASEAREA**.
In the Prompt field:
Type **Area**.
In the Default field:
Type **0000 M2**.
Set the Justification to **Center**.
Set the Text style to **RomanS**.
Disable **Annotative**.
Set the Text height to **300.**

30. Enable **Align below previous attribute definition** for the insertion point.
Click **OK**.

Rooms and Sheets

The attribute is placed.

SPACEOBJECTS:STYLE
SPACEOBJECTS:BASEAREA

31. SPACEOBJECTS:STYLE
    SPACEOBJECTS:BASEAREA
    000 X 000

    Place some text below the existing attributes to help you locate the length and width attributes.

    You can then modify the text to only show the X.

32. Switch to the Insert ribbon.

    Click **Define Attributes**.

33.

    In the Tag field:
    Type **SPACEOBJECTS:LENGTH**.
    In the Prompt field:
    Type **Length**.
    In the Default field:
    Type **0000**.
    Set the Justification to **Left**.
    Set the Text style to **RomanS**.
    Disable **Annotative**.
    Set the Text height to **250**

34.

    Enable **Specify on-screen** for the insertion point.
    Click **OK**.

35. Place below and slightly left of the previous attributes.

    Use the text to help you locate the attribute.

36. Copy the length attribute and place to the right.

9-31

37. Double click on the copied attribute.
Change the tag to **SPACEOBJECTS:WIDTH**.
Change the prompt to **Width**.
Click **OK**.
Click **ENTER** to exit the command.

38. Double click on the text and edit to leave only the X.

   SPACEOBJECTS:STYLE
   SPACEOBJECTS:BASEAREA
   SPACEOBJECTS:LENGTH X SPACEOBJECTS:WIDTH

39.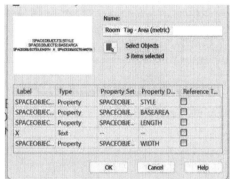
Activate the Annotate ribbon.

Select the **Create Tag** tool from the Scheduling panel in the drop-down area.

40. Select the attributes and the text.

   SPACEOBJECTS:STYLE
   SPACEOBJECTS:AREA
   SPACEOBJECTS:LENGTH X SPACEOBJECTS:WI

41. Type **Room Tag – Area (metric)** for the name.
Verify that the property sets and definitions have been assigned correctly.

If the property definitions are not correct, you may need to double check your attribute definitions.

42. Click **OK**.
Select the center of the attribute list to set the insertion point for the tag.

43. The tag is created.

   Lobby
   0000 M2
   0000 x 0000

Save the drawing to your work folder.

Exercise 9-6:
Create a Room Tag Tool

Drawing Name: schedule tags_metric.dwg
Estimated Time: 5 minutes

This exercise reinforces the following skills:

- Tags
- Palettes
- Blocks

1. Open *schedule tags_metric.dwg*..

2. Launch the **Document** tool palette.

3. Locate the **Room Tag** tool on the Document tool palette.

   Right click and select **Copy**.

4. Move the cursor to a blank space on the palette.

   Right click and select **Paste**.

5. Highlight the copied Room Tag tool.

   Right click and select **Rename**.

6. Rename it **Room Tag (w/Dimensions)** and move it below the original wall tag.

7. Highlight the **Room Tag (w/Dimensions)** -

   Right click and select **Properties**.

Rooms and Sheets

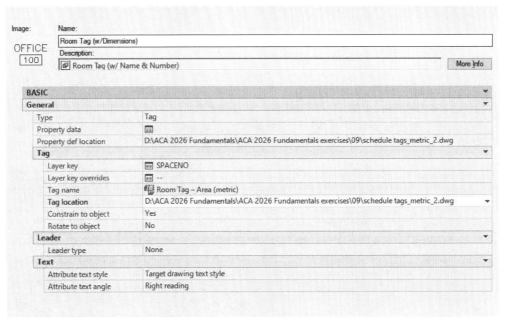

8. Set the Tag Location as *schedule_tag_metric.dwg*.
   Set the Tag Name to **Room Tag-Area (metric)**.
   Set the Property def location as *schedule_tag_metric.dwg*.

   Be sure to select the drawing you saved to your work folder that was modified.

   Click **OK**.
9. Close and save the drawing.

Exercise 9-7:
Adding Room Tags - Reprised

Drawing Name: A-FP01-Rooms.dwg
Estimated Time: 5 minutes

This exercise reinforces the following skills:

- Tags
- Tool Palette
- Content Browser

1. *The current project is the Brown Medical Clinic.*

   Open the Project Navigator.

   Highlight **A-FP01-Rooms** on the Views tab.
   Right click and select **Open**.

9-35

2. Go to the Manage ribbon.
   Launch the **Style Manager**.

3. Open the *schedule tags_metric.dwg*.

   Locate **SpaceObjects** under Property Set Definitions.

   Copy and Paste the SpaceObjects to the *A-FP01-Rooms.dwg*.

4. Enable **Overwrite Existing**.

   Click **OK**.

5. Verify that the new Property Set Definitions have been added.

   They were:

   - BaseArea
   - Length
   - Name
   - Style
   - Width

6. Locate the Property Data Formats under Documentation Objects in the *schedule tags_metric.dwg*.

   Copy and Paste the SpaceObjects to the *A-FP01-Rooms.dwg*.

Rooms and Sheets

7.

Enable **Leave Existing**.

Click **OK**.

Close the Style Manager.

If you don't copy the property set definitions and formats to the current drawing the custom room tag won't work properly.

8.

On the Document palette:

Highlight **Room Tag (w/Dimensions)**.
Right click and select **Import Room Tag (w/Dimensions) Multi-View Block Definition**.

9.

Select an existing room tag.
Right click and **Select Similar**.

All the room tags are selected.

Right click and select **Properties**.

10.

Change the tag definition to **Room Tag – Area (metric).**

Change the scale to **.2**.
Adjust the scale as needed.

Click **ESC** to release the selection.

11. The tags all update.

12. 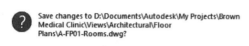 Highlight **A-FP01-Rooms** in the Project Navigator.
    Right click and select **Close**.

13. Click **Yes**.

Extra: *Create room plan views with tags for the ground, first and second floors in the Tahoe Cabin project. You will need to use the schedule tags – imperial.dwg.*

Exercise 9-8:
Create a Room Schedule Style

Drawing Name: schedule tables (metric).dwg
Estimated Time: 20 minutes

This exercise reinforces the following skills:

- Schedules
- Schedule Styles
- Property Set Definitions

1. 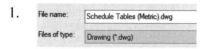 Open *Schedule Tables (Metric).dwg*.

   This is one of the downloaded exercise files.

2. Activate the Manage ribbon.

   Select **Style Manager**.

Rooms and Sheets

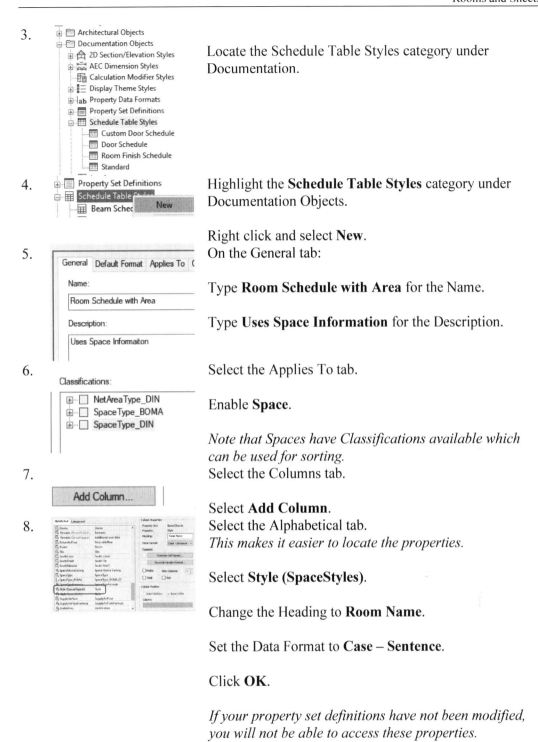

3. Locate the Schedule Table Styles category under Documentation.

4. Highlight the **Schedule Table Styles** category under Documentation Objects.

   Right click and select **New**.

5. On the General tab:

   Type **Room Schedule with Area** for the Name.

   Type **Uses Space Information** for the Description.

6. Select the Applies To tab.

   Enable **Space**.

   Note that Spaces have Classifications available which can be used for sorting.

7. Select the Columns tab.

   Select **Add Column**.

8. Select the Alphabetical tab.
   This makes it easier to locate the properties.

   Select **Style (SpaceStyles)**.

   Change the Heading to **Room Name**.

   Set the Data Format to **Case – Sentence**.

   Click **OK**.

   If your property set definitions have not been modified, you will not be able to access these properties.

9. Select **Add Column**.

10. 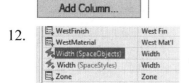 Select the Alphabetical tab to make it easier to locate the property definition.

    Locate and select **Length**.
    Set the Data Format to **Length – Short**.

    Click **OK**.

11. 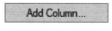 Select **Add Column**.

12. Select the Alphabetical tab to make it easier to locate the property definition.

    Locate and select **Width**.
    Set the Data Format to **Length – Short**.

    Click **OK**.

13. Select Add Column.

14. Select the Alphabetical tab to make it easier to locate the property definition.

    Select **BaseArea (SpaceStyles)**.

    Change the Heading to **Area**.

    Click **OK**.

15. 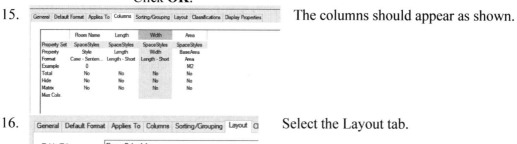 The columns should appear as shown.

16. Select the Layout tab.

    Change the Table Title to **Room Schedule.**

17. Select the **Sorting/Grouping** tab.
    Highlight **Sort**.
    Select the **Add** button.

18. Select **SpaceStyles: Style** to sort by Style name.
    Click **OK**.

    The panel should fill in with the sort information.

19. Select the Columns tab.

    Highlight **Area** and select **Modify**.

20. Enable **Total**.

    Click **OK** to close the dialog.

    Click **OK** to close the Style Manager dialog.

    Save the drawing to your work folder.

    Close the drawing.

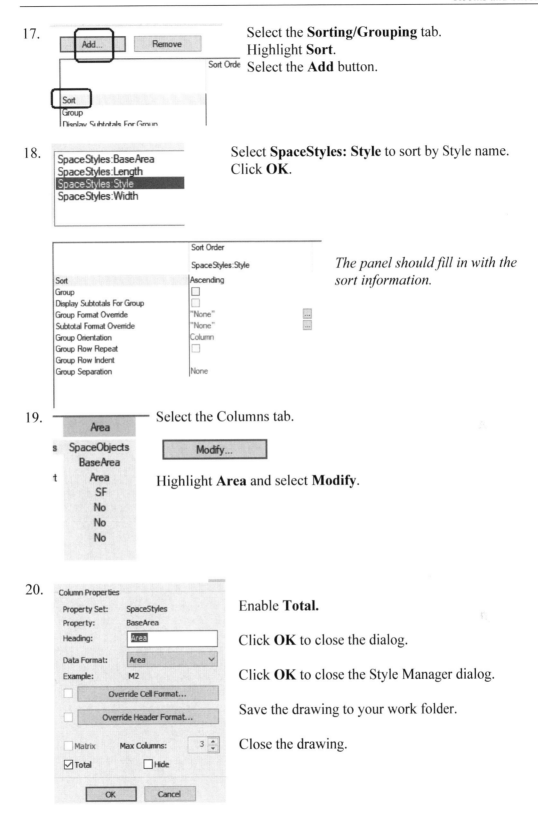

Exercise 9-9:
Create a Room Schedule Tool

Drawing Name: A-FP01-Rooms.dwg
Estimated Time: 10 minutes

This exercise reinforces the following skills:

- Schedules
- Tool Palettes

1. *The current project is the Brown Medical Clinic.*

   Open the Project Navigator.

   Highlight **A-FP01-Rooms** on the Views tab.
   Right click and select **Open**.

2. Launch the Annotation Tools palette from the Annotate ribbon.

3. 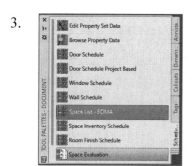 Select the Scheduling tab.

4. Highlight the **Space List – BOMA**.

   Right click and select **Copy**.

5. Move the mouse off the tool.

   Right click and select **Paste**.

6. Select the copied tool.

   Right click and select **Rename**.

7. Type **Room Schedule w/Area** for the name.

8. Highlight the new tool.

   Right click and select **Properties**.

9. Set the Style location to the **Schedule Tables (Metric).dwg** in your work folder.
   In the Style field, select the **Room Schedule** style which you just created.
   In order to use the Room Schedule style you created, you need to reference the drawing you saved the style in.
   By default, ACA will reference a different drawing.
   If you want to be able to use this style in other projects, use the Style Manager to copy and paste the style to the default schedule style drawing.

   Click **OK**.

10. Close and save the file using the Project Navigator.

Exercise 9-10:
Create a Room Schedule

Drawing Name: A-FP01-Rooms.dwg
Estimated Time: 50 minutes

This exercise reinforces the following skills:

- Schedules
- Tool Palettes
- Creating Tools
- Schedule Styles
- Property Set Definitions
- Add viewport
- Named Views
- Project Navigator
- Project Views
- Room Tags

1. 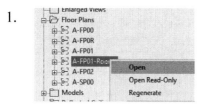 *The current project is the Brown Medical Clinic.*

   Open the Project Navigator.

   Highlight **A-FP01-Rooms** on the Views tab.
   Right click and select **Open**.

2. Go to the Annotate ribbon.

   Launch the **Annotation Tools** tool palette.

3.

Room Schedule			
Room Name	Length	Width	Area
Bath_small	2017	2069	4.2 M2
Bath_small	1610	2192	4.0 M2
Business office	4871	4080	17.5 M2
Business office	2711	1450	3.9 M2
Business office	1409	1812	2.6 M2
Closet	343	1812	0.6 M2
Corridor	10543	4284	23.3 M2
General_exam	2703	2509	6.8 M2
General_exam	2724	2509	6.8 M2
General_exam	2691	2509	6.8 M2
Lab	3408	643	2.2 M2
Nurse station	2321	771	1.8 M2
Physician office	2703	3926	10.6 M2
Reception	3910	4922	19.2 M2
Staff breakroom	2401	3157	7.6 M2
			117.8 M2

Select the **Room Schedule w/Area** tool.

Window around the building.

Click **ENTER**.

Pan over to an empty space in the drawing and left pick to place the schedule.

Click **ENTER**.

If there are any ? symbols in the table, you have some spaces which are unassigned.

You may have placed duplicate spaces or empty spaces.

To update: select the schedule. Right click and select **Edit Table Cell**. Click on the cell with the question mark.

The table should update with the correct information.

Repeat for each question mark.

It may be easier to select all the spaces using QSELECT and delete them and then replace all the spaces.

4.

Your area values and room sizes may be slightly different from mine depending on how you placed the walls.

If you placed duplicate spaces, you will see too many rooms with the same names.

You can use QSELECT to help you to locate the duplicate spaces and delete them.

Then, select the schedule and select UPDATE on the ribbon.

Go to the View ribbon.
Launch the **View Manager**.

5.

Create a Named View for the **Room Schedule**.

Click **OK**.

6.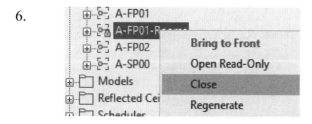

Highlight **A-FP01-Rooms** in the Project Navigator.
Right click and select **Close**.

Rooms and Sheets

7. Click **Yes**.

8. The named views that are in the drawing are listed.

9. Highlight the **Top Model Plan** named view.
Right click and select **Rename**.

10. Rename the view **Room Floor Plan**.

11. Right click on A-SH01 under Schedules. Select **Open**.

12. Type **XREF** to launch the XREF Manager.

   Highlight all the external references.

   Right click and select **Detach**.

   Close the XREF Manager.

13. Switch to the Model layout tab.

9-47

14. 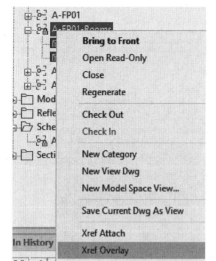   Highlight **A-FP01-Rooms**.

    Right click and select **Xref Overlay**.

15.   Go to the View ribbon.
    Open the View Manager.

    Create a view of the Room Schedule.

    Close the View Manager.

16. 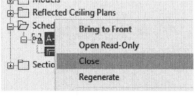   In the Project Navigator:
    Highlight **A-SH01**.
    Right click and select **Close**.

17.   Click **Yes**.

18. 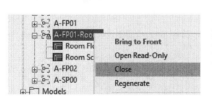   In the Project Navigator:
    Highlight **A-FP01-Rooms**.
    Right click and select **Close**.

19.   Click **Yes**.

20. Right click on the **Room Schedule** named view under **A-FP01-Rooms**. Select **Delete**.

21. Each named view is now saved in a separate drawing file.

Extra:

For the Tahoe Cabin project:

Create a named view for the room schedule.

Create a different room schedule style.

Create a new layout with the floor plan and the new room schedule.

You can insert blocks into model or paper space. Note that you did not need to activate the viewport in order to place the Scale block.

➤ By locking the Display you ensure your model view will not accidentally shift if you activate the viewport.

➤ The Annotation Plot Size value can be restricted by the Linear Precision setting on the Units tab. If the Annotation Plot Size value is more precise than the Linear Precision value, then the Annotation Plot Size value is not accepted.

Most projects require a floorplan indicating the fire ratings of the building walls. These are submitted to the planning department for approval to ensure the project is to building code. In the next exercises, we will complete the following tasks:

- Load the custom linetypes to be used for the exterior and interior walls
- Apply the 2-hr linetype to the exterior walls using the Fire Rating Line tool
- Apply the 1-hr linetype to the interior walls using the Fire Rating Line tool
- Add wall tags which display fire ratings for the walls
- Create a layer group filter to save the layer settings to be applied to a viewport
- Apply the layer group filter to a viewport
- Create the layout of the floorplan with the fire rating designations

Exercise 9-11:
Create a Fire Rating Floor Plan

Drawing Name: new
Estimated Time: 15 minutes

This exercise reinforces the following skills:

- Layers
- Edit an External Reference In-Place
- View Manager
- Project Navigator Views

1. Launch the Project Browser. Set the **Brown Medical Clinic** as the current project.

Current Project	
Name	Brown Medical
Number	2026-102
Description	medical clinic

2. Start a new drawing using a Metric template.

3. Save as *Level 1 Fire Rating.dwg*.

File name:	Level 1 Fire Rating
Files of type:	AutoCAD 2018 Drawing (*.dwg)

4. 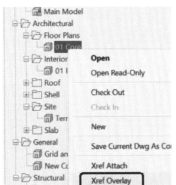 Open the Project Navigator.

   Right click on the **01 Core** construct.
   Select **Xref Overlay**.

   Double click the mouse wheel to **Zoom Extents**.

5. Freeze the **PDF Images** layer.

6. Select the **Freeze Layer** tool on the Home ribbon.

7. Select the grid lines indicated located at the lower left of the drawing.

   Select the ceiling lights if you placed them.

   Freeze the layer for the spaces you placed.

8. Go to the View ribbon.

   Launch the **View Manager**.

9. Create a Named View of the top plan view of the building.

   Click **OK**.

10. Click **OK**.

11. 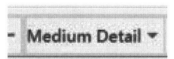 Set the Display Configuration to **Medium Detail**.

12. 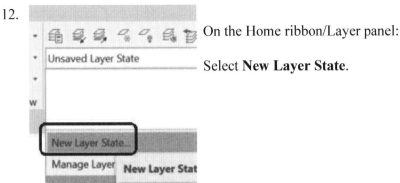 On the Home ribbon/Layer panel:

    Select **New Layer State**.

13. Type **Fire Rating** for the layer state name.

    Type **fire rating for walls** for the description.

    Click **OK**.

14. 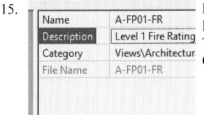 Open the Project Navigator.
    Open the **Views** tab.
    Right click on **Floor Plans**.
    Select **Save Current Dwg As View→General**.

15. For Name: Type **A-FP01-FR**.
    For Description:
    Type **Level 1 Fire Rating Plan**.
    Click **Next**.

16. Enable **First Floor**.

    Click **Next**.

17.   Disable all selections except for Floor Plans.

    Click **Finish**.

18.   Highlight **A-FP01-FR** on the Views tab in the Project Navigator.
    Right click and select **Close**.

19. 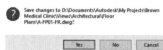 Click **Yes**.

Exercise 9-12:
Applying a Fire Rating Line

Drawing Name: A-FP01-FR.dwg
Estimated Time: 25 minutes

This exercise reinforces the following skills:

- Adding a Layout
- Layers
- Edit an External Reference In-Place
- Adding Fire Rating Lines
- Creating a tool on the tool palette

1.   *The current project is the Brown Medical Clinic.*

    Launch the Project Navigator.

2. 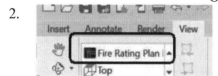 Open the **A-FP01-FR** view drawing.
    Restore the **Fire Rating Plan** named view, if needed.

Rooms and Sheets

3. Restore the **Fire Rating** layer state.

4. Select an exterior wall.

5. Select **Edit Reference In-Place** from the ribbon.

6. Click **OK**.

7. Launch the **Design Tools** palette from the Home ribbon if it is not available.

8. Right click on the Design Tools palette title bar.

   Enable **Document**.

9.

   Select the Annotation tab.

   Locate and select the **Fire Rating Line** tool.

   Copy and Paste two copies.

10. Rename one copy **1-hr Fire Rating Line**.
    Rename one copy **2-hr Fire Rating Line**.

11. Right click on the **1-hr Fire Rating Line**.
    Select **Properties.**

    Set the Line width to **130.00**.

    Set the Linetype to **Aec_Rating_1Hr.**

    Click **OK.**

12. Right click on the **2-hr Fire Rating Line**.
    Select **Properties.**

    Set the Line width to **170.00**.

    Set the Linetype to **Aec_Rating_2Hr.**

    Click **OK.**

13.

    Turn **ORTHO** ON.
    Select the 2-hr Fire Rating Line from the tool palette.

14. Select the end points of the exterior walls and trace around the building to place the fire rating line.

    Go slowly and wait for the preview to place each line segment. You can't undo if you make a mistake on a segment selection.

15. Set the Display Configuration to **Low Detail.**

    This is on the status bar.

16. Select the polyline that is the fire rating line.

    Right click and select **Properties**.

    Note that the line is placed on the F-Wall-Fire-Patt layer.

17. Click **ESC** to release the selection.
    Select the 1-hr Fire Rating Line tool from the tool palette.
    Carefully trace over the interior walls.

    Change the View Scale to **1:100**.

    You should be able to see the hatch pattern of the fire rating line.

18. Place the 1-hr polyline on all the interior walls.

    You will need to place more than one polyline as the interior walls are not all connected.

    You won't be able to add a fire rating line to the curtain walls unless the properties are modified. We will do this in the next lesson.

19. Select **Save Changes** from the ribbon.

20. Click **OK**.

21. 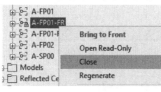 Open the Project Navigator.
Highlight **A-FP-FR**.
Right click and select **Close**.

22. Click **Yes**.

Exercise 9-13:
Assigning Fire Rating Properties to Wall Styles

Drawing Name: 01 Core.dwg
Estimated Time: 30 minutes

This exercise reinforces the following skills:

- Wall Properties
- Style Manager
- Property Sets

1. 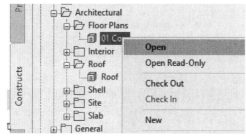 *The current project is the Brown Medical Clinic.*

   Launch the Project Navigator.

   Open the **01 Core** Construct drawing.

2. Activate the Manage ribbon.

   Select the **Style Manager**.

Rooms and Sheets

3. Locate and select the **exterior** Wall Style.

4. On the General tab:

   Select **Property Sets**.

   Property sets control the values of parameters which are used in schedules and tags.

5. Type **2-hr** in the FireRating property.

   Click **OK**.

   When defining the attribute to use this value, we use the format WallStyles:FireRating. The first word is the property set and the second word is the property.

6. 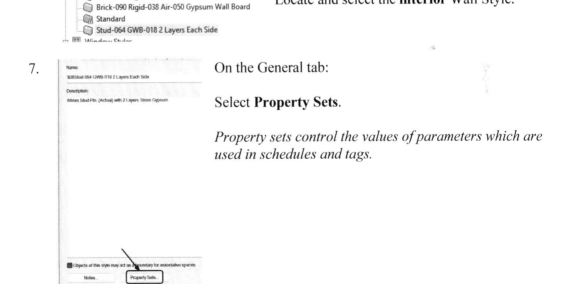 Locate and select the **interior** Wall Style.

7. On the General tab:

   Select **Property Sets**.

   Property sets control the values of parameters which are used in schedules and tags.

9-59

8. Type **1-hr** in the FireRating property.

Click **OK**.

9. Locate the **Property Set Definitions** under Documentation Objects.
Right click and select **New**.

10. Rename **CurtainWallStyles**.

11. Open the Applies To tab.

Enable **Styles and Definitions.**
Enable **Curtain Wall.**

12. Open the Definition tab.

Select the **Add Manual Property Definition** tool.

13. Type **FireRating** in the Name field.
Click **OK**.

14. Set Type to **Text**.
Set Format to **Case – Upper**.

15. Select the **Add Manual Property Definition** tool.

16. Type **Type** in the Name field.
Click **OK**.

Rooms and Sheets

17. Set Type to **Text**.
    Set Format to **Case – Upper**.

18. You should see two property set definitions listed.

19. Select the **Add Automatic Property Set Definition** Tool.

20. Enable **Style.**

    Click **OK.**

21. Click **Apply.**
    Locate the Curtain Wall style used in the drawing.

22. Click the General tab.

    Click **Property Sets.**

23. Click **Add Property Set.**

24. Enable **CurtainWallStyles.**

    This is the Property Set Definition you just created.
    Click OK.

25. Type **2-hr** in the FireRating field.

    Click **OK.**

26. Close the Style Manager.

27. Set the Current layer to **F-Wall-Fire-Patt**.

28. Use a polyline to trace over the curtain wall.

    Select the polyline.
    Right click to select **Properties**.
    Change the Linetype to **Aec_Rating_2Hr**.
    Change the Global width to **30.00**.
    Click ESC to release

29. Highlight **01 Core** in the Project Navigator.
    Right click and select **Close**.

30. Click **Yes**.

Exercise 9-14:
Creating a Schedule Tag

Drawing Name: new.dwg
Estimated Time: 15 minutes

This exercise reinforces the following skills:

- Wall Tags
- Attributes
- Create a Schedule Tag

1. Create a new drawing called *fire rating tag.dwg*.

2. Activate the **Model** layout.

3. Set the view scale to **1:1**

4.

   On the Application Menu:

   Go to **Drawing Utilities→Drawing Setup**.

5. Select the Scale tab.
   Highlight **1:1**.
   Set the Annotation Plot Scale to. **3.5**
   Click **OK**.

6. Draw a 200 x 200 square.

   Hint: Use the Rectangle tool. Click one corner and for the second corner, type **@ 200, 200**.

7. Select the square.
   Right click and select **Basic Modify Tools→Rotate**.

   When prompted for the base point, right click and select **Geometric Center**.

   Then select the center of the square.

   Type **45** for the angle of rotation.

8. Go to the Manage ribbon.

   Open the **Style Manager**.

9. Open the *schedule tags_metric.dwg*.

10. Locate the **Wall Styles** under Property Set Definitions.

    Copy and paste into the active drawing.

    Close the Style Manager.

11. Activate the Insert ribbon.

    Select the **Define Attributes** tool.

12.

Type **WALLSTYLES:FIRERATING** for the tag. *This is the property set definition used for this tag.*
Type **Fire Rating** for the prompt.
Type **2-hr** for the Default value.

Set the Justification for the **Middle cente**r.
Set the Text style to **RomanS**.
Disable **Annotative**.
Set the Text Height to **20**.

Enable **Specify on-screen** for insertion point.

Click **OK**.

13. Select the Geometric Center of the Square to insert the attribute.

14.

Activate the Annotate ribbon.

Select the **Create Tag** tool from the Scheduling panel in the drop-down area.

15. Select the square and the attribute you just created.

Press **ENTER**.

16. 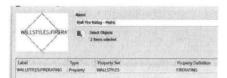 Name the new tag **Wall Fire Rating - Metric**.

    You should see a preview of the tag and you should see the Property Set and Property Definition used by the tag based on the attribute you created.

    Click **OK**.

17. You will be prompted for the insertion point for the tag.

    Select the bottom vertex of the rectangle.

18. *The tag will convert to a block and you will see the default attribute.*

    Notice that when it converts, the size will change.

    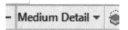

    If you don't see the tag, check that the Display Property is set to Medium Detail on the status bar.

    This tag will only work on walls, NOT curtain walls.

19. Go to the Manage ribbon.
    Launch the **Style Manager**.

20. Locate the **Property Set Definitions** under Documentation Objects.
    Right click and select **New**.

21. Rename **CurtainWallStyles**.

22. Open the Applies To tab.

    Enable **Styles and Definitions**.
    Enable **Curtain Wall**.
    Enable **Curtain Wall Unit Style**.

23. Open the Definition tab.

    Select the **Add Manual Property Definition** tool.

24. Type **FireRating** in the Name field.
    Click **OK**.

25. Set Type to **Text**.
    Set Format to **Case – Upper**.

26. Select the **Add Manual Property Definition** tool.

27. Type **Type** in the Name field.
    Click **OK**.

28. Set Type to **Text**.
    Set Format to **Case – Upper**.

29. You should see two property set definitions listed.

30. Select the **Add Automatic Property Set Definition** Tool.

31. Enable **Style**.

    Click **OK**.

    Click **Apply**.
    Close the Style Manager.

32. Copy the fire rating tag.

    Explode the copy.
    Repeat exploding until you see the attribute definition.

    It is a tag with a nested block, so it needs to be exploded multiple times to get to the rectangle and attribute level.

33. Double click on the attribute.
    Change the Tag to
    CURTAINWALLSTYLES:FIRERATING.
    Click **OK**.

34. Activate the Annotate ribbon.

    Select the **Create Tag** tool from the Scheduling panel in the drop-down area.

35. Select the square and the attribute you just created.

    Press **ENTER**.

36. Name the new tag **CurtainWall Fire Rating - Metric**.

    You should see a preview of the tag and you should see the Property Set and Property Definition used by the tag based on the attribute you created.

    Click **OK**.

Rooms and Sheets

37. You will be prompted for the insertion point for the tag.

    Select the bottom vertex of the rectangle.

38. Change the scale of the curtain wall tag to **0.3**.

39. Save the drawing as **fire rating tag.dwg**.
    Close the file.

Exercise 9-15:
Adding a Schedule Tag Tool to the Document Palette

Drawing Name: A-FP01-FR.dwg
Estimated Time: 20 minutes

This exercise reinforces the following skills:

- Wall Tags
- Create a Tool on the Tool Palette
- Property Sets

1. *The current project is the Brown Medical Clinic.*

    Launch the Project Navigator.

    Open the *A-FP01-FR.dwg* on the Views tab.

2. Switch to the Annotate ribbon.

    Launch the **Annotation Tools**.

9-69

3. Click on the **Tags** tab of the Tool Palette.

   Locate the **Wall Tag (Leader) tool** on the Document tool palette.

4. Highlight the **Wall Tag (Leader) tool**.
   Right click and select **Copy**.

5. Move the cursor to a blank space on the palette.

   Right click and select **Paste**.

6. Highlight the copied Wall Tag tool.

   Right click and select **Rename**.

7. Rename it **FireRating Wall Tag (Leader)** and move it below the original wall tag.

8. 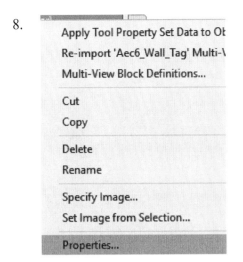 Highlight the **FireRating Wall Tag.**

   Right click and select **Properties**.

9. In the Tag location field:

   Click **Browse**.

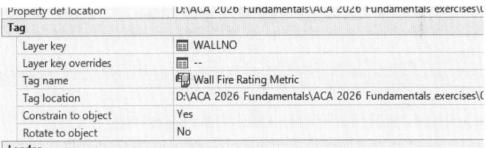

10. Set the Tag Location as *fire rating.dwg*.
    Set the Tag Name to **Wall Fire Rating - Metric**.

    You may want to create a drawing to store all your custom schedule tags and then use that drawing when setting the tag location. In this case, I created the drawing and loaded the tag we created in the previous exercise.

11.

    Set the Property definition location to the fire rating.dwg.
    Click **OK**.

12. 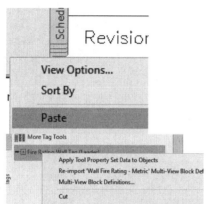 Highlight the **Fire Rating Wall Tag (Leader) tool**.

    Right click and select **Copy**.

13. Move the cursor to a blank space on the palette.

    Right click and select **Paste**.

14. Highlight the copied Wall Tag tool.

    Right click and select **Rename**.

15. Rename it **Fire Rating Curtain Wall Tag (Leader)** and move it below the original wall tag.

16. 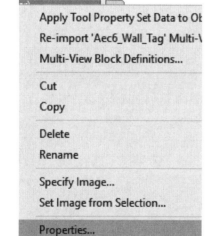 Highlight the **FireRating Curtain Wall Tag**.

    Right click and select **Properties**.

17. 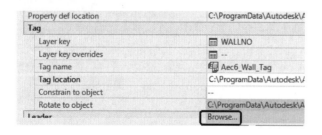 In the Tag location field:

    Click **Browse**.

18.

Tag	
Layer key	WALLNO
Layer key overrides	--
Tag name	CurtainWall Fire Rating - Metric
Tag location	D:\ACA 2026 Fundamentals\ACA 2026 Fundamentals exercises\09\co
Constrain to object	Yes
Rotate to object	No

19. Set the Tag Location as *fire rating.dwg*.
    Set the Tag Name to **Curtain Wall Fire Rating - Metric**.

20.

General	
Type	Tag
Property data	
Property def location	D:\ACA 2026 Fundamentals\ACA 2026 Fundamentals exercises\09\completed exercises\fire rating t.

Set the Property definition location to the fire rating.dwg.
Click **OK**.

21. 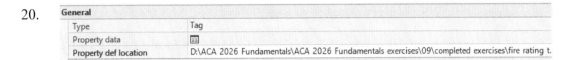 Highlight **A-FP01-FR** in the Project Navigator.
Right click and select **Close**.

22. 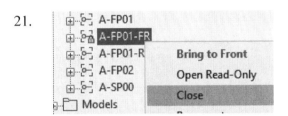 Click **Yes**.

Exercise 9-16:
Adding Property Sets to Walls

Drawing Name: A-FP-FR.dwg
Estimated Time: 20 minutes

This exercise reinforces the following skills:

- Wall Tags
- Create a Tool on the Tool Palette
- Property Sets

1. Launch the Project Navigator.

   Open the **A-FP-FR** on the Views tab.

2. Open the Project Browser.
   Right click on the Brown Medical Clinic Project and select **Properties**.

   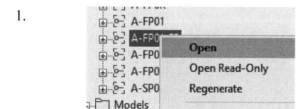

   Notice the folder where the project files are stored.

   Click **OK**.
   Close the Project Browser.

3. Go to the Manage ribbon.

   Open the **Style** Manager.

4. Open the 01 Core drawing.

   Locate the Curtain Wall style and copy into A-FP01-FR.

   Close the Style Manager.

5. Set the Display Configuration to **Medium Detail**.

6. Set the Scale to **1:1**.

7. Select the **FireRating Wall Tag** tool and click on an exterior wall.

   Click a point outside the wall to place the tag.

8. *You should see the Property Set Data dialog pop-up.*

   Click **OK**.

9.

   Hint: *Enable **Selection Cycling** to make it easier to select a wall.*

10. Left click to place the tag and then click **OK** to accept the properties.

    You should see the updated tag.

11. Right click and select **Multiple.**
    Window around the entire building.
    Click **ENTER**.
    Click **No.**

12. Click **OK**.

    Exit the command.

13.

Select one of the curtain walls. Select the **Fire Rating Curtain Wall Tag**
Click to place the end of the leader. **(Leader)** tool.
Click **ENTER**.

Click **OK** to accept the property sets.

14.

15.

Repeat to tag the second curtain wall.

Select the two curtain wall tags.
Right click and select **Basic Modify Tools→Scale.**

16.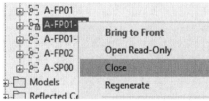

Select the end point of one of the tags.
Set the scale value to 0.3.
Click ENTER

17.

The drawing should appear like this.

If you like, you can go through and use grips to reposition any of the tags.

18.

Highlight **A-FP01-FR** in the Project Navigator.
Right click and select **Close**.

19. Click **Yes** to save.

Exercise 9-17:
Modify a Dimension Style

Drawing Name: A-FP01.dwg
Estimated Time: 30 minutes

This exercise reinforces the following skills:

- Dimension Styles
- AEC Dimensions

1.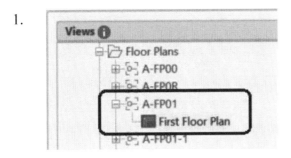

    The current project is the Brown Medical Clinic.

    Launch the Project Navigator.

    Open the **A-FP01.dwg** view.

2.

    Select the XREFs.

    Position the xref so it is centered between the elevation and section lines.

    Move the view title below the XREFs.

3.

    Launch the Layer Properties Manager.
    Perform a search for layers with ***fire*** in their name.
    Freeze those layers.

4. Perform a search for layers with ***iden*** in their name.
    Freeze those layers.

    Close the Layer Properties Manager.

5. Perform a search for layers with ***lite*** in their name.
    Freeze the ceiling lights.

6. Go to the View ribbon.

   Launch the **View Manager**.

7. Highlight the **First Floor Plan**.

   Click **Edit Boundaries**.

8. Window around the floor plan.

   Click ENTER.

   Click **OK** to close the View Manager.

9. 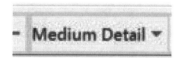 Set the Display Configuration to **Medium Detail**.

10. On the Home ribbon/Layer panel:

    Select **New Layer State**.

11. Type **Floor Plan** for the layer state name.

    Type **Floor Plan with dimensions** for the description.

    Click **OK**.

12. Use the grips to adjust the location of the view title and scale attributes.

13. Activate the Annotate ribbon.

    Select the **Dimension Style Editor** on the Dimensions panel.

14. Highlight **Annotative**.

15. Select **Modify**.

16. On the Lines tab,
    set the Baseline spacing to **15**.

    Use the Preview window to check your settings.

17. Set Extend beyond dim lines to **1**.
    Set Offset from origin to **1.5**.

18. On the Symbols and Arrows tab,

    Select **Architectural** tick for the arrowheads.
    Set the Arrow size to **1.5**.

19. On the Text tab,
    Set the Text style to **Arial**.

    You will have to create that text style using the Arial font.
    Set the Text height to **2.5**.

20. Set the Vertical placement to Centered.
    Set the Horizontal placement to Centered.

    Set the Offset from dim line to **3**.

21. Set the Text alignment to **Horizontal.**

22. Activate the Primary Units tab.

    Set the Unit format to **Decimal.**
    Set the Precision to **0**.

23. Click **OK** and **Close**.

24. Close the drawing in the Project Navigator and save.

Exercise 9-18:
Dimensioning a Floor Plan

Drawing Name: A-FP01.dwg
Estimated Time: 30 minutes

This exercise reinforces the following skills:

- Drawing Setup
- AEC Dimensions
- Title Mark
- Attributes
- Design Center
- Dimension Styles

1.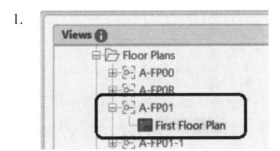

   The current project is the Brown Medical Clinic.

   Launch the Project Navigator.

   Open the Views tab.

   Open the **A-FP01** view drawing.

   The floor plan should look like this.

   Doors, windows, and walls should be visible in the viewport.

   Detach any unneeded XREFs.

2.

   Activate the Home ribbon.

   In the Layers panel drop-down, select **Select Layer Standard**.

3. 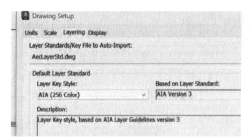 Set the Layer Key Style to **AIA (256 Color)**.

   Click **OK**.

4. On the Status Bar: Set the Global Cut Plane to **1400**.

   That way you see the doors and windows in the floor plan. You can only set the global cut plane in model space.

5. Left click on the Global Cut Plane icon.

   Set the Cut Height to **1400**.

   Click **OK**.

6. Verify that the **Add Annotative Scales** is enabled on the status bar.
   Show Annotative Objects should also be enabled.

7. `for use current <"use current">: A-Anno-Dims`   Type **DIMLAYER**.

   Type **A-Anno-Dims**.

   This ensures any dimensions are placed on the A-Anno-Dims layer, regardless of which layer is current.

8. Launch the Design Center by typing **ADC**.

   Or toggle ON from the Insert ribbon.

Rooms and Sheets

9. Click the **Open Drawings** tab.

Highlight **DimStyles** for the A-FP01.dwg.

You will see the available dimension styles in the drawing.

10. 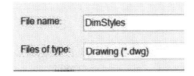 Open the *DimStyles.dwg* file located in the exercises folder.

11. Highlight **DimStyles** in the DimStyles.dwg file.

Change the Views to **List**.

12. Highlight **AEC-Arch-M-100**.
Drag and drop into the A-FP01 drawing window.

13. Look at the A-FP01.dwg in the Design Center.

Verify that the dimstyle has been added.

14. Close the Design Center.

9-83

15. Switch to the Annotate ribbon.

    Set the Dimension Style to **AEC-Arch-M-100**.

16. Select the **Linear Dimension** tool on the Home ribbon.

17. Click **ENTER** to select an object.

18. Select the right side of the building.

19. Drag and place the dimension away and to the right of the building.

20. Select the **Linear Dimension** tool on the Home ribbon.

21. Select the upper right corner of the building.

    Select the midpoint of the window.

    Drag and place the dimension away and to the right of the building.

22. Select **DIMCONTINUE**.

23. Select the endpoint of the wall below the window.

24. Select the wall below the door.

25. Select the endpoint of the bottom wall.

    Use grips to align and position the dimensions.

    It's OK if your dimensions are slightly different from mine.

26. Hover over a dimension.

    The dimension should automatically be placed on A-Anno-Dims because the DIMLAYER system variable was set to that layer.

27. Close the drawing in the Project Navigator and save.

Exercise 9-19:
Creating a Custom Title Block

Drawing Name: Architectural Title Block.dwg
Estimated Time: 30 minutes

This exercise reinforces the following skills:

- Title blocks
- Attributes
- Edit Block In-Place
- Insert Image
- Insert Hyperlink

1. Select the **Open** tool.

2. Set the Files of type to *Drawing Template*.

3. Open the *Tutorial-iArch.dwt*.
   Verify that *Files of type* is set to Drawing Template or you won't see the file.

   This file is included in the downloaded exercise files.

4. Perform a **File→Save as**.

   Save the file to your work folder.
   Rename **Arch_D.dwt**.

5. Enter a description and Click **OK**.

9-87

6. Zoom into the Firm Name and Address rectangle.

7. Select the **MTEXT** tool from the **Annotation** panel on the Home ribbon.

   Draw a rectangle to place the text.

8. Set the Font to **Verdana**.

   Hint: If you type the first letter of the font, the drop-down list will jump to fonts starting with that letter.

   Set the text height to ⅛".
   Set the justification to **centered**.
   Enter the name and address of your college.

9. Extend the ruler to change the width of your MTEXT box to fill the rectangle.

   Click **OK**.

10. Use **MOVE** to locate the text properly, if needed.

    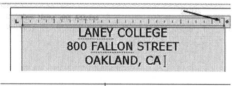

11. Activate the **Insert** ribbon.

    Select the arrow located on the right bottom of the Reference panel.

12. The External Reference Manager will launch.

    Select **Attach Image** from the drop-down list.

Rooms and Sheets

13. Locate the image file you wish to use.
    There is an image file available for use from the publisher's website called *college logo.jpg*.
    Click **Open**.

14. 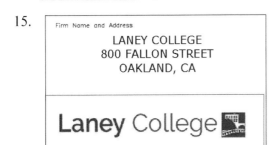 Click **OK**.

15. Place the image in the rectangle.

If you are concerned about losing the link to the image file (for example, if you plan to email this file to another person), you can use **INSERTOBJ** to embed the image into the drawing. Do not enable link to create an embedded object. The INSERTOBJ command is not available on the standard ribbon.

16. Select the image.
    Right click and select **Properties**.

17. 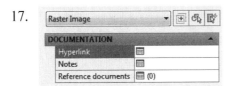 Select the **Extended** tab.
    Pick the Hyperlink field.

18. 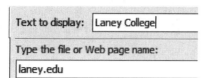 Type in the name of the school in the Text to display field.

    Type in the website address in the *Type the file or Web page name* field.

    Click **OK**.
    Close the Properties dialog.

19. If you hover your mouse over the image, you will see a small icon. This indicates there is a hyperlink attached to the image. To launch the webpage, simply hold down the CTRL key and left click on the icon.

If you are unsure of the web address of the website you wish to link, use the Browse for **Web Page** button.

20. To turn off the image frame/boundary, type **IMAGEFRAME** at the command line. Enter **0**.

Rooms and Sheets

IMAGEFRAME has the following options:
- 0: Turns off the image frame and does not plot
- 1: Turns on the image frame and is plotted
- 2: Turns on the image frame but does not plot

21. Select the titleblock.
    Right click and select **Edit Block in-place**.

22. Click **OK**.

23. Change the text for Project to **Drafter**.
    To change, simply double click on the text and an edit box will appear.

24. Select the **Define Attribute** tool from the Insert ribbon.

25. Select the **Field** tool.

26. Highlight Author and Uppercase.

    Click **OK**.

27. In the Tag field, enter **DRAFTER**.
    In the Prompt field, enter **DRAFTER**.
    The Value field is used by the FIELD property.
    In the Insertion Point area:
    In the X field, enter **2' 6.5"**.
    In the Y field, enter **2-1/16"**.
    In the Z field, enter **0"**.
    In the Text Options area:
    Set the Justification to **Left**.
    Set the Text Style to **Standard**.
    Set the Height to **1/8"**.

    Click **OK**.

28. Select the **Define Attributes** tool.

29. In the Tag field, enter **DATE**.
    In the Prompt field, enter **DATE**.

    In the Insertion Point area:
    In the X field, enter **2' 6.5"**.
    In the Y field, enter **1-9/16"**.
    In the Z field, enter **0"**.
    In the Text Options area:
    Set the Justification to **Left**.
    Set the Text Style to **Standard**.
    Set the Height to **1/8"**.

30. Select the Field button to set the default value for the attribute.

    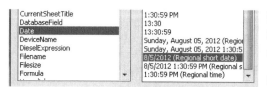 Select **Date**.
    Set the Date format to **Regional short date**.

    Click **OK**.

Rooms and Sheets

31. Select the **Define Attributes** tool.

32. In the Tag field, enter **SCALE**.
In the Prompt field, enter **SCALE**.
In the Insertion Point area:
   In the X field, enter **2′ 6.5″**.
   In the Y field, enter **1-1/16″**.
   In the Z field, enter **0″**.
In the Text Options area:
   Set the Justification to **Left**.
   Set the Text Style to **Standard**.
Set the Height to **1/8″**.

33. Select the Field button to set the default value for the attribute.

Select **PlotScale**.
Set the format to **1:#**.

Click **OK**.

Click **OK** to place the attribute.

34. Select the **Define Attributes** tool.

35. In the Tag field, enter **SHEETNO**.
In the Prompt field, enter **SHEET NO**.
In the Insertion Point area:
   In the X field, enter **2′ 8.25″**.
   In the Y field, enter **1-9/16″**.
   In the Z field, enter **0**.
In the Text Options area:
   Set the Justification to **Left**.
   Set the Text Style to **Standard**.
   Set the Height to **1/8″**.

9-93

36. Select the Field button to set the default value for the attribute.

    Select **CurrentSheetNumber**.
    Set the format to **Uppercase**.

    Click **OK**.

    Click **OK** to place the attribute.

37. Select the **Define Attribute** tool.

38. In the Tag field, enter **PROJECTNAME**.
    In the Prompt field, enter **PROJECT NAME**.
    In the Insertion Point area:
    In the X field, enter **2′ 7-9/16″**.
    In the Y field, enter **4″**.
    In the Z field, enter **0**.
    In the Text Options area:
    Set the Justification to **Center**.
    Set the Text Style to **Standard**.
    Set the Height to **1/8″**.

39. Select the Field button to set the default value for the attribute.

    Select **AEC Project** for the field category.
    Set the Field Name to **Project Name**.
    Set the format to **Uppercase**.

    Click **OK**.

A common error for students is to forget to enter the insertion point. The default insertion point is set to 0,0,0. If you don't see your attributes, look for them at the lower left corner of your title block and use the MOVE tool to position them appropriately.

Your title block should look similar to the image shown.

If you like, you can use the MOVE tool to reposition any of the attributes to make them fit better.

40. Select **Save** on the ribbon to save the changes to the title block and exit the Edit Block In-Place mode.

41. Click **OK**.

42. Save the file and go to **File→Close**.

Tips & Tricks

> Use templates to standardize how you want your drawing sheets to look. Store your templates on a server so everyone in your department uses the same titleblock and sheet settings. You can also set up dimension styles and layer standards in your templates.

> ADT 2005 introduced a new tool available when you are in Paper Space that allows you to quickly switch to the model space of a viewport without messing up your scale. Simply select the **Maximize Viewport** button located on your task bar to switch to model space.

> To switch back to paper space, select the **Minimize Viewport** button.

Exercise 9-20:
Adding Views

Drawing Name: A102 Floor Plans.dwg
Estimated Time: 30 minutes

This exercise reinforces the following skills:

- ❏ Project Browser
- ❏ Project Navigator
- ❏ Title blocks
- ❏ Viewports
- ❏ Layer Properties

1.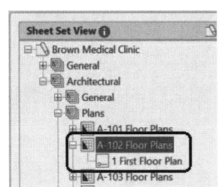
Set the **Brown Medical Clinic** project Current.

Launch the Project Navigator.
Open the Sheets tab.

Open the **A102 Floor Plans** sheet.

2. Insert the *Architectural Title Block w Attributes.dwg* into the drawing.

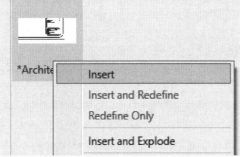

When prompted for an insertion point, click **ESC**.

This loads the block without placing it.

3.

Open the layout tab in the drawing.
Select the title block.

Type **BREPLACE**.

4.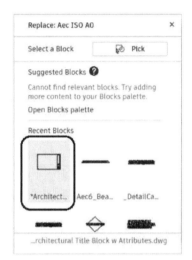

There will be a pause while ACA searches for blocks and brings up the dialog.

Select the *Architectural Title Block w Attributes.dwg*.

5.

The title block is inserted.

Right click and select **Basic Modify Tools→Scale**.

6.

Select the lower left point of the title block as the base point.

7. Right click and select **Reference**.

8. Select the lower left point of the title block.
Select the lower right point of the title block.

9. Select the lower right corner of the layout as the new size.

10. Select the viewport.
Right click and select **Basic Modify Tools→Delete.**

Rooms and Sheets

The goal is to place four viewports.

One viewport will show the room schedule.

One viewport will show spaces with room tags.

One viewport will show the fire rating patterns and the wall tags with fire ratings.

One viewport will show the floor plan with dimensions.

11. Create a new layer called **Viewport.**
    Set the color to **Cyan**.
    Set it to **No Plot**.

12. Select the Model tab.

    Type **XREFs** to see which XREFs are loaded in the drawing.

13. In the Project Navigator:

    Right click on **A-FP-01-Rooms** view and select **Xref Overlay**.

14. Move the **A-FP-01-Rooms** XREF on top of the 01 Core XREF,

15. 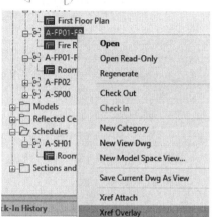 In the Project Navigator:

    Right click on **A-FP01-FR** view and select **Xref Overlay**.

16. Move the **A-FP01-FR** XREF to align with the 01 Core XREF.

17. Locate the Room Schedule.
    Create a Named View for the Room Schedule.

18. Set the View scale to 1:1.

    Set Viewport as the current layer.

19. Open the **A-102 Floor Plans** layout.

    Open the Layout ribbon.

    Select the **Rectangular** viewport tool.

20. 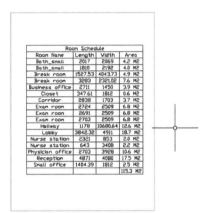 Place the viewport on the viewport layer.

    Activate the model space inside the viewport.

    Zoom into the Room Schedule using the View Manager.

21. Exit model space.
    Select the viewport.
    Set the Display to **Locked**.
    Release the selection by clicking **ESC**.

22. Open the Layout ribbon.

    Select the **Rectangular** viewport tool.

23. Zoom into the floorplan.

    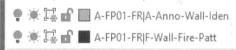

    Freeze in the active viewport:
    A-ANNO-DIMS
    A-Anno-Wall-Iden
    F-Wall-Fire
    F-Wall-Fire-Pat

    Verify that G-Area-Spce-Iden is ON and THAWED.
    Verify that A-Area-SPCE is ON and THAWED.
    Lock the Display.

24. Open the Layout ribbon.

 Select the **Rectangular** viewport tool.

25. Set the viewport to use 1:50 scale.
 Set the Annotation Scale to 1:1.

 Freeze in the Active Viewport:
 A-ANNO-DIMS
 G-Area-Spce-Iden
 G-Area-SPCE

26. Open the Layout ribbon.

 Select the **Rectangular** viewport tool.

27. Freeze in the Active Viewport:
 G-Area-Spce-Iden
 G-Area-SPCE
 A-Anno-Wall-Iden
 F-Wall-Fire-Pat

28. The layout should look similar to this.

 One viewport should show the spaces with room tags.
 One viewport should show the room schedule.
 One viewport should show the fire rating lines and fire rating tags.
 One viewport should show the floor plan with dimensions.

29. Go to the Project Navigator.

 Open the Sheets tab.
 Close **A-102 Floor Plans**.
 When prompted to save, click **Yes**.

Exercise 9-21:
Creating a Sheet in a Project

Drawing Name: new
Estimated Time: 30 minutes

This exercise reinforces the following skills:

- Project Browser
- Project Navigator
- Title blocks

1. 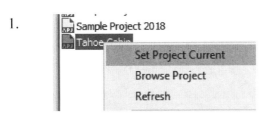 Set the **Tahoe Cabin** project Current.

   Close the Project Browser.

2. 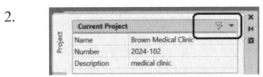 Go to the Project Navigator.
   Select the Project tab.
   Click on **Edit Project**.

3. 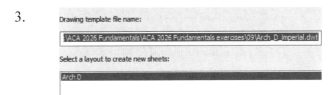 Set the template to use the *Arch_D_imperial.dwt* template.

   Click **OK**.

4. Select **Apply changes to selected subset only**.

5. 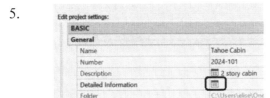 Click on the **Detailed Information** button.

6. Fill in as you like.

   Why is the Detailed Information different from the metric project? Because we used a template for the metric project and it automatically created all those fields.

   Click **OK**.

   Close the Project Properties.

7. Open the Sheets tab.

   Highlight **Architectural**.

   Right click and select **Properties**.

8. Set the Sheet Creation Template to the *Arch_D_imperial.dwt*.
   Set Prompt for Template to **Yes**.

   This way you can select what template to use every time you create a sheet.

9. Click **Apply changes to nested subsets**.

10. Highlight **Plans**.
Select **New→Sheet**.

11. You will be prompted to select a template.
Select the *Arch_D_imperial.dwt*.

Click **OK**.

12. Type **A102** for the Number.
Type **Framing Plan** for the Sheet Title.

Click **OK**.

13. 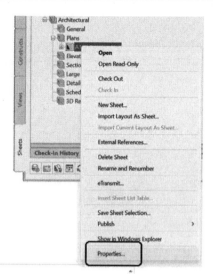 Highlight the **A102 Framing Plan**. Right click and select **Properties**.

14. Fill in the fields.

    These fields can be utilized by the title block attributes.

    Click **OK**.

15. 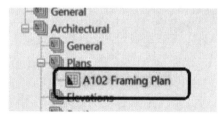 Highlight the **A102 Framing Plan**. Right click and select **Open**.

16. The sheet opens to the layout tab.

Rooms and Sheets

17. Switch to the Views tab on the Project Navigator.
Locate the **Framing Plan** view.

18. Right click and select **Place on Sheet.**

19. Scale the viewport so it fits onto the sheet.

20. If you are having difficulty seeing the elements, activate model space inside the viewport.

    Check the Global Cut Plane settings.

21. 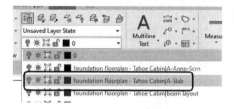 Freeze the **A-Slab** Layer.

22. 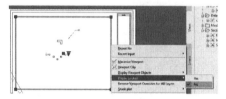 Select the viewport.
    Right click and select **Display Locked→No**.

23. Set the viewport Standard scale to **1/8" = 1'-0"**.
    Set the Annotation scale to **1/8" = 1'-0"**.

    Display needs to be unlocked to modify the scales.

    The view should look similar to this.

24. You can change the colors of layers in the viewport to make the labels easier to read.

25. Launch the Document tool palette.
Open the Callouts tab.
Select the **Title Mark** tool.

26. Modify the attributes for the view title.

    Note that the View title is placed in Paper Space not model space.

27. Switch to Model Space.

    Locate the column detail view in the Project Navigator.

    Drag and drop it into the window.

28. If you see this dialog, you can ignore it.

    If you don't want to see this warning, type LAYERNOTIFY and set to 0.

    This basically is telling you new layers are being added to the drawing.

29. Go to the View ribbon.
    Launch the View Manager.
    Create a Named View for the **Column Detail**.

30. Return to the A102 Framing Plan layout.
31. Open the Layout ribbon.
32. Click **Make Object's Layer Current** on the Home ribbon.

    Select the viewport on the layout.

The G-Anno-Nplt layer becomes current.

33. Select the **Rectangular** viewport tool.

34. Draw the new viewport next to the framing viewport.

35. Click inside the new viewport to activate model space.
Use the Named view to zoom into the Column Detail.

Verify that the Annotative Objects are enabled on the status bar or you won't see them.

36. Unlock the viewport display.
Zoom into the column detail.
Set the viewport scale to **1/2" = 1'-0"**.
Set the annotation scale to **1/2" = 1'-0"**.
Lock the display.

37. Your sheet should look similar to this.

Rooms and Sheets

38. Go to the Project Navigator.
Highlight **A102 Framing Plan**.
Right click and select **Close.**

Click **Yes** to save.

Exercise 9-22:
Creating a Framing Schedule Style

Drawing Name: foundation floor plan – Tahoe Cabin.dwg
Estimated Time: 30 minutes

This exercise reinforces the following skills:

- Project Browser
- Project Navigator
- Style Manager
- Property Set Definitions
- Schedules

1. Set the **Tahoe Cabin** project Current.

2. Go to the Project Navigator.
Select the Constructs tab.
Click on **foundation floorplan – Tahoe Cabin**.
Right click and select **Open**.

3. 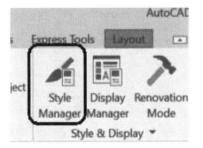 Go to the Manage ribbon.

Click **Style Manager**.

9-111

4. Click **Open**.

5. Open *schedule_styles.dwg*.

    This is a downloaded exercise file.

6.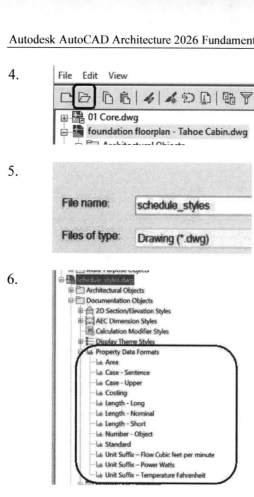

    Expand the Documentation Objects category.

    Highlight **Property Data Formats**.

    Copy and paste the Property Data Formats from *schedule_styles.dwg* to *A102 Framing Plan.dwg*.

    Hint: Go to the source drawing. Highlight Property Data Formats. Right click and select Copy. Go to the target drawing. Highlight Property Data Formats. Right click and select Paste.

7. Enable **Leave Existing**.

    Click **OK**.

8. Expand the Documentation Objects category in the **foundation floorplan – Tahoe Cabin** drawing.

    Highlight **Property Set Definitions**. Right click and select **New**.

9. Select the General tab.

    Type **Structural Members** in the Name field.

Rooms and Sheets

10. Select the Applies To tab.

Enable **Styles and Definitions**.
Enable **Structural Member Style**.

11. Select the Definition tab.

Click **Automatic Definition**.

12.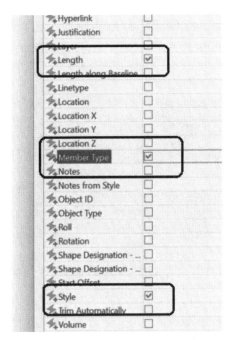

Enable:
- Length
- Member Type
- Style

Click **OK**.

13.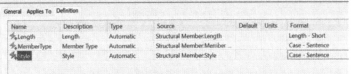

Set the Format for Length to **Length-Short**.

14. Set the Format for Member Type to **Case – Sentence.**
Set the Format for Style to **Case – Sentence**.
Click **Apply**.

9-113

15. 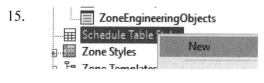 Expand the Documentation Objects category.

Highlight **Schedule Table Styles**.
Right click and select **New**.

16. Select the General tab.

Type **Foundation Framing Schedule** in the Name field.

17. Select the Default Format tab.

Set the Text Style to **Comic Sans**.

If you don't like that font, assign your preferred text style. If the desired font is not available, create the text style and assign it later.

18. Select the Applies To tab.

Enable **Structural Member.**

19. Select the Columns tab.

Click **Add Column**.

20. Look under StructuralMemberObjects.

Highlight **Style**.
Change the Heading to **Style**.
Set the Data Format to **Case – Sentence**.
Click **OK**.

21. 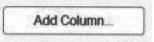 Click **Add Column**.

Rooms and Sheets

22. Look under StructuralMemberObjects.

Highlight **Member Type**.
Change the Heading to **Type**.
Set the Data Format to **Case – Sentence**.

Enable **Insert After**.
Click **OK**.

23. Click **Add Column**.

24. Look under StructuralMembers.

Highlight **Length**.
Enable **Total**.
Change the Heading to **Length**.
Set the Data Format to **Length - Short**.

Enable **Insert After**.
Click **OK**.

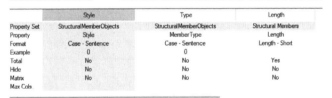 The columns tab should look like this.

25. Highlight the Style column.

Enable **Include Quantity Column**.

A column for quantity will be added.

9-115

26. Select the Sorting/Grouping tab.

Highlight **Sort**.

Click **Add**.

27. Highlight **Style**.

Click **OK**.

28. Select the Layout tab.

Change the Table Title to:

Foundation Framing Schedule.

Click **OK**.

29. Close and save the file in the Project Navigator.

Exercise 9-23:
Creating a Framing Schedule Tool

Drawing Name: foundation floorplan – Tahoe Cabin.dwg
Estimated Time: 30 minutes

This exercise reinforces the following skills:

- Project Browser
- Project Navigator
- Style Manager
- Property Set Definitions
- Schedules

1. 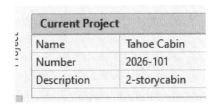 Set the **Tahoe Cabin** project Current.

2. Go to the Project Navigator.
Select the Constructs tab.
Click on **foundation floorplan – Tahoe Cabin.**
Right click and select **Open**.

3. Launch the Annotation tool palette.

Open the **Scheduling** tab.

4.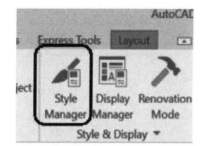

   Go to the Manage ribbon.

   Open the **Style Manager**.

5.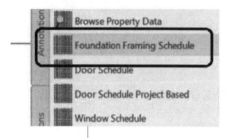

   Drag and drop the **Foundation Framing Schedule** onto the tool palette.

   Close the Style Manager.

6. Open the Model layout.

   Zoom into the upper right corner of the model.
   Locate the concrete column block.
   Select the block.
   Right click and **Select Similar** to select all the blocks in the drawing.
   Type **EXPLODE**.

7.

   Once the block is exploded, you should be able to hover over the elements to see the structural members.

8.

   Click the **Foundation Framing Schedule** tool on the Document toll palette.

   Window around the model.

   Click ENTER.

   Click to place the schedule.

   If you see any ?s in the schedule, select the schedule. Select Edit Table Cell on the ribbon. Left click in the cell with the ?. The schedule should update with the correct information.

Rooms and Sheets

9. Create a named view for the schedule.

10. In the Project Navigator:
Highlight the **foundation floorplan – Tahoe Cabin** drawing.
Right click and select **Close**.
When prompted to save, click **Yes**.

Sheet Set Manager

The Sheet Set Manager provides a list of layout tabs available in a drawing or set of drawings and allows you to organize your layouts to be printed.

The Sheet Set Manager allows you to print to a printer as well as to PDF. Autodesk does not license their PDF creation module from Adobe. Instead, they have a partnership agreement with a third-party called Bluebeam. This means that some fonts may not appear correct in your PDF print.

Exercise 9-24:
Adding a Sheet

Drawing Name: new (Tahoe Cabin Project)
Estimated Time: 15 minutes

This exercise reinforces the following skills:

- Creating Views
- Add Sheet
- Add Elevation
- Xref Manager

1. Set the **Tahoe Cabin** project Current.

Current Project	
Name	Tahoe Cabin
Number	2026-101
Description	2-storycabin

2.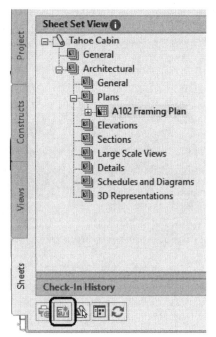
Launch the Project Navigator.
Open the Sheets tab.

Click **Add Sheet** at the bottom of the palette.

3. You will be prompted to select a template.
Browse to the Arch_D_imperial.dwt template.

This is one of the exercise files you downloaded.

Click **Open**.
Click **OK**.

4. Type **A201** in the Number field.
Type **Exterior Elevations** in the Sheet Title.
Enable **Open in drawing editor**.
Click **OK**.

5. 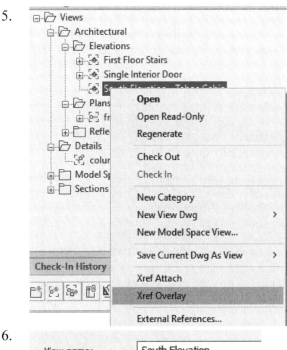 Switch to Model Space.
Switch to the Views tab on the Project Navigator.
Locate the **South Elevation** view.
Right click and select **Xref Overlay**.

6. Create a Named view of the elevation view.

7. Set the **G-Anno-Stnd-Nplt** layer current.

8. Switch to the A201 layout tab:
Open the Layout ribbon.
Place a Rectangular viewport.
Activate Model Space.
Select the South Elevation Named View.

9. Select the viewport.
Right click and change the Display Locked to **No**.

10. Switch to Model space and zoom extents.
You will see the south elevation.

   Set the View Scale to 1/8" = 1'-0".
   Set the Annotation Scale to 1/8" = 1'-0".

   Position the elevation in the viewport.
   Lock the viewport display.

11. 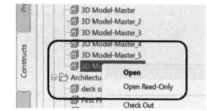 Add a view title in paperspace.
Change the view title as shown.
The title should read **South Exterior Elevation**.
The scale should read Scale: **1/8" = 1'-0"**.

12. Can you create North/West/East Exterior elevation views and add them to the sheet?

   Hint: Open the Master 3D construct. Restore the Model Only layer state.
   Create the elevation views and then add as new view drawings.

13. Select the **Elevation** tool from the Annotate ribbon.

14.

    Place the elevation at the desired location.

    Point it towards the building model.

15.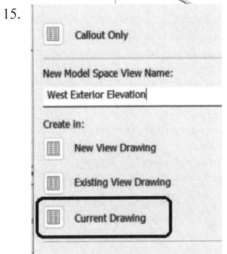

    Give the elevation a name.

    Click **Current Drawing**.

16.

    Window around the entire building.
    Click to place the view in the drawing.

17.

    Update the attributes for the view title.

18. 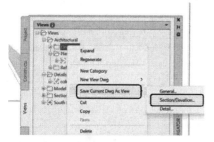 Save the **Current Dwg As View→Section/Elevation**.

19. Provide a name and Description.

    Click **Next**.

20. Enable all the levels.

     Click **Next**.

    Click **Finish**.

    Save and close the view drawing.

21. Return to the **A201 Exterior Elevations** sheet.
    Add the exterior view to the sheet.
    Repeat for the remaining exterior views.

22. Go to the Project Navigator and close A201 Exterior Elevations on the Sheets tab.
    Click **Yes** when prompted to save.
    Close 3D Model-Master.
    Click **Yes** when prompted to save.

Exercise 9-25:
Creating a PDF Document

Drawing Name: none
Estimated Time: 5 minutes

This exercise reinforces the following skills:

- Printing to PDF

1.
   Open the Sheets tab.

   The Tahoe Cabin is the current project.

   Launch the Project Navigator.

2.
   Switch to the Sheets tab.
   Click the Sheet Set icon to switch to the Sheet Set View.

3.
   Open the two sheets.

4.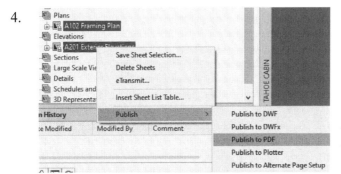
   Highlight the two sheets.

   Right click and select **Publish→Publish to PDF.**

   By default, sheet sets are published to DWF files. To publish to other file types, you need to open the files.

5.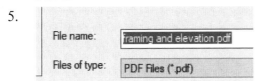
   Browse where you want to store your PDF file.

   Give your file a name and click **Select**.

6.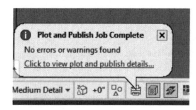

    All **sheets** that exist in the project will be converted to PDF. You will see a notification when the plot is complete.
    Click the link.

    The sheets that were plotted are listed.

    Close any open files and save.

7. Locate the pdf and open it to review.

Extra:

1) Update the view titles with the correct sheet numbers based on the sheets where the views are placed.

2) Create additional elevation and section views for the kitchen, the second bathroom, the exterior elevations, and windows.

3) Add the new views to existing sheets or new sheets.

4) Add window tags to all the windows.

5) Create a window schedule.

6) Create a window legend.

7) Create a detail view for window framing.

8) Create a callout to the window framing detail view.

9) Create a section elevation view of an interior wall.

10) Add keynotes to the interior wall section elevation view.

11) Update the attributes on each title block with the correct sheet number and title information.

Notes:

QUIZ 9

True or False

1. You can create a view drawing by selecting constructs from the Project Navigator palette and using them as external references in a View drawing.

2. A construct drawing can be used as a view drawing.

3. View drawings are usually created after you have defined the project's levels and basic construct drawings.

4. In order to create a schedule, you need to add schedule tags to the objects to be included in the schedule first.

5. Property set definitions must be attached to an object or style before they can be added to a schedule.

Multiple Choice

6. The three types of views that can be created in a project are:

    A. General
    B. Architectural
    C. Detail
    D. Section/Elevation
    E. Floor Plan
    F. Reflected Ceiling Plan

7. To display the external references for a view drawing:

    A. Highlight the view drawing in the Project Navigator, right click and click External References
    B. Open the view drawing, bring up the XREF Manager
    C. Launch the Layers Properties Manager, highlight XREFs
    D. Go to the View ribbon, click on XREFs

8. Space Styles: (select all that apply)

    A. Control the hatching displayed
    B. Control the name displayed when spaces are tagged
    C. Cannot be modified
    D. Have materials assigned

9. When placing a wall tag:

   A. Tags are positioned relative to the midpoint of a wall
   B. Tags are positioned relative to the end of a wall
   C. Tags are positioned relative to the center of a wall
   D. Tags are positioned based on user input.

10. When placing a space tag:

    A. Tags are positioned based on user input
    B. Tags are hidden behind the space hatch and need to have the display order changed
    C. Tags are positioned relative to the center of the geometric extents of the space
    D. Tags are positioned above the space hatch

ANSWERS:

1) T; 2) F; 3) T; 4) F; 5) T; 6) B, C, and D; 7) A; 8) A, B; C, and D 9) A; 10) C;

Lesson 10:
Rendering & Materials

AutoCAD Architecture divides materials into TWO locations:

- Materials in Active Drawing
- Autodesk Library

You can also create one or more custom libraries for materials you want to use in more than one project. You can only edit materials in the drawing or in the custom library—Autodesk Materials are read-only.

Materials have two asset definitions—Appearance and Information. Materials do not have to be fully defined to be used. Each asset contributes to the definition of a single material.

You can define Appearance independently without assigning/associating it to a material. You can assign the same assets to different materials. Assets can be deleted from a material in a drawing or in a user library, but you cannot remove or delete assets from materials in locked material libraries, such as the Autodesk Materials library or any locked user library. You can delete assets from a user library – BUT be careful because that asset might be used somewhere!

You can only duplicate, replace or delete an asset if it is in the drawing or in a user library. The Autodesk Asset Library is "read-only" and can only be used to check-out or create materials.

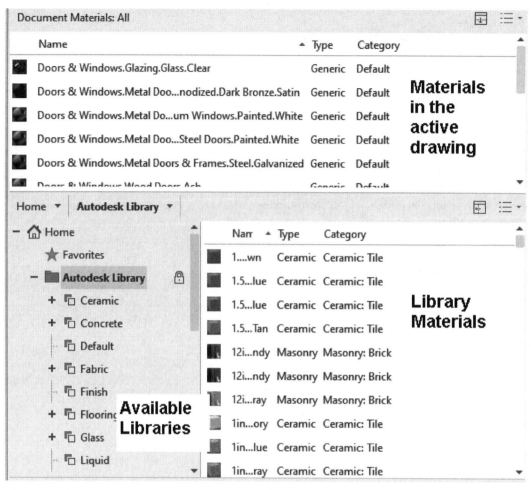

The Material Browser is divided into three distinct panels.
The Document Materials panel lists all the materials available in the drawing.
The Material Libraries list any libraries available.
The Library Materials lists the materials in the material libraries.

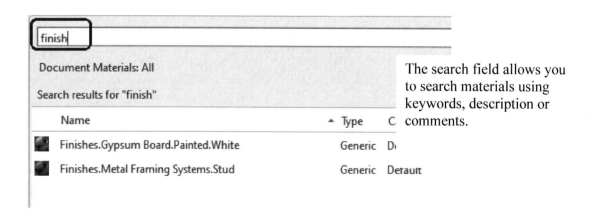

The search field allows you to search materials using keywords, description or comments.

Rendering & Materials

The View control button allows you to control how materials are sorted and displayed in the Material Libraries panel.

Material Editor

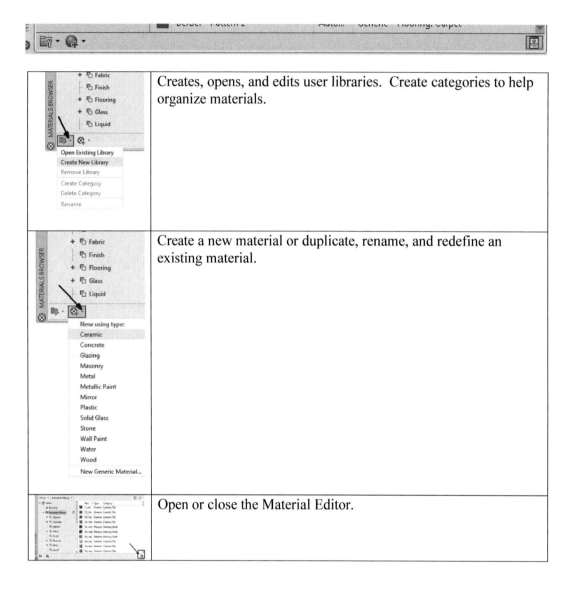

	Creates, opens, and edits user libraries. Create categories to help organize materials.
	Create a new material or duplicate, rename, and redefine an existing material.
	Open or close the Material Editor.

Rendering & Materials

Exercise 10-1:
Modifying the Material Browser Interface

Drawing Name: material_browser.dwg
Estimated Time: 10 minutes

This exercise reinforces the following skills:

❑ Navigating the Material Browser and Material Editor

1. 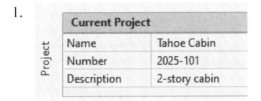 Set the **Tahoe Cabin** project current.

2. Open *3D Model-Master.dwg*.

3. Activate the **Render** ribbon.

   Select the small arrow in the lower right corner of the materials panel.

   This launches the Material Editor.

4. 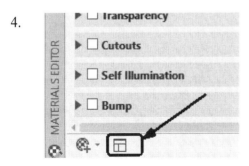 Launch the Material Browser by selecting the button on the bottom of the Material Editor dialog.

10-5

5. Make the Materials Browser appear as shown.

6. 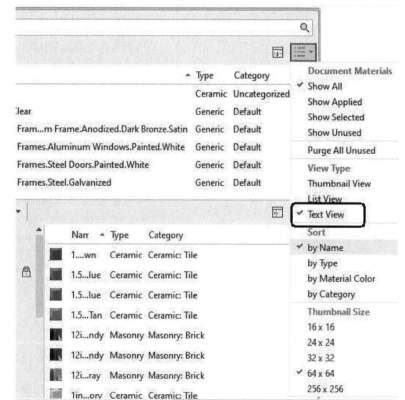 Change the top pane to use a Text view.

7. 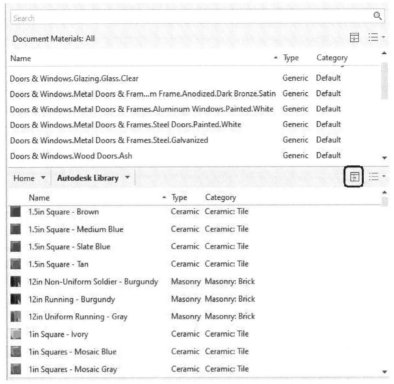 Toggle the Materials Library list OFF by selecting the top button on the Documents pane.

8.

Change the upper pane to a **List View**.
Set the Thumbnail size to **16x16**.

9. 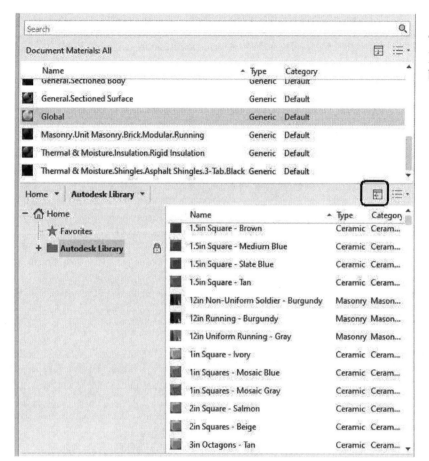 Toggle the Library tree back on.

10. In the Document Materials panel, set the view to **Show Unused**.

Scroll through the list to see what materials are not being used in your drawing.

11. In the Material Library pane, change the view to sort **by Category**.

12. Close the Material dialogs.

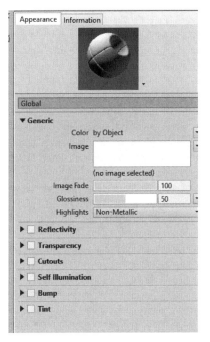

The Appearance Tab

Appearance controls how material is displayed in a rendered view, Realistic view, or Ray Trace view.

A zero next to the hand means that only the active/selected material uses the appearance definition.

Different material types can have different appearance parameters.

The Information Tab

The value in the Description field can be used in Material tags.

Using comments and keywords can be helpful for searches.

Use this flow chart as a guide to help you decide whether or not you need to create a new material in your project.

Exercise 10-2:
Copy a Material from a Library to a Drawing

Drawing Name: First Floor Plan.dwg
Estimated Time: 10 minutes

In order to use or assign a material, it must exist in the drawing. You can search for a material and, if one exists in the Autodesk Library, copy it to your active drawing.

This exercise reinforces the following skills:

- ❑ Copying materials from the Autodesk Materials Library
- ❑ Modifying materials in the drawing

1. 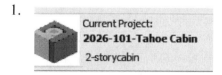 Set the **Tahoe Cabin** project current.

2. Open *First Floor Plan.dwg*.

   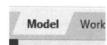 Open the Model tab.

3. Go to the **Render** ribbon.

4. 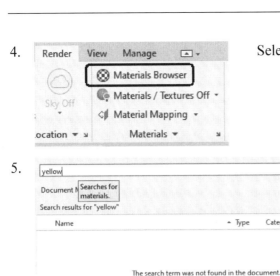 Select the **Materials Browser** tool.

5. Type **yellow** in the search field.

   There are no yellow materials in the drawing.

6. Highlight **Wall Paint** under Autodesk Library.

   There are three yellow wall paints.

   Locate the **Yellow Matte Wall Paint**.

7. 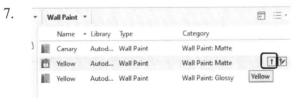 Select the up arrow to copy the material up to the drawing.

 The yellow paint material is now listed in the Document Materials.

8. Type **blue** in the search field.

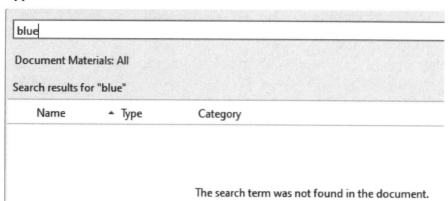

9. The Autodesk Library has several different blue materials available.

10. 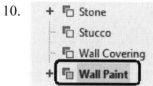 Highlight the Wall Paint category in the Library pane.

This confines the search to blue wall paints.

Rendering & Materials

11. Locate the **Periwinkle Matte** Wall Paint and then copy it over to the drawing.

    Notice the lock symbol next to the material name. Materials in the library cannot be modified. However, once you import a material into your document, it can be edited.

The blue wall paint is now available in the drawing.

You have added material definitions to the active drawing ONLY.

12. Close the Materials dialog.

13. In the Project Navigator:

    Right click on **First Floor Plan** and select **Close**. Click **Yes** when prompted to save.

Exercise 10-3:
Adding Color to Walls

Drawing Name: First Floor Plan.dwg
Estimated Time: 30 minutes

This exercise reinforces the following skills:

- Edit External Reference
- Materials
- Colors
- Display Manager
- Style Manager

1. *The Tahoe Cabin is the current project.*

   Open *First Floor Plan* in the Project Navigator.

2. Switch to a **SE Isometric** view.

3. Go to the Manage ribbon.

   Launch the **Style Manager**.

4. 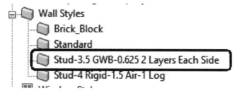 Locate the Stud-3.5 GWB… wall style.

   Create a copy of the wall style.

5. 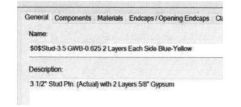 Rename the copy **3.5 GWB…Blue-Yellow**.

10-14

Rendering & Materials

6. Open the Components tab.

   Rename the exterior components **GWB-Yellow** and **GWB-Blue**.

   Just click in the field to modify the names.

7. Activate the Materials tab.

   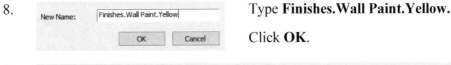

   Highlight the **GWB-Yellow** component.
   Select the **New** button.

8. Type **Finishes.Wall Paint.Yellow.**

   Click **OK**.

9.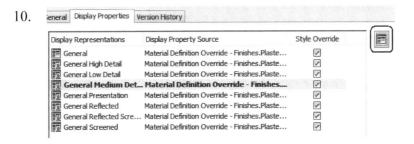

   Highlight the **GWB-Yellow** component.
   Select the **Edit** button.

10. Activate the **Display Properties** tab.
    Select the **Edit Display Properties** button.

10-15

11. Activate the **Layer/Color/Linetype** tab.

    Highlight **3D Body**.

    Left pick on the color square.

12. Select the color **yellow**.

    Click **OK**.

13. Select the **Other** tab.

14. Select **Yellow** in the drop-down list next to Render Material under Surface Rendering.

    Note that the materials are in alphabetic order.

15. Click **OK**.

Rendering & Materials

16. Verify that there is a check in the Style Override box.

Click **OK** again.

17. Repeat the settings for all the Display Representations.

18. Highlight the **GWB-Blue** component.
Select the **New** button.

19. Type **Finishes.Wall Paint.Periwinkle**.

Click **OK**.

20. Highlight the **GWB-Blue** component.

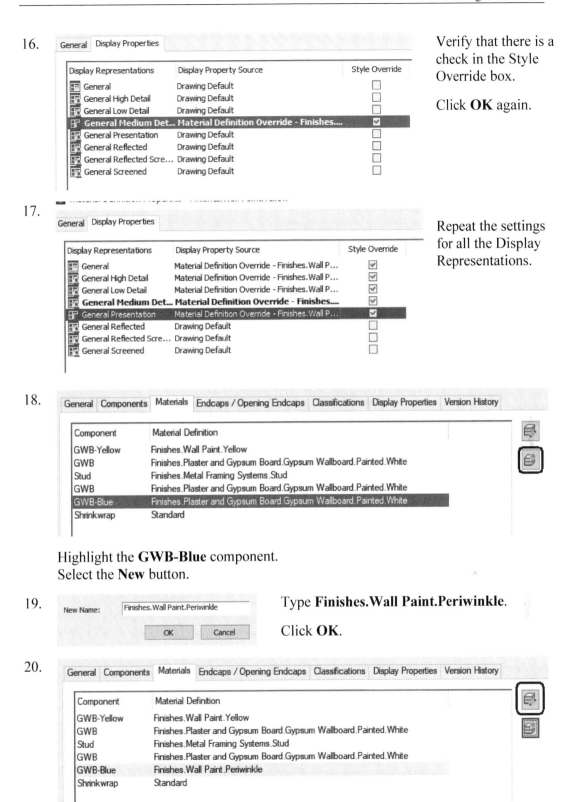

10-17

Select the **Edit** button.

21.

    Activate the **Display Properties** tab.
    Select the **Edit Display Properties** button.

22.

    Activate the **Layer/Color/Linetype** tab.

    Highlight **3D Body**.

    Left pick on the color square.

23.

    Select the color **blue**.

    Click **OK**.

24.

    Select the **Other** tab.

    Use the drop-down list to select the color Periwinkle.

    Click **OK**.

25.   Verify that there is a check next to the Style Override.

    Click **OK**.

26.   Repeat the settings for all the display representations.

Rendering & Materials

27.

Your components should show two different material definitions for the GWB components.

Click **OK**.

Close the Style Manager.
Select a wall.
Right click and select **Properties**.
Change the wall style to use the **Blue-Yellow** wall style.

Click **ESC** to release the selection.

28.

29.   On the View ribbon, change the display to **Realistic**.

30. Inspect the wall.

Notice that all walls using the new wall style have blue on one side and yellow on the other.

In order to apply different colors to different walls, you would have to create a wall style for each color assignment.

31.

To flip the color so walls are yellow/blue, simply use the direction arrows.

32. Open the Project Navigator.
    Highlight **First Floor Plan**.
    Right click and select **Close**.
    Click **Yes** to save the drawing.

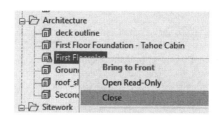

Elements

An element is a generic building block for multiple use. For example, you can create an element for a repeating design object like a desk/chair combination to place in a number of cubicles. You can also create an element for a typical bathroom layout and reference it multiple times into one or more constructs. Because you can annotate individual instances of an external reference, you can use the same element and annotate it differently in different locations. Unlike constructs, elements are not assigned to a level/division in the building.

Elements are dwg files. When you convert or add a dwg file as a project element, an additional XML file with the same name is created. The accompanying XML file contains information to connect the drawing file to the project.

Note: The XML file is created and updated automatically. You do not need to edit it, but be careful not to accidentally delete it in File Explorer.

Exercise 10-4:
Adding Elements

Drawing Name: woman1.dwg
Estimated Time: 15 minutes

This exercise reinforces the following skills:

- Project Navigator
- Elements

1. | Current Project | |
   |---|---|
   | Name | Tahoe Cabin |
   | Number | 2026-101 |
   | Description | 2-storycabin |

   Set the **Tahoe Cabin** project current.

2.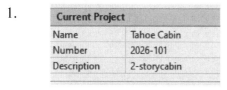

   In the Project Navigator, open the Constructs tab.
   Highlight **Elements**.
   Right click and select **New→Category**.

10-20

3. Name the category: **Entourage**.

4. 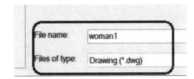 Open *woman1.dwg*.

   I have included several 3D drawings of men, women, a dog, etc. in the exercise files that can be used as elements in your projects.

5. Locate 0,0,0 in the drawing.

   I locate this by drawing a line from 0,0,0.

6. Move the figure so it is standing at the 0,0,0 location.

   This will make it easier to insert and position the block.

7. Highlight the **Entourage** category in the Project Navigator.

   Right click and select **Save Current Dwg As Element**.

8. Type a Description for the element: **3D woman figure standing**.

   Click **OK**.

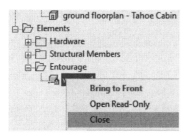
The element is now listed in the Project Navigator.
Right click on the woman1 element.
Close the file.

Click **Yes** to save.

9.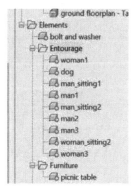
Add additional files to the Project Navigator as elements.

Exercise 10-5:
Adding Topography

Drawing Name: 3D Model_Master
Estimated Time: 15 minutes

This exercise reinforces the following skills:

- Content Browser
- Xrefs
- Mass Elements

1.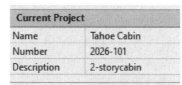
Set the **Tahoe Cabin** project current.

2.
Open the 3D Model_Master Construct.

10-22

3. Highlight Topography.

Right click and select **Xref Overlay**.

4. Position the topography so it is under the building.

Use Properties to adjust the elevation of the topography.

You can modify the topography to add a mass element for the fill below the driveway, if desired.

5. Open the Content Browser.

Locate the pine tree and add to the topography.

You can change the scale of some of the trees, so some of the trees are larger and some are smaller.

6. Close and save the file.

Camera

You can place a camera in a drawing to define a 3D view.

You can turn a camera on or off in a drawing and use grips to edit a camera's location, target, or lens length. A camera is defined by a location *XYZ* coordinate, a target *XYZ* coordinate, and a field of view/lens length, which determines the magnification, or zoom factor.

By default, saved cameras are named sequentially: Camera1, Camera2, and so on. You can rename a camera to better describe its view. The View Manager lists existing cameras in a drawing as well as other named views.

Exercise 10-6
Camera View

Drawing Name: 3D Model-Master.dwg
Estimated Time: 60 minutes

This exercise reinforces the following skills:

- Camera
- Display Settings
- Navigation Wheel
- Saved Views
- Adjust Camera

1. *The Tahoe Cabin is the current project.*
   Open **3D Model-Master** Construct.

2.

   The model should appear like this.

   Save as a new layer state.

3. Use the View Cube to orient the floor plan to a Top View with North in correct position. *You can also use the right click menu on the upper left of the display window.*

   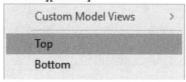

Rendering & Materials

4. Set the elevation to the **First Floor**.

5. Activate the Render ribbon.

   On the Camera panel,

   select **Create Camera**.

6. Place the Camera so it is looking toward the southwest corner of the building.

   Click ENTER.

7. 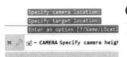 Click Height and set the Height of the camera to **15'-0"**.

8. 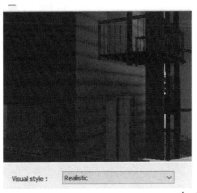 Select the camera so it highlights.

   A Camera Preview window will open.

   If you don't see the Camera Preview window, left click on the camera and the window should open.

   Set the Visual Style to **Realistic.**

   Close the Camera Preview window.

9. 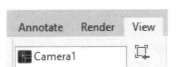 Activate the View ribbon.

   Notice the Camera1 view has been added to the view lists.

   Left click to activate the Camera1 view.

10-25

10. Switch to the Render ribbon.

    Click **Adjust**.
    Click ENTER to see a list of cameras.

11. 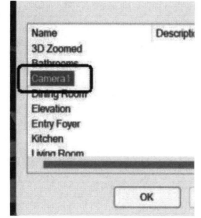 Highlight **Camera1**.

    Click **OK**.

12. You can use the dialog to adjust the view to your liking.

    Click **OK**.

13. Switch to the View ribbon.

    Change the Display Style to **Realistic**.

14. Set Materials/Textures **On**.

15. Set **Full Shadows** on.

16. 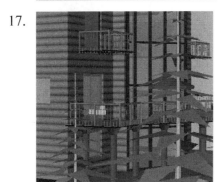 Switch to the View ribbon.

    Set **Realistic Face Style** on.

17. The Camera view should update as the different settings are applied.

18. Select **Full Navigation**.

19. *Use the controls on the navigation wheel to adjust the view.*

    Try LOOK to look up and down.

    Click the small x in the upper right to close when you are satisfied with the view.

20. 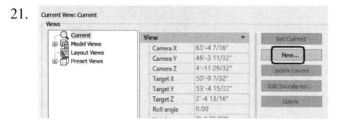 Click the bottom arrow on the view list.

    Select **View Manager** located at the bottom of the view list.

21. Select **New**.

22. Name the view **Outside Deck.**

    Select the down arrow to expand the dialog.

23. Set the Visual style to **Realistic**.

    Set the background to **Sun & Sky**.

24.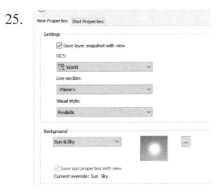

Click **OK** to accept the default sun & sky settings.

I have several different sky images in the exercise files you can use for your renderings.

25.

Click **OK**.

26.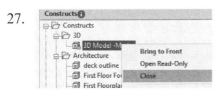

The saved view is now listed under Model Views.

Click **OK**.

27. Go to the Project Navigator.

Right click on **3D Model-Master**.
Select **Close**.
Click **Yes** to Save when prompted.

Rendering

Rendering is the process where you create photo-realistic images of your model. It can take a lot of trial and error to set up the lighting and materials as well as the best camera angle before you get an image you like. Be patient. The more you practice, the easier it gets. Make small incremental changes – like adding more or less lighting – turning shadows off and on – changing materials – and render between each change so you can understand which changes make the images better and which changes make the images worse.

If you have created a rendering that is close to what you want, you may be able to use the built-in image editor to make it lighter/darker or add more contrast. That may be enough to get the job over the finish line.

Exercise 10-7
Create Rendering

Drawing Name: 3D Model-Master
Estimated Time: 5 minutes

This exercise reinforces the following skills:

- Render
- Display Settings
- Set Location

You need an internet connection in order to perform this exercise.

1. The Tahoe Cabin is the current project. Open **3D Model-Master** construct.

2. Set the **Top** view active.

3. Activate the Render ribbon.

Rendering & Materials

4. Select **Sky Background and Illumination**.

5.

In the drop-down panel under Sky Background and Illumination, select

Set Location→From Esri Maps.

6.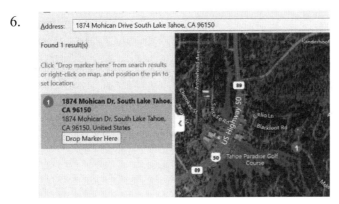

Type in an address in the search field where your project is located.

Once it is located on the map, select **Drop Marker here.**

Click **Next**.

7. Select the coordinate system to be applied to the project.

Highlight **CA-III**, then Click **Next**.

8.

Click ENTER to accept the origin.

Click ENTER to accept the default North location.

Your building model will appear on a satellite image of the address you provided.

This is useful to provide an idea of how the model will look in the area where it will be constructed.

9.

Under Esri Imagery:

Click **Map Off**.

10. Open the Render ribbon.

    On the Render to Size drop-down, select the **More Output Settings**.

11. 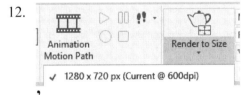 Set the Image Size to **1280x720 px**.
    Set the Resolution to **600**.
    Click **Save**.

12. Click on **Render to Size**.

    Note the setting you created is enabled.

13. Select the small arrow in the right corner of the Render panel on the ribbon.

14. Set the Preset Info to **Medium**.

    Notice that ACA gives you an idea of how long the rendering will take depending on the preset.

15. 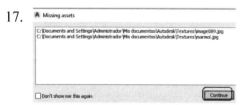 Set the Render Accuracy for the Lights and Materials to **Draft**.

16. Click on the **Render** button.

17. If a dialog comes up stating some material images are missing, Click **Continue**.

    If you get an error message stating you are missing assets, go to Options, select the Files tab.

    Look for The Textures search path, add your exercise folder to the list.

18. A window will come up where the camera view will be rendered.

    If you don't see the window, use the drop-down to open the Render Window.

Rendering & Materials

19. ![save icon] Select the **Save** icon to save the rendered image.

20. By default, the image will be saved to the 3D category under Constructs.

21. File name: southwest outside.jpeg
    Files of type: JPEG(*.jpeg;*.jpg)

    Type in a name for the image.
    Save as a jpg file.

    Click **Save**.

22. JPG Image Options
    Quality: 100
    Draft   Best
    File Size: 465.4 KB
    OK   Cancel

    Set the quality of the jpg file.

    Click **OK**.

10-35

23. Close the Render Window.

24. Go to the Project Navigator.

    Highlight **3D Model- Master**.
    Right click and select **Close**.
    Click **Yes** when prompted to save.

Exercise 10-8
Render in Cloud

Drawing Name: First Floor Plan.dwg
Estimated Time: 5 minutes

This exercise reinforces the following skills:

- Render in Cloud
- Design Center
- Blocks

    Autodesk offers a service where you can render your model on their server using an internet connection. You need to register for an account. Educators and students can create a free account. The advantage of using the Cloud for rendering is that you can continue to work while the rendering is being processed. You do need an internet connection for this to work.

1. *The Tahoe Cabin is the current project.*

    Open the **First Floor Plan** construct.

Rendering & Materials

2. Switch to a top view.

Restore the **Space Planning** layer state.

3. Use the **Freeze layer** tool to freeze the elevation/section markers and lines.

Update the Layer State.

4. 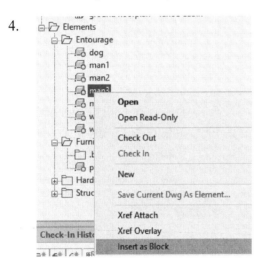 Locate an entourage element to add to the kitchen area.

I selected man3.

10-37

5. 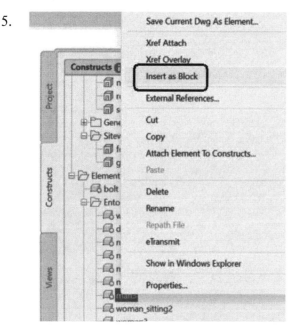 Highlight **man2** (or your preferred element).

6. Position the two male blocks in the kitchen/dining room area.

   Scale them to fit into the room.

7. Switch to a Top view.
   Open the Render ribbon.

   Select **Create Light**→**Spot**.

8.   Click **Turn off the default lighting**.

9.

Place the light above the kitchen island.

Click **ENTER** to accept the default values.

Select the light.
Right click and select **Properties**.

10.

Geometry	
Position X	24'-3 5/32"
Position Y	37'-10 7/8"
Position Z	8'-0"
Target X	24'-3 5/32"
Target Y	37'-10 7/8"
Target Z	4'-0"
Targeted	Yes

Change the Position Z to **8'-0"**.
This locates the light at the ceiling.

Change the Target Z to **4'-0"**.
This positions the light to fall to the kitchen island.

Click **ESC** to release the selection.

11. 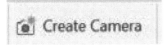   Select the **Create Camera** tool on the Render ribbon.

12.

Position the camera so it is looking into the kitchen towards the upper left corner of the building.

13.

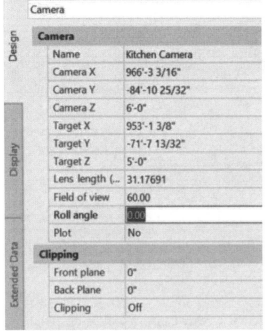

Select the camera.
Right click and select **Properties**.
Change the Name to **Kitchen Camera**.
Change the Camera Z to **6'-0"**.
Change the Target Z to **5'-0"**.
Change the Field of view to **60.0**.
This widens the angle of the view.

Click **ESC** to release the selection.

14.

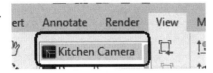

Go to the View ribbon.

Select **Kitchen Camera**.

Rendering & Materials

15. Use the Full Navigation Wheel to adjust the view as needed.

16. *You should see the 3D figure inside the kitchen.*

    Change the visual style to **Hidden** to make it easier to see.

17. Save the file.

    You must save the file before you can render.

18. Activate the Render ribbon.
    Enable **Full Shadows**.
    Set **Sky Background and Illumination** ON.
    Enable **Materials/Textures On**.
    Save the drawing.

19. Select **Render in Cloud**.

20. Set the Model View to render the current view.

    Click the **Start Rendering** model.

21. *A small bubble message will appear when the rendering is completed.*

10-41

22. *You will also receive an email when the rendering is complete. The email is sent to the address you used to sign into your account.*

23. Select **Render Gallery** on the Render ribbon to see your renderings.

24. Click on the My Renderings tab on the browser to review your renderings.

25. You can also select View completed rendering from the drop-down menu under your sign in.

26. Close and save *First Floor Plan.dwg*.

You may need to sign into the gallery in order to see your rendering.

Compare the quality of the rendering performed using the Cloud with the rendering done in the previous exercise.

I have found that rendering using the Cloud is faster and produces better quality images. It also allows me to continue working while the rendering is being processed.

Walk-Through

You can create 3D preview animations and adjust the settings before you create a motion path animation.

Preview animations are created with the controls on the Animation panel found on the ribbon and the 3D navigation tools. Once a 3D navigation tool is active, the controls on the Animation panel are enabled to start recording an animation.

Walk-through animations are useful when reviewing building sites or discussing building renovations.

The easiest way to create a walk-through is to sketch out the path using a polyline. Then, attach a camera to follow the desired path.

Exercise 10-9:
Create an Animation

Drawing Name: animation.dwg
Estimated Time: 5 minutes

This exercise reinforces the following skills:

- Walk-Through

It will take the software several minutes to compile the animation. It is a good idea to do this exercise right before a 30-minute break to allow it time to create the animation during the break.

1. Open *animation.dwg*.

2. Activate the View ribbon.

   Switch to a **Top** View.

3. Set the view display to **Hidden**.

10-43

4. Activate the Home ribbon.

Set the layer named **Walkthrough** Current.

This layer is set so it doesn't plot.

5. Select the **Polyline** tool located under the Line drop-down list.

6. Draw a polyline that travels through the floor plan to view different rooms.

7. Select the polyline.

Right click and select **Properties**.

Rendering & Materials

8. Set the elevation of the polyline to **5' 3"**.

   If you don't raise the line, your camera path is going to be along the floor.

   Click **ESC** to release the selected polyline.

9. Switch to a **SW Isometric Realistic** view.

10. Activate the Render ribbon.

    Select **Animation Motion Path**.

11. Set the Frame Rate to **10**.

    Set the Number of frames to **3000**.

    Set the Duration to **300**.

    Set the Visual Style to **Realistic**.

    Set the Format to **AVI**.
    This will allow you to play the animation in Windows Media Player.

    Set the Resolution to **1024 x 768**.

12. For Camera:

    Enable **Path.**

    Left click on the select button.

13. Select the polyline.

    Name the camera path.

    Click **OK**.

14. For Target:

    Enable **Path.**

    Left click on the select button.

    Select the polyline.

    Name the camera path.

    Click **OK**.

15. Click **OK**.

    Browse to your classwork folder.

    Name the file to create *walkthrough1.avi*.

    Click **Save**.

16. 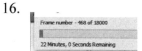 You will see the animation preview as it processes.

    This will take several minutes.

17. When it is complete, open Windows File Explorer.

    Browse to the folder where it is saved.

18. Right click on it and select **Open with Windows Media Player**.

19. Try creating different walkthroughs using different visual styles.
    You can use different video editors to edit the files you create.
20. Save as *ex10-10.dwg*.

Exercise 10-10:
Using the Sun & Sky

Drawing Name: sun_study.dwg
Estimated Time: 15 minutes

This exercise reinforces the following skills:

- Create a saved view
- Apply sunlight
- Add an image as background
- Adjust background

1. Open *sun_study.dwg*.

2. 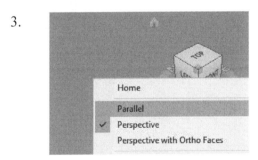 Right click on the ViewCube and select **Parallel**.

   How does the view shift?

3. Right click on the ViewCube and select **Perspective**.

   How does the view shift?

4. Double click the wheel on the mouse to Zoom Extents.

   Adjust the view so that the back edge of the slab is horizontal in the view.

   Hint: Switch to a Front view then tip the view slightly forward.

5. Switch to the View tab.

   Launch the **View Manager**.

6. Click **New**.

7. Type **Front Isometric** for the View Name.

8.

   Expand the lower pane of the dialog.

   Under Background:

   Select **Image**.

9. Set image to *sky.JPG*.

   You may need to change the Files of type to JFIF. This file is included in the downloaded exercise files.

   Click **Open**.

Rendering & Materials

10.

    Click **OK**.

11.

    Click **OK**.

    Set the Front Isometric as the Current View.

    You have now saved the view.

    Close the View Manager.

12.

    Type **Render** to render the view.

    A preview window will open and the view will render.

    Close the preview window.

13.

    Switch to the Render tab.

    Enable **Sky Background and Illumination**.

14. Enable **Materials/Textures On**.

15. Type **Render** to render the view.

    A preview window will open and the view will render.

    Close the preview window.

16. Enable **Full Shadows**.

17. Click the small arrow in the lower right corner of the Sun & Location panel.

18. Set the Intensity Factor to **1.25**.
    Set the Ground color to **110,219,0**.
    (This is a light green.)
    Set the Disk Intensity to **2**.

    Close the dialog.

19. Type **Render** to render the view.

    A preview window will open and the view will render.

    Close the preview window.

20. Save as *ex10-11.dwg*.

This exercise lets you try different settings and compare the rendering results. Try applying different backgrounds and lighting to see how the rendering changes.

Exercise 10-11:
Applying Materials

Drawing Name: materials.dwg
Estimated Time: 45 minutes

This exercise reinforces the following skills:

- Navigate the Materials Browser
- Apply materials to model components
- Edit Styles
- Change environment
- View Manager
- Render

1. Open *materials.dwg*.

2. [–][SW Isometric][Realistic]   Set the display to **Realistic**.

   If you don't set the display to Realistic, you won't see the material changes.

3. Switch to the Render ribbon.

   Click on **Materials Browser**.

4. Locate **Beechwood – Honey** and load into the drawing.

   This is for the flooring.

5. Locate **Glass Clear - Light** and load into the drawing.

   This is for the window glazing.

10-51

6. Locate **Wall Texture - Salmon** and load into the drawing.

   This is for the walls.

7. 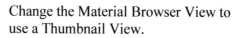 Locate **Sand Wall Paint** and load into the drawing.

   This is for the wall and window trim.

8. 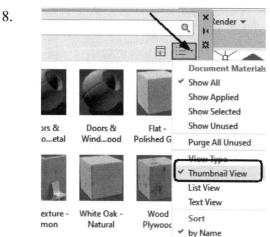 Change the Material Browser View to use a Thumbnail View.

   Now you can see swatches of all the materials available in your drawing.

   Close the Materials Browser.

9. Select a wall.

   On the ribbon:
   Select **Edit Style**.

10. Click the Materials tab.

    Highlight the top component for the wall.
    Click on the **Edit Material** button.

11. Click the Display Properties tab.

    Click on the override button.

12. Click the Other tab.

Set the Render Material to **Wall Texture – Salmon**.

Click **OK**.

Close all the dialogs.

Click ESC to release the selection.
You should see the new material on the walls.

If you don't see the material change, verify that your display is set to **Realistic**.

This only changes the wall style used in this drawing.

13.   Click on a window.
On the ribbon:
Select **Edit Style**.

14. Click the Materials tab.

Highlight the **Frame Component**.
Click on **New Material**.

15. Create a new material called **sand paint**.

Click **OK**.

16. The Frame is now assigned the new material.

10-53

17. Highlight the Glass Component.
    Click on **New Material**.

18. Create a new material called **Glass – Clear Light**.

    Click **OK**.

19. The Glass is now assigned the new material.

20. Highlight the Frame and select **Edit Material**.

21. Place a Check next to the General Medium Detail to enable Style Override.

22. Click on the Other tab.
    Set the Render Material to the **Sand** material.

    Click **OK**.

    Close the Display Properties dialog.

23. Highlight the Glass and select **Edit Material**.

24. Place a Check next to the General Medium Detail to enable Style Override.

Rendering & Materials

25. Click on the Other tab.

    Set the Render Material to the **Clear - Light** material.

    Click **OK**.

    Close the Display Properties dialog.

26. Verify that:

    Set the Frame to **sand paint**.

    Set the Glass to **Glass – Clear Light**.

    Close all the dialogs.

27. Click ESC to release the selection.
    Select the floor slab.

28. On the ribbon:
    Select **Edit Style**.

29. On the Components tab:

    Click **Add component**.

30. Rename **wood flooring**.

31. Make sure the Thickness Offset is set to 0" or you won't see the new material.

32. Switch to the Materials tab.

    Highlight the wood flooring Component.
    Click on **New Material**.

33. Name the new material **beechwood floor**.

    Click **OK**.

34. Highlight the wood flooring component and select **Edit Material**.

35. Place a Check next to the General Medium Detail to enable Style Override.

36. Click on the Other tab.
    Set the Render Material to the **Beechwood - Honey** material.

    Click **OK**.

37. Close the Display Properties dialog.
    Click **ESC** to release the selection.

    Verify that you see all the material changes that you made. The walls should appear salmon colored, the windows should have a light brown frame, and the floor should have a wood surface.

38.

    Switch to the Render tab.

    Enable **Sun Status**.

Rendering & Materials

39. Click on **Keep the default lighting turned on.**

40. Click on **Adjust exposure settings**.

41. Turn the Environment **On**.

    Enable **Use Custom Background.**

    Click on **Background…**

42. Set Type to **Image**.

    Click **Browse**.

    Select the *Beach.jpg* file in the downloaded exercise files.

    Click **Open**.

    Click on **Adjust Image**.

43. Select **Stretch** for Image position.

    Enable **Scale**.

    Click **OK**.

    Close the dialogs.

44. Orbit, pan and zoom to position the model on the beach so it appears proper.

45. Switch to the View tab.

Launch the **View Manager**.

46. Click **New**.

47.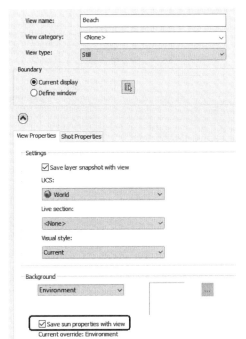

Save the view as **Beach**.

Enable **Save sun properties with view**.

Click **OK**.

48.

Click **OK**.

49.

Type **RENDER**.

The preview window will appear and the view will render.

Save as *ex10-12.dwg*.

Exercise 10-12:
Applying Materials to Furniture

Drawing Name: Wicker chair and sofa.dwg
Estimated Time: 15 minutes

This exercise reinforces the following skills:

- Navigate the Materials Browser
- Apply materials to model components
- Customize materials

1. Open the *Wicker chair and sofa* in the downloaded exercises folder..

2. Use explode to explode the blocks until you see solids when you hover over the elements.

   Type **EXPLODE, ALL, ENTER**.

   Repeat until you see 3D solid when you hover over each item.

3. Switch to the Render ribbon.

   Click on **Materials Browser**.

4. Locate **Pebbled – Mauve** and load into the drawing.

   This is for the chair fabric.

5. Locate **Chrome - Satin** and load into the drawing.

   This is for the chair frame.

Rendering & Materials

6. Highlight the Pebbled – Mauve fabric.

   Right click and select **Duplicate**.

7. Right click on the duplicate material.

   Select **Rename**.

8. Rename **Sea Fabric**.

9. Select the Sea Fabric material.

   Right click and select **Edit**.

10. Click on the image name and set to *sea fabric.jpg*.
    This file is available as part of the exercise downloads.

    Change the Color to **255,255,255**.
    This is white.

    Close the Materials Editor.

10-61

11. Select one of the cushions.

    Right click and select **Properties**.

12.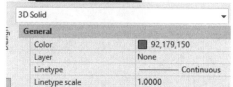

    On the Properties palette:

    Note the color is set to **92, 179,150**.

    Click **ESC** to release the selection.

13.

    Type **QSELECT** for quickselect.

    Set the Object type to **3D Solid**.

    Set the Color Equals to **92, 179, 150**.

    Click **OK**.

    All the chair cushions are selected.

14.

    Highlight the Sea Fabric material in the Materials Browser.

    Right click and select **Assign to Selcction**.

    Click ESC to release the selection.

Rendering & Materials

][Realistic]

If the view is set to Realistic, you should see the material as it is applied.

15. Select one of the chair frame elements.

General	
Color	White
Layer	None
Linetype	Continuous
Linetype scale	1.0000

The Color is set to White.

Click ESC to release the selection.

16.

Type **QSELECT** for quickselect.

Set the Object type to **3D Solid**.

Set the Color Equals to **White**.

Click **OK**.

The chair frames are selected.

10-63

17. Highlight the **Chrome - Satin** material.

    Right click and select **Assign to Selection**.

    Click **ESC** to release the selection.

18. The drawing has been redefined with new materials.

    Save as *Wicker chair and sofa – Sea Fabric.dwg*

Exercise 10-13:
Replace a Block

Drawing Name: replace_block.dwg
Estimated Time: 10 minutes

This exercise reinforces the following skills:

- Insert a block
- Replace a block
- Render

   In order to sync blocks, you need to have access to the internet and you need to be signed in to your Autodesk account.

1. Open *replace_block.dwg*.

2. Type **INSERT**.

   Click ENTER.

3. 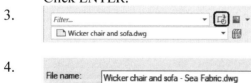 Select the **Browse** button next to the Filter box.

4. Locate the *Wicker chair and sofa – Sea Fabric.dwg*.

   Click **Open**.

Rendering & Materials

Click a point in the view to place the block away from the room.

Click ENTER when prompted for a rotation angle.

5. Type **BLOCKREPLACE**.

   Scroll down and select *Wicker chair and sofa*.

   Click **OK**.

6. Scroll down and select the *Wicker chair and sofa – Sea Fabric* block.

   Click **OK**.

7. Click **ENTER** to purge the replaced block.

8. The block is replaced using the same location and orientation.

   Delete the block that was inserted and isn't needed any more.

   Note that you had to fully insert the new block into the drawing before you could replace the block.

9. Type RENDER.

   The preview window will appear and the view will render.

   Save as *ex10-14.dwg*.

Exercise 10-14:
Using Artificial Light

Drawing Name: lights.dwg
Estimated Time: 15 minutes

This exercise reinforces the following skills:

- Add lights to a model
- Edit light properties

1. Open *lights.dwg*.

2. Switch to the Render ribbon.

   Select the **Point** light tool.

3. Select the center of the circle on the left as the location for the point light.

   Click ENTER to accept all the default settings for the light.

   If you have difficulty placing the lights, freeze all the layers except for Light Locator.

4. Select the point light.
Right click and select **Properties**.

Change the Name to **Dominant Light**.

Change the Lamp intensity to **15.00 Cd**.

Did you notice that the size of the light glyph updates?

Click ESC to release the selection.

5. Enable **Full Shadows**.
Enable **Sky Background and Illumination**.

6. Click on **Sun Status**.
Click on **Adjust exposure settings**.

7. Set Environment to **On**.

Set the Image Based Lighting to **Warm Light**.

Enable **Use IBL Image as Background**.

Close the palette.

8. Click **Render to Size** on the ribbon.

The Render Window will appear.

You will see a new rendering.

Close the Render Window.

9. Select the **Point** light tool.

10. Select the center of the circle in the middle of the room as the location for the point light.

    Click ENTER to accept all the default settings for the light.

    If you have difficulty placing the lights, freeze all the layers except for Light Locator.

11. Select the point light.
    Right click and select **Properties**.

    Change the Name to **Secondary Light**.

    Change the Lamp intensity to **5.00 Cd**.

    Click ESC to release the selection.

12. Switch to the Home ribbon.

    Use **Thaw All** to thaw any frozen layers.

13. Switch to the Render ribbon.

    Enable **Full Shadows**.
    Enable **Sky Background**.

    If you can't enable the Sky Background, check that the Viewcube is set to Perspective.

14. Click on **Sun Status**.

15. Click on **Adjust exposure settings**.

16. Set Environment to **Off**.

    Set the Exposure to **8**.

    Set the White Balance to **15000**.

    Close the palette.

17. Click **Render to Size** on the ribbon.

    The Render Window will appear.

You will see a new rendering.

Close the Render Window.

Save as *ex10-15.dwg*.

Exercise 10-15:
Mapping Materials

Drawing Name: medallion.dwg
Estimated Time: 15 minutes

This exercise reinforces the following skills:

- Create a material
- Apply material to a face.

1. Open *medallion.dwg*.

2. Switch to the Render tab.

   Click on Materials Browser.

3. Select the **Create Material** tool at the bottom of the palette.

4. Create the new material using the **Stone** template.

Rendering & Materials

5. Change the name to Medallion.

Change the Scene to **Canvas**.

Click on the image name.

6.

Locate the *stone medallion* file in the downloaded exercise files.

Click **Open**.

7.

Click on the down arrow next to the preview and select **Edit Image**.

8.

Set the Scale to **4' 0"**.

Under Repeat:

Set the Horizontal and Vertical to **None**.

9. You should see a preview of what the medallion will look like.

   Close the dialog.

   Close the Materials Editor.

10. Type **SOLIDEDIT**.

11. Click on **Face**.
12. Click on **Material**.
    Click on the disk.

    We only want the top face selected, so click **Remove**.

13. Click on the bottom of the disk.

    Click ENTER when only the top face is highlighted.

14. Type **Medallion** for the material to be applied.
    Click **ENTER** to exit the command.

15. Change the display to **Top Realistic**.

Rendering & Materials

16. Switch to a Top view.

    The material is placed, but it didn't map properly.

    Open the Materials Browser.

    Double click on the material in the Material Browser to open the editor.

17. Select **Edit Image**.

18. Move the dialogs so you can see the solid.

    Adjust the Position and the Scale until the preview looks correct.

    Close the dialogs.

19. Save as *flower medallion.dwg*.

Extra: *Place the medallion in the beach scene you did in the previous exercise and see if you can create a nice rendering.*

Notes:

QUIZ 10

True or False

1. When rendering, it is useful to save named views using the View Manager.
2. Sky illumination can be used to add extra light to a scene.
3. You can use an image or a color to change the background of a scene.
4. To change the material used in a wall, you need to modify the wall style.
5. When mapping a material, you can only use grips to adjust the placement.

Multiple Choice

6. Materials can be displayed in the following views: (select all that apply)

    A. plans
    B. sections
    C. elevations
    D. renderings

7. Surface Hatches can be displayed in the following views: (select all that apply)

    A. model
    B. plan
    C. section
    D. elevation

8. Identify the tool shown.

    A. Expand Render Window
    B. Expand Tea Kettle
    C. Scale
    D. Render to Size

9. When there are no lights placed in a scene, the scene is rendered using:

    A. Default lighting.
    B. Sun & Sky.
    C. Nothing, it is really dark.
    D. Sun only, based on location.

10. Spotlights and point lights are represented by:

    A. Glyphs (symbols used to indicate the position and direction of the light)
    B. Nothing
    C. Blocks
    D. Linework

11. When mapping a material, you can adjust: (select all that apply)

    A. The X position
    B. The Y position
    C. Rotation
    D. Scale

12. Once you place a camera, you can adjust the camera using: (select all that apply)

    A. Properties
    B. The Adjust tool on the Render tab
    C. Using the MOVE and ROTATE tools
    D. You can't modify a camera once it has been placed

ANSWERS:

1) T; 2) T; 3) T; 4) T; 5) F; 6) A, B, C, D; 7) A, C, D; 8) D; 9) A; 10) A; 11) A, B, C, D; 12) A, B, C

Lesson 11:
Collaboration

Drawing Management

Project Navigator allows drawing versioning for AutoCAD Architecture drawings. This ensures informed collaboration between multiple users and prevents unauthorized modifications to the drawings.

When a project involves multiple users working together on a set of drawings, it is essential to have a file locking and versioning mechanism to ensure that all changes are recorded and there are no access clashes. When you check out a drawing from the Project Navigator, other users only have read-only access to the drawing and can view the last saved version of the drawing, till you check the drawing back in. This ensures that there are no file access conflicts and each modification made to a drawing is recorded.

Changes being made to the checked out drawing are not dynamically visible to other users and as the checked out file is saved, no xref notifications are sent to others which can be an interruption to their work.

Hovering over a file in the Project Navigator shows you the status of the file, the name of the drawing, its location, the size of the file, the date and time the file was last checked in, the name of the user who last checked-in the file, and the check in version history with the check-in comments. Red checkmarks indicate that the drawing is checked out by another user, and a green checkmark indicates that the drawing is checked out by you.

When you check out a file, make modifications and check it back in, you are prompted to add comments on the changes you have made. This information is displayed in the Check-In Version History, along with your username, your domain or computer name, and the date and time of the check-in.

Every time you check-in a file, AutoCAD Architecture creates a backup file in the same folder where the drawing is stored, with the drawing name appended with check in time. If during the course of a project, you wish to revert to an earlier version of the drawing, the comments history makes it easier for you choose the backup file version you wish to roll back to.

If you open a drawing and make changes without checking it out, ACA will not create a backup file or update the version history. Even if you are a solo user on a project, it might be useful to check in and check out drawings, so that you can maintain a version history.

Exercise 11-1:
Set the Number of Backup Files in a Project

Drawing Name: Brown Medical Clinic
Estimated Time: 10 minutes

This exercise reinforces the following skills:

- Project Navigator
- Drawing Management
- Changing the appearance of the Project Browser
- Changing the number of backups

1.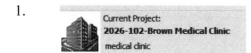

   Launch **ACA (US Metric)**.

   Set the **Brown Medical Clinic** project current.

   Close the Project Browser.

2.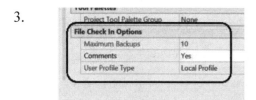

   In the Project Navigator palette, Project tab, click the **Edit Project** icon, on the top right corner.

3.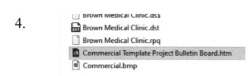

   In the Project Properties dialog box, **Advanced→File Check In Options→Maximum Backups**.

   Set the Maximum Backups to **10**.
   Set Comments to **Yes**.

4. Click **OK**.
   Browse to your My Projects/Brown Medical Clinic folder.

   By default it is located under Documents/Autodesk.

   Locate the *Commercial Template Project Bulleting Board.htm* file.

Collaboration

5. [screenshot of file browser] Open using Notepad.

6. [screenshot of HTML code] Scroll down to the bottom of the document.

   Modify the text to provide instruction on how to work in the Brown Medical Clinic folder.

7. [screenshot of HTML code] Type:
   This clinic must comply with VA standards and regulations.
   Go to https://www.cfm.va.gov/til/projReq.asp for more information.

   Save the file as **Brown Medical Clinic**.htm in your exercise files.

8. [screenshot showing Brown Medical Clinic.htm] You should see the new htm file listed in the File Explorer.

9. [screenshot of Project Browser settings] In the Project Navigator, Click the **Edit Project** icon, on the top right corner.

10. Change the Bulletin Board file to the **Brown Medical Clinic.htm.**
    Change the Project image using the bmp file provided in the exercise files.
    Click **OK**.

11. [screenshot of toolbar icons] Launch the **Project Browser**.

12. The bulletin board has updated.

Use the bulletin board to provide contact information for team members, project standards, scheduling updates, and other announcements.

Exercise 11-2:
Checking out and Checking in a Drawing

Drawing Name: Brown Medical Clinic
Estimated Time: 25 minutes

This exercise reinforces the following skills:

- Project Navigator
- Drawing Management
- Checking out a drawing
- Ceiling grids
- Checking in a Drawing

1. Set the **Brown Medical Clinic** project current.

2. Open the Project Navigator.
   Open the Constructs tab.
   Highlight **Main Model**.
   Right click and select **Check Out**.

3. Highlight **Main Model**.
   Right click and select **Open**.

Collaboration

4. Switch to the **Model** tab.

5. 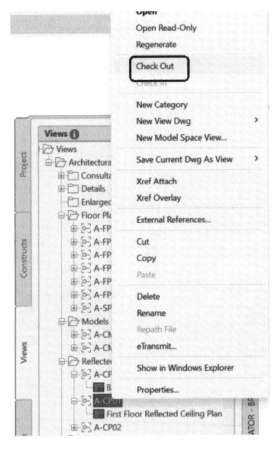 On the Project Navigator, open the **Views** tab.

Locate the **A-CP01** under Reflected Ceiling Plans.
Right click and select **Check Out**.

Then Right click and select **Open**.

6. Notice that co was added to the drawing name to indicate it was checked out.

7. Switch to the Model tab.

Turn off GRID and SNAP.

8. Move the view title into the correct location in the drawing.

9. Change the Display Representation to **Reflected**.

10. Move the XREFs to the center of the views.

11. In the Project Navigator:

    Right click on **A-CP01**.

    Click **Check In.**

12.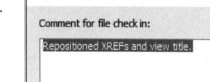

    Type in a comment when the dialog appears.

    Click **OK.**

13.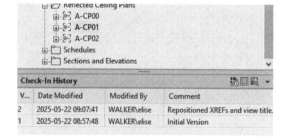

    Highlight A-CP01 in the Project Navigator.

    Expand the Check-In History.

    You will see the version history.

Note the Main Model file name indicates it has been checked out.

14. On the Home ribbon:

    Go to **Manage Layer States**:

15. Click **Import**.

    Note: Even if you created a layer state in a different project, you can use them in this project as the layer naming standards are the same in both projects. So, if you exported your layer states from one project, you can import them into another project and save time!

16. 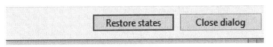 Change the files of type: to .las.

    Then select the *Model Only.las* file in the downloaded exercise files.

17. Click **Restore States**.

18. 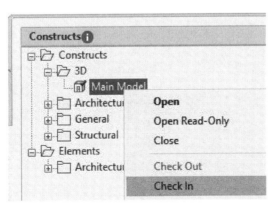 In the Project Navigator:

    Highlight Main Model on the Constructs tab.

    Right click and select **Check In**.

19. 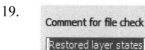 Type in a comment.

    Click **OK**.

Exercise 11-3:
Version History

Drawing Name: A-CP01.dwg
Estimated Time: 10 minutes

This exercise reinforces the following skills:

- Project Navigator
- Drawing Management

1. 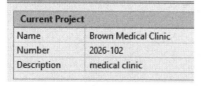 Set the **Brown Medical Clinic** project current.

2. 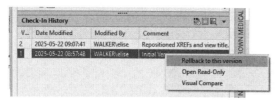 Open the Project Navigator.
   Open the Views tab.
   Highlight **A-CP01**.
   Right click on Version 1.
   Select **Rollback to this version.**

3. Click **Yes.**

4. 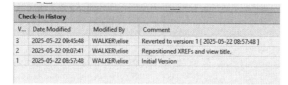 A version has been added that shows it is back to the previous version.

Collaboration

5. Check Out **A-CP01.dwg** view.

   Open the file.

   Notice that checking out a file doesn't open it.
   You can use Check Out to prevent other users from editing a file.

6. *You see it is an earlier version of the reflected ceiling plan.*

   Check in the drawing.

7. Add a comment.

   Click **OK**.

When a drawing is opened and closed, it does not create a new version. The drawing must be checked out and then checked in to create a new version.

Shared Views

A shared view allows users to share in the cloud a viewable, read only document. The recipient doesn't need an AutoCAD application, just a system with a current browser application and an internet connection. Viewers can mark up and add comments to the views. The shared document is outside of the project and any mark-ups and comments are not part of the document management system.

You need to be signed in to an Autodesk account and have internet access in order to create and use shared views.

Exercise 11-4:
Shared Views

Drawing Name: Main Model.dwg
Estimated Time: 15 minutes

This exercise reinforces the following skills:

- Project Navigator
- Drawing Management

1. *The current project is the Brown Medical Clinic.*

   Open the Project Navigator.

   Highlight the **Main Model** 3D construct.
   Right click and **Check Out**.
   Right click and **Open**.

2. 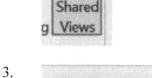 Open the Collaborate ribbon.
   Click **Shared Views**.

3. Click **New Shared View**.

4. Enable **Share model view and all layout views**.
   Enable **2D views only**.

   Click **Share**.

5. Click **Proceed**.

6. Click **View in Browser**.

7. A browser window will open with the views.

   Click the **Share** button located in the upper right.

8. Sign in to your Autodesk account.

   A link is displayed that you can copy and email to a team member for review.

9. Click **Markup** at the bottom of the browser window.

10. Place a cloud, arrow and some text at the east/right side of the building model.

11. Click **Save**.

12. Click on the **Comments** icon.
    Notice you can toggle any mark-ups on and off.

13. Return to AutoCAD Architecture.

    Back in the drawing, click the Refresh icon at the top of the Shared Views palette.

    You will see the shared view that was created.

14. 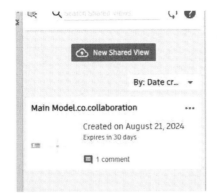 Click the ... next to the view name.

    Click **View in Browser**.

15. 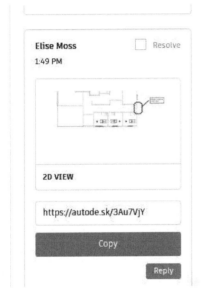 Toggle Comments on.

    You will see the markup and the comment.

    Close the browser window.

16. Highlight the **Main Model** construct in the Project Navigator.

    Right click and select **Close**.

17. Highlight the **Main Model 3D** construct. Right click and **Check In**.

18. Type **Created Shared Views**.

    Click **OK**.

Trace

Trace provides a safe space to add changes to a drawing in the web and mobile apps without altering the existing drawing. The analogy is of a virtual collaborative tracing paper that is laid over the drawing that allows collaborators to add feedback on the drawing.

Create traces in the web and mobile apps, then send or share the drawing to collaborators so they can view the trace and its contents.

Traces can be viewed in the desktop application but can only be created or edited in the mobile apps.

Markup Import

Markup Import attaches an image file or pdf to use as a trace for an existing drawing.

You can convert elements of the trace to AutoCAD elements using the Markup Import tool to make changes quickly and easily.

To create a markup, print out the drawing to be modified. Use a RED pen to indicate the desired changes. Then scan it to a pdf or take a picture with your phone and email it to the person who needs to make the changes.

Exercise 11-5:
Use Markup Import

Drawing Name: A-102 Floor Plans.dwg, A-102 Floor Plan_trace1.pdf
Estimated Time: 5 minutes

This exercise reinforces the following skills:

- markups
- Trace
- Project Navigator
- Drawing Management

1. 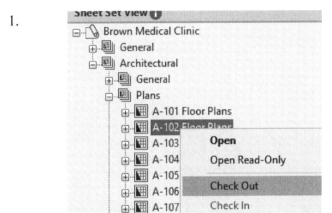 *The current project is the Brown Medical Clinic.*

   Launch the Project Navigator.
   Open the Sheets tab.
   Locate the **A-102 Floor Plans** drawing.
   Right click and select **Check Out**.
   Right click and select **Open**.

2. Activate the Collaborate ribbon.

   Click **Markup Import**.

3. Click **I understand**.

4. 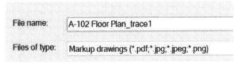 Locate the *A-102 Floor Plan_trace1.pdf* file downloaded from the publisher.

   Click **Open**.

5. Zoom in to see the mark-up.

   Move to place over the view in the lower left corner of the sheet.

6. Click **ENTER** to accept the placement.

7. Verify that the Trace mode is enabled.

   Notice that the trace is now active.

8. Go to the Home ribbon and select the MTEXT tool.

   Add Mtext below the schedule note.

9. 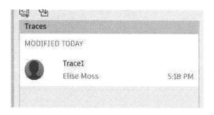 Switch back to the Collaborate ribbon.

   Click on the **Traces Palette**.

10. The trace is listed on the palette.

11. Close the Traces toolbar.
Zoom out.
The markup is no longer visible.

12. Click the Trace1 listed on the palette.

The markup reappears.

Notice that the MTEXT that was added is now part of the mark-up.

13. Toggle the Traces palette OFF on the ribbon.
The markup is still visible.

14. Close the Traces toolbar.
Zoom out.
The markup is no longer visible.

15. Open the Project Navigator.
Locate the **A-102 Floor Plans** drawing.
Close the drawing.
Click **OK** to save changes.

Right click and select **Check In**.

16. Type a comment.

Click **OK**.

Exercise 11-6:
Use Trace

Drawing Name: A-EL01_02.dwg, A-201 Building Elevations_02.dwg, mark-up.pdf
Estimated Time: 20 minutes

This exercise reinforces the following skills:

- markups
- Trace
- Project Navigator

You can share a drawing with a colleague or client and have them add notations for your review using the free mobile app available to smart phones and tablets.

1. Open A-EL01_02.dwg.

   This is included in the exercise files.

2. Click **Open the External References palette**.

3. Bring up the XREF Manager.

   Highlight the **01 Column Grid** file.
   Right click and **Select New Path**.

   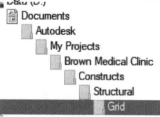

   Browse to the Structural folder where you are storing your project files.
   Click **Open**.

   You will be asked if you want to re-path all the other external references.
   Click **Yes**.

Collaboration

All the path errors should be corrected now.
If there are still errors, repeat by pointing to the correct folder.

4.

   Close the XREF Manager.
   Open the Project Navigator.
   Open the Views tab.
   Highlight **Sections and Elevations**.
   Right click and **Save Current Dwg As View→Sections/Elevation.**

5. Click **Next**.

6. Enable all the floors.
   Click **Next**.

11-19

7. Click **Finish**.

8. 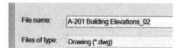 Open *A-201 Building Elevations_02.dwg*.

   This file is in the downloaded exercises.

9. 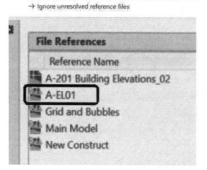 Click **Open the External References palette**.

10. Highlight A-EL01.

Collaboration

11. Right click and **Select New Path**.

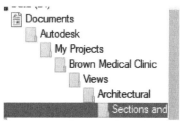

Browse to the new location for the file.

12. Select *A-EL01_02.dwg*.

Click **Open**.

13. *All the errors are now corrected.*

Close the XREF Manager.

Save the file.

14. Open the Sheets tab of the Project Navigator.
Highlight Elevations.
Right click and select **Import Current Layout As Sheet**.

15. Open the Collaborate ribbon.

Click **Markup Import**.

16. 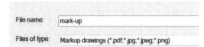 Select the *mark-up.pdf*.
Click **Open**.

This is a downloaded exercise file.

17. Click ENTER to accept the placement of the mark-up.

Some callouts have been added.

18. Enable **Drawing** mode.

19. If you hover over the text, you will see a tooltip.
Click at the edge of the dashed rectangular border.

20. ACA will automatically add the note.

21. Hover over the markup for the stucco.

Click the left mouse button.

22. Click **Insert as Mleader**.

23. Click to place the start of the leader at the wall.

    Click to the right of the building to place the text.

24. Click on the SHINGLES markup.

    Click **Fade Markup**.

25. Click on the leader markup.

    Click **Fade Markup**.

26. Click on the arrow for the stucco markup.

    Click **Fade Markup**.

The markup is shown as faded.

The mleader notes have been added.

27.

Click the x on the toolbar to close the trace.

28.

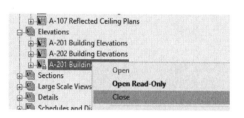

Open the Project Navigator.
Highlight **A-201 Building Elevations**.
Right click and select **Close**.

29. Click **Yes**.

30.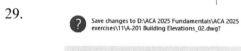

Switch to the Views tab.
Highlight **A-EL01_02** under Sections and Elevations.
Right click and select **Close**.

When prompted to save, click **Yes**.

Exercise 11-7:
Use Autodesk Docs

Drawing Name: 01 Core
Estimated Time: 10 minutes

This exercise reinforces the following skills:

- Collaboration
- Autodesk Docs

> *More and more companies are utilizing Autodesk Docs. BuildingConnected, Autodesk Construction Cloud, and other applications use the Autodesk Docs cloud storage. You may be asked to upload your files to Autodesk Docs, so you can share information with other team members. You do need access to the internet for this exercise. Autodesk provides a limited amount of storage to students and faculty so they can use Autodesk Docs. Other users require a subscription.*

1. 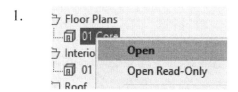 The current project is the Brown Medical Clinic.

   Go to the Constructs tab in the Project Navigator.
   Open the **01 Core Floor Plan**.

2. Open the Collaborate ribbon.

   Click **Push to Autodesk Docs.**

3.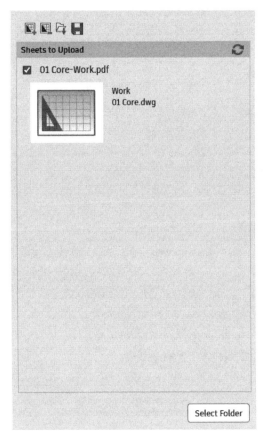

   DWG files are automatically converted to PDF files for upload.

   Click on **Select Folder**.

4.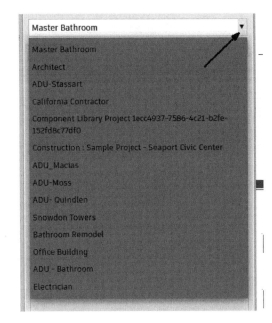

   If you click on the down arrow, you will see any folders you may have created in Autodesk Docs.

   You won't see these folders. These are my projects in my Autodesk Docs account.

5. *Each of my project folders is divided into subfolders for the project.*

   Select the subfolder to place the file and click Upload Sheets.

6. *The file is uploaded.*

   Click on the link to view the uploaded file in the browser.

7. The file is listed.

   To view it, click on the file.

   Return to AutoCAD Architecture.

8. Close and save the file.

eTransmit

eTransmit in AutoCAD is a feature that packages a drawing file (.dwg) and all its associated files into a single folder or ZIP file. This is especially useful when you need to share a drawing with someone else (e.g., a colleague, contractor, or client) and want to make sure they have all the necessary files to view and work with it correctly.

This is especially useful when you are using Projects within AutoCAD Architecture because of the heavy reliance on external references.

When you use eTransmit, AutoCAD collects and bundles:
- The main DWG file.
- All externally referenced drawings (Xrefs).
- Image files or raster references.
- Fonts (TrueType and SHX).
- Plot styles (.ctb or .stb files).
- Sheet set files (.dst) if applicable.
- Custom linetypes, materials, and other dependencies.

Exercise 11-8:
Use eTransmit

Drawing Name: 01 Core.dwg
Estimated Time: 5 minutes

This exercise reinforces the following skills:

- Collaboration
- eTransmit

1. The current project is the Brown Medical Clinic.

   Open the Constructs tab of the Project Navigator.

   Let's say you want to set the 01 Core model to the electrical sub-contractor so they can use the drawings to determine the best placement of lighting and wiring.

2. Highlight **01 Core** under Floor Plans. Right click and select **eTransmit.**

3.

Note 41 files are included in the package. If you wanted to add additional files, for example, a contract or correspondence, you could add additional files as well.

Type in any notes to accompany the transmittal.

Click **OK**.
A zip file is created.

4. Browse to a folder where you want to save the file and click **Save**.

Notes:

QUIZ 11

True or False

1. A shared view is not linked to the drawing where the view originates.
2. You can install an AutoCAD app on your phone and use Traces to Markup a drawing.
3. A trace allows you to make edits directly in the drawing file.
4. You can have more than one trace in a drawing.
5. A drawing is checked out by one of your team members. If you click Refresh or Reload for the checked out drawing, you will see the changes.

Multiple Choice

6. You have received an AutoCAD drawing from the plumbing contractor for your building design. You want to change the color and linetype of the external reference using his drawing file so it is easy to identify. To do this:

   A. You create a new construct using his drawing.
   B. You create a new view using his drawing and change the colors and linetypes in the view.
   C. You create a new construct using his drawing, attach his drawing to the Building Model as an xref overlay, then apply a layer filter to control the appearance of his drawing.
   D. You open the plumbing drawing and modify the layer colors and linetypes.

7. A shared view can be accessed in a browser for:

   A. One week
   B. A user-specified amount of time
   C. A year
   D. 30 days

8. You have checked out a file and you are ready to check it in. ACA will provide a prompt. The prompt allows you to:

   A. Add comments regarding the changes that were made.
   B. Email your team members to let them know that you are checking in the drawing.
   C. Verify that the changes you made are correct.
   D. Save the drawing file as a new file.

9. You wish to revert to an earlier version of a drawing. You select the earlier version, right click and select Rollback to this version.

    A. ACA creates a new file based on the older version that you can open and adds it as the most recent version of the drawing.
    B. ACA deletes all saved versions of the file that were created after the selected version and makes the selected version the most recent version.
    C. ACA creates a new file based on the older version and deletes all saved versions that were created after the older version.
    D. ACA creates a new file based on the older version and purges all the changes that were made.

10. You open the Project Navigator and want to work on one of the construct files. However, you see a lock on the file. What does this mean?

    A. The file is currently set to Read-Only because it has been released.
    B. The file is checked out, open and is currently being edited – either by you or another team member.
    C. You do not have the security permissions to make changes to this file.
    D. The file is checked out and is unavailable for viewing.

11. You see a red check mark next to a file in the Project Navigator. This means:

    A. The external reference has lost its path and needs to have a new path specified,
    B. Changes have been made to the file and it needs to be reloaded.
    C. The file is checked out by another team member.
    D. The file needs to be audited.

ANSWERS:

1) T; 2) T; 3) F; 4) T; 5) False – you will only see the changes once the drawing is checked in and you will see a notification when the drawing has been checked in 6) C; 7) D; 8) A; 9) A; 10) B; 11) C